W9-BJV-383

Dirt and Desire

Patricia Yaeger

Dirt and Desire

Reconstructing Southern Women's Writing 1930–1990

THE UNIVERSITY OF CHICAGO PRESS
Chicago & London

PATRICIA YAEGER is professor of English and women's studies at the University of Michigan. She is author of *Honey-Mad Women: Emancipatory Strategies in Women's Writing* (1988), coeditor of *Nationalisms and Sexualities,* and editor most recently of *The Geography of Identity* (1996).

THE UNIVERSITY OF CHICAGO PRESS, CHICAGO 60637
THE UNIVERSITY OF CHICAGO PRESS, LTD., LONDON

Printed in the United States of America

09 08 07 06 05 04 03 02 01 00   1 2 3 4 5

ISBN: 0-226-94490-5 (cloth)
ISBN: 0-226-94491-3 (paper)

Library of Congress Cataloging-in-Publication Data

Yaeger, Patricia.
Dirt and Desire : reconstructing southern women's writing, 1930–1990 / Patricia Yaeger.
p. cm.
Includes bibliographical references and index.
ISBN 0-226-94490-5 (alk. paper)—ISBN 0-226-94491-3 (pbk : alk. paper)
1. American fiction—Southern States—History and criticism. 2. Women and literature—Southern States—History—20th century. 3. American fiction—Women authors—History and criticism. 4. American fiction—20th century—History and criticism. 5. Southern States—In literature. 6. Race in literature. I. Title.

PS261.Y34 2000
810.9'9287'09750904—dc21   99-085969

The paper used in this publication meets the minimum requirements of the American National Standard for Information Sciences—Permanence of Paper for Printed Library Materials, ANSI Z39.48-1992.

To Kiri and Noah

Contents

Prologue

We have rather ordinary expectations about the South and what we will find in southern literature. The goal of this book is to make the usual expectations strange—to explore the density and peculiarity of southern women's fictions across racial boundaries. As Susan Goodman proclaims in her 1998 biography of Ellen Glasgow: "Glasgow defined many of the elements we now associate with a larger pattern of Southern literature: a tragic sense of life, a deep-rooted pessimism, a recognition of human capacity for evil, and the decrees of history and place" (1).

I'm tired of these categories. When I open a story by a southern woman writer I find figures and ideas that astonish. Sarah E. Wright, a southern writer whose work has been largely unsung, captures the material deprivations of black agricultural laborers in southern Maryland as well as her heroine's dense interiority, the sweetness of her mind: "Dirt flying in her face? Well, honies, she wasn't even gonna mind. She'd eat that dirt and hustle on. She wouldn't even mind how the dirt got packed under whatever fingernails she had left . . . she was just gonna suck her fingers every now and then—dirt and all—and keep on tearing down those rows" (1969, 3).[1]

Southern women write dirt-eating, finger-sucking fiction—an image that plays into still more stereotypes about southern women as crackers, "folk" artists, or the writers of regionally limited fictions. But dirt-eating has a transatlantic as well as a regional basis. In a recent gallery show focused on memory, the African American artist Marianetta Porter displayed embossed silver muzzles covered with filigree: objects so beautiful that

I gasped at their source. These mouth-stopping talismans recreated the muzzles that white southern slave owners used to silence or starve disobedient slaves—and to prevent the eating of dirt. Since soil can provide nourishment and oral pleasure, why was it so dangerous? In Africa and the Americas, dirt-eating "bedeviled masters who used muzzles to discourage its ill effects. Done in moderation it was apparently an indulgence, like chewing gum or tobacco and had possibly developed as a means of allaying hunger in times of famine. Consumed in quantity clay was supposed to be a means of suicide" (Starkey 1964, 56–57). In *Travels in the Interior Districts of Africa* Mungo Park explains that a woman and a girl who were about to be sold into slavery had used dirt more aggressively. When they fell ill their master "had no choice but to lead them home again," where they vomited clay—a substance ingested in order to produce "an illness serious enough to defeat their master's purpose of selling them to African traders" (Starkey 56–57).

What are the remnants in southern women's fiction of such desperate practices? To describe this disturbing writing, a nostalgic invocation of the South's "tragic sense of life" or "the decrees of history and place" no longer suffice. In *This Child's Gonna Live* Sarah E. Wright follows the example of other southern women in foregrounding a history of terrifying embodiment, of "altered human tissue" (Spillers 1994, 458). Mariah not only eats dirt, she also sucks the excrement from her children's faces. When her eldest son Rabbit breaks one of her few possessions, a small china plate, she attacks him: "*Meant to hold her hands back, but Jesus, Jesus. My hands is killing him. . . . Cut off my hands, Jesus.* The woman wept. *I ain't meant to hurt up his face like I did. . . .* She grabbed that little old body quivering the same as it did when he was first born . . . and she sucked her knuckles where she cut them on Rabbit's teeth. Licked the slobber and the snot and the blood from his face" (1969, 31). We stumble across torn, wounded flesh in Wright's writing, but we also find an epistemology of astonishment, an act of wonder at the power of flesh-eating, dirt-eating kindredness in which strangeness is a permanent property of the hard-bitten everyday and writing a magical theater of terror.

Modern southern women writers evoke, in their fictions, the oracular power of Zora Neale Hurston's Queen of Sheba, "an Ethiopian just like Jethro, with power unequal to man. She didn't have to deny herself to give gold to Solomon. She had gold-making words. But she was thirsty, and the country where she lived was dry to her mouth" (1990a, 185). In *Dirt and Desire* I want to find new legends to characterize these gold-making words, this fiction written from a country that instigates prolific writing and yet insists on an ideology that is "dry" to the mouths of black and white women alike.

How should the models for examining southern women's fiction change? First, instead of sustaining a belief in the belle or female "miniature" as the prototypical southern female figure, I want to put in her place a procession of giant women, from Hurston's Big Sweet as she refuses to let a white man take away her weapon ("'You wuz uh whole woman and half uh man. You made dat cracker stand off a *you.*' 'Who wouldn't?' said Presley. 'She got loaded muscles. You notice he don't tackle Big Sweet lak he do de rest round here'" [1990a, 152–53]) to Carson McCullers's Miss Amelia, "a dark, tall woman with bones and muscles like a man" (1971, 4). By placing black and white writers side by side, I do not want to insist on a continuum but to shake up a narrow and male-defined southern "tradition," to construct a wide terrain from which to explore southern women's racial differences and their unevenly shared symbol and language systems, erected so boldly across differing topographies of power.[2] Thus Hurston turns the white ideal of a powerful, hard-working black woman—someone seen from a white perspective as a dangerously labile, commodity-producing body—back on white culture itself while McCullers's gargantuan image explodes and exposes the cult of true white womanhood.[3]

Second, instead of sustaining a lustrous southern preoccupation with family, I want to examine the problem of neglect, of the throwaway. In Wright's *This Child's Gonna Live* a hurricane ravages the local graveyard, until "the rotted bones and rags of their kin and friends [were] just a-swinging in the winds." The living pull "the bones and rags—some crumbling and dry, some still squirming with the worms eating away at them—from those once mighty roots" and place them back in the ground. But when Mariah finds the bones of her dead baby daughter with "pieces of that pink dress they'd put her away in," she collects "the little old bones for to keep with her" (1969, 269). Wright's novel struggles to gather up the child's blasted remains: the little girl's bones become a weird pen or prosthesis that stays with Mariah for the rest of the novel, a talisman for other children who should not die. This novel presents the black child as someone who is invaluable and yet becomes white culture's throwaway, and we will see that this throwaway child reappears as a painful motif in both black and white women's fictions.

Third, I want to initiate new ways of thinking about racial epistemologies in American women's literature, about the importance of the unseen everyday, as well as the struggle to articulate an "obscene" species of racial blindness that I will call "the unthought known." Toni Morrison suggests that the most "spectacular" question of American literary studies is not why she as an African American is absent but "what intellectual feats had to be performed by the author or his critic to erase me from a society seething with my presence, and what effect has that performance had on the work? What are the strategies of escape from knowledge? Of willful oblivion?" (1994, 378). One of my hypotheses about white southern women's writing is that it creates bizarre and frequent emblems for white southerners' racial blindness in images of fractured or scattered whiteness, in scenes filled with partial bodies, cotton lint, flour dust, displaced snow, or facial masking, whereas black southern women are less interested in what white people know than in surrogated knowledges, in histories that have been lost or cast away. This suggests that it is time to subordinate the familiar debate about "the mind" or "the idea" of the South to an examination of the ways the South has helped encode American ways of racial knowing: of both overconceptualizing and refusing to conceptualize an obscene racial blindness.[4]

Still, in juxtaposing black and white writers I face a continued dilemma. Won't these juxtapositions "filter out [a black text's] embeddedness in black cultural and political tradition" and foreground, instead, the agendas of white feminism? (Abel 1997, 118). What I'm doing is, I hope, more promiscuous. First, I'm following the path mapped by black feminist scholars such as Thadious Davis, who argues that the term *southern* has been whitened, or shorn of its African American connotations, and that African American writers need to be reexamined under the rubric of region (1988, 5). When *southern* becomes an occlusive term that pertains only to white southern culture, black southern writers are often deregionalized as "black" or "African American." This skews our reading of southern literature and skewers the complex racial texture of women's writing coming out of the South. Second, we need to look at this fiction interracially precisely because of the different conundrums and inequities that black and white writers unearth. The South is, after all, a region where race has been at the heart of aesthetic practice.

These paradigms have only become possible because of recent discoveries in southern and African American history, the work of black feminist critics, and the growing literature on the history of whiteness.[5] Black feminists, in particular, have opened new space for rethinking both black and white women's literature. In "Mama's Baby, Papa's Maybe" Hortense

Spillers describes the sociopolitical order of the New World as a sequence written in blood that produces not figurative grotesques but scenes of "*actual* mutilation, dismemberment, and exile." We will see that the grotesque is omnipresent in southern women's fiction not as a decorative filigree but as a space of political obsession. As Spillers explains, "New-World, diasporic captivity was marked by a *theft of the body*—a willful and violent . . . severing of the captive body from its motive will, its active desire" that seems "unimaginable from this distance." In diaries and logbooks "the anatomical specifications of rupture, of altered human tissue, take on the objective description of laboratory prose—eyes beaten out, arms, backs, skulls branded . . . as the calculated work of iron, whips, chains . . . the canine patrol" (1994, 457–58). This is the deep background for yards of southern literature: not only for black women but also for white. Sarah Wright's Mariah dreams of her father's lacerated body, while Katherine Anne Porter catalogues the nonchalance of white caretakers who overlook the sudden deafness of an ailing black child. Flannery O'Connor's sawed-off, deregulated bodies flailing in space represent not only icons of mutilated saints but histories of southern mutilation that the economy she writes about is heir to. This is to argue that older models of "the" southern grotesque are due for a paradigm shift. In *Dirt and Desire* I will explore the prevalence in southern women's writing of flesh that has been ruptured or riven by violence, of fractured, excessive bodies telling us something that diverse southern cultures don't want us to say. That is, instead of the grotesque as decadent southern form, I want to examine the importance of irregular models of the body within an extremely regulated society and to focus on figures of damaged, incomplete, or extravagant characters described under rubrics peculiarly suited to southern histories in which the body is simultaneously fractioned and overwhelmed.[6]

But in crushing black and white literatures together in order to challenge stereotypes for thinking about "southern" literature, what else gets left out? Ann duCille, Cherrie Moraga, and Valerie Smith argue that people of color have been misappropriated by white critics; they have been fashioned into a bridge to be cast across the abyss of "tormented history" (Moraga 1981, xv) in order to allow white critics to feel au courant or save face, enabling "scholars working in exhausted fields to cross over into the promised land of the academy" (duCille 1997, 49).[7] Southern literary studies can certainly be accused of debility, enervation, or fatigue, especially when its scholars have not kept pace with recent developments in feminist theory, African American studies, and the growing consciousness of the racialization and history of whiteness.[8] But the goal of *Dirt and Desire* is not to build a bridge across an abyss but to depend on an already developed architecture that incorporates the recent work of the white studies industry, of southern and African American historians, and of black feminist critics. I want to ask: Why have the troubling crypts and verbal honey of southern women's fictions been so segmented and split off from rest of American writing—especially since literature written out of the South not only represents prime territory for thinking about the intersecting histories of whiteness and blackness but also offers dynamic examples of a hypervisible, hypercamouflaged whiteness?[9]

For example, the white writer Sarah Barnwell Elliott begins her racially obsessed story "The Heart of It" with a rather dull image: a white woman is walking down a "broad, white road" that has been hidden under floodwaters. She becomes a "blur" as Elliott tries to find an image that can reflect the heroine's just-discovered secret that she is descended from African Americans. In the wake of this ambivalent image, Elliott has her heroine follow the example of Frances Watkins Harper's *Iola Leroy*—a novel that disrupts the forms of tragic mulatto fiction by making Iola Leroy "defend the system of slavery" before she discovers that she herself is black and will be forced to return to the South as a slave (Carby 1987, 74). Elliott's heroine also asserts that blacks are deeply inferior, and her words come back to haunt her: "'Slavery raised your race,' she had said sharply; 'you came to this country, savages!'" (1991, 121). Elliott's text is riddled with racial anxiety and contradiction. "Darkness" represents ignorance and lack of illumination, whereas enlightenment is associated with ideas of whiteness. And yet the white road remains obscure while the outlines of the surrounding "darkness" are comforting; the story's most knowing character is an educated black woman, and the most ignorant character is a white aunt who has known for years about her niece's lineage and refused to allow her to visit or eat with other plantation owners: "I could not take her there any more than I could take a disease there." The white author's formal choices (especially her disavowal of the aunt's weird racist diatribes by inverting them temporally, installing them in the painful partitions of the story that occur *after* the heroine discovers that she is object of her aunt's disdain) construct whiteness itself as a disease.

To examine a story by a white woman written in the 1890s that depends so completely on a plot invented by a black writer of the same period deepens a series of debates already vigorous in the American academy. In "The Occult of True Black Womanhood" duCille criticizes feminists who continue to see racial identity as a property only of nonwhites. "Unless the object of study happens to be the Other, race is placed under erasure as something outside immediate consideration, at once extratextual and extraterrestrial . . . 'as a woman' in main stream feminist discourse all too often continues to mean 'as a white woman'" (1997, 35). But in southern women's fiction, such meaning is never "extraterrestrial"; it is rarely taken for granted. For the white writer Sarah Barnwell Elliott as for the black writer Sarah E. Wright, white is always the color of danger.[10]

Elizabeth Abel has argued that white critics plunge into these comparative territories for selfish reasons, that any theory of "reading across race" must be marked by "white desires" (1997, 118). But I want to add this proviso: white southern women's fiction is worth examining precisely because it is continually overwhelmed by racial desires (for racial blending, for racial purity, for appropriating difference, for keeping difference at bay), whereas black women's fiction about the South annotates complex economic and social differences among women in aesthetically fascinating ways. Still, isn't Abel vertiginously right? Isn't *Dirt and Desire* moored in—and marred by—its own integrationist dreams? Perhaps, but this book also gestures toward an intellectual field that needs to be reopened, one that does not mitigate the differences between black and white women.

My goals in *Dirt and Desire* are threefold. First, I want to undomesticate southern women's fiction by inventing more dangerous, up-to-date, culturally acute terms for examining a rich and underread literature. Second, I look at black and white women writers using similar rubrics to map out the regional geographies that they do and do not share—a crucial strategy because southern studies has, until very recently, focused its attention on whiteness without admitting its exclusive agenda. Finally, the field of southern literary studies has been dominated by a huge Faulkner industry that both overshadows and tames the terms we use for reading southern women's fiction. What is missing from Faulkner's epic fiction but present in writers such as Alice Walker or Eudora Welty is a sense of the ways race functions in the nonepic everyday.

Models are microsystems designed to represent aspects of a "larger" reality; they are powerful proscriptive fields suggesting what one can and cannot observe. The central thesis of this book is that older models of southern writing are no longer generative, that they don't yield interesting facts about women's fictions, about the struggle of some southern women to make sense of a society seething with untold stories, with racist loathing; nor do they help place this fiction within its "American" context. Concomitantly, looking at southern women's writing via a new set of paradigms changes the rules critics have used for thinking about (1) southern fiction, (2) the place of women writers in North America's racial history, and (3) our sense of the relations between black and white women's writings.

Finally, I want the models that I develop here to have the power of Picasso's portrait of Gertrude Stein. To numerous complaints about the portrait's lack of resemblance to its original, Picasso replied: "Everybody thinks she is not at all like her portrait, but never mind. In the end she will manage to look just like it" (Casti 1997, 22). In the end, she did.

This book represents the work of many minds. My friends have been endlessly patient in listening to and working through its ideas with me. I am especially grateful for luminous Sunday nights spent with P. A. Skantze, as well as brainstorms with Arlene Keizer, Yopie Prins, and Marlon Ross that changed my paradigms and my internal weather. Liz Barnes and Suzanne Raitt bestowed ideas, read chapters, and helped to mend them, while Michael Awkward, Sarah Blair, Phil Blumberg, Matthew Fink, Simon Gikandi, Ian Grandisson, Linda Gregerson, Marjorie Levinson, Aamir Mufti, Anita Norich, Tobin Siebers, Valerie Traub, and Athena Vrettos helped me respond with greater depth and clarity to topics ranging from vernacular landscapes to the uncanny.

My knowledge of the South has been amplified by Thadious Davis, Susan Donaldson, Drew Faust, Sharon Holland, Ann Goodwyn Jones, Michael O'Brien, Ann Romines, Peter Schmidt, Dawn Trouard, and Jay Watson. Without the wisdom of their conversations and books none of this would have been possible. My readers, Tara McPherson and Philip Weinstein, provided impeccable critique that helped sharpen and redirect the manuscript's focus. Joseph Boone, Ardis Cameron, Laura Doyle, Richard Godden, Anne Howells, Barbara Johnson, Judy Kleinman, Seth Koven, Andy Parker, Mary Russo, Jani Scandura, Carroll Smith-Rosenberg, and Bryan Wolf have all contributed ideas that helped me formulate this project. I want, especially, to thank Harriet Chessman for my title and her brilliance.

My undergraduates at Harvard University and the University of Michigan have asked demanding questions and made unexpected connections among texts. I want to single out Jennifer Weil and Matt Schmitt, who have become part of my daily life. A group of remarkable graduate students—especially Colin Johnson, Peter Kalliney, Bradley Kodesh, J. Samaine Lockwood, Jocelyn Stitt, Hilary Thompson, and Mako Yoshikawa—have been amazing in their sophisticated, insightful criticism of my most protracted obsessions, while my most recent graduate classes on southern writing (including Stan Barrett, Louis Cicciarelli, Kirk Davis, Francesca Delbanco, Katie Halverson, Emily Harrington, Laura Kopchick, Brandi Lewis, Jamesie McNaughton, Shani Mott, Patrick O'Keeffe, Jess Roberts, Madeleine Vala, and Cynthia Wu) bestowed a passel of new ideas. I am also grateful to Alan Thomas, my editor at the University of Chicago Press, for his unflagging interest in this project, and Jane Zanichkowsky, the most precise and empathic copyeditor I've known. Shani Mott showed exquisite initiative as my research assistant in the final stages of this project. I am also grateful to the National Endowment for the Humanities and the University of Michigan for funding this project. An earlier version of chapter 3 first appeared in *Southern Cultures* 5 (spring 1999): 1, published for the Center for the Study of the American South at the University of North Carolina by the University of North Carolina Press. Chapter 4 is reprinted with permission of the University Press of Virginia from *Haunted Bodies: Gender and Southern Texts,* edited by Anne G. Jones and Susan Donaldson (Charlottesville: University Press of Virginia, 1998).

There are other debts to pay, first and foremost to my father, Cecil Smith, for his stories about Cartersville, Virginia, and for providing daily lessons in how to transform a conservative, segregationist past into a future of activism and liberalism, and to my mother, Cecile Gaddis Smith, for never playing the part of a southern lady and for always refusing to behave. My siblings, David and Nancy Smith and Kathryn Rightor, have been exemplary southern expatriates whose joie de vivre keeps me grounded. Finally, I want to thank Selma and Bernie Miller for their constancy, Richard Miller for being always a little honey mad, and Kiri and Noah for giving me a heartbeat.

Chapter One

Southern Women Writers: A Confederacy of Water Moccasins

This is a book about the South: a book driven by the pleasures and costs of my family's own southern past—lived in northern Florida, northern Georgia, and eastern Virginia. In writing it I have been mesmerized by a spectacle of regional trauma that may be shared with others but remains peculiarly my own. Like Faulkner's Quentin Compson, I feel unable to refuse a lingering passion for the South that has drawn me into this book-length affair with southern women, an affair compounded by nostalgia for moon-pie and grits, for the smell of mildew and the itch of Spanish moss, by a never-ending desire to come home to some Sunbelt town that is humid as hell, humming with summer bees, and covered with kudzu. But this longing for something like home remains in constant tension with my own dixiephobia: a horror bred from the cruelties of the autocratic, segregated ways of my childhood, with its acrid memories of "Colored Town"—our habitual route to church every Sunday (as if my father longed to connect with the hard-baked deprivations of his youth—or were we just saving gas?), and its muffled recollections of the convicts haunting the roads between Micanopee and Ocala—were they chained? Not in North Florida, not in the fifties, but I remember them chained; they were, of course, in chains. My memories of the South are also filled with not-to-be-spoken-of longings, with a confused desire for connection with the dignified African American women our family knew only by their first names—Belle, Star, Willie Mae—who fussed with my hair and then departed forever, leaving precipitously after quarrels with my imperious and demanding mother.[1]

To explore the remnants of nostalgia clinging to such a time and place may seem unspeakable. And yet the chapters that follow flow inevitably from my own private quarrels with the South—from a sense that I was gargantuan or oversized in a world of petite and belle-like little girls; from a sense that my own right to testify, to speak out against familial, racial, and religious injustice was censored in school and at home; from a sense, as well, that I did not want to testify, or could not, or did not know how; from memories of the bizarre pressures of being a middle-class southern white girl caught between my father's southern Methodism and the world of my mother's hymn-singing, Bible-swinging Baptist past and of being someone destined by the age of five for my family's peculiar Scylla and Charybdis—the fatal need to choose between the Tri Delts, my Aunt Mary Louise's sorority, or Kappa Delta, my mother's—and clearly unfit, in my anger and awkwardness, for either institution. My identities and sympathies, then, are all with the southern grotesque, having been one and known more than a few. But I also hope that this personal take—these cumbersome private investments—will intensify rather than distract from the validity of these quarrels with the Souths I have known. Although caught in the delinquencies of my own southern past, the chapters that follow seek out a language for other people's experiences. I need to know: Why did the best women writers in the American South turn away from the beautiful body and toward the grotesque? Why do we encounter such consistent reconfigurations of southern body politics among a coterie of black and white women writers who felt at home within and yet deeply estranged from the South of the twentieth century? Why did these women write a series of in-your-face fictions that mangle, mar, and mistreat bodies of all shapes, sizes, cultural positions? What happened during this period to give women this fierceness, this power, this flagrant desire to abuse a form of cultural capital not traditionally their own?

Monstrosity

If we are to see this fiction in all of its power, we need to change the categories we use to think about southern literature. I want to begin with a parable—a story about beauty ravaged into bestiality, about the eruption of monstrosity in a climate and setting where one least expects it. We encounter this monstrosity in Ellen Douglas's *Can't Quit You, Baby,* in a tale within a tale that suggests new strategies for thinking about the relation between southern culture and the female body. The story is, first and foremost, about leisure and who has the freedom and space to enjoy it. The setting sizzles with the usual "southern" vividness of place: it is a beautiful summer day, filled with "white August cumulus," "green mist of willows," "sickle of jet trail." And yet something ominous has accumulated around the edges of this "apocryphal tale of a water-skier that rolled like ball lightning through the Mississippi Delta during the late sixties." The heroine is a "a beautiful young [white] girl" who "is flying along the surface of one of the innumerable oxbow lakes that mark changes in the course of the Mississippi River." These changes marked on the landscape of the sixties, suggest a story laden with allegory. In a state altered by the civil rights movement, this body skating on surfaces prepares us for a crisis of whiteness in a place in which it has become impossible to be white in the old, accustomed ways. In fleeing these changes "something happens" to the white woman skimming the surface of the lake:

> the rope breaks or she loses her balance and falls. No big deal. It's happened hundreds of times before. But this time is different: screams of agony—a thrashing and churning in the water. The lover spins the wheel, brings the boat about in less time than it takes to write this sentence. The young girl's lovely face is contorted with pain. Barbed wire, she gasps. I'm caught in barbed wire.
>
> But there isn't any barbed wire. No. It's a writhing, tangled mass of water moccasins. She holds out a hand and he seizes it.
>
> Wait! Wait! she says.
>
> She's dead before he can drag her into the boat, snakes dropping away as she slips over the side. (1988, 130–31)

The skier becomes both a corpse and a female predator, a serpent-woman, or lamia, a southern Medusa who invokes predatoriness and pathos. By reinflecting archaic tropes to refigure a Sunbelt version of the southern gothic, Douglas gets the best of both worlds—she veers toward the southern grotesque while making her story au courant, clever, up-to-date. She gives us both the mystique of the white belle and vestiges of an older world of property relations: the speaker describes pieces of barbed wire—ruined estuaries—clinging to the white girl's fingers. But this is also an eerie description of a woman who, instead of striving to get back in the boat, refuses to get in. Intimating what?—a sudden opening of her eyes to the deadly conditions she inhabits? a desire to save her boyfriend from the grotesque fact of her death? Or does she secretly want to stay there, beneath the surface, communing with the water moccasins, imbibing their knowledge with their power?

Whatever the answer, the most remarkable aspect of this passage is its insistent, languid connection of change with the sudden eruption of monstrosity. This is a pattern we will see repeated in numerous tales by southern women. In a culture dealing with crisis, unable to handle changes in the course of everyday life—the growing demand (from the thirties into the nineties) for African American equality, for greater access to education, citizenship, and economic resources—change erupts abruptly, via images of monstrous, ludicrous bodies.

In Flannery O'Connor's "The Displaced Person," a story published in 1954 in the *Sewanee Review,* images of monstrosity seem incredibly raw and vigorous. Here ethnicity, class, and the bizarre habitus of Jim Crow explode with premonitions of change when a Catholic property owner, Mrs. McIntyre, agrees to sponsor the Guizacs, a Polish family consigned to Europe's displaced persons camps. The story's images turn most ludicrous when a backwater region of Georgia has to contend with a minuscule immigrant population. As local gossip lumps Germans and Poles together as easy-to-identify enemies, old regional categories are thrown into disarray.

These changes are mediated by two monstrous events. When the hardworking Mr. Guizac displaces Mr. Shortley, the shabby white man who does chores around Mrs. McIntyre's farm, *Mrs.* Shortley sees future apocalypse: "Legs where arms should be, foot to face, ear in the palm of the hand. Who will remain whole? . . . Who?" (1971, 210). She fulfills these visions herself when she dies of a heart attack, creating a signature monstrosity as she grabs her loose-limbed daughters "and beg[ins] to tug and pull on them as if she were trying to fit the two extra limbs onto herself" (213).

But the story approaches a more frightening moment of domestic and political change when Mr. Guizac arranges for one of Mrs. McIntyre's black laborers to marry his blonde, pale-faced cousin, who is still suffering in Europe's displaced persons camps. Mrs. McIntyre is aghast: "'Mr. Guizac . . . that nigger cannot have white wife from Europe. You can't talk to a nigger that way. You'll excite him and besides it can't be done. Maybe it can be done in Poland but it can't be done here and you'll have to stop. It's all foolishness. That nigger don't have a grain of sense and you'll excite . . . ' After a second he shrugged and let his arms drop as if he were tired. 'She no care black,' he said. 'She in camp three year'" (222–23). Suddenly everyone conspires to break Mr. Guizac's body: "She had felt her eyes and Mr. Shortley's eyes and the Negro's eyes come together in one look that froze them in collusion forever, and she had heard the little noise the Pole made as the tractor wheel broke his backbone" (234). We return to the pattern that emerges at the death of Douglas's water skier. When new ideas are born, when new practices and ideologies make their way into public discourse against resistance, what emerges is the figuration of monstrosity.

We gather an even larger sense of how this rhetoric of monstrosity works in a story Grace Paley tells about taking a bus trip to Florida to meet her husband during the war. Again we encounter a South confronting change. It is 1943, a time of rising expectations coupled with the painfully segregated mingling of black with white soldiers. Although Paley is not by any stretch of the imagination a southern writer, what I want to capture is the volatility of the world she rides into—the sense of encountering a political space so combustible it is ready to explode with violence or vulnerability. The result is an encounter not only with the South but with southern habits of troping. Paley connects with a racial imaginary that seems unthinkable and uninhabitable: she comes face to face with a rhetoric of monstrosity invented to cope with a situation of change.

On the bus, now deep in South Carolina or Georgia, Paley "had been sleeping, waking, reading, writing, dozing, waking. So many hours, the movement of the passengers was like a tide that sometimes ebbed and now seemed to be noisily rising." Like Douglas's water skier she is inundated—this time by a human tide—out of which struggles a black woman "holding a large sleeping baby, who, with the heaviness of sleep, his arms tight around her neck, seemed to be pulling her head down." Barely awake, and now in the last seat in the whites-only section of the bus, Paley offers this woman her seat with no thought of the segregationist anger such an act might incite. "She looked to the right and left as well as she could. Softly, she said, 'Oh, no.' I became fully awake. A white man was standing right beside her, but on the other side of the invisible racial border. Of course she couldn't accept my seat." Warding off the bad dreams all around her, Paley asks to hold the baby until "out of sheer exhaustion," the black woman "disengaged the child from her body and placed him in my lap. He was deep in child-sleep. He stirred, but not enough to bother himself or me. . . . I was so comfortable under his nice weight." She starts to doze but is jolted awake by the "face of a white man talking. In a loud voice, he addressed me: 'Lady, I wouldn't of touched that thing with a meat hook'" (1997, 43).

Everything is startling about this turn of speech. A baby, drifting into sleep, returns as a monster child in this man's lacerating invective; the child is objectified, made mechanical.[2] This forceful, repulsive image creates a category of pollution in which something very familiar—a sleeping baby—is made completely unfamiliar, estranged.[3]

But what is most uncanny about this behavior is that it is also a version of the norm. Because of the shift Paley enacts in the plane of reality, something familiar and expected in the southern order of things—a black women nurturing white babies—turns into its mirror image—a white woman nurturing a black baby. In this new and threatening form it is denied or cast away; it returns as monstrosity.

This stretching of speech into oblivion is designed to create odd sensations in listeners and readers alike. An ordinary child, sleepy, at home on a white woman's lap, is made freakish, attacked by disanimating rhetoric, envisioned as a corpse, as pollution, as a "thing." This act has a variety of consequences. First, it becomes a metaphor for somatic knowledge, for the ways in which an entire culture has taught itself to think about race. Second, it suggests the bizarreness, the inherent uncanniness, of a culture that thinks this way, that produces such knowledge (in violent acts as well as violent rhetoric) as power. Third, Paley suggests the ways in which even small events can have the power of history making. "That is how history is made," says Julius Lester. "Ordinary people make a simple, human decision to live differently than their parents lived. Ordinary people make a decision to assert their humanness instead of continuing to live in deference to a collectivity that denies it" (1991, 31).

And yet collectivity triumphs here. Although the white man's rhetoric gives this story its edge, what startles most is Paley's and her black companion's inability, within these labyrinths of subordination, to meet one another's eyes: "I thought, Oh, this world will end in ice. I could do nothing but look straight into his eyes. I did not look away from him. Then I held that little body a little tighter, kissed his curly head, pressed him even closer, so that he began to squirm. So sleepy, he reshaped himself inside my arms. His mother tried to narrow herself away from that dangerous border, too frightened to move at all. After a couple of minutes, she leaned forward a little placed her hand on the baby's head, and held it there until the next stop. I couldn't look up into her mother face" (43). The allusion to Robert Frost ("Some say the world will end in fire, / Some say ice") is Paley's way of circulating a counterrhetoric; her need to say "*mother* face" suggests the importance of reanimating this mother's and child's humanity to disavow the force of the white man's lacerating words. And yet Paley also notes the Medusan power of a white man's metaphor. Petrified, unable to look, these women hover on a dangerous border where monstrosity squats in one man's eyes, ready to explode. (His words are not just linguistically intimidating; the meat hook is an implement of loathing; it intimates violence to come.) Warding off this petrifaction, we welcome the black woman's care:

"her hand on his head is quite small, though she tries by spreading her fingers wide to hide him from the white man" (43).

The anthropologist Mary Douglas explains that many cultures respond to anomaly by reordering unexpected events, reducing ambiguity to a new set of rules. The southern stories we've begun to analyze suggest an equally heightened response to dissonance. Instead of reducing disorder to rule, dissonance gets magnified or multiplied; anomaly gets figured as monstrosity, and monstrosity itself becomes a way of casting out or expelling the new. This suggests a poverty within southern culture's political idiom—an idiom that is not enriched by change but made hysterical. I am arguing that Douglas's and Paley's stories are primarily about resistance to change. When crisis erupts, when change grapples toward history, it is configured via appalling body images as something excessive, as monstrosity.

We see this clearly in Douglas's story about the skier and the water moccasins. Like Paley, Douglas touches on the power of local, vernacular speech by insisting on the repeatability of the water skier's story—its circulation as rumor or gossip, its shift from locale to locale. The snake-woman's fate changes into an incredible story about white panic—a sensational diatribe about convulsive white bodies.

By focusing on local rhetoric Douglas reins her story in; she flattens out her own anecdote, de-dramatizes it, insists that what's most interesting about the white woman's fate isn't her denouement but the valence of this story as gossip—its strange repeatability at a fragile moment of historical change:

> This tragedy, they say, occurred on Lake Bolivar, Lake Washington, Lake Jackson, Lake St. John, Catahoula Lake, Lake Chicot, Moon Lake, Horn Lake, Eagle Lake, Lake Providence, Lake Concordia. Sometimes there is another boat nearby, a crowd of witnesses. Again, the two young people are alone on the lake. Or only the narrator of the tale witnessed the accident. Or he heard it from a cousin of the girl's.
>
> But *you*—you're the one, I hear you say. You're the driver of this boat. You're pulling the skier. Is the story true?
>
> It's always true. Always true that a tangle of water moccasins lies in wait for the skier. Always, always true. (1988, 131)

Douglas turns her own gothic filigree into a question about public culture and the circulation of signs within this culture. By foregrounding this story's power as rumor, Douglas asks, Why does this story keep circulating, why does it keep reemerging in new locations as an effervescence of the local? Douglas fingers the source of these southern monster stories; she asks, Where do they come from? Who invents them, what keeps them circulating? And what about the role of both black and white southern women writers in this circulation? In *Can't Quit You, Baby,* the white writer becomes the "real" driver of the boat—no longer the skier's helpless female double, but her antagonist, unsettling her bland southern beauty with a writhing mass of serpentine trauma. Why?

Answering this question will constitute the journey of this book. We will investigate a group of women writers from very different southern localities who keep circulating and recirculating grotesque stories about the South—stories preoccupied with figures of dirt, monstrosity, the throwaway, gargantuan women, old children, and the problem of arrested systems of knowledge. These common themes have a great deal to teach us about the intersections between race and gender in twentieth-century America, where racism has become the dominant economy. These fictions ferret out subsemantic obsessions about race and gender that invite a rethinking of some of the most basic categories that we use to think about American literature.

These texts deploy a series of strategies—the explosion of monstrosity or violence, the flickery image of injustice (which remains unconceptualized, unacknowledged but also well known), discomforting emblems of neglect, disregard, elision, the throwaway, gargantuan women, or hybrid bodies that try to move the reader toward unregistered precincts of knowledge. But beyond this, my interest in monster stories, in recurrences of the grotesque and repeated tales of dirt and desire, also emanates from the incredible suspense that these tales generate, from a sense that whenever you're riding through the lake of southern culture, some confederacy of water moccasins awaits you—intimations of occluded drama that disoccludes itself, that wells up—attacking the body and misshaping it.

In Alice Walker's *Meridian* this monstrosity erupts in a slave woman's tale, a story told to a group of spellbound white children:

> Encouraged by the children to become more and more extravagant in her description, more pitiless in her plot, Louvinie created a masterpiece of fright . . . the intricate, chilling story of the old man whose hobby was catching and burying children up to their necks and then draping their heads—which stuck up in rows, like cabbages—with wriggly eels dipped in honey. Long before the culprit received his comeuppance, young Saxon had slumped dead to the ground of a heart attack. He was seven years old. . . .

> Louvinie's tongue was clipped out at the root. Choking on blood, she saw her tongue ground under the heel of Master Saxon. Mutely, she pleaded for it, because she knew the curse of her native land: Without one's tongue in one's mouth or in a special spot of one's own choosing, the singer in one's soul was lost forever to grunt and snort through eternity like a pig. (1976, 43, 44)

Once again the convulsive white body marks the "southernness" of this story. As for Louvinie, her tongue is buried beneath a scrawny tree that grows huge and sacred. Its fate is duplicated in Charles Chesnutt's *The Conjure Woman,* a tale in which a slave becomes a tree to escape his master's cruelty—a transformation that, finally, yields no protection. Both trees are chopped down, their great-rooted music riven. But these trees also turn into stories: Walker suggests that a scrap of Louvinie's tale has been saved in the library, its words copied out—ironically—in a white child's shaky hand.

The story of Louvinie's severed tongue finds its own bizarre cognate in Douglas's *Can't Quit You, Baby.* Whereas Louvinie is a black woman who loses her power of speech, in Douglas's novel we meet a white woman who refuses to hear. We first encounter the middle-aged Cornelia in the kitchen, trying *not to listen* while Julia, a black woman who has worked for her for more than a decade, recounts the sexual harassment she endured at another job. Julia's story about a sex-driven white man is so shocking to her white listener (how could Julia have been molested by someone Cornelia knows, how could Julia have complained to his *wife*?) that Cornelia refuses to take it all in: "The white woman is deaf and wears a hearing aid, a tiny shell in her ear with a cord running down to the battery and receiver clipped to her brassiere strap," making it easy to retreat into silence when Julia tells her about Wayne Jones: "He was a damn crazy man—crazy for black women." But the white employer hears nothing of this: "Such behavior is inappropriate even to Wayne Jones. The white woman does not wish to credit it. You mean he got after you down there—at the cafe? No" (4).

Douglas's narrator does not identify with Julia (or "Tweet," as she is known throughout the story), even though Tweet is one of the novel's best narrators. Instead, she allies herself, shamefacedly, with the not-hearing, self-deafening white woman, whose disabilities become a symbol for the fiction-writing disabilities of the author herself:

> Now . . . as I struggle with my own difficulties, with the near impossibility for *me* of grappling with these events—I think that perhaps—no, certainly—I am the one who is skiing, who cannot ac-

> knowledge or express the complexity of all those layers of circumstance and imagining—in all our lives, but particularly in Tweet's. I thought I was at home in Tweet's life, that when she spoke, I heard her speak with her own authentic voice. . . .
>
> But of course I never heard her speak, *except to Cornelia.* Does that trouble you as it does me? Again and again I have turned aside, shied away from knowing how she spoke at home, in bed at night with Nig, sitting in their crowded little house, the gas heater pulsing, with Robert and Rosa and their friends and neighbors. I wrote nothing, for example, of Martin Luther King's death, except that Tweet turned away from Cornelia's gesture of sympathy. What tangle of snakes have I been skiing over? (239–40).

Here, late in the novel, the author becomes both driver and skier, trying to navigate southern imponderables while deaf to African American culture's encyclopedic knowledge of race and class prejudice, its habits of protest and economic fortitude. "She is black," the narrator writes. "Cornelia is white. She is servant, Cornelia is mistress. She is poor. The measure of her poverty is that she considers Cornelia (who thinks of herself as modestly well off) immensely wealthy" (240).

The question that Douglas unearths, a question driving many of the stories we will read in this study, is frighteningly simple. *How do you write a story everyone knows but nobody hears?* How do you write annals for the very histories you want to annul? This white obliviousness, this act of writing without listening, finds its emblem in the deaf white heroine-employer, her hearing aid hooked to her brassiere, who becomes, in turn, the deaf white author, the nib of her pen deployed in criticism of southern culture but still refusing to encounter its margins.

Once again: How do you write a story everyone knows but white people rarely hear? How do you speak a story when your tongue as been severed? The grotesque offers one answer. It offers a figure of speech with the volume turned up, a body that entices one's hearing and speaking because of its anomalousness. But I want to add to this analogy by insisting that critics of American fiction are also at fault; we have been reading modern literature by southern women with its tongue cut out, ignoring the blood at the root; we have been reading this fiction with its volume turned down. Writers as diverse as Porter, Hurston, Welty, McCullers, O'Connor, Walker, Williams, Douglas, Gilchrist, and Ansa (not to mention the black women who write in equally stirring ways about ancestral southern roots, including Morrison, Clifton, Lorde, and Naylor) produce vociferous writing that is incredibly responsive to political silence, body talk, and object obsession as well as to a series of ontological questions about rights to citizenship and self-possession that not only plague the South but have spread throughout the nation. The goal of this book is to turn up the volume on southern studies by providing a new set of categories for examining southern women's fiction, to find new terms for cataloguing its arrested systems of knowledge. How do we reinscribe a literature that keeps repeating stories about race-thinking that everyone knows but no one wants to hear?

Turning Up the Volume on Southern Women's Writing

Why do the categories dominating the study of southern literature need reshaping? We know the litany of terms associated with southern letters, the truisms. "The South [has] a tradition which is more oriented toward history, toward the family . . . toward storytelling, and toward tragedy," Walker Percy intones (1965, 95). But are these really the most interesting repetitions in southern women's writing? Let me suggest some alternatives.

Let's say, instead, that southern literature has a tradition that is oriented toward crises of whiteness: toward convulsive white bodies and the portrayal of white panic. Louvinie's story capitalizes on this panic. As she tells her white wards: "In deepest Africa, there lived a man blacker than the night, whose occupation was catching little white children . . . and planting them in his garden . . . because he liked to hear them wail and scream and call for their mothers" (1976, 44). The "shock" of discovering African Americans in unexpected places induces a strange sense of trauma for white characters in literature by both black and white writers.[4]

Are the uses of history, the family, storytelling, and the past as tragedy still more of a magnet than the "theme" of white panic? Then let's explore the ways that southern literature is tantalized by the discovery of hidden black mothers, not only at the end of "The Little Convent Girl" (where everyone who "wanted to say good-by" was also curious about "the mother. . . . Some expressed surprise in a whistle; some in other ways. All exclaimed audibly, or to themselves, 'Colored!'" [1995, 175]), but also at the end of O'Connor's "Everything That Rises Must Converge" and Cather's *Sapphira and Slave Girl.*[5] Or say that southern fiction is larded with portraits of throwaway bodies, or that it is obsessed with unusual morphological types—with female gargantua and dwarfish child narrators who tell uncanny stories ("Miss Amelia crossed the porch with two slow, gangling strides . . . and stood looking thoughtfully at the stranger. Gingerly, with one long brown forefinger, she touched the hump on his back" [McCullers 1971, 9]).

Is this too slender a paradigm shift? Then let's go on. Say that southern literature is obsessed with arrested systems of knowledge, with redefining racialized object relations in a post-Lockean world where people's identities are always coterminous with what they own. Or say that this literature is obsessed, especially post-emancipation, with describing the objects and people who pass back and forth between black and white culture. Say that southern literature is most itself *not* when it re-creates miscegenation as tragedy but when it examines genealogies of labor—foregrounding the extraordinary costs to African Americans of lives trapped between the spaces of domestic and agricultural labor.

To these new categories—(1) convulsive white bodies, (2) covert or hidden black mothers, (3) jettisoned bodies pointing to (4) arrested systems of knowledge or "the unthought known," (5) crossover objects defining a weird zone of contact between black and white cultures filled with anxiety, and (6) stories attesting to the daily trauma of domestic and agricultural labor, add a seventh, (7) a sense of blackness as something to be inventoried—that is, reduced, in white fiction, to an atmosphere or part of a list. Whereas southern literature by white women is obsessed with rehearsing (and sometimes criticizing) the lists in which African Americans figure as objects, get turned into atmosphere, southern literature by black women is obsessed with extracting blacks from such lists.[6] Or, while we're on the subject of lists, say that white southern literature is obsessed with (8) repetition—with stories that will not go away, that keep repeating themselves endlessly, helplessly, in a kind of literary stutterance that creates a rich field of intertextual neurosis, while black literature about the South contributes to the exorcism of this repetition by ringing these stories backwards, providing white nannies for black babies and digging children out of ditches as fast as white culture flings them in.[7] Is it any wonder that (9) southern literature is obsessed with migration and with the problem of public time in unexpected ways? ("'Been waiting long?' Sam Guidry asked me. 'About two and a half hours, sir,' I said. I was supposed to say, 'Not long,' and I was supposed to grin; but I didn't do either." Gaines, *A Lesson Before Dying* [1993, 47].)

If we want to emphasize the ways women's writing challenges the public sphere, have we noticed that southern women are more interested in (10) the secrets of political economy, with the ways in which politics gets discussed in the kitchen, than in who is playing politics at the state house? Or that it portrays the civic discussions parleyed between white children and their black caretakers as more progressive or, at any rate, more daring?[8] No? Then say that (11) literature by southern women often eschews romance but asks about who gets to work at the post office, who owns the ballot box, who gets to plan utopias; or (12) that southern literature is obsessed with dirt—who owns it, who cleans it; with bodies that go into the ground but also with white pollution: with landscapes so glaring in their whiteness that they lacerate any reader who cannot turn away. Say that (13) southern literature is concerned with the usual sites of American commerce—agriculture, factory work, domestic labor, sales, construction—but that this literature explores the ways in which each of these sites is inflected by race. Say that (14) place is never simply "place" in southern writing, but always a site where trauma has been absorbed into the landscape, or that (15) bodies of water—the great Mississippi, Lake Okeechobee, the Pearl River, Moon Lake, Silver Lake, Lake Okatukla—are never simply sites for leisure or hauling cotton or crossing over but sites for recycling sadness. Say that (16) the grotesque is not just another trope designed to confirm our belief in the South as "the Sahara of the Bozart" but a technique for positioning texts at the edges of southern disorder, and that this disorder is worth studying because it has become an American habit of disorder as well. Finally, say that southern women writers are interested in (17) occluded knowledge—for white women, the gender and race practices that their characters know by heart and yet rarely acknowledge, for black women, a longing for lost epistemologies—the names, customs, revenants, and remnants of Africa.[9]

Or, if you still can take a breath, say that (18) this is a literature obsessed with its own limitations, that asks us to think about America's burgeoning brands of consumerism as we move from the South of the twenties to the South of the seventies and eighties,[10] or note that (19) southern women's literature carries a double burden: it focuses on the mechanical, the expected, the everyday, and yet it represents this world in terms that are fantastic, unexpected, and perpetually uncanny.

If this list feels exhausting, still, it is only half done—and this raises a crucial question. Can we really change the categories we use to analyze southern literature so easily—or, for that matter, so compendiously? In another of the memorable, axiom-producing interviews that famous writers are prone to give, Eudora Welty provides these moving maxims: "We in the South have grown up being narrators. We have lived in a place—that's the word, Place—where storytelling is a way of life. . . . Our concept of Place isn't just history or philosophy; it's a sensory thing of sights and smells and seasons and earth and water and sky as well" (1984, 95).[11] Let's begin this transformation of categories at their root, by examining the sensory resonances of place, of "earth and water" in southern literature.

Since every literature with a setting invents or reflects a locality, the southern claim to "place" always strikes me as peculiar. And yet, perhaps we can find a smidgen of truth here; perhaps there is a different phenomenology of place in southern literature? If so, it is not a vision of place associated with romanticism or the virtues of rootedness that Welty describes.

Take the figure of the dead white woman who gets pulled from the lake in Douglas's novel, her lost body clinging to a waterscape that becomes a cover for white anxieties about the changing South. This trope about a body that merges with water or earth occurs frequently in southern literature; it is an event, a preoccupation, shared by white and black writers alike, one that takes diverse forms.[12] But for the most part the bodies merging with southern landscapes are black—or at least, culturally defined as black. The white-looking mother who discovers she has given birth to a black-looking child in "Désirée's Baby" presupposes her own African Americanness and commits simultaneous suicide and infanticide:

> She did not take the broad, beaten road which led to the far-off plantation of Valmonde. She walked across a deserted field, where the stubble bruised her tender feet, so delicately shod, and tore her thin gown to shreds.
>
> She disappeared among the reeds and willows that grew thick along the banks of the deep, sluggish bayou; and she did not come back again. (1979, 406)

The white woman who discovers in "The Little Convent Girl" that her mother is black drops into the landscape:

> No one was looking, no one saw more than a flutter of white petticoats, a show of white stockings, as the little convent girl went under the water.
>
> The roustabout dived, as the roustabouts always do, after the drowning . . . but she had gone down in a whirlpool. Perhaps, as the pilot had told her whirlpools always did, it may have carried her through to the underground river, to that vast, hidden, dark Mississippi that flows beneath the one we see; for her body was never found." (1995, 176)[13]

The black youths playing at the swimming hole in Richard Wright's "Big Boy Leaves Home" are cruelly flung into the water:

> CRACK!
>
> Buck stopped at the edge of the embankment, his head jerked backward, his body arched stiffly to one side; he toppled headlong,

> sending up a shower of bright spray to the sunlight. The creek bubbled. (1965, 28–29)

Easter, the dirt-bespangled white orphan in Welty's "Moon Lake," is haplessly knocked off the dock by a black youth who works at her summer camp:

> She dropped like one hit in the head by a stone from a sling. In their retrospect, her body, never turning, seemed to languish upright for a moment, then descend. It went to meet and was received by blue air. It dropped as if handed down all the way and was let into the brown water . . . and went out of sight at once. (1949, 141)

Finally, Gus, the black child in Ellen Gilchrist's "President of the Louisiana Live Oak Society," is invited by Robert, his white friend, to stay at Robert's mansion while his parents are away. Found out by Robert's parents, Gus jumps from the third-story window:

> Gus jumped into the heart of the crepe myrtle tree. He dove into the tree and swayed in its branches like a cat. He steadied, grabbed for a larger branch, found a temporary footing, grabbed again, and began to fall through the upthrust branches like a bird shot in flight. As Robert watched, Gus came to rest upon the ground, his wet black hair festooned with the soft pink blossoms of the crepe myrtle. (1981, 37)

In general parlance, literary characters who submerge themselves in water or earth provide a litany of romantic transcendence or transfiguration. But in southern literature extraordinary numbers of women, men, and children fall into the landscape and disappear. It is as if the foundation or basis for this world is made out of repudiated, throwaway bodies that mire the earth: a landscape built over and upon the melancholic detritus, the disposable bodies denied by white culture.

"Sights and Smells and Seasons"

How should we describe the sense of "place" that dominates southern women's writing? The answer will inevitably change across temporalities and localities, but let's look at four different ways in which southern characters inhabit space.

Reverse Autochthony

Autochthonous means "sprung from the earth, self-born"; it describes Cadmus's action at the founding of Thebes as he sows dragon's teeth to create a pure race of men; it recurs in the powerful moment from *Paradise Lost* when, at the creator's touch, gallant creatures claw their way up from the earth: "The grassy Clods now Calv'd, now half appear'd / The Tawny Lion, pawing to get free / . . . the swift Stag from under ground / Bore up his branching head" (VII, ll. 463–64, 469–70). In Milton's poem the inanimate strains to get free; in contrast, Faulkner uses the myth of Theban autochthony to mythologize or hyperanimate Thomas Sutpen: "He now had a plantation; inside of two years he had dragged house and gardens out of virgin swamp, and plowed and planted his land with seed cotton which General Compson loaned him" (1936, 40).[14]

But in southern women's writing we see a movement from relative freedom to disanimation, from the attempt to found a pure race by sewing dragon's teeth or dragging "house and gardens out of virgin swamp" to descriptions of bodies that fall in the opposite direction. The examples are legion: "In de swamps dey used to stake 'em out all day and all night, and all day and all night and all day wid dey hans and feet tied so dey couldn't scretch and let de muskeeters eat 'em alive" (Porter 1972, 342); Ellen Fairchild "felt as if the cotton fields so solid to the sight had opened up and swallowed her daughter" (Welty 1946, 89); "He knew . . . that he had to baptize the child even as he drowned him" (O'Connor 1964, 422–23); "Mr. Paradise's head appeared from time to time on the surface of the water. Finally, far downstream, the old man rose like some ancient water monster and stood empty-handed, staring with his dull eyes as far down the river line as he could see" (O'Connor 1971, "The River," 174). In *Delta Wedding* Pinchy seems to disappear into thin air when Troy Flavin gives her an inedible morsel to eat: "Eat it or give it to the other Negroes. Now scat!" the foreman growls at her. "He clapped his hands at her skirt. Pinchy, with the cake, moved stiffly, out into the light, like a matchstick in the glare, and was swallowed up in it" (1946, 197). Finally, before the Okeechobee starts swallowing people in *Their Eyes Were Watching God,* Hurston defines the pleasures of life on the muck: "Work all day for money, fight all day for love. The rich black earth clinging to bodies and biting the skin like ants" (1990b, 125). But when Lake Okeechobee is unleashed by the hurricane and feeds on everything in sight, this rich earth becomes a graveyard: "corpses were not just found in wrecked houses. They were under houses, tangled in shrubbery, floating in water, hanging in trees, drifting under wreckage" (162). Once again African American women and men are flung into the earth:

> "Hey, dere, y'all! Don't dump dem bodies in de hole lak dat! Examine every last one of 'em and find out if they's white or black."
>
> ". . . Whut difference do it make 'bout de color? Dey all needs buryin' in uh hurry."
>
> "Got orders from headquarters. They makin' coffins fuh all de white folks. . . . Don't dump no white folks in de hole jus' so."
>
> "Whut tuh do 'bout de colored folks? Got boxes fuh dem too?"
>
> "Nope. They cain't find enough of 'em tuh go 'round. Jus' sprinkle plenty quick-lime over 'em and cover 'em up." . . .
>
> "They's mighty particular how dese dead folks goes tuh judgment," Tea Cake observed to the man working next to him. "Look lak dey think God don't know nothin' 'bout de Jim Crow law." (162–63)

We can now describe reverse autochthony as a site where both grownups and children are hurled into water or earth without proper rituals, without bearing witness to grief, without proper mourning. Oddly, this story was repeated as recently, as grimly, as 1998, when three white men dragged James Byrd Jr. to death behind their pickup truck. It was repeated as recently as 1996, almost sixty years after the publication of *Their Eyes Were Watching God,* in the story of Whitney Elaine Johnson, a baby born to a black father and a white mother, who was buried in Thomasville, Georgia, in an all-white cemetery. Three days later Logan Lewis, deacon of the Barnetts Creek Baptist Church, informed the family that the newborn's coffin had to be moved to another resting place. "He said they don't allow half-breeds in their cemetery," the baby's maternal grandmother told the press. "That's a 100 percent white cemetery." In his interview with the *Atlanta Journal-Constitution* Lewis explained: "there's not any mixing of cemeteries anywhere in this area. If someone white asked to be buried in a black cemetery, he'd be a laughing stock" (*New York Times,* 21 March 1996, 1). The deacons also argued that a black child's presence desacralized their holy ground, that "their tradition was in pieces," and the only way to make themselves whole was to move "the tiny coffin" elsewhere.

"Reverse autochthony" presents a peculiar literary pattern in which figures of speech lose their shape and are put back into the ground, into the space of earth and materiality, revealing a Machiavellian allegiance with base rather than superstructure. (When Daphne becomes a laurel tree she becomes a named, locatable entity; she is not equated with inchoate matter, nor, for that matter, is Wordsworth's Lucy.) But these southern, subterranean bodies are kin to the throwaway bodies I will describe in chapter 3, and they present "place" not as the nostalgic location of "sights and smells and seasons" but as a trash heap with profound economic resonance, describing a world whose foundations have been built on men and women who have "worked all day" and been thrown away.

Landscapes of Melancholy or Occluded Sadness (Or, Place as Crypt)

If "reverse autochthony" founders as jargon, presenting a gladiatorial mouthful, I still want a phrase describing a southern pastime that is anything but glamorous: people disappearing into water or earth—bodies disposed of, cast away without funerals, left unmourned. I've suggested that a deliberative accumulation of capital is at work here, but if we find a rapacious economy, we also discover a frightening psychology: the creation of landscapes loaded with trauma unspoken, with bodies unhealed or uncared for, with racial melancholia.

This melancholy (rather than the self-magnifying guilt we sometimes find in Faulkner's or Warren's fiction) is the particular subject of Katherine Anne Porter's short stories, which depict white children digging in the earth—with no strong sense of what they're after. In "The Fig Tree," a story from *The Old Order,* Miranda, an avatar for Porter herself, buries a baby chick who "was spread out on his side with his eyes shut and his mouth open. . . . 'Lazy,' said Miranda, poking him with her toe. Then she saw he was dead" (1972, 355). The children in Porter's fiction are always making coffins, climbing in and out of open graves, and scratching about in the earth:

> It wasn't hard work digging a hole with her little spade in the loose dry soil. Miranda wrapped the slimpsy chicken in tissue paper, trying to make it look pretty, laid it in the box carefully, and covered it up with a nice mound, just like people's. She had hardly got it piled up grave shape, kneeling and leaning to smooth it over, when a strange sound came from somewhere, a very sad little crying sound. It said Weep, weep, weep, three times like that slowly, and it seemed to come from the mound of dirt. (356)

Miranda is haunted by something, but what does she hear?

> "Hurry up, Baby, you'll get left!" Miranda felt she couldn't bear to be left. She ran all shaking with fright. Her father gave her the annoyed look he always gave her when he said something to upset her and then

> saw that she was upset. . . . "Stop getting so excited, Baby, you know we wouldn't leave you for anything." Miranda wanted to talk back . . . but she was still listening for that tiny sound: "Weep, weep." She lagged and pulled backward, looking over her shoulder, but her father hurried her toward the carry-all. But things didn't make sounds if they were dead. They couldn't. That was one of the signs. Oh, but she had heard it. (356)

"You'll get left." This threat, and the exorbitant threats of the former slave, Uncle Jimbilly, echo throughout Miranda's obsessions with creaturely weeping.

The suspicion that Miranda participates in a world where living things can be buried alive drives her story toward the borders of the fantastic, mingling ghost story with realist melodrama. This is an ambiguous tale about a little girl who is too sensitive and overreacts to everything, but it is also a fantasmatic tale about a world filled with factual ghosts, with disobedient slaves staked out in the swamps, black babies malnourished when their mothers suckle white children: a material foundation for a culture that contains too many uncounted bodies. Which of these two readings should we believe—the psychoanalytic or the historical? Avery Gordon argues that they must be read simultaneously: "Freud's science will try, once and for all, to rid itself of all vestiges of animism by making all the spirits or the hauntings come from the unconscious, from inside the troubled individual. . . . Freud will try to demystify our holdover beliefs in the power of the *world at large*, hoping to convince us that everything that seems to be coming at us from the outside is really coming from this now shrunken inside" (1997, 47–48). In other words, these uncanny experiences are both internal and relentlessly social, reminding us that "what lies between society and psyche is hardly an inert empty space" (47–48).

This is a world encumbered with endless melancholy.[15] While Miranda's grandmother has given birth to eleven children and lost three of them, Nannie Gay, a slave purchased to be Granny's playmate and then forced to nurse Granny's white infants, has lost more; out of her nine children only three remain. Is it any surprise that Miranda hears weeping? The grown-ups may be dead to these voices, but Miranda hears sorrow without ceasing. The landscape of *The Old Order* is filled with real and hypothetical bodies—with buried children, buried chickens, and the bodies of tortured slaves.[16] In the secret world of the child, these voices come to life again. Their weeping marks not only the child's individual loss but her culture's predations.

If for Welty "place does endow," what it endows in Porter's landscape is the burning sense that all around us, and all around the child, there is an excess or remainder. Something is calling out from Miranda's past that escapes the control of its concepts, that continues to weep. The child becomes the agonized vehicle for this lost remainder.[17]

White Detritus

If the depths of southern "place" yield the remains of foundation-bearing black folks who lie beneath the earth (the subjects of lynching, shooting, drowning, murder, beating, suicide, being ignored, or being worked to death), what's going on for the white folks at the surface, in the exterior spaces of this world? Given the literary patterns we've examined, one would expect a white landscape in which blackness becomes the core around which concentric, dominant whitenesses can be formulated. But instead, literature by southern women explores a radically dislocated surface landscape filled with jagged white signifiers and pallid detritus that bespeaks a constant uneasiness about the meaning of whiteness.[18]

This suggests a third gestalt for examining a "southern" phenomenology of place—one in which an odd white pollution hangs in the air, as if these writers are hyperconscious about trying to thematize something about whiteness that passively resists articulation. I want to argue that a series of uncanny white surfaces fill women's texts with fragmentation and unevenness. In *Delta Wedding* the air is heavy with cotton lint from the compress, requiring constant black labor. In *Sapphira,* the air is flecked with flour dust—freckled with scraps of dead, unusable skin—floating signifiers of whiteness that possess a form but lack any narrative trajectory.

This suggests a new take on Toni Morrison's descriptions of the ways whiteness works in American fiction. In her analysis of "the parasitical nature of white freedom" (1992, 57) Morrison describes what happens "at the end of literary journeys into the forbidden space of blackness" (58). She argues that the usual suspects (white male canonical authors) portray their heroes as "the inheritors of the blood of African Kings" as they dance over fields of "frozen whiteness." Snow becomes "the wasteland of unmeaning, unfathomable whiteness" in Poe or, in Bellow's *Henderson the Rain King,* the sign of "a new white man in a new found land." In each of these fictions (by Melville, Faulkner, and Hemingway, as well as Poe and Bellow) blackness is "evil and protective . . . fearful and desirable—all the self-contradictory features of the self. Whiteness, alone, is mute, meaningless, unfathomable, pointless, frozen, veiled, curtained, dreaded, senseless, implacable. Or so our writers seem to say" (58).

But images of frozen whiteness speak very differently in fictions by white southern women. When Frankie dispenses with her black caretaker, Berenice, frost silvers "the brown grass and the roofs of neighbors' houses, and even the thinned leaves of the rusty arbor" (McCullers 1975, 151). Miss Snowdie MacLain, a white albino, is the epitome of protected femininity who lives in a shower of whiteness in Welty's *Golden Apples,* while in Douglas's *Can't Quit You, Baby,* Cornelia begins to talk to an imaginary Tweet—for the first time—in a New York snowstorm: "I'm cold. The wind is blowing. This crosstown wind. . . . And I have to watch my step every minute or I'll fall down. Listen. Cornelia put her foot on a slanting icy mound, slipped, recovered her balance" (1988, 193). As Tweet begins to speak and Cornelia to listen, what she hears are Tweet's hallucinatory stories about the heaviness of things:

> Wait, Cornelia says, This is heavy. Too heavy. . . .
>
> You think you know heavy? You hadn't drug a cotton sack twelve or fourteen hours a day, have you? Carried a load of somebody else's wash on your head. Carried two buckets of water from the cistern? That's heavy.
>
> Whatever this is, it's heavy, too, Cornelia says.
>
> If it's wash, carry it home, wash it and iron it. Get you a red wagon and a basket and carry it back. Hold on, that's the message. Keep your hand on the plow, hold on. If it's water, drink with it, wash with it, cook with it. If it's a cotton sack, hmmm. . . . My advice, if it's a cotton sack, go get you a better job. (196)

Here whiteness becomes a burden, not because whites are victims but because they have no perspective on their own skins. Throughout southern women's fiction we find these weird images—part bodies, fragments of face paint or skin, texts where images of pallor spill out of the atmosphere like ghosts going to the wrong wedding.[19]

Instead of a gestalt in which "whiteness, alone, is mute, meaningless, unfathomable, pointless, frozen, veiled, curtained, dreaded, senseless, implacable," in the landscapes imagined by these women writers, whiteness speaks in water moccasin tongues; it erupts with too much meaning; it is terrifyingly dynamic, vulnerable, agitated, tortured, vertiginous. Or, it is partial, fragmented, an intensive source of labor, a site of confusion that gums up the works. In *Sapphira and the Slave Girl* the miller's clean-shavenness is reputed to be "unusual in a man of his age and station" because "a miller's beard got powdered with flour-dust, and when the sweat ran down his face this flour got wet and left him with a beard full of dough" (Cather 1968, 4). Things migrate or coagulate where they do not belong. This coagulation recurs in Sapphira's swollen white legs, and her body parts become near-totemic objects requiring black labor and vibrating with revulsion and fixation—as if some demonic aura of whiteness has dropped down on her body and immobilized it forever.

I've already suggested that this flour floats through the air like so much dead skin, like the leavings of some decaying albino body. It creates an intriguing sense of disconnection, unanchored identity, and fragmentation—an "anguished preoccupation with the mobility of meaning" (Bersani 1977, 59), a bizarre self-scattering. Why have we failed to recognize these persistent landscapes that are already in pieces but cling to the body like a funky, disintegrating amnion and cannot be brushed away?

Southern Geographies

These maps for tracing alternative phenomenologies of place in southern women's writing need not be multiplied exhaustively, but they do suggest several ways for redistricting a southern social geography that should make the quiddity of "southern" places more interesting.[20] First, in many of Flannery O'Connor's stories "place" is given a weird animistic force; it bites into the story's ending, gaining a bizarre oral power ("Behind them the line of woods gaped like a dark open mouth" [1971, "A Good Man Is Hard to Find," 127]). Second, as we've seen in Porter and Welty (but also rediscover in *Dessa Rose* and *Beloved*), southern whites may encounter African Americans as landscape, background, atmosphere—as part of the furniture—although these perceptions may also be shared by bourgeois blacks in urban African American fictions: "Zulena, a small mahogany-coloured creature, brought in the grape-fruit" (Larsen 1986, 184). Third, in looking again at *Their Eyes Were Watching God,* we get a bifocal sense of place as the novel moves from dreams of a black town's self-creativity to the nightmare of the hurricane's earth-shattering volatility. After constructing a town out of nothing (Eatonville, like Sutpen's Hundred, seems magically dragged from the earth), Hurston reproduces an incredible instability of place; she sends her African American characters southward and lurching for shelter as the hurricane explodes and white people seize the only locus of safety ("White people had preempted that point of elevation and there was no more room," 156). Finally, in "Neighbors," Diane Oliver's story about the violence surrounding desegregation, a bomb as destructive as a

Florida hurricane rakes the home of a black family who have been preparing their little boy for his first day at a whites-only public school. In the bomb's aftershock "Ellie stood up and crept toward the living room crying to prepare herself for what she would see. . . . There were jagged holes all along the front of the house and the sofa was covered with glass and paint" (1991, 479).

This litany of places could go on, from the commercial romance of the Louisiana racetracks in "Old Mortality" to the diverse rural and urban spaces described in *Meridian,* to the losing battles over Mississippi property rights depicted in *Can't Quit You, Baby,* to the bulldozer revolution that dominates the end of *The Golden Apples.* We need to contemplate both the *phenomenologies* of place that bind such texts together and the multiregional facts and perspectives on place that change from decade to decade and blow texts apart. (As Foner comments, "from the earliest days of settlement, there had never been a single white South [but] areas with sharply differing political economies" from the plantation belt to the up-country inhabited by small farmers and herdsmen engaged in mixed or subsistence agriculture [1988, 11].) We could add that there has never been a single black South either, and that the "sharply differing political economies" involving race have become even more distinct over time. And yet some critics might argue that this very diversity confirms Welty's sense that "place does endow," since southern writers, black and white, are so caught up in writing out of and redefining the meaning of place. Very well. But I would add one more proviso. If place is so weighty and important in twentieth-century southern literature, it is because its central feature (even after the sixties) is so constant. It is, and remains, the specter of segregation.

In Thomasville, Georgia, after a great deal of press coverage and pressure from the Southern Baptist Convention, the church fathers of the Barnetts Creek Baptist Church allowed Whitney Elaine Johnson to stay in the white cemetery where she was buried. The minister, Mr. VanLandingham, insisted that "we are all aware that God is no respecter of persons. We are also aware that we are part of an imperfect world and in our own imperfection we find ourselves having to make uninformed and or misinformed decisions and then having to live with the outcome" (*New York Times,* 21 March 1996, 1). Here doctrinal equality—a God who does not discriminate—meets with barely veiled contempt for the baby's "imperfections" and a regret about the loss of this graveyard as the site of a ghostly white autochthony. As Rick Bragg reported in the *Times* article, "Unlike schools and lunch counters, it was just one of those invisible lines in Southern life that no one seemed to care to cross, for as long as people here can recall."

Place, then, may be beautifully limned in southern fiction, but what it endows is almost always racially marked, as we discover on a trip to the cemetery in Welty's *Golden Apples:* "Virgie leaned out to look for a certain blackened lamb on a small hump of earth that was part of her childhood. It was the grave of some lady's stillborn child (now she knew it must have been Miss Nell Loomis's)" (1949, 260). The least visible but most prominent thing about this hallowed place is its "invisible line," the fact that there are no African Americans here except for the laborers. As Virgie moves closer to her mother's burial site, she sees her father's grave "and the red hole torn out beside it. In spite of the flowers waiting, the place still smelled of the sweat of Negro diggers and of a big cedar root which had been cut through and glimmered wetly in the bed of the grave" (262). Sights and smells and seasons, indeed.

Anatomizing the Grotesque

If "place," that time-honored term for thinking about southern literature, can be so variegated, what should we do about the "southern grotesque," a form that is often reviled? Flannery O'Connor began to diminish our appetite for this southern stereotype in her well-known lecture "The Grotesque in Southern Fiction": "Of course, I have found that anything that comes out of the South is going to be called grotesque by the Northern reader, unless it is grotesque, in which case it is going to be called realistic" (1961, 40).

More recently, and with a progressive politics in mind, Mab Segrest urged lesbians and other minority writers to steer away from the grotesque's obtuseness and decadence. In *My Mama's Dead Squirrel: Lesbian Essays on Southern Culture,* Segrest argues that the grotesque characters who populate southern literature only marginalize the already marginal. "I knew in my guts that my strongest feelings, for women and girls, put me somehow on the outside, set me apart. Although I did not know what *lesbian* was, I felt myself a closet freak" (1985, 20). For years Segrest found an outlet for her "freakishness" in an affection for the outlaws, deaf-mutes, and idiots of southern writing. "If paint peeled or a porch sagged on my parents' house, I would sigh, 'Ah, Compson, Oh, Sartoris.' [Faulkner] seemed to be dealing with race more than any other Southern writer I knew, so I thought his politics were profound" (21).

But in "Southern Women Writing: Toward a Literature of Wholeness,"

Segrest argues that the grotesque appeals to outlaw southerners for neurotic reasons. To identify with the grotesque is physically dangerous when southerners tortured by their own "normalcy" choose "the most vulnerable among [us] to punish for their own secret alienation, to bear the burden of strangeness" (24). For Segrest the grotesque serves reprehensible political ends: "It fastens the creative imagination on images of deformity and despair. Backed by patriarchal myth, it persuades us that this is reality, i.e. not to be questioned or changed. People in power stay in power: it's god-ordained. The grotesque limits the creative imagination by causing divisions within the self so that the individual is cut off from her deepest parts, from those oracles and visions that could tell of a different reality, of the possibility of wholeness" (29). After such indictment, what forgiveness? Why salvage the southern grotesque?

First, the grotesque is worth looking at simply because southern literature displays such an extraordinary penchant for broken bodies and peculiar corporeal citations. It is fascinated with a set of metaphors that describe local cultures by means that are not entirely local but shared across regions and nationalities. In other words, the South has no special purchase on the grotesque; other cultures call on its features as well. But grotesque bodies provide a particularly condensed and useful figure of thought for presenting a set of problems plaguing the South; it offers, among other advantages, a way of previewing what is known but not thought—a set of unacknowledged political coordinates.

Segrest, of course, grants the grotesque's omnipresence; what she rues is its political intent. But I want to describe the grotesque's political fierceness as well as its transitivity: it has great mobility across a range of fields and feelings. Although I'm convinced that the grotesque reproduces the possibility for confronting the strangeness of southern culture, other theorems suggest its liabilities as well as its refining fires.

The Grotesque as Semiotic Switchboard

First and foremost, the grotesque can be understood as a prose technique for moving background information into the foreground of a novel or story. We see this most clearly in that famous *northern* story about the South, *Uncle Tom's Cabin.* Two men sit "alone over their wine, in a well-furnished dining parlor"—a slave dealer and slave owner who are bickering over the price of Uncle Tom. With his uncouth diction and slovenly dress, the slave dealer Haley ("a short thick-set man, with coarse commonplace features") speaks in obscene aphorisms while Mr. Shelby has "the appearance of a gentleman." Stowe heightens the contrast between these men only to drive home their similarities. When an African American child enters the room—a beautiful boy with eyes "full of fire and softness" who becomes another object for sale, the two men toss him bits of food:

> "Hulloa, Jim Crow!" said Mr. Shelby, whistling, and snapping a bunch of raisins towards him, "pick that up, now!"
>
> The child scampered, with all his little strength, after the prize, while his master laughed.
>
> "Come here, Jim Crow," said he . . . the master patted the curly head, and chucked him under the chin.
>
> "Now, Jim, show this gentleman how you can dance and sing." The boy commenced one of those wild, grotesque songs common among the Negroes, in a rich, clear voice, accompanying his singing with many evolutions of the hands, feet, and whole body, all in perfect time to the music.
>
> "Bravo!" said Haley, throwing him a quarter of an orange.
>
> "Now, Jim, walk like old Uncle Cudjoe when he has the rheumatism," said his master.
>
> Instantly the flexible limbs of the child assumed the appearance of deformity and distortion, as, with his back humped up, and his master's stick in his hand, he hobbled about the room, his childish face drawn into a doleful pucker, and spitting from right to left, in imitation of an old man.
>
> Both gentlemen laughed uproariously. (1966, 11–14)

Bent over and gray, this sudden grotesquing of the child's body skewers the "background" features of slavery and shoves them into the foreground; the child's old body maps for the reader the slaveholders' predations. Little Harry becomes a "semiotic switchboard" (Eagleton 1981, 145) for a world of grief and pain; this world's primary code—a child playing games before a jovial adult audience—is scrambled into its antithesis: a child who becomes old before his time, and two men who are bent on his aging. The body of this "southern" child becomes a site for reading cultural depravity; in the superimposition of Uncle Cudjoe on Harry's young body, the very young are swallowed by the very old, and the horrendous implications of Haley's and Shelby's everyday acts come to life. Ground is turned into figure as the child assumes the burden of future deformities.

The Grotesque as Monstrosity, as a Figure Resisting Change

If the grotesque serves primarily as a figure of condensation that helps us read a particular character's social or political sphere (inscribing the social on the ungainly parameters of the body), we have also seen the ways in which its avatars can be less than politically progressive. Instead of recreating repressed ground as figure, tropes of monstrosity can create so much distraction that emerging politics (especially those that might become ground-breaking or foundational) simply recede. Monster tropes become switching points in a stratified culture overloaded with change: a culture whose categories have short-circuited precisely because they carry too much information.

If monstrous bodies connote (and produce) social explosions, they are also the stuff of rumor, allowing entire populations to resist social change. As we've already seen, O'Connor's "Displaced Person" plays out this hysteria (displacing it from race to ethnicity) when Mrs. Shortley has a vision of two languages—Polish and English—at war with one another. "She began to imagine a war of words, to see the Polish words and the English words coming at each other, stalking forward . . . gabble gabble gabble, flung out high and shrill and then grappling with each other. She saw the Polish words, dirty and all-knowing and unreformed, flinging mud on the clean English words until everything was equally dirty. She saw them all piled up in a room, all the dead dirty words . . . piled up like the naked bodies in the newsreel" (1971, 209), as if the only result of political disagreement can be dirt and atrocity.

When monstrous images roar in, political contestation becomes so heightened, so labile, that a sense of civil or political content disappears and what emerges instead are chaos-centered paradigms that deride or banish the possibility of reasoned political speech. A monstrous public response can have this result: ideas that are trying to make their way into public space disappear—overtaken by the chimera of horror. Still, the messy, untidy, fiendish bodies that emerge suggest the eruption of forces outside the system. And the result, at least in fiction, is a brilliant imagistic strategy for defining the ways in which conservative white southern populations deal with change.

The Grotesque as Figure for the Literal

Already we're acquiring a sense of the rich field this body-bent fiction tries to work over and through. But amid these hyperbolic figurations, a third version of the grotesque may seem at first woefully short on imagination. The wounded, nonintegral body becomes a trope for reproducing the literal—that is, for displaying what happens to bodies in real time and space. As Farah Jasmine Griffin describes black migration narratives from the twenties and thirties: "The texts are filled to the brim with the portrayal of an institutionalized terrorism that daily inflicts itself on the lives of black characters. Lynching becomes a metaphor for all such acts of violence on Southern blacks. The black body—be it lynched, raped, working in the fields, working in kitchens, or acting in resistance—is a site of struggle. The power of the South is one of spectacle and torture. It infiltrates black bodies, leaving them dismembered, bent, old beyond their years" (1995, 16). We see this attempt to find metaphors for the literal in Porter's Uncle Jimbilly, whose hands are so gnarled from working that he cannot unbend them. We also find a "figural literalism" in Welty's Pinchy as her body follows the automaton of the law; when she is expelled into the noontime heat for a white woman's convenience, her body provides a spectacle "like" that of torture or lynching. The sweatbox in *Dessa Rose* offers more literalism. Sherley Ann Williams focuses on the implements slave-owning cultures designed for creating pain: "Know what that is, Mis'ess? It's a closed box they put willful darkies in, built so's you can't lie down in it or sit or stand in it. . . . I don't know how long they had her in that box. Her face was swolled; she was bloody and dirty, cramped from lying up in there. I didn't think she could stand up; but she did" (1986, 142–43). In *Dessa Rose* Williams invents a Dantesque punishment for a white slave dealer who has been purchasing house slaves and field hands. Set upon by the slaves in his coffle, he loses an arm: "The slave dealer . . . was quite literally mad. . . . A crackle of laughter or perhaps only the blinking of an eye and he would be plunged into tears and raving. . . . Most often Wilson cursed the darky, 'treacherous nigger bitch,' and her cohorts, 'fiends,' 'devils'—'Oh stop the bloody bastards, Nate!' his empty right sleeve waving as the nub within it jerked. It was an affecting spectacle. To see a white man so broken by nigras went quite against the grain" (14–15). Here, the grotesque becomes a quick way of presenting the beggarliness of this white man's worldview (fitting the parameters of the grotesque as semiotic switchboard) but also suggesting what happens when "institutionalized terrorism" turns back on itself.

Why describe as "literal" a prosody so highly wrought, so figurative? I'm suggesting that these highly embroidered bodies offer a way of reproducing official terrorism that is both surrealistic and all too real. Confronted with the spectacle of torture, of the body bent, overworked, suffering, tossed aside, it may be difficult to find metaphors exaggerated enough to describe systematic oppression.

The Grotesque as a Figure for the Horror of Whiteness

So far these images seem racially interchangeable, deployed by black and white authors alike. But don't racial differences also inflect the southern grotesque? For example, African American fiction often uses dismembered or monstrous bodies as a figure for the horror of whiteness. In Hurston's *Their Eyes Were Watching God* and Wright's "Big Boy Leaves Home," ferocious, open-mouthed dogs inculcate the costs of a predatory whiteness:

> He braced himself, ready. Then, he never exactly knew whether he had lunged or the dog had lunged—they were together, rolling in the water. The green eyes were beneath him, between his legs. Dognails bit into his arms. His knees slipped backward and he landed full on the dog; the dog's breath left in a heavy grasp. Instinctively he felt the dog twisting between his knees. The dog snarled, long and low. (Wright 1965, 50)

> The dog shook up and growled like a lion, stiff-standing hackles, stiff muscles, teeth uncovered as he lashed up his fury for the charge. Tea Cake split the water like an otter, opening his knife as he dived. . . . They fought and somehow he managed to bite Tea Cake high up on his cheek-bone once. (1990b, 157)

In each instance the dog offers a somatic alphabet for the angry white world each author wants to depict with swiftness and economy. The grotesque becomes a figure of condensation and displacement in which a fragment represents a whole gamut of actions that, in Hurston's case, define white cruelties both after and during the storm. In her novel the dog is, in fact, a miniature version of the hurricane, "lashed up [in] his fury"; like the white people who claim the hill, he commands the high ground and turns on Tea Cake with vituperative fury (just as the white men do when the waters have subsided and Janie and Tea Cake walk into town).

What formal power do these figures offer? In *Their Eyes Were Watching God,* Hurston has no desire to dwell on white culture's dominance across the breadth of her text. Instead she uses the dog and the hurricane to acknowledge white culture's power and momentum before exploring the results of this momentum on black communities. In contrast, Wright wants to show his black hero tackling white culture, defeating it, taking it on in the labyrinthine depths of the earth, where, Theseus-like, Big Boy battles this culture's Minotaurs before escaping north in a truck that looks nothing like kingdom come.

The Grotesque as a Figure for the Horror of Being White

Whereas black fiction uses the grotesque to reproduce the horror of whiteness, fiction by white southern women often deploys frightening, nonintegral bodies to depict the horror of being white in a culture that abuses people according to their place in the color line. When Porter's Miranda goes to the segregated circus (accompanied by her family and by Dicey, her black caretaker), "the flaring lights burned through her lids, a roar of laughter like rage drowned out the steady raging of the drums and horns." She opens her eyes to see a creature dressed "in a blousy white overall . . . with bone-white skull and chalk-white face" who is balancing precariously on a very high wire. As he pretends to fall, "the crowd roared with savage delight, shrieks of dreadful laughter like devils in delicious torment. . . . Miranda shrieked too, with real pain. . . . The man on the wire, hanging by his foot, turned his head like a seal from side to side and blew sneering kisses from his cruel mouth. Then Miranda covered her eyes and screamed, the tears pouring over her cheeks and chin" (1972, 344–45). Is this an image of self-loathing that communicates the horror of whiteness without self-recognition? Yes and no. Miranda is put upon by white grownups who send her home when her scream unleashes their cruelty. But when Dicey is forced to take her away, Dicey herself suffers an extraordinary sense of loss; her ticket into the whites-only circus is revoked, her demeanor legislated by this white child's needs. Thus Miranda reenacts the very thing that frightens her most. Her own terror about white sadism, masochism, repetition, and loss is reenacted by a clownish white body—one that becomes her own, in its cruelty and vertigo.

I'm suggesting that white writers investigate half-glimpsed, invisible ideologies of whiteness using metaphors of grotesqueness that differ from the grotesque valences of African American fiction. There the grotesque frequently offers a terrifying condensation of the forces that a range of black protagonists find themselves up against. White writers, in contrast, are both in and of the world they are trying to define or critique. Images of leakage, a sense of being unable to locate the self in the midst of a nameless, floating field of chalky, bone-white faces, create in Miranda feelings of vertigo, frightened overidentification, and nausea. These images of whiteness have the effect of the uncanny, in which something all too familiar is strangely defamiliarized.

The Grotesque and the Stripe of Segregation

Clearly the grotesque is not a static form. I've suggested five different ways this figure is useful to southern writers: in the first a predatory background becomes available for progressive acts of reading and perhaps even for change. The second involves the reenactment and exposition of a reactive politics, while the third reveals the grotesque's mimetic powers. Fourth and fifth, I've suggested that the grotesque's nonintegral bodies can be racially motivated or inflected: handled differently by black and white writers. To these I want to add a sixth mode of politicized writing, namely, the ways in which some southern bodies take on the stripe of segregation and are, quite literally, divided in half: split between white and black cultures—transgressively hybrid. I'm not speaking about mulatto figures here (although characters like Joe Christmas may well carry a grotesque valence in fiction by men). Instead, I'm interested in bodies that offer a literalization of Jim Crow ideology by incorporating the line of segregation itself, bringing apartheid deep into the self.

We'll see instances of these bisected figures in the fictions of McCullers, O'Connor, and Gilchrist, as well as a fascination with twinned bodies, suggesting a crucial point. As we move from the nineteen-twenties to the forties and fifties we find an increasing interest in hybridity. This is hardly surprising, given the South's ongoing political turmoil and the strange, unaccountable stories that emerge from this turmoil. Even though economic deprivation and Jim Crow illogic persisted as the twenties trudged into the thirties, during the New Deal, ideologies and expectations changed. As Arthur Raper, one of the founders of Southern Conference for Human Welfare, explained: "A lot of folks were standing on their feet and talking and expecting things that they had never expected before. . . . Here was a ferment, a very basic, vital ferment, and people needed to respond to it in some way" (Sullivan 1996, 67).

Southern literature responded to this ferment with increasingly bizarre bodily tropes:

> It had been a freak with a particular name but they couldn't remember the name. The tent where it was had been divided into two parts by a black curtain, one side for men and one for women. The freak went from one side to the other, talking first to the men and then to the women but everyone could hear. . . . The girls heard the freak say to the men, "I'm going to show you this and if you laugh, God may strike you the same way." The freak had a country voice, slow and nasal. . . . "God made me thisaway and if you laugh He may strike you the same way. . . . I never done it to myself nor had a thing to do with it but I'm making the best of it. I don't dispute hit." Then there was a long silence on that side of the tent. (O'Connor 1971, "The Temple of the Holy Ghost," 245)

These hybrid bodies multiply in the fiction of the forties and fifties, a time of angst about women's shifting roles and the slow redistricting of the color line. By the sixties and seventies hybridized bodies often separate into two distinct but interconnected characters. Instead of McCullers's Berenice, a domestic worker with one brown and one blue eye, we meet characters like Gilchrist's Gus and Robert—black and white children whose bodies and fates are inseparable, or the purple hat ladies from "Everything That Rises Must Converge," or the drowning women from Ellen Douglas's "On the Lake."

This observation carries within it a simple proposition that "the" southern grotesque is subject to a wide range of historical variation. If the demeanor of these hybrid bodies is subject to historical whim, we see another dimension of change in *Can't Quit You, Baby,* where the main characters cease to be stereotypical grotesques and become characters who are disabled. Clearly the language used to describe southern bodies changes with time; by the eighties it no longer seems appropriate to throw about disabled bodies as tropes without an awareness of the harm to be done in using such bodies as symbols.

"God Made Me Thisaway"

At the beginning of this chapter I offered to round up the usual suspects of southern studies and send them all packing. Instead, I've gussied them up, reinflecting place and "the southern grotesque" by providing lexicons to confound the habitual. In the next chapters I will be less conciliatory. Chapter 2 asks what happens if you dynamite the tracks separating an "African American" from a "southern" tradition and rethink southern literary critical habits of periodization. Chapter 3 redefines the economy of dirt avoidance that Mary Douglas invents in *Purity and Danger;* it describes a semiotics of southern pollution that foregrounds rags and cloth remnants as racialized emblems of soul murder. Chapter 4 examines "the mind of the South" from the perspective of women's writing, investigating (1) the abyss between white and black ways of knowing the South, (2) the importance of the "unthought known" as an index of white culture's arrested systems of knowledge, and (3) the need to explore entire systems of surrogated knowledge about race and gender that have been subjugated to "official" ways of knowing. Chapter 5 will take on an undernoticed morphology in southern women's fiction: the prominence of gargantuan women whose giant bodies become a remarkable way of redistricting earth and reclaiming new southern territory; they involve the production of terrain for the disenfranchised but also conjure up a passel of old southern children who become a route to the politics of the everyday. Chapter 6 redefines southern literature's relation to "History"; it explores women writers' refusal of monumental and empirical chronicles of the southern past—of the South as "past." In casting Eleanor Roosevelt as an artist of the surreal, I explore the ways in which Carson McCullers's *The Member of the Wedding* contributes to and revises our reading of Roosevelt as an icon of the thirties and forties.

Chapter 7 is about the object history shared between black and white women; it creates a space where very disparate fictions about the South come together, and it moves outside the South, to the rim of Ohio: "*Nothing nastier than a white person!* / She mutters as she irons alterations / in the backroom of Charlotte's Dress Shoppe." In Rita Dove's *Thomas and Beulah,* white objects inspire invective as the air fills with white women's odors, the iron awakening "perspiration / and stale Evening of Paris" (1986, 63). Here I want to explore another kind of bodily residue: namely, what happens when an object owned by one culture crosses over—is split, shared, appropriated, or handled by another culture? What does it mean for southern women—black and white—to handle the same things, to address a similar object world of commodities and children, but from radically different political, economic, and semiotic perspectives?

If these chapters demonstrate that what gets mapped onto southern minds, bodies, and objects is always overinvested and overdetermined, chapter 8 explores the grotesque as a figure of testimony; it asks how bodies that bear witness become racially or sexually marked. But I also want to suspend the politics of the grotesque for a reading of its shivers and shiftiness and ask—what is the role of revulsion in southern women's writing? Finally, chapter 9 questions the relevance of southern studies within a world of globalized localities and explores the dirt-based economy—the pollution-play—that Zora Neale Hurston embraces in *Their Eyes Were Watching God.*

Chapter Two

Dynamiting the Rails: Desegregating Southern Literary Studies

Describing his recent book on southern literary studies, Michael Kreyling says that "*Inventing Southern Literature* is . . . not a counternarrative that seeks to dynamite the rails on which the official narrative runs; rather, it is a metanarrative, touching on crucial moments . . . where the official narrative is made or problematically redirected" (1998, ix). This goal is unevenly achieved within Kreyling's book. But in *Dirt and Desire* I'm driven by another animus. I want to dynamite the rails.

The iron path, the official narrative along which the Dixie Limited has been bound, suggests that southern literature is about community (and not contestation), about place and the past (and not about the burden of underpaid domestic and agricultural labor, or the Great Migration, or the effects of the New Negro Renaissance on southern writing), about the preoccupations of an established white patriarchy (and not the weird conversations that take place among black and white women writers), about the epic of race (and not about the recognition of patrilineal mystifications of miscegenation, or of "the" southern family, or of "the" spirit of the land, or of a peculiarly southern sense of place). I want to argue that these traditional categories represent mystifications in order not to know, mystifications designed to overlook the complexities of southern fiction—its exploration of throwaway bodies, of a culture of white neglect, of the ways in which gender and racial politics work in the everyday, the commonplace. But if these old categories have become the mystic self-certainties that I want to blow up, what can I use for nitroglycerine? And where shall I plant it?

Looking at the detritus of chapters and papers that surround me I see a hundred paths for amplifying the South's differences with itself; these stories seem self-multiplying rather than linear. "I can smell you the minute you walk in the house without even looking to see if it is you. Like a hundred flowers," John Henry says to Frankie in Carson McCullers's *Member of the Wedding*. "'I don't care,' she said. 'I just don't care.' 'Like a thousand flowers,' said John Henry, and still he was patting his sticky hand on the back of her bent neck" (1975, 11) But I will need to get away from floral metaphors if I'm going to keep my head straight about these explosives. And where better to begin than with the train tracks themselves? In Zora Neale Hurston's 1934 novel *Jonah's Gourd Vine,* when John Pearson first glimpses a train, he is frightened out of his mind: "John stared at the panting monster for a terrified moment, then prepared to bolt. But as he wheeled about he saw everybody's eyes upon him and there was laughter on every face. He . . . tried to look unconcerned, but that great eye beneath the cloud-breathing smoke-stack glared and threatened" (1962, 34–35). Does this portrait of a black youth who has never seen a train seem excessively naïve, a depiction of the black southerner as primitive, or is Hurston capturing a new phenomenology: the myriad ways the southern world was changing for African Americans born just after emancipation who were still harnessed by the scarcity and immobility of the sharecropping system? As late as 1965, visiting a plantation in Alabama, Martin Luther King Jr. was incredulous when he met sharecroppers who had only handled plantation scrip, who had never seen U.S. currency (Dittmer 1995, 17). Critics have argued that Hurston does invaluable work in associating the train's jazzy rhythms with folk traditions ("Wolf coming! Wolf coming! Opelika-black-and-dirty! Opelika-black-and-dirty! Ah—wah-oooon," 77), but I will also argue that she is rewriting black public history—capturing the train's historic meaning for southern black men and women longing for that "great away that gave John's feet such a yearning for distance" (77).

What would it mean to organize one's reading of the mind or meaning of "the" South around Hurston's texts rather than, say, Faulkner's? The train tracks that William Faulkner describes in *Go Down, Moses* furnish fuel for older readings of southern literature; they fan Agrarian flames.[1] Here the train becomes an emblem of the disappearing "wholeness" of a mythic southern experience—a space-devouring monster, a force ruining the southern wilderness. "The caboose still slowing, creeping, although the engine's exhaust was already slatting in mounting tempo against the unechoing wilderness. . . . Then it was gone. It had not been. . . . The wilderness soared, musing, inattentive, myriad, eternal, green; older than any mill-shed, longer than any spur-line. 'Mr Boon here yet?' he said" (1973, 322). Even here, in the "inattentive, myriad" wilderness, Isaac MacCaslin is careful to call his white sidekick, Boon Hogganbeck, "Mr Boon" when he speaks to Ash, the black cook. Pastoral does not eviscerate hierarchy and racism but crystallizes them, so that a white nostalgia for lost wilderness, for the spaces devoured by this train also includes a yearning for the hierarchy enforced by this "Mr." In contrast, when Hurston's John Pearson finally rides on a train, its progress covers him in splendor. He "forgot the misery of his parting from Lucy in the aura of it all. That is, he only remembered his misery in short snatches, while the glory lay all over him for hours at the time. He marvelled that just anybody could come along and be allowed to get on such a glorified thing. It ought to be extra special. He got off the train at every stop so that he could stand off a piece and feast his eyes on the engine. The greatest accumulation of power that he had ever seen" (168–69).[2] The train that roars through the wilderness in *Go Down, Moses* comes to mean loss and transition—a transition that denotes something entirely different for the white men who continue to populate Faulkner's hunting camps than it does for the black cook's descendants. The train becomes John Pearson's alter ego, a great cipher in his efforts to construct the edifice of black patriarchy in a world where all the power seems sewn up by whites. This is a crucial fact about southern literature. African and Anglo Americans often experienced a world of similar objects—but from within completely different semiotic and cultural systems.

For example, in Harper Lee's *To Kill a Mockingbird* when Jem and Scout find the clumsy gifts that Boo Radley leaves for them in the knothole of a tree, Lee seems obsessed with whiteness: "Something white was inside this time. Jem let me do the honors: I pulled out two small images carved in soap. One was the figure of a boy, the other wore a crude dress" (1960, 58). In Lee's novel, these white children dream of themselves, but in Horton Foote's 1962 screenplay for *Mockingbird,* they dream of someone else. This time the children reach into the tree trunk and discover the figures of a boy and girl carved not in white soap but in black. The camera focuses on the white children's hands as they hold these black dolls and imagine these images as their doubles, as images of themselves.

Set against the information on black children's preference for white dolls as idealized self-images that became so crucial in the 1954 case *Brown v. Board of Education,* this portrait of white children treasuring black dolls is, at its core, political. But if the movie idealizes these multicolored children and their not-yet-realized future in a desegregated world where blacks are treasured by whites, the novel brings us back to a more sodden reality. During an unexpected snow shower in Maycomb, Alabama, Jem and Scout try to make a snowman:

> When we had five baskets of earth and two baskets of snow, Jem said we were ready to begin.
>
> "Don't you think this is kind of a mess?" I asked.
>
> "Looks messy now, but it won't later," he said.
>
> Jem scooped up an armful of dirt, patted it into a mound on which he added another load, and another until he had constructed a torso.
>
> "Jem, I ain't ever heard of a nigger snowman," I said.
>
> "He won't be black long," he grunted.
>
> Jem procured some peachtree switches from the back yard, plaited them, and bent them into bones to be covered with dirt. (66)

These messy armfuls of earth are buried, extinguished under a flimsy veneer of whiteness. "Jem scooped up some snow and began plastering it on. He permitted himself to cover only the back, saving the public parts for himself. Gradually Mr. Avery turned white" (67). Black children whose intrinsic worth and cleanliness are denied but who are made out of soap, snow-white characters extrinsically associated with cleanliness but who are secretly made out of earth: southern literature trades on these confusions.

These images, aiming at comedy, carry a traumatic subtext: the historical association of African Americans with earth or dirt.[3] Lee represents an abstracted black body that has both created and has been forced—through its work and its traumas—to become a landscape. As Farah Griffin suggests in *"Who Set You Flowin'?": The African-American Migration Narrative,* "The juxtaposition of the sweet and bitter affirms the basic contradictions of the South. On the surface it is a land of great physical beauty and charm, but beneath it lay black blood and decayed black bodies. Beneath the charm lay the horror. Like the cotton they pick, the lynched black bodies are also a southern crop" (1995, 16). In this snowman Lee is trying both to gloss and gloss over a history beyond the power of her images—the white surface of the snowman depends entirely upon the body of the black snowman—but in this body black subjectivity is utterly extinguished.[4]

In *Sula* Toni Morrison takes these traumas north in order to challenge the repressive legacy of Harper Lee's color fantasies. But the vestiges of southern labor history, the association of Africans and African Americans with the soil that they tilled, the earth in which they were buried, continues to hector her novel. For Sula, the value of Ajax's body resides in an intricate layering of precious metals and water-seeking earth:

> If I take a chamois and rub real hard on the bone, right on the ledge of your cheek bone, some of the black will disappear. It will flake away into the chamois and underneath there will be gold leaf. I can see it shining through the black. I know it is there. . . . And if I take a nail file or even Eva's old paring knife—that will do—and scrape away at the gold, it will fall away and there will be alabaster. The alabaster is what gives your faces its planes, its curves. . . . Then I can take a chisel and small tap hammer and tap away at the alabaster. It will crack then like ice under the pick, and through the breaks I will see the loam, fertile, free of pebbles and twigs. For it is the loam that is giving you that smell. . . . I will put my hand deep into your soil, lift it, sift it with my fingers, feel its warm surface and dewy chill below. . . . I will water your soil, keep it rich and moist. But how much? How much water to keep the loam moist? And how much loam will I need to keep my water still? And when do the two make mud? (1973, 130–31)[5]

Black to gold to alabaster to loam: Morrison insists on the treasuring, the revaluing of African American characters who possess layers and layers of complex subjectivity and not just the brute subjected stuff from which whiteness is made. Morrison may move her character north, but what lingers from the southern past is the need to reassess black subjectivity as a site of struggle. Morrison's quarrel with Harper Lee and the "tradition" she writes from is contestatory; repudiating the binary portrait of black and white implicit in Lee's snowman, she creates an entirely different black hero, a new kind of Tom Robinson: a black man with layers and layers of complexity to separate him from Atticus's paternalism. As Griffin suggests, "The power of the South" has been "one of spectacle and torture. It infiltrates black bodies, leaving them dismembered, bent, old beyond their years. It also reaches into the very depths of the land which they occupy" (1995, 16), becoming, in effect, a part of the soil. Moving north these layers and associations can change; Toni Morrison takes this landscape and fashions it again into a character.

This act of refashioning a southern literary tradition is also the work of *Dirt and Desire*. At the heart of this book is the insistence that southern literature, at its best, is not about community but about moments of crisis and acts of contestation, about the intersection of black and white cultures as they influence one another and collide. This has not been the dominant methodology of southern literary studies. Instead, when feminist scholars such as Thadious Davis have opened the door to such comparisons, other critics of southern literature have closed them.

In *Inventing Southern Literature,* Kreyling insists on "the difficulties in accomplishing cultural crossover from African American to southern literary heritage and history"; he suggests that the project of reimagining African Americans as writers involved in "the southern self-interpretation" is deeply problematic—difficult to argue for and even harder to imagine (1998, 77).[6] For Kreyling, it seems simpler to divide "southern" and "African American" writers into competing traditions. "To make [Ernest] Gaines a redeeming southern writer is to delete much of this interpretation of his work. His 'place'—pardon the problematic echoes . . . seems to be in another tradition" (97).[7] Within this gestalt black male writers' "southernness" becomes "peripheral to the fiction many of them have written" (98), while black women writers become most "southern" when they write within a utopian tradition that affirms a female world of love and ritual. But the black writers we will explore here are obsessed with the South and the ways it has been shaped by African American subjects. When Kreyling asks, "What interest could exist that might persuade a black southern writer that his identity is to be found in an ideology so consistently exclusionary and prejudicial to him and to images of him?" (77), I would answer with another question. Is it possible to write about black and white versions of the South apart from one another? That is, can you read *Go Down, Moses* (1942) without thinking about what *Jonah's Gourd Vine* (1934) teaches us about the train's possible meanings for Ash, the black cook? Can you read *Jonah's Gourd Vine* without thinking about the difference between Isaac MacCaslin's and John Pearson's visions of southern progress? What happens if you dynamite the spaces separating these tracks? Describing the white mobs who rioted against freemen and slaves at the time of Nat Turner's rebellion, Linda Brent tells of the violent envy of poor whites for her grandmother's possessions, her relative bounty:

> My grandmother had a large trunk of bedding and tablecloths. When that was opened, there was a great shout of surprise; and one exclaimed, "Where'd the damned niggers git all dis sheet an' table clarf?"
>
> My grandmother, emboldened by the presence of our white protector, said, 'You may be sure we didn't pilfer 'em from *your* houses."
>
> "Look here, mammy," said a grim-looking fellow without any coat, "you seem to feel might gran' 'cause you got them 'ere fixens. White folks oughter have 'em all." (Jacobs 1973, 66)

A century later, in "Everything That Rises Must Converge" (a story about the conflicts dividing blacks and whites during the civil rights movement in Georgia), Flannery O'Connor tells a very different story about racial unrest that points to a continuous drama of class and race violence over possessions, leading to the same insistence that "white folks oughter have 'em all." This time two women—one black, the other white—get on a city bus wearing identical purple hats, and one of them dies. There are several themes to unlock here. First, it seems amazing that practices so salient in the 1840s—the anxiety about race and ownership not only as a mark of rising class status but as a mark of equality, a brand of self-ownership threatening to white culture—are still so salient in the postbellum South. Second, we encounter the problem of repetition, or stutterance—of a literature that keeps recycling the same themes in increasingly violent and macabre settings. Third, these stories suggest the difficulty white southern culture has in freeing itself from specters of ownership—from its obsessions with African Americans as objects, as things to be owned—and the question of whether whites can allow a person who has been so commodified to ascend to the status of possessive individualism. Fourth, this object-obsession (this use of "things" to investigate questions of self-ownership and self-extension in space) is one site where fiction by black and white women is both similar and utterly unlike. That is, both Brent and O'Connor share a fascination with objects that cross back and forth between cultures; both writers note the violent results of this passage. But Brent is describing her own struggle within the devastating climate of deprivation experienced by most antebellum blacks, whereas O'Connor lived part of her life in a house that, as Alice Walker tells us, was built with bricks made by slaves.

To thrust black and white writers together (to jump into the abyss separating writers by history, culture, geographical location, and race) does very strange things. For instance, black and white women differ in their retellings of political conversion narratives. Coming-into-knowledge-about-race is a typical story for white liberals who grew up in the pre–civil rights South. *The Long Walk Home,* a film set during the Montgomery bus boycotts, envisions its white heroine's prejudice-changing revelation on a bus trip to Oregon in the 1930s:

> It was midsummer and it was hot and this bus driver found us a public pool and we went swimming and then these two colored boys came and got in the water, and let me tell you, you've never seen twenty girls get out of the water so fast in all your life. We just didn't know any better. But I remember watching the other kids in the water, and they just

> kept right on swimming with the colored boys. They didn't seem any the worse for it. The rest of the world is living this way and so you just don't question it.

Here we find the same terror of bodily contamination through contact with a racial "other" that we will explore in Maya Angelou's visit to a white dentist, or Molly Ivins's coming to consciousness at a black water fountain, or Virginia Durr's coming of age. When Durr, the future civil rights activist, went to Wellesley from the white enclaves of Birmingham in the 1920s, her greatest shock was to encounter a new way of eating. Her dining table was integrated—that is, it included a single black student. As she said to Patricia Sullivan, "I nearly fell over dead" (Sullivan 1996, 110).

This coming to knowledge about race (almost always invoking white convulsiveness) is a repeated story, not just a phenomenon of the thirties or the fifties. The century is pockmarked by whites going north and seeing the world through different eyes. Take the case of the white southern activist Clark Foreman in the years before he became an advocate for voting rights and progressive labor politics: "Foreman's first break from southern tradition came when he joined a group of students for dinner with W. E. B. Du Bois before a talk Du Bois delivered to [Harvard's] Liberal Club. Foreman had planned to attend the talk but did not know that a dinner was involved. At first he refused to go. He had never sat down to a meal with a black person before and said he could not do it. But his friends and roommates argued with him 'until [he] had no rational defense'" (Sullivan 1996, 28). In reading these conversion narratives, we gather an immediate sense of the schism between black and white writers contemplating the South.[8] The glimmer for whites of blacks' equality and common humanity comes across in these narratives as discovery or surprise. But this story is, for African Americans, already a very old story. Black narratives of racial discovery demonstrate a very different rhetoric of racial confusion. In *Their Eyes Were Watching God,* Hurston describes Janie's sudden discovery amidst the narcissistic bliss of childhood of being defined on the sloping side of the color line. "'Ah couldn't recognize dat dark chile as me. So Ah ast, 'where is me? Ah don't see me.' . . . Miss Nellie . . . pointed to de dark one and said, 'Dat's you, Alphabet, don't you know yo' ownself?'" (1990, 9). The oldness and weariness of the story of prejudice, its wearing out and wearing thin, marks black narratives about the South (as opposed to the humor and logical shamefacedness of once-naïve white people as they happen upon the demons of racism).

These contrasts are instructive but hardly astonishing. And yet comparisons between black and white southern narratives can also produce juxtapositions that seem more mysterious. In 1894, Kate Chopin sends one of her characters into a landscape that is already, as Farah Griffin tells us, filled with the dead. Désirée has recently discovered that her baby (and perhaps she herself) is black. Taking her child from its nurse and walking along "the still fields [where] negroes were picking cotton," Désirée walks to her death. As she disappears, she begins to disaggregate: her dress (a commodity whose raw materials were produced by workers from these very fields?) comes apart:

> Désirée had not changed the thin white garment nor the slippers which she wore. Her hair was uncovered and the sun's rays brought a golden gleam from its brown meshes. She did not take the broad, beaten road which led to the far-off plantations of Valmonde. She walked across a deserted field, where the stubble bruised her tender feet, so delicately shod, and tore her thin gown to shreds.
>
> She disappeared among the reeds and willows that grew thick along the banks of the deep, sluggish bayou; and she did not come back again. (1979, 406)

This thin rim of whiteness followed by an encounter with earth, this image of shredded cloth blanching into the landscape, is something we will encounter again.

In Alice Walker's *The Third Life of Grange Copeland,* published eighty years later, we encounter a similar scene, a strange amalgamation of solid earth and flimsy whiteness. Margaret Copeland, like Désirée, has been abandoned by her husband; she is the mother of a mixed-race baby whose skin "was shadowed pale gold and chocolate like a little animal," and she, too, takes her child and walks out into the dirty beyond. "'Well. He's gone,' his mother said without anger at the end of the third week. But the following week she and her poisoned baby went out into the dark of the clearing and in the morning Brownfield found them there. She was curled up in a lonely sort of way, away from her child, as if she had spent the last moments on her knees" (1988, 29).

Chopin and Walker describe different worlds. Désirée is a "white" woman ejected from her husband's aristocratic privilege who kills herself and her child when she suspects they both are black. Margaret Copeland is a "black" woman locked into her race, stuck in a sharecropper economy supplemented by factory work that keeps her family on the edge of starvation. She kills herself out of self-hatred born from economic, romantic, and ideological hopelessness. She is forced to neglect her oldest child in order to work—under horrific conditions—to feed him. Her husband has been brutalized by the unjust conditions of southern sharecropping; he alternately abandons and brutalizes her. In contrast, Chopin's tale is a new take on the tragic mulatto tale. She redefines the lines of descent for black children, tracing this line through the father's "blood"; she locates, within Désirée's husband, a white man who is also a black father; she gestures toward the power of the letter when it is wielded by a black woman. But Walker's and Chopin's texts, across decades, regions, and races, use shared image clusters to excavate these different valences of race and class as they play across the horizons of gender.

This work of doubling between white and black texts offers an uncanny effect. On a train, seeing his own image in a mirror and confusing this image with the intrusion of an irascible, dangerous old man, Freud began to invent the idea of the uncanny in order to investigate the problem of doubling, or mirroring; he discovered what happens when "his own self" becomes "strange." As Avery Gordon explains, "Freud's haunting experience consists of his looking into a mirror and seeing an alienating figure that turns out to be him too. What Freud calls the archaic here is the recognition of himself as another, as a stranger, the arrival of the person from . . . the world outside himself, from what we call the social." For Gordon the social is "ultimately what the uncanny is about: being haunted in the *world of common reality*" (1997, 54). It is this haunting in the world of common reality—a world of striking gender inequality, a world unevenly shared by two races—that I want to address in *Dirt and Desire*. Both Chopin and Walker invent heroines who respond to racism by destroying themselves and their children and "becoming" a landscape. These common tropes suggest a common haunting that demands a new set theory for assessing the scripts that we use to connect black and white women's writing. But to invoke these texts' commonality is not to make them the same. Hazel Carby cautions that "any feminist history that seeks to establish the sisterhood of white and black women as allies in the struggle against the oppression of all women must also reveal the complexity of the social and economic differences between women" (1987, 3), especially in a world where "fragility was valorized as the ideal state" of white woman, whereas "strength and ability to bear fatigue . . . were positive features to be emphasized in the promotion and selling of a black female field hand at a slave auction" or in hiring a family of sharecroppers (25). Thus Désirée is the picture of aristocratic domesticity, while Margaret Copeland has been sentenced to hard labor to support herself and her family. Chopin's story comes to a close with Désirée's death; her husband's about-to-be-discovered blackness creates a sensational dénouement. In contrast, Walker begins her novel with Margaret Copeland's death. The sensations that accumulate around this dead mother and child are extraordinary but not mysterious; their resolution must be emphatically social.

We need to get over the idea that writing by African Americans has to fit a certain mold before it can be considered "southern." Instead, this writing should change our definitions of what southern literatures are and the categories we use to analyze these literatures. We also need to get over the prejudice that literature by southern women is "minor," for in these texts by Anglo and African American women, we will discover the ammunition we need to blow up the rails: a wealth of images unread, undersung, giving us a world that swerves from official narratives. In the intersections, constellations, and contestations between writings by black and white southern women, in their focus on throwaway babies, giant bodies, epistemological surfaces (rather than depths) and the unseen everyday, we find new routes for thinking about the complexities of southern time and space. Is southern literature about family and community? Sometimes. But it is more likely to be about struggle, crisis, cultural emergence and emergency.

Until very recently, southern literary studies has been driven by a series of refusals. Its central ideas about the modern period have been built upon a strangely restricted way of examining the relation of modern literature to southern history. As we will see in chapters 5 and 6, "history" is a concept to which southern women writers are imagined to be immune or allergic. But this is because scholars have not witnessed these writers' attentiveness to subsemantic history, nor have they challenged the conservative scope of the histories that many southern literary critics invoke.[9] I've already suggested that the segregation of black writing changes the way critics read southern literature. Now I want to address the problem of periodization and the uses of history. Nineteen-thirty has remained a magical date for studies of modern southern literature, and so it is with 1930 that *Dirt and Desire* just as magically begins. *The Sound and the Fury* was published in 1929; in 1930 we are said to have entered a new era in southern self-consciousness sparked by that down and dirty dogfight between H. L. Mencken and the Nashville Agrarians. Even if "the Sahara of the Bozart"'s critique of a Cro-Magnon southern mentality jump-started a great deal of white writing in the 1920s, even if it culminated in the 1930 publication of *I'll Take My Stand*, other things were happening in the South during this period—events that influenced the shape of women's writing to an uncanny degree.

In *A Southern Renaissance,* when Richard King locates the beginning of an efflorescence of southern letters in 1930, when he asks "What was the Southern Renaissance?" his answer is skeptical, but it is also driven by the Agrarians' conservative project. "The writers and intellectuals of the South after the late 1920s were engaged in an attempt to come to terms not only with the inherited values of the Southern tradition but also with a certain way of perceiving and dealing with the past, what Nietzsche called 'monumental historical consciousness.' It was vitally important for them to decide whether the past was of any use at all in the present; and if so, in what ways" (1980, 7).

This focus on the uses of the past has had two important effects on southern literary studies. First, it has created a scenario in which many critics continue to focus on intellectual history—on a set of ideas about the South constructed by a group of conventional white men—and continue to overlook the uses of contemporary events in modern southern literature. This circling of the wagons around the same issues creates something worse than déjà vu; it creates "the return of sameness over and over again, in all its psychological desolation and tedium" (Jameson 1990, 16), producing wild-eyed critics who get the Agrarians' number and then keep calling them again and again. But the opposite path can be just as dangerous: "To shed our defenses and give ourselves over absolutely to this terrifying rush of the non-identical is of course one of the great ethical fantasy-images of the postmodern and the very delineation of the 'schizophrenic hero'" (19). What happens if, as heroines, we risk this schizophrenia?

Second, in 1930 America was also in the midst of another intellectual movement, the New Negro Renaissance, a literary movement that rayed out from Harlem in the 1920s but was hardly restricted to the Northeast. By the 1930s this movement had come into its own and come south; Sterling Brown's *Southern Road* was published in 1932, Zora Neale Hurston's *Jonah's Gourd Vine* in 1934 and *Mules and Men* in 1935, followed by *Their Eyes Were Watching God* in 1937 and *Uncle Tom's Children* in 1938. What were white southerners to make of this gathering of black artists and intellectuals who wrote so beautifully and so freely challenged stereotypes about black resistance and intellect, rewriting old southern monologues about race? Black middle-class southerners formed reading groups to absorb these new texts, while white writers such as William Faulkner and Caroline Gordon wrestled with a new vision of African American creativity in their fictions and in their midst.

In considering these texts, what difference might it make to register the importance of this explosion of African American creativity on the white South? Admitting the New Negro Renaissance into a southern literary lexicon changes things in several ways. First, it complicates the notion that there ever was (or can be) an "officially imagined" tradition of southern writing that does not include the writing of African Americans.[10] For example, in his eloquent essay about *Absalom, Absalom!* Philip Weinstein looks to the past to explain the white Henry's murder of his supposedly black brother, Charles Bon, suggesting that if Bon "'were' black, he would be a slave and none of this would be possible. Since he 'is' black, we see simultaneously the absurdity and the brutality of racial prejudice, brutal because the normative imposition of that prejudice prevented Southern blacks from ever becoming Charles Bon. Faulkner has created, in the guise of this socially impossible figure (once identified he must self-destruct), so much that the social cannot possibly put together" (1995, 40). Never mind the fact that figures like Charles Bon—privileged, upper class, learned, mixed race—did inhabit the South of the nineteenth century. The point I want to make is that Bon looks rather different if Faulkner is thinking about the past *and* glancing over his shoulder at the New Negro Renaissance. Bon's use of stove polish ink becomes, simultaneously, a joke about the Confederacy and an exemplum of the very difficult material world that some American blacks had to write their way out of. In the context of the New Negro Renaissance, Bon is not at all impossible. He possesses the urbanity of a Sterling Brown and the elegiac eloquence of a Countee Cullen—although the ironies of war, not race, become his subject matter. Could Faulkner (who worked in a New York City bookstore in 1921 as the Harlem excitement was building) be using the story of miscegenation as a screen for his own competition with these new black voices in the landscape—killing off the competition in a racialized version of the anxiety of influence? Perhaps Bon must self-destruct because he has become, in the context of the New Negro Renaissance, so very possible.[11]

Or look at Caroline Gordon's "One Against Thebes," published in 1929 and 1930 and then revised and republished in 1961 and 1963. This is a story obsessed with the heroic stature of Son, a black youth who enters Gordon's narrative like an infant Hercules. The story's white protagonist admires, avoids, and imitates his examples; she slips him a book, walks in his footsteps, and keeps an eye on the tracks he makes over and over again in the dust (1990, 121–33). By 1930 black intellectuals were fully in control of their own intellectual landscapes and stirring up new identities and new ideas for white writers as well. I'm suggesting that the New Negro Renaissance had an enormous impact on the flowering of white southern writing, that the newly visible identity politics represented in Harlem produced, in the South, both defensiveness and a deeply bifurcated, multi-interested white writing.

There are additional problems with reading the early 1930s as a literary moment defined primarily by a group of traditionally racist white men. King suggests that Mencken and the Vanderbilt crowd catapulted white writers into a bewildering inquisition: First, how does one deal with the past? Second, what form should the South's "monumental historical consciousness" take? And finally, how does one decide "whether the past was of any use at all in the present; and if so, in what ways"? Michael O'Brien argues that we need to question "the simple insistence that historical consciousness and rootedness are characteristic of the South" (1993, 169). But I will argue that we must ask a prior question. Whose histories or memories do we refer to as an "inheritance"? Whose history counts as "monumental"? What history does history itself consist of? In *Jonah's Gourd Vine,* when a black sharecropper moves off the plantation to go farther south—all the way to the Florida frontier—why can't Zora Neale Hurston's account of his first train ride count as "monumental"? What about this man's labor in constructing southern railroad lines? Does this count as an "inheritance"?

> That night John slept in the railroad camp and at sun-up he was swinging a nine-pound hammer and grunting over a lining bar. . . .
>
> All day long it was strain, sweat and rhythm. When they were lining track the water-boy would call out, "Mr. Dugan!"
>
> The straining men would bear down on the lining bars and grunt, "hanh!"
>
> "Hanh!"
> "Got de number ten!"
> "Hanh!"
> "Got de pay-car."
> "Hanh!"
> "On de rear end."
> "Hanh!"
> "Whyncher pick 'em up!"
> "Hanh!"
> "Set it over."
> "Hanh!"

> And the rail was in place. Sometimes they'd sing it in place, but with the same rhythm. (1962, 171)

The fuss about whether or not black literature belongs in a "southern" tradition seems, from the perspective of Hurston's text, ridiculous. The argument for Hurston's southernness is usually constructed around her role as a collector of southern folk culture. But in *Jonah's Gourd Vine* she is also recording and recovering black economic history. O'Brien comments that "jazz, though a traditional form, is not remarkable for historicism. There is little history in the lyrics of the Mississippi blues except personal history" (1993, 169). But as Alan Lomax argues in *The Land Where the Blues Began,* these railroad chants are loaded with labor history. Lomax explains: "Railroading was the best job available to blacks in the Deep South." In fact, "it was sometimes hard to get a real railroad man to talk about anything else. . . . A railroad man got some respect from his bosses, who needed skilled men and a happy gang to get the work done so the trains could run on time. The money was steady and better than on any other job, and a woman considered herself lucky if her man worked on the railroad" (1993, 72). Working on the railroad line, John Pearson is able to send money home, and this money creates the conditions for another set of migrations. As men from a Mississippi section-gang told Lomax, "It's a good job, I mean, you can raise a family with the job," which provided not much money, but enough to get by. In this atmosphere of penury, the role of railroad songs remained contested among the workers. As one said: "Singing comes according to what job you're doing. Now you take lining track, that singing was just a rhythm that the labor used in keeping the time and getting the track lined like the bossman wanted. But wasn't no joy in singing whatsoever. I mean that it was just a part of the way we men set up to work, to get the job done" (72). Others disagreed: the singing was like the sound of a band that could give your team its spirit to play, its spirit to work.

What counts as history? Hurston's novel is about the difficulty of lining track, as well as the difficulty of constructing new modes of black patriarchy after emancipation; it is about the holes in the self, the potential dangers for a young boy raised amidst the poverty of black sharecropping, and the familial violence that can follow from the white-imposed violence of slavery. These psychological and material constraints push John Pearson into a series of emotional blind alleys and economic advances, ranging from cotton cropping to the rough world of turpentine gangs to railroads to preaching. If Hurston conveys the immediacy of folk forms in this novel, she supplies a great deal about black political and economic history as well. To cite a single example, in 1933 (the year before *Jonah's Gourd Vine* was published), Benjamin Mays and Joseph W. Nicholson published *The Negro's Church,* in which they describe African American churches as the source of five mobilizing themes for black communities. Four of these ("periods of growing racial consciousness, group and individual initiative, splits and withdrawals from established churches," and black migration [Burton 1987, xxxvii]) form the backbone of *Jonah's Gourd Vine.* The second half of Hurston's novel describes an incredible flurry of political activity—a dizzying round of fissures within and withdrawals from John Pearson's church, including the effects of northward migration and the changing role of the church as the center for community life. Mays defined the haven that black churches provided from everyday discrimination; he insisted that to "be recognized and to be 'somebody,' has stimulated the pride and preserved the self-respect of many Negroes who would have been entirely beaten by life, and possible completely submerged. Everyone wants to receive recognition and feel that he is appreciated. The Negro church has supplied that need" (Mays 1968, 15). In the midst of Pearson's unsuccessful marriages, his congregation and his magnetic preaching provided a crucial place for self-definition.

This is all to the good as "local" history, but does Hurston's novel illuminate similar religious-political themes in other southern novels? Indeed it does, for the complexity of African American church politics proves central to Richard Wright's *Uncle Tom's Children,* Eudora Welty's *Delta Wedding,* Harper Lee's *To Kill a Mockingbird,* Flannery O'Connor's novellas and short stories, Ernest Gaines's *A Lesson Before Dying,* and James Agee's *Let Us Now Praise Famous Men;* fissures within the black church also construct the plot of southern spirituals (such as "Scandalize My Name") that Roland Hayes and Paul Robeson recorded.

The "cultural crossover from [an] African-American to [a] southern literary heritage and history" is only difficult because scholars have conflated "southern" with "white." In order to change these categories, we need to invent new archives, new "laws" about what can and cannot be said about texts scattered across and under the "official" literary canon of southern studies. For Foucault, archives are the frameworks that allow things to be "grouped together in distinct figures, composed together in accordance with multiple relations . . . that which determines that they do not withdraw at the same pace in time, but shine, as it were, like stars"; it is a "system of enunciability" that allows the re-creation of "possible sentences" and lets statements emerge "as so many regular events, as so many things to be dealt with and manipulated" (1972, 129–30).

These "possible sentences" must be expanded, for the New Negro Renaissance and *I'll Take My Stand* were not the only stories driving "southern" literature in the 1930s. The beginning of this decade marks the end of the first wave of the Great Migration and the approach of the New Deal: a new era of southern poverty and activism, of greater consciousness about the politics of race and labor. The massive movement of African Americans from South to North figures catastrophically in Faulkner's *The Unvanquished* (that is, it is figured proleptically when Faulkner portrays a post-emancipation exodus from slavery in the midst of the Civil War as a tragedy that results in massive loss of life). This panic about an African American exodus also frames *Jonah's Gourd Vine* as black churchmen struggle over how to respond to the loss of their congregations:

> "Lawd, Sanford gettin' dis Nawth bound fever lak eve'ywhere else," Hambo complained one Sunday in church. "Elder, you know we done lost two hund'ed member in three months?"
>
> "Co'se Ah knows it, Hambo. Mah pocketbook kin tell it, if nothing else. Iss rainin' in mah meal barrel right uh long."
>
> "Dat's awright. De celery farms is making good. All dese folks gone Nawth makes high wages 'round heah. Less raise de church dues," and it was done.
>
> But a week later Hambo was back. "Looka heah, John, dis thing is gittin' serious sho 'nuff. De white folks is gittin' worried too. Houses empty eve'ywhere. (235–36)

The Great Migration becomes a metaphor for white women writers as well as black. Carson McCullers's Frankie longs to go north; O'Connor's Hazel Motes is irked by a black porter who insists: "'I'm from Chicago.' 'Yeah, I bet you are,' Haze said with a leer. . . . Haze got up and hung there a few seconds. He looked as if he were held by a rope caught in the middle of his back and attached to the train ceiling. . . . He knew him to be a Parrum nigger from Eastrod" (1949, 12). Alice Walker begins *The Third Life of Grange Copeland* with the story of a child who yearns for migration: "They had bombarded him with talk about automobiles and street lights and paved walks and trash collectors . . . he had been dazzled by this information and at last overwhelmed. They taunted him because . . . his father worked for a cracker and . . . this cracker owned him. They told him that their own daddy, his Uncle Silas, had gone to Philadelphia to be his own boss" (1988, 4–5).

The southern literary landscapes of the 1930s look much less regionally insular if, instead of zeroing in on events in white intellectual history, we broaden the date to include the influences of black intellectual history as well as the pressures of material histories from black church politics to the effects of the Great Migration to the impact of the New Deal on race, gender, and the politics of segregated labor—a territory recently excavated by Patricia Sullivan. For example, in 1930, when the rates of lynching of black men in the South had doubled (following a gradual decline in the 1920s) and Mary McLeod Bethune signaled her intent "to issue a statement to the press demanding that southern white women assume responsibility for halting the rise in racial violence" (Hall 1993, 161), Jesse Daniel Ames mobilized twenty-six white women to meet in Atlanta to form the Association of Southern Women for the Prevention of Lynching (ASWPL). This organization's important work in combating images of white female fragility, as well the ASWPL's deployment of tactics more euphemistic and less shattering to white populations than those of the NAACP, influenced the work of writers such as Porter, Welty, and O'Connor.[12] In focusing on the uses of the climactic southern past (of the Civil War and its aftermath), literary scholars have overlooked the importance of the southern present—the way that even past-driven fictions such as *The Unvanquished* are immensely worried about black mobility and contemporary struggles for voting rights. The political fantasies Frankie has in *The Member of the Wedding* look very different when her dreams are set against the political projects of Eleanor and Franklin D. Roosevelt; *A Curtain of Green* clamors for a more extended accounting of what happened to southern aristocracies during the depression, as well as an anatomy of white women's responses to jazz and hoboes and spectacle lynchings; Zora Neale Hurston's short stories are filled with details from the new consumer culture that reached into the South with catalogues, advertisements, and objects that blacks (at least, those who had money) could purchase from mail order catalogues as easily as whites—without the threat of bad service or discrimination (Hale 1998, 121–98). These events point to the arbitrariness of any date as "the" beginning of southern literary modernity—especially when this modernity circumscribes women's fiction. Hurston, Julia Peterkin, and Ellen Glasgow created important fiction in the twenties that could serve equally well to mark the beginning of a new southern modernism. (Nella Larsen's reflections on the South in *Quicksand* [1928] and *Passing* [1929] offer still wider reference points for gendered remappings of the New South's racial coordinates.) But 1930 still offers, for the purposes of this book, an imaginary beginning, a premasticated, predefined date that needs, above all, to be chewed over, reruminated, undefined: a year *in the midst of* several tidal events changing the face of the South—events that should also change the ways southern scholars perform their overviews of southern literature.

Finally, in the 1930s an incredible onslaught, a locomotion of women, began publishing fiction. In 1930 Katherine Anne Porter published *Flowering Judas and Other Stories,* while Caroline Gordon issued some of her finest short stories, among them "The Long Day" and "One Against Thebes." These were followed by Fielding Burke's *Call Home the Heart* and Grace Lumpkin's *To Make My Bread* (1932); *Jonah's Gourd Vine,* Gordon's *Aleck Maury, Sportsman,* and Lillian Hellman's *The Children's Hour* (1934); Hurston's *Mules and Men* (1935); Juanita Harrison's *This Great, Wide, Beautiful World,* Margaret Mitchell's *Gone with the Wind,* and Welty's "Death of a Travelling Salesman" (1936); Hurston's *Their Eyes Were Watching God* and Gordon's *None Shall Look Back* (1937); Hur-ston's *Moses, Man of the Mountain*; Marjorie Kinnan Rawling's *The Yearling,* Porter's *Pale Horse, Pale Rider,* and Hellman's *The Little Foxes* (1939); McCullers's *The Heart Is a Lonely Hunter* and Willa Cather's *Sapphira and the Slave Girl* (1940); and Welty's *Curtain of Green* (1941). During the forties Lillian Smith published two major books and Welty three, McCullers produced *The Member of the Wedding* (1946), Knopf published Katherine De Pre Lumpkin's *The Making of a Southerner* (1946), Porter's and Gordon's careers continued to flourish, and Hurston wrote her crazy and underappreciated novel about Florida crackers, *Seraph on the Suwanee* (1948).[13] *The Golden Apples* and *Killers of the Dream,* both richly problematic, both published in 1949, should have changed the South's universe; these books' strange evocations of gender and racial injustice rhyme with the ethos of Simone de Beauvoir's *The Second Sex,* published in France the same year.

The list is absolutely partial, but it is also completely formidable, and it moves us toward 1955, the end of the period covered by Richard King's influential *Southern Renaissance: The Cultural Awakening of the American South, 1930–1955.* King himself points to the arbitrariness of his dates: "Although Woodward suggested no point at which the literary well ran dry, one might conveniently locate the end of the main phase of the Renaissance somewhere around 1955. . . . This is not to say that Southerners stopped writing or that nothing of worth appeared after the mid-1950s. Far from it. But by this point the figures dealt with in my study were either dead or past their creative peaks" (1980, 3). But 1954 is the date of *Brown v. Board of*

Education; 1955 marks the death of Emmett Till, 1956 the Montgomery bus boycott, 1961 the year of the freedom riders, 1962 Fannie Lou Hamer's application to vote and her eviction from the Marlowe plantation, 1963 her beating in the Winona jail. For a southern renaissance to be said to be over in 1955 suggests that the best southern writers could not respond to the civil rights movement with any complexity—a benighted portrait of the South indeed. In 1955 the story of Anglo and African southern women's writing had just begun—or, it had been begun so many times that it started up again, and then again.

During the fifties white southern women published *The Ballad of the Sad Café* (1951), *Wise Blood* (1952), *The Dollmaker* (1954) and *The Black Prince* and *A Good Man Is Hard to Find* (1955), followed by *To Kill A Mockingbird* and *The Violent Bear It Away* (1960) and *Black Cloud, White Cloud* (1963), followed by major story collections by Gordon, Porter, and O'Connor in 1965. Also in 1965 Margaret Walker published *Jubilee,* and women's writing experienced another sea change. Initially, in this rewriting of Civil War and Reconstruction history from an Africanist perspective, "black" and "white" children are twinned:

> Would Marster bring her in his house as he had done all his other bastards? Even though they never lasted long in the Big House. . . . Aunt Sally looked again at the child sleeping in Mammy Sukey's arms and thought how much she and the little Missy Lillian in the Big House looked alike. In her mind she thought, "They could pass for twins—same sandy hair, same gray-blue eyes, same milk-white skin. One of them was Hetta's child, and one of them was Big Missy Salina's. But they were both Marse John's and there was no mistake about that. (1965, 13)

"Same . . . same . . . same." So much gets explored here: the intensity of the racial gaze, an excavation of the mind of the South, but from a black woman's perspective ("Aunt Sally looked . . . and thought. . . . In her mind she thought"). Labor, genealogy, the magic of names, the status of African Americans as they move from being to holding property: What, Walker asks, is the nature of the African American "real"?

> The real name of my maternal great-grandfather, Randall Ware, free black man of Georgia and a blacksmith of Dawson has been retained in the story. The records of his transactions in real estate during the Reconstruction are in the County Courthouse of Terrell County in Dawson, Georgia. The Bank of Dawson and the Bus Depot now

> stand on what was his property. The Bus Depot covers the spot where his smithy and grist mill stood. (x)

As Lee does in *To Kill a Mockingbird,* Walker focuses on black foundations that have been hidden—although institutions such as banks and bus depots rather than dirt snowmen become the tegument of a covering whiteness. But Walker exposes the histories of these foundations, no longer focusing on black men and women who have been disposed of as throwaways or turned into earth but on African American possessors who have owned the earth itself. Four years later Sarah E. Wright explores the elusiveness of this ownership in *This Child's Gonna Live* (1969).

In the sixties, black southern women writers reopened the question of what, precisely, was "monumental" about the Civil War, Reconstruction, the New Deal, and African Americans' acts of migration and urbanization, while white women investigated the politics—and the complicitous aesthetics—of racist guilt. In Ellen Douglas's "On the Lake" (1961) Estella, a former black domestic, does not know how to swim. She goes out in a boat with Anna, her white employer, who can swim but cannot cope with Estella's bulk once both women start to go under; they are drawn together in a terrible twinning:

> They went down. This time they stayed under so long, deep in the softly yielding black water, that Anna thought she would not make it back up.
>
> . . . *She's going to drown me. I've got to let her drown, or she will drown me.* She drew her knee up under her chin, planted her foot in the soft belly, still swollen from pregnancy, and shoved as hard as she could, pushing herself up and back and Estella down and away.
>
> . . . They had been together, close as lovers in the darkness or as twins in the womb of the lake, and now they were apart. Anna shot up into the air with the force of her shove and took a deep, gasping breath. Treading water, she waited for Estella to come up beside her, but nothing happened. . . .
>
> Before she had to decide to dive, something nudged lightly against her hand, like an inquiring, curious fish. She grabbed at it and felt the inert mass of Estella's body, drained of struggle, floating below the surface of the water. She got hold of the belt of her dress and pulled. (391)

Douglas uses, once again, the metaphor of doubling, but this time to push her readers under the water to catch sight of a white woman kicking a black woman to her probable death. Although Anna eventually saves Estella's life, Douglas wants the reader to know that it is the white woman who has put Estella under. When Estella loses consciousness and become fishlike, Douglas stages a trip to the outer zones of disposability to investigate white women's complicity in jettisoning African Americans and their culture during the racist mayhem of Mississippi in the 1960s.

In this changing climate, 1970 is a banner year, with publication of *The Third Life of Grange Copeland, I Know Why the Caged Bird Sings,* and *The Bluest Eye* (set in Ohio, but with traumatic, life-stealing scenes set in the South), as well as *Losing Battles.* From 1970 on the deluge of women's writing from and about the South continues with *The Optimist's Daughter* (1972), *Rubyfruit Jungle* and *Pentimento* (1973), *Corregidora* and *Sister Gin* (1975), *Meridian* and *Generations: A Memoir* (1976), *Song of Solomon* (1977), *In the Land of Dreamy Dreams* (1981), *The Color Purple* (1982), *One Writer's Beginnings* (1984), *My Mama's Dead Squirrel* (1985), *Dessa Rose* and *Thomas and Beulah* (1986), and *Beloved* (1987), *Mama Day* and *Can't Quit You, Baby* (1988), and *Baby of the Family* (1989)—as well as *Bastard Out of Carolina* (1992), *Daughters of the Dust* (1992) and *Eve's Bayou* (1997).

What's wrong with this list? Besides the books and films it leaves out, it commingles texts that *are* with those that *are not* strictly "southern." Is this what happens when someone tries to dynamite the rails? Why do novels by black women raised in the South stand side by side with novels by black writers from the North and the West? If these tracks really run parallel, why hang onto the appellation "southern" at all? Am I simply repeating Hazel Motes's parochial inability to let the black porter in *Wise Blood* be *from* Chicago?

This list includes texts by Clifton, Dove, Morrison, Naylor, and Williams because each of these writers has changed our notion of the mind of the South: of African Americans' relations to the South and to southernness.[14] In addition, Morrison is deeply absorbed by and in dialogue with an "official" southern literary tradition; she is constantly rewriting Faulkner—changing Clytie's ragged body into Circe's rage, rerouting Judith's and Rosa's tattered trousseau into Sethe's bold re-creation of a pieced-together wedding dress. Meanwhile, Clifton and Dove invoke autobiographical connections to the South in memoirs and poetry that describe slave ancestors and relatives who traveled to the North or the Midwest during the Great Migration but were still aiming south in their heads. These writers are included as black women who locate an origin for themselves or for their ancestors in the South, and are therefore absorbed in redefining, as much as any white male agrarian, the uses of the southern past.[15] Still, in clinging to "southern" as a system of classification, have I also effaced region altogether—precisely in order to construct some African American women writers as more "southern" than others? But I also aim to make this distinction. Writers such as Morrison and Clifton may hail from elsewhere, but they are invested in thinking about the South, in rereading and rewriting a Southland that emerges both as ancestral torture chamber and as ancestral home. Starting in the late sixties (although we could go all the way back to ex-slave narratives, or to the ending of Nella Larsen's *Quicksand,* or to Gwendolyn Brooks's statements about black poets who cannot invoke the image of a tree without thinking about the trauma of lynching), we discover a set of African American women writers who needed to think about the South as a way to think about the meaning of being black and who needed to think about the meaning of being black as a way of thinking about the South.[16]

Do I want to take this a step farther, to assert that books by black and white women writers constitute a "tradition"? Not at all. Instead, I will argue that moving back and forth between Anglo and African American texts will teach us something crucial about both "southern" and American literature that we have not seen before. My project is not to examine women's writing decade by decade but to create a new archive—to project a series of image clusters that will help us rechart the strange world "southern" women both reflect and invent in their peculiar, separate, intertwined, and internecine fictions. But the problem is still before me. If I try to dynamite the rails, how do I know if I'm on the right track? Given the dangers of misrepresenting everyone, why embark on this project at all?

First, the abyss between black and white ways of knowing—between these starkly different "minds of the South"—is conflictual, but it can also be symbiotic. In *The Third Life of Grange Copeland* Ruth tries to calm her "severe case of jitters" by "reading *Bulfinch's Mythology*" (325). In Diane Oliver's "Neighbors" an African American child who will be the first to desegregate a white school sits "crosslegged, pulling his ear lobe as he turned the ragged pages of *Uncle Wiggily at the Zoo*" (1991, 474). In contrast, when Juba, Miss Lizzie Starks's black maid, visits the white Virgie Rainey to pack things away after her mother's funeral, Virgie benefits from Juba's tales. At first Juba talks about ghosts in a way that seems utterly irrelevant to Virgie's tentative mourning. For Virgie (and perhaps even for the educated reader), Juba's talk seems primitive and parochial. But this ghost talk has an unerring effect: it allows Virgie to start working through her rage at her mother and her sorrow at her mother's death:[17]

> "Juba, take it all. . . . Plates, knives and forks, the plants on the porch. . . . And what's in the trunks. You and Minerva divide." Then she had to burst out and say something to Juba. "And I saw Minerva! I saw her take Mama's hair switch—her young hair that was yellow and I never saw when it matched any more and she could do anything but keep it in that trunk, and I saw it put down in that paper sack. And my brother's baby clothes and my own, yellow and all the lace—I saw all stolen and put with Minerva's umbrella to take home, and I let them go. You tell that Negro. Tell her I know I was robbed, and that I don't care."
>
> Juba nodded and changed the subject. "Thank you, Miss Virgie, for men's clothes. That salt-and-pepper of poor Mr. Rainey."
>
> "Mama kept everything," Virgie said after a moment.
>
> "Glory."
>
> "Now you can go."
>
> "Why, it's a-rainin'. Do hate rain."
>
> Juba left. But she came back.
>
> "That's it," she called softly. . . . "That's right. Cry. Cry. Cry" (1949, 270).

African American spirit beliefs provide Virgie with superior psychological knowledge. Through Juba's talk, Virgie's anger about what's been taken—her mother's life, her own childhood—gets stirred up and expressively deranged, and two epistemological problems get jammed together. First, we are asked to contemplate the power of a way of knowing death that seems conceptually absurd but emotionally powerful. Wisdom that looks ersatz from one perspective becomes quite effective once it is put to work.

But Virgie is also irritated by what she feels; she tries to repudiate her connections to Africanist systems of knowing by reasserting her whiteness. As the discounted messages about ghosts go to work in Virgie's psyche, Welty explores the ways in which white fantasies about African Americans become ways of coping with metaphysical conundrums. Here, the painful fact of death, the act of necessary grief-work, gets pushed onto an African American woman's body: "And my brother's baby clothes and my own, yellow and all the lace—I saw all stolen and put with Minerva's umbrella to take home, and I let them go. You tell that Negro. Tell her I know." As Virgie's grief wells up, it gets displaced onto her certitude about a domestic worker's pilfering, as if grief can only be handled through surrogacy—via anger at the acts of a subordinate. Welty presents her readers with toxic knowledge that is at once repugnant and epistemologically telling.

Second, comparisons between texts by black and white women writers are full of surprises. In both the African American writer Juanita Harrison's *My Great, Wide, Beautiful World* (1936) and in the white writer Eudora Welty's *Delta Wedding* (1946) a young white girl is killed by a train. In Welty's text the girl dies forgotten, a throwaway, but in Harrison's travelogue the death of a white girl becomes a site of open-eyed, unrestricted trauma.

Class inflects one important difference between Welty's and Harrison's texts. The wealthy Fairchilds can afford to ignore the death of a white trash girl who has flitted across their property:

> "You know what's in my satchel?" He patted it until they all attended. "Train victim. I got a girl killed on the I. C. railroad. My train did it. Ladies, she was flung off in the blackberry bushes. Looked to me like she was walking up the track to Memphis and met Number 3."
>
> "Change the subject," commanded Aunt Tempe, who was the right-end figure of the group.
>
> "Yes ma'am. Another picture of the same pose. . . . Everybody looking at the bride and groom." (1946, 287)

Well fed but impoverished, this young woman is neither recognized nor mourned by the Fairchilds—although one of the Fairchild men has slept with her and Ellen Fairchild treats her with peremptory concern once she knows she is white. That is, Welty's white family is willing to abandon a girl of their own race to a photographers' portmanteau; as a poor white traveler who is not from their class or neighborhood she can easily be discarded. In contrast, Harrison feels a deep sense of sympathy with a wealthy white girl who becomes, in the moment of her death, a fellow traveler. Harrison, who was born and raised in Mississippi, worked as a domestic laborer until she read about the world's nonsouthern spaces in an employer's magazine and decided to take a look for herself. She captured her round-the-world epic (still subsidized by itinerant stints as a lady's maid or domestic laborer) in a roughly spelled memoir excerpted in the *Atlantic Monthly* and published by Macmillan in 1936.

On the day of the white girl's death Harrison is, once again, on a train: "I was studying the book that means everything to me Bradshaws Continental guide all of the sudden I was throwd across the compartment and hit my head. . . . I was very dizzy but I thought about nothing but this book and kept calling my book, my book I was stunted" (1996, 50–51). When she gets off the train Harrison sees many dead and injured passengers:

> It was a hot day and it happen in a turnip patch we used the turnip tops to put under the engured ones heads. I stayed with a German Girl

> that had been torned into thread from the waist down She lived a half hour in that half hour I just loved her she was not more than 21 and had beautiful great blue eyes. she were well dressed and had a beautiful engagement ring on. . . . She kept saying the same thing over and over But . . . a phesant woman . . . couldn't stand the sight and ran away . . . The doctors came and said there was no use trying to do anything for her. I felt terrbly heartbroken to think they left her. finally she died on my arm. had I been killed it would have been absolutely nothing compared to that girl. (51)

How do we read this? We find at least two echoes of what one might think of as a southern aesthetic: the eccentric turnip tops used for pillows (parallel to Welty's odd image of a body stuffed in a portmanteau) and Harrison's self-effacing sense that "had I been killed it would have been absolutely nothing compared to that girl." And yet while Harrison may be from a region where she counts as "absolutely nothing," the South is most conspicuous in its absence from her story: a travelogue in which almost every other place on Earth gets visited, celebrated, named.

Harrison left the South as fast as she could; she wrote very little about this mother-region but a great deal about her global journeys. Like John Pearson, she gathers a powerful sense of self from the trains she travels in. And she is fascinated with her own ability to cross boundaries that would have been restricted in the South. When she describes the act of spending the night in a depot in Bratislava where she "had on a little white crepe waist and it was very cold but the station had a beautiful First Class waiting room" (52), do we take this passage back to the United States and remember that she would not have been allowed to enter a "beautiful First Class waiting room" in the Jim Crow South of the 1930s? Or, when she explains that she often started her trip in third class but made her way into second or first class, does this preoccupation with trains and social mobility suggest the Jim Crow South as one ground against which the figure of her journey gains meaning?

In fact, Harrison remembers the South as the place of another train wreck: "I was in a Reck in 1903 on Sept. 1st when I was a little girl also a Monday but it was twice as bad about 100 killed and many wounded I din't get hurt but many in the coch did so I knew just what to do. I cant bear staying in the hotel room long I . . . imagin the hotel may catch fire and I'd be wraped in flames so I stay out as much as possible" (53). In the South, in 1903, she could only have been seated in a Jim Crow car. How do we read this travelogue in the context of other southern writing? First, Harrison mentions a southern train wreck that has taught her to handle trauma, to recognize and identify with a woman torn below the waist to a thread, and she accompanies this story with a description of terror that mimics a lynching: the possibility of being "wraped in flames so I stay out as much as possible." Part of staying out (of the South) means traveling the rails as much as possible—going away from a place where so many were killed, where somebody dynamited the rails.

The official southern literary narrative, in which black and white southern women writers are minor players, and Harrison a mere curiosity, misses the best part of the journey. My book offers a preliminary effort to use women's writing as lens to rethink the literary "mind" of the South, to invent categories that bring black and white fiction together, and to recognize the ways in which women's writing provides a trip to geographies rarely visited by the white men who've been riding the rails, who've traveled so far on the Dixie Limited.

Chapter Three

"And Every Baby . . . Was Floating Round in the Water, Drowned": Throwaway Bodies in Southern Fiction

Why "dirt and desire"? I take the opening of this chapter from the Jewish writer Edmond Jabès: "'Don't get yourselves all dirty,' mothers tell their children. 'Play with your ball. It's more fun.' But the children would rather dig their fingers into the mud roof of the dead" (1984, 87). This summarizes the way many readers and critics think about southern literature; it is a route to the dead, to the embarrassing, disavowed American past, a space with no exit—a literature replaying stories we're trying (as multiculturalists, feminists, queer theorists, students of globalization) to transcend. To revisit the white texts spawned in the Jim Crow South of the thirties and forties—or even the fifties, sixties, and seventies—is to exit from the contemporary excitements of African, Asian, or Latin American studies, to go south to a very Old Place. This is a fiction always hovering too close to the mud roof of the dead and too nostalgic about its traumas. (Don't we know enough already about the South's torments—about its lynchings and poverty, about Quentin Compson panting—I don't hate the South, I don't, I don't.)

But to turn away from this literature is also to turn away from a world we barely understand: a site where racism happens in some of its most brutal forms, and this brutality, in turn, produces extraordinary works of art. It is also to turn away from obsessions shared by black and white women writers: a preoccupation with the grotesque, with old children and gargantuan women, with objects that pass—or do not pass—the boundaries of race and class.

I have already suggested that my goal in *Dirt and Desire* is to invent categories that will allow us to see southern texts differently, to provide a new etiology of pollution and bodily obsession in southern women's writing, to examine a set of unexpected connections between black women who write about the South and white southern women writers. This register of new and mended terms for analyzing southern literature will include a growing obsession with disfigured bodies, with the culture of neglect and landscapes made out of throwaway bodies, with the law as automaton, with whiteness as pollution, and with the demonics of the racial gaze. But first I want to turn to another question that will haunt me: Why hasn't this work been done before? Why is the work of white southern women writers so domesticated, so hemmed in, while black women who write from or about the South are marginalized, minoritized—not quite counted as southern?

Let's begin with the problem of domestication. Why is it that a writer as freak-obsessed and fiercely disturbing as Eudora Welty can consistently be described as "one of our purest, finest, gentlest voices" (Tyler 1992, 144), her fiction made over in the image of her endearing private persona: the friendly, generous, sweetly intellectual white lady? In her review of Welty's collected short stories, Ann Tyler describes Welty as someone who "tells stories like a friend, someone you're fond of—sitting on her porch shelling peas, you imagine, and speaking up in the South, longingly gazing over the fence at the rich, tangled lives of the Southern neighbors" (144). But what is neighborly about the title story from Welty's first volume, *A Curtain of Green,* in which a middle-aged white lady advances on her black yardman and threatens to kill him, her hoe raised menacingly over his head?

> The clumsy sleeves both fell back, exposing the thick, unsunburned whiteness of her arms, the shocking fact of their youth.
>
> She gripped the handle tightly, tightly, as though convinced that the wood of the handle could feel, and that all her strength could indent its surface with pain. The head of Jamey, bent there below her, seemed witless, terrifying, wonderful, almost inaccessible to her, and yet in its explicit nearness meant surely for destruction, with its clustered hot woolly hair, its intricate, glistening ears, its small brown branching streams of sweat, the bowed head holding so obviously and so fatally its ridiculous dream. (1979, 216)

This avenging white woman hardly seems pitiable, and yet she is filled with voiceless terror about the death and unpredictability of the natural world. Her husband has been killed by a falling tree; her response is to teeter on the edge of an ontological abyss, facing down the puzzle of life and death by tending her garden, until one day she decides to thrust her private anguish onto the body of a black man. Welty suggests the outlines of a psyche and a society that allow such projections; she describes the ways in which the contempt white southerners heaped on African Americans has a complex genesis; here it assuages the metaphysical conundrums of commonplace lives. Welty does not focus on southern racism as an epic event but as a quotidian praxis, a sadistic solution to the ordinary riddles of everyday life.[1]

Welty's horrific story is, then, exactly the opposite of Tyler's honorifics. "A Curtain of Green" says nothing about the comforts of friends shelling peas, looking with affection at the "rich, tangled lives of the Southern neighbors." It says a great deal about nonepic confrontations between the races: the ways in which the available forms of southern racism can convert almost anyone into a borderline personality.

The blow threatening Jamey and the lack of consequences accruing to such a blow (that is, the certainty that any white person who committed such a murder in Mississippi in the thirties would and could get away with it) rhymes unexpectedly with the stricken memories in Audre Lorde's 1981 poem about Emmett Till: "the length of gash across the dead boy's loins / his grieving mother's lamentation / the severed lips, how many burns / his gouged out eyes / sewed shut upon the screaming covers" (1997, 340).[2] "Screaming covers" refers to the graphic images of Till's body that filled northern tabloids after his murder in the summer of 1955. And yet what Lorde gives witness to is a sensational media event rather than a moment of national mourning. In "A Curtain of Green" Welty asks us to think about the melancholic sources of such an event, but not in the usual terms of white culture's sexual psychoses or the South's economies of racial guilt; instead, she dramatizes the nonevents, the meditative unreason driving a white woman to contemplate a murder that is, from the perspective of her grief and her whiteness, emotionally logical. In bearing witness to these unthinkable incidents, both Lorde, a black northern writer, and Welty, a white southerner, evoke the ungrieved grief, the throwaway bodies whose loss hovers in the margins of pre- and post–World War II American culture. That is, Lorde focuses on the shadow cast by Till's death and her own inability to stop aestheticizing it, her well-reasoned need for both physical and aesthetic vengeance. In contrast, Welty investigates the cognitive mechanisms within white southern culture that might allow such an event to recur, to be normative.

Given the violence of Welty's story and its resonance with Lorde's devastating and politically charged poem, how do we account for this double blow: the domestication of white southern women's fiction and the marginalization of black women's writing about the South? Why have powerfully revisionist black writers such as Zora Neale Hurston, Margaret Walker, or Alice Walker become marginal to definitions of a southern tradition? Why have the extraordinary books and short stories white southern women produced in this century been softened, diminished, palliated by even the best of critics? To answer these questions we need to pursue several strategies. First, we must reinvent the categories that have been used to keep southern literature in its place. I have already begun to challenge some of the truisms that have dominated southern literary studies—such as nostalgia for place, the burden of southern history, a propensity for storytelling, and miscegenation as the core of the South's family romance—in light of new maps of genocide, gender, race, and migration that have transformed the study of American regionalism. Can the worn-out categories that have dominated southern studies still account for the ravaged bodies that wash up again and again in stories by black and white southern women? What happens when we look past these truisms to the strange particulars of their writing?

For example, the emotional anatomy of the cast-off, discarded body becomes a repeated figure for angry meditation among black women who write about the South. In *Beloved,* Ella is finally drawn to help Sethe when she remembers her own throwaway child—an infant brutally fathered by the white men who owned her: "She had delivered, but would not nurse a hairy white thing, fathered by 'the lowest yet.' It lived five days never making a sound. The idea of that pup coming back to whip her too set her jaw working" (1987, 258–59).[3] The black child as rubbish, as a waste product, as a residue of white culture's neglect, cries out again in Alice Walker's *Meridian:* "It was Meridian who had led them to the mayor's office, bearing in her arms the bloated figure of a five-year-old boy who had been stuck in the sewer for two days before he was raked out with a grappling hook. The child's body was so ravaged, so grotesque, so disgusting to behold, his own mother had taken one look and refused to touch him. . . . [Meridian] had placed the child, whose body was beginning to decompose, beside [the mayor's] gavel" (1976, 191). Here a little boy's decomposing flesh stands in for a world of African Americans who have vanished without trace. As Farah Griffin explains so tersely in *"Who Set You Flowin'?":* "When authorities dragged the Mississippi River for the bodies of civil rights workers James Chaney, Andrew Goodman, and Michael Schwerner, they pulled from the river numerous black bodies, whose disappearances had never been investigated" (1995, 20). By politicizing a little boy's body, by taking a corpse that is untouchable and making its decomposition both a literary figure and a motive for political action, Walker suggests the public-sphere politics that still attach themselves to the southern grotesque. Following her lead, I want to revise the ways we read the ravaged bodies so dominant in southern women's fiction, the ways in which southern women invent and reinvent the formal structures that have been gathered loosely under the rubric of the southern grotesque. But I also want to suggest that this rethinking demands a very different way of circulating the politics of disgust, refuse, pollution, and dirt in southern literature.

Voncille Sherard, a black domestic worker, corroborates these theories when she describes her experiences cleaning white southern homes:

> I think they all just categorized me—as a servant, a black. I only remember one household in which I ate with the family. And they always opened the back door of the car for you so you'd know not to get in the front seat. I think the bad things that happened did so more because of the individuals involved and because you were a domestic than a black working for whites, but it is hard to separate them all out. The things that hurt the deepest were racially motivated—like the lady who the first day I got there took out a fork and a plate and told me that this was mine to always use. They gave me the impression that I wasn't clean enough. (Tucker 1988, 221)

Here we find a preliminary answer to the question: Why dirt and desire? Dirt comes into play in southern literature because of its metaphoric power in day-to-day life; it offers a category of alienation that has peculiar powers of abjection. But it is also a category that has special transparencies—a cognitive category to see over and through. Dirt is central to white conversions to racial liberalism, as in Molly Ivins's sudden recognition of the illogic supporting Jim Crow:

> I believe all Southern liberals come from the same starting point—race. Once you figure out they are lying to you about race, you start to question everything.
>
> If you grew up white before the civil rights movement anywhere in the South, all grown-ups lied. They'd tell you stuff like, "Don't drink out of the colored fountain, dear, it's dirty." In the white part of town, the white fountain was always covered with chewing gum and the marks of grubby kids' paws, and the colored fountain was always clean. Children can be horribly logical. (1991, xiv)

We know a great deal from anthropology and cultural studies about the social specificity of dirt. In *Purity and Danger* Mary Douglas focuses on the social rules that the signifiers "clean-dirty" uphold. "Pollution beliefs can be used in a dialogue of claims and counter-claims to status. But as we examine pollution beliefs we find that the kind of contacts which are thought dangerous also carry a symbolic load. This is a more interesting level at which pollution ideas relate to social life. I believe that some pollutions are used as analogies for expressing a general view of the social order" (1984, 3). One need not be an anthropologist or a cultural critic to understand the authority that collects around such ordinary pollution metaphors. Both Sherard, the domestic worker, and Ivins, the journalist, recognize dirt as a potent symbol, as a set of proscriptive categories whites have invented for ends that are not only hurtful but epistemologically and politically powerful. But I want to push Douglas's categories further, to ask, What do we do with bodies and experiences that fall *outside these categories*—that refuse the category "dirty-clean" as a paradigm with a readable political topography? Is there a pollution outside pollution, a remainder beyond this remainder, a politics of dirt that falls outside such structuralist transparencies, outside the libels of status?

This question resonates powerfully in Maya Angelou's early autobiography, *I Know Why the Caged Bird Sings,* in a scene where the young Angelou, immobilized by an aching, swollen tooth, finally accompanies her grandmother to the local dentist. This trip begins with a painstaking ritual cleansing: the toothache, ongoing for days, is aggravated by the child's careful washing of her mouth and body before visiting the white dentist—someone who is expected to treat the child with care because he is in her grandmother's debt for a loan generously made during the depression. Identifying with this black child's pain, one can only be stunned by the white dentist's stomach-turning refusal: "He let go of the door and stepped nearer Momma. The three of us were crowded on the small landing. 'Annie, my policy is I'd rather stick my hand in a dog's mouth than in a nigger's.' He had never once looked at me. He turned his back and went through the door into the cool beyond" (1970, 160).

Considered from a structuralist perspective, this is a story with all-too-"clean" lines, suggesting that even though pollution metaphors are culturally variable (the by-products of permeable systems of rules about proper and improper, reaction formations against "matter out of place"), pollution is also a politically disreputable category that allows ascendant peoples to put those who are less powerful in their place. That is, dirt becomes the arbiter of cultural categories that are both offensive and arbitrary. But pollution is also a highly contaminating medium to work with. In *The Politics and Poetics of Transgression* Stallybrass and White argue that when "superior" classes depend on pollution-ridden "low-Others" to bolster prestige, they are caught in a loop in which "the top *includes* that low symbolically, as a primary eroticized constituent of its own fantasy life" (1986, 5).[4] That is, people in power consolidate their sense of power by obsessing about the distasteful lives of those with less power. Describing this unexpected psychological dependence of ascendant castes on the very persons of lower caste who are rigidly excluded, Stallybrass and White invent the powerful maxim that "what is socially peripheral is frequently symbolically central. The low-Other is despised and denied at the level of political organization and social being whilst it is instrumentally constitutive of the shared imaginary repertoires of the dominant culture" (5–6).

But is this always the case? What does this maxim leave out? I want to focus on a bleaker moment in Angelou's story: "He turned his back and went through the door into the cool beyond." Here the companion text is neither Ivins's discoveries about race at the blacks-only water fountain nor Sherard's story of ostracism while laboring in a white household, but a moment from W. E. B. Du Bois's description of his trip south in *The Souls of Black Folk:* "Was not all this show and tinsel built upon a groan? 'This land was a little Hell,' said a ragged, brown, and grave-faced man to me. We were seated near a roadside blacksmith-shop, and behind was the bare ruin of some master's home. 'I've seen niggers drop dead in the furrow, but they were kicked aside, and the plough never stopped. And down in the guard-house, there's where the blood ran'" (1989, 102). If dirt defines matter out of place, a matter of classification distinguishing high from low, what happens to those who pass beyond classification, who slip outside structure altogether?

In answer I want to invoke a series of categories that have been overlooked and underdisseminated in the analysis of southern women's writing—namely, the ways in which this literature provokes the uncanny presence of disposable bodies—and these, in turn, suggest (1) the exceeding strangeness of the figures of thought this literature invents to think about race and gender, (2) the inadequacy of current critical languages for accounting for these figures, and (3) the ways in which southern women's writing opens up a different way of thinking about the relation between American history and the body—particularly, what happens to the body within a culture of neglect.

We must pay attention to the difficult figure of the throwaway body—to women and men whose bodily harm does not matter enough to be registered or repressed—who are *not* symbolically central, who are looked over, looked through, who become a matter of public and private indifference—neither important enough to be disavowed nor part of white southern culture's dominant emotional economy.

Although Angelou and Du Bois describe human beings intended to be discarded after use, let me hasten to add that the literary counterparts to their stories are not always so tragically represented. Often we learn little or nothing about the black characters who float through white southern stories—except for their atmospheric density. In Welty's *Delta Wedding,* "Pinchy was setting the table and Aunt Mac was at the china closet loudly counting the glasses of each kind. Horace was hosing down the Summer's car. . . . Howard, with Maureen running about the foot of his ladder, was with almost imperceptible motions hanging paper lanterns in the trees, gradually moving across the yard like the movement of shade under the clinging sun" (1946, 260). Blacks and whites commingle to such a degree in *Delta Wedding* that an unwary reader may not know that Howard, Horace, and Pinchy are black, and Aunt Mac and Maureen are white. But African Americans can always be separated out in Welty's story, not only because of the constancy and degree of their labor but because of their habit of fading away; they inhabit novelistic worlds that can change them, in the twinkling of an eye, from a character into an atmosphere.

The wavering of Howard's body into the landscape "like the movement of shade" echoes the moment when Pinchy disappears "out into the light, like a matchstick in the glare, and was swallowed up in it." Welty continually replays these gestures of white minds that consign African Americans to ambience, mood, holding environment. Robbie Reid, one of *Delta Wedding*'s many white ingenues, watches Pinchy blister in the heat: "her eyes fastened hypnotically on the black figure that seemed to dangle as if suspended in the light, as she would watch a little light that twinkled in the black, far out on the river at night, from her window, waiting" (194). This conversion of a young girl's pain (her body associated with the trauma of lynching) into lyric or pastoral is shocking. Welty not only lingers at a point of unregistered trauma where Pinchy fades into background or atmosphere, she explores a part of white southern cognition that sees this disappearing act—the evacuation of Pinchy's pain and materiality, as well as the loss of her story (in this scene she is isolated because she is in the midst of an emotionally charged conversion experience)—as normative, expected, not worthy of repression, problem-free.[5] Later I will argue that the simultaneous gift and horror of the grotesque is its ability to reverse this moment of fading—as throwaway bodies reaccelerate from ground into figure. But for the moment I want to ask another set of questions. First, how does a writer—white or black—create adequate icons for describing human beings whose lives are not properly registered, who are disposed of, taken for granted, not present (in the terms of the dominant culture—not really there)? How does a writer dramatize a world dense with unnoticed trauma? I am suggesting, first, that societies are driven by gestures that are often less sensuous and psychoanalytically thrilling than the metaphors of soiling that are so often invoked when critics study subaltern cultures via the magic of pollution. Second, I will argue that we lack an adequate critical language to explore the literary attempt to dramatize a southern culture of neglect.[6]

To see how this culture empties itself into southern women's writing, I want to turn to Kate Chopin's "La Belle Zoraïde," a story from the turn of the century that is, in its own peculiar way, very much about dirt and desire. In this object-laden world, Manna-Loulou, a servant "black as night," is preparing to tell one of her stories "to Madame, who lay in her sumptuous mahogany bed, waiting to be fanned and put to sleep in the sound of one of Manna-Loulou's stories. The old negress had already bathed her mistress's pretty white feet and kissed them lovingly, one, then the other" (1991, 102). Here we find the invocation of pollution behavior dividing caste from caste, but we also find evidence of the black storyteller's "aphanisis," or fading. Even though Manna-Loulou is the teller of Zoraïde's tale, from the very beginning of Chopin's story she slips into the background. When Madame goes to sleep in a mahogany-colored bed (a reflection of the nurturing environment provided by her servant), Chopin suggests that in this Louisiana culture, African Americans are not so much people, characters, human beings as an atmosphere, a background, a mood.

"La Belle Zoraïde" exemplifies the plight of the disposable body: the body that is neither symbolically nor socially central, that is intended to be discarded after use. Chopin's story is framed by a narrative that uses images of cleanliness and dirt to schematize the degree of intimacy permissible between whites and blacks. But inside this carefully built frame such structuralist analogies fall apart; the story shifts from a description of Manna-Loulou washing and kissing the feet of her white mistress to an obsession with rubbish, trash, and throwaway bodies. In this culture of disposability a black woman makes a baby out of a bundle of rags and holds it to her bosom until she dies; she is defined as insane by a culture that has thrown away her lover and her biological child.

Even more brutally than Welty's "Curtain of Green," Chopin's story prefigures Lorde's "Afterimages"; it replicates the poem's ritual mourning for Emmett Till, a brutalized, thrown-away child:

> his 15 years puffed out like bruises
> on plump boy-cheeks
> his only Mississippi summer
> whistling a 21 gun salute to Dixie
> as a white girl passed him in the street
> and he was baptized my son forever
> in the midnight waters of the Pearl.

I have already explored southern landscapes mired with disposable bodies, suggesting a redefinition of the southern romance with "place." But Lorde focuses on these landscapes of occluded grief to describe the ways in which—even when discovered—Till's body still becomes paltry and immaterial. On street corners everywhere

> . . . the secret relish
> of a black child's mutilated body
> fingered by street-corner eyes
> bruise upon livid bruise
> and wherever I looked that summer
> I learned to be at home with children's blood
> with savored violence
> with pictures of black broken flesh
> used, crumpled, and discarded
> lying amid the sidewalk refuse
> like a raped woman's face.

The extremity of this verse reflects not just the body *in extremis*—gouged-out eyes, flayed skin, "bruise upon livid bruise"; it also corroborates the ideas about pollution we have just examined: the ways in which defilement makes a child who has been socially peripheral become symbolically central. The South enacts horror, the North consumes it. But Lorde, like Chopin, changes focus. Instead of a polluted, broken body that becomes the object of everyone's gaze, Emmett Till becomes the body as throwaway—its image, the child's newspaper-afterlife, turned to refuse: "crumpled . . . discarded." Chopin's Zoraïde also reenacts this shift in economy, from the commodified body of a beautiful black woman capable of reproducing children whose bodies can be turned into capital, to a woman who reads her culture too well and creates icons that reflect what has been so easily discarded.

The story Manna-Loulou tells begins with all the bittersweet promise of a fairy tale. Zoraïde is a mulatto slave "so dusky, so beautiful" that "she even had her own little black servant to wait upon her." But her destined husband, the light-skinned body servant, M'sieur Ambrose, is a man she detests. Instead, she loves "le beau Mezor," a man proud as a king, whose body "was like a column of ebony," who, when he was not dancing Bamboula in Congo Square, was "hoeing sugar-cane, barefooted and half-naked, in his master's field outside the city." (Once again African Americans become atmosphere, architecture, foundation; Mezor is a column-like figure supporting this banal surface world.)

While Zoraïde's lightness establishes her mistress's high social standing, Mezor is a field slave, a worker producing the wealth that makes such status possible. Furious at the idea of marrying her "cafe-au-lait" slave with one so low in rank, her mistress forbids the union. But Zoraïde meets Mezor privately and becomes pregnant by her lover. As she argues with her mistress: "I am not white . . . then . . . let me have from out of my own race the one whom my heart has chosen." Instead, the mistress persuades Mezor's owner to sell him at once: "Naturally, he lost no time in disposing of le beau Mezor, who was sold away into Georgia, or the Carolinas, or one of those distant countries far away, where he would no longer hear his Creole tongue spoken, nor dance Calinda, nor hold la belle Zoraïde in his arms" (104). It is this "disposal" that I want to draw attention to, because it becomes the primary metaphor of the story—and of the southern world Chopin describes.

To dispose of is to get rid of or to throw away; it is the fate of detritus, of garbage, of objects generally thought to be unclean or dirty, debris-ridden, worthless. As a young male sugar-worker, Mezor is very valuable, and yet this value accrues to his labor power and not to the young man himself, who remains within the phylum of the disposable, the interchangeable, the throwaway. He not only loses his friends and his lover but the connections with his own African history, fitfully embedded in his dances in the public square and his beloved Creole tongue.

This embedding of African Americans in the category of the disposable or the interchangeable did not end with emancipation. In *The Land Where the Blues Began* Alan Lomax describes the "Delta levee world" of the turn of the century as "the last American frontier, even more lawless than the Far West in its palmiest days, partly because there was, so to speak, open season on blacks, considered less valuable than the mules they drove: 'Kill a nigger, hire another; kill a mule, you got to buy another one'" (1993, 216).[7]

In Susan Tucker's *Domestic Workers and Their Employers in the Segregated South,* a black domestic worker named Clelia Daly describes her own participation in this homicidal economy: "I always had a feeling that people like you as long as you're able to do their work. My mother told me that. I told you she worked for a very rich family, and she was up in their house one day helping out with the old grandmother. And this old black man who had worked for them since he was a boy, he passed up there in the house with them. So my mother said, 'Oh, I know they're going to miss him.' And the old lady said, laughing: 'I don't know, Margaret. You can always get another darky, just as good or better'" (200). These stories are especially sobering because they involve loss of life, but I want to capture the indiscriminateness of this everyday rhetoric of disposability. One of Tucker's white subjects, Margaret McAllister, describes a similar relationship with her family's maid that progresses well past her childhood: "Today I feel so tired. I have these two children, and I'm pregnant, and I'd love someone to bring me breakfast! And Rachel came every day—well, six days a week—and did that. I can never remember her going on vacation, or anything. . . . She came at seven in the morning and left at six-thirty; after she'd fed us and had us all cleaned up" (62). The one who handles the family's dirt also makes its good life possible: "And so then Mama and Daddy would have their time alone." What's unexpected is the way in which Rachel, the black worker, and Margaret, her white ward, also make themselves into an optative couple; they dream of transcending the narrow grip of a culture that divides people into dirty and clean by fantasizing that Rachel will sing prophecies at the white child's wedding. In this story the black grownup and little white girl work to subvert the ideology of pollution—and yet these dreams die as easily as the Delta's muledrivers:

> She'd always said she was going to sing the Lord's Prayer at my wedding. That was the thing we talked about, all the way growing up. She'd always sing it around the house, and we'd talk about it. That was her dream.
>
> Well, when it came time, I just couldn't let her. When I called her, she said, "Oh, I'll get to sing at your wedding!" I mean, she had a nice voice, but . . . I didn't want her to sing at my wedding. It would have been real different, for Mississippi especially. But I think I hurt her feelings. It was one of those childhood promises, but you still worry about breaking it. (62–63)

What's notable is the casualness of this disregard, the easy neglect of this "childhood promise." It is this random sense of neglect that I want to return to in "La Belle Zoraïde," for the pyrotechnics of disposability do not end with the heart-breaking loss of le beau Mezor. Desolate at her beloved's absence, Zoraïde waits for consolation, for the birth of her child. She almost dies in its delivery, but back from the dead she asks to hold the baby in her arms. "'Où li, mo piti a moin? (Where is my little one)' she asked imploringly." Mistress and nurse each reply in turn "'To piti à toi, li mouri' ('Your little one is dead')."[8] But Zoraïde's child is not dead; it has been thrown away, disposed of, "removed from mother's side" and sent to "Madame's plantation, far up the coast" so that Madame can "have her young waiting-maid again at her side free, happy, and beautiful as of old" (105). We return to Du Bois's metaphor: all this "show and tinsel" is simply "built upon a groan." But what climbs out of this rubble is not a ghost body but rubbish, waste, a "senseless bundle of rags."

Finally acquiescing to her betrothal to M'sieur Ambrose, Zoraïde makes an icon out of disposability itself. On the eve of her ceremony, "with a look of strange and vacuous happiness on her face," she asks for quiet, insisting that her young one is sleeping. "Upon the bed was a senseless bundle of rags shaped like an infant in swaddling clothes. Over this dummy the woman had drawn the mosquito bar, and she was sitting contentedly beside it. In short, from that day Zoraïde was demented. Night nor day did she lose sight of the doll that lay in her bed or in her arms" (106). These rags become a kind of fantasmatic supplement, knitting together the fates of her family's thrown-away bodies. This "senseless bundle" also suggests a high degree of unthought, castaway material that white Creole culture overlooks, that it refuses to think.

Desperate to undo the spell of this rubbish, Madame tries to reawaken her slave; she brings back Zoraïde's flesh-and-blood child—a little "griffe girl": "Keep her; she is yours. No one will ever take her from you again." But Zoraïde only clutches her rag bundle more tightly and suspects that a plot is afoot to deprive her of her child. The little girl of flesh and bone is sent back to the plantation, "never to know the love of mother or father" while Zoraïde lives to be very old—"always clasping her bundle of rags—her 'piti.'" In making such a moving icon out of everyday refuse, what does this story accomplish? First, it punctures the myth of replaceability ("You can always get another darkie") by divesting the gothicism of Mezor's and Zoraïde's story of any shred of romance. Gothicism survives, but in a sad, revolting form: to discard is to be haunted by rubbish. Zoraïde's bundle of rags becomes a patchy emblem of the throwaway bodies that have collected throughout this story. As an aesthetic object as well as a "child," it defamiliarizes the "pity" we normally associate with such stories, creating an alienation effect that invades the reader's complacency that such events are bygone, that they took place in the past.

Second, although these rags are worthless items, of no importance to the culture that produced them, here they become the kernel of the real, as if this remnant of identity, this remainder (something we think of as very small) is really quite large and carries enormous material freight.

Third, this story uses emblems of the throwaway body to get at the question of the gap between what is articulable and what has been lived. Hearing the end of Zoraïde's story, Manna-Loulou's white mistress continues to use the language of disposability: "Ah, the poor little one, Man Loulou, the poor little one! better had she died!" (107). In response, I want to suggest that southern women's fiction strives to create a history for these disposable bodies—for a world too easily experienced, too little conceived.

I have suggested that in "Zoraïde" the rag becomes a fantastic supplement describing a high degree of unthought, castaway material that white Creole culture overlooks, that it refuses to think. In the rest of this chapter I want to associate the rag as "supplement" with the throwaway, to argue that rags perform unexpected work in several southern cultural traditions, and that we need to pay attention to the enormous symbolic properties invested in so minor an object. In *A Narrative of the Life and Adventures of Charles Ball, A Black Man* (1854), Ball recalls a morning in which an overseer drove 168 near-naked slaves into the fields to work:

> A wretched looking troop we were. There was not an entire garment among us.
>
> More than half of the gang was entirely naked. . . . There was neither bonnet, cap, nor headdress of any kind amongst us, except the old straw hat that I wore. . . . Some of the men had old shirts and some ragged trousers, but no one wore both. Amongst the women several wore petticoats and many had shifts. Not one of the whole number wore both of these vestments. We walked nearly a mile through one vast cotton field before we arrived at the place of our intended day's labor. (1837, 146–47)[9]

Ball contemplates a moment from his own past: a group of half-clothed people walk through a vast cotton field where they are forced to produce the material for other people's clothing. Are there words wide enough to describe the abyss between owner and owned? Here rags become an emblem for a lacerating inequity, an emblem of the separation between white profiteers and black laborers who are naked in each other's eyes and must endure without clothing's shelter and dignity. Rags take on an extra political valence in an economy in which African Americans labor for white capitalists to produce cotton as a cash crop. "His clothes is full of patches, / His hat is full of holes, / Stoopin down picking cotton / From off the bottom boll." This Texas sharecropper's song suggests how frequently rags come into play in southern culture as an index to the object-poor, sub-subsistence world spawned by the lower South's surreal one-crop economy: "Po farmer, po farmer, / Po farmer, / They get all the farmer make" (Lomax 1993, 96). In songs as well as stories, remnants of clothing surface emblematically at moments of everyday crisis, describing subjects at the limit of their status as subjects, and objects at their limit as artifacts. "Give my clothes to my sister, give Papa my diamond ring, / Give my shoes to my sister, don't give my wife a doggone thing. / If my mother don't want my body, cast it in the deep blue sea / Where the catfish and the alligators can fight over me" (299).

We will see that clothing in general and rags in particular offer another language, a subset of overlooked images, for the discarded body in a variety of southern texts. But before embarking on this project, we need to note the complex analysis that African American singers and speakers have already bestowed on the trauma of witnessing or becoming a discarded body.

Ida Hutchinson, a former slave, describes the connection between murdered children and the unstinting labor performed by African American subjects prior to emancipation.

> Blackshear had them take their babies with them to the field and it was two or three miles from the house to the fields. He didn't want them to lose time walking backward and forward nursing. They built a long trough like a great long old cradle and put all these babies in it every morning when the mother come out to the field. It was set at the end of the rows under a big cottonwood tree. When they were at the other end of the row, all at once a cloud no bigger than a small spot came up and it grew fast, and it thundered and lightened as if the world were coming to an end, and the rain just came down in great sheets. And when it got so they could go to the other end of the field, that trough was filled with water and every baby in it was floating round in the water, drowned. They never got nary a lick of labor and nary a red penny for any of them babies. (Lester 1968, 38)

Hutchinson demonstrates a complex understanding of slavery as economic practice; she insists that white slaveholders registered these deaths neither as personal nor as moral trauma but as the loss of labor and capital. As Julius Lester says, "To the slaves it was clear that slavery existed for two reasons: free labor, and the money that was gotten from . . . that free labor and from selling slaves" (38). Black narrators in fiction and autobiography are hyperconscious about the connection between throwaway bodies and the commodification of African American subjects. Moreover, once African Americans cease to be viewed as commodities and demand the status of free subjects, white culture's violence and neglect become even more vehement. In a book published almost seventy years after emancipation, *Mules and Men,* Zora Neale Hurston tells about the murder of black men in tones as ironic and matter-of-fact as Ida Hutchinson's:

> During the Christmas holidays of 1926 [Babe] had shot her husband to death, had fled to Tampa were she had bobbed her hair and eluded capture for several month but had been traced . . . and lodged in Bartow jail. After a few months she had been allowed to come home and the case was forgotten. Negro women *are* punished in these parts for killing men, but only if they exceed the quota. I don't remember what the quota is. Perhaps I did hear but I forgot. One woman had killed five when I left that turpentine still where she lived. The sheriff was thinking of calling on her and scolding her severely. (1990a, 60)

This is the quintessence of the throwaway body: the quick translation of white-on-black murder into economic terms, the quicker translation of black-on-black murder into nothing.

The throwaway bodies of men who "drop dead in the furrow" may be symbolically central to Hutchinson, Hurston, Du Bois, and Chopin, but they do not seem to matter to mainstream white southern culture. To assess this difference we need to examine two parallel economies of representation. First, we've looked at stories depicting white people who take these throwaway bodies for granted—who participate in a culture of violence or neglect. But other stories seek a language or genre to describe the history of the throwaway. Thus if Hurston describes white officials' casual approach to murdered black men satirically in *Mules and Men,* Ben Simpson, a former slave, recounts this story flatly, as tragedy:

> Massa have a great, long whip platted out of rawhide, and when one of the slaves fall behind or give out, he hit him with that whip. It take the hide every time he hits a slave. Mother, she give out on the way, 'bout the line of Texas. Her feet got raw and bleeding, and her legs swoll plumb out of shape. Then massa, he just take out his gun and

> shot her, and while she lay dying, he kicks her two, three times, and say, "Damn a nigger what can't stand nothing." You know that man, he wouldn't bury Mother. Just leave her laying where he shot her at. (Lester 1968, 55)

Who can make the throwaway matter in a world in which it did not matter? Who can respond to a world where a man could "just leave her laying where he shot her," where "every baby . . . was floating round in the water, drowned"?

In Caroline Gordon's "The Long Day," Henry, a white child, is forbidden to go inside the cabin of Joe, a black man sentenced to life on Henry's parents' plantation. Faced with this interdiction, Henry has intensive fantasies about the cabin's meager cloth contents: "Inside the cabin Joe walked to and fro. Blang—blang—blang! There was one loose board that flopped up and down every time he stepped on it. All that walking around was to wait on Sarah. But how could he wait on her? There wasn't anything in the cabin but the pallet that Sarah was lying on and a table that Joe had made and one chair. There was a closet in one corner, though. Maybe they kept their clothes there. Sarah changed her dress sometimes, and Joe had some Sunday clothes" (1990, 78). (Juxtaposed with this absolute penury, the carnivalesque scenes of pants-making in *The Color Purple* take on new dimensions.) As in "La Belle Zoraïde," a number of texts by black and white southern women coalesce, surprisingly, unexpectedly, around images of rags—a contradictory site for measuring the effects of black sharecroppers' trauma.[10]

In "The Long Day" Joe's face has been cut and Sarah remains invisible; she is "feeling po'ly"—badly hurt in a domestic dispute. But Sarah's pain and the couple's turmoil remain opaque to Henry, a white child who fishes with Joe and confides in him. Throughout Gordon's story Joe is abstracted and distressed ("I never cut that woman," he said. "Before God, I never cut that woman!"), but the pace of the story is slow, almost languorous, as the reader waits, with Henry, for Joe to gather up his pole and go fishing:

> "Joe," he said, "you want to go fishing?"
>
> "Yes," Joe said, "I'd like to go fishing." He stepped down from the porch and walked a little way toward the sycamore tree, then stopped. "I can't go fishing right now, Hinry," he said. "I have to stay round here a while and wait on Sarah. She's feeling po'ly."
>
> "All right," Henry said. "I'll go dig some worms."
>
> He picked up a can and went around the back to the hen house. The hen house hadn't been used for so long that it was falling to pieces. The best worms were there under the fallen planks. (76)

As Henry digs in the warm earth Gordon strikes a contrast between the emotional richness that Joe's house and company provide for the white child and the object-poverty and quiet misery of the black man. Henry is in love with Joe and his way of life, but slowly, sentence by sentence, the damage this environment wreaks on its black inhabitants seeps into view. Sarah moans soundlessly while the boy and the hungry man share Henry's lunch; Henry shares the cloth contents of the big house with Joe as well:

> "Yo ma has got some old rags up at the house, hasn't she?" Joe said. "Clean, white rags?"
>
> "Yes," Henry said, "she's got a whole drawerful. In the entry."
>
> "Can you get 'em without anybody seein' you?" (79)

Rags are objects reduced to their material nature, to denatured stuff. But as material that used to have a form, rags still have a purpose—to absorb dirt and bodily fluids, to stuff the cracks in broken windows, to keep sweat out of a laborer's eyes or wrap her head, to take the place of shoes. As disintegrating objects, rags seem quite separate from the world of solid objects, which protect and stabilize human life. Men and women, as Hannah Arendt says, "can retrieve their sameness, that is, their identity, by being related to the same chair and the same table" (1958, 137). In fact, the rags hidden in the white folks' entryway also offer a kind of object-continuity. Clean and white, they have the status and solidity of implements used to keep this entry beautiful. But once they cross the boundary into Joe's house something disturbing happens; they scatter into emblems of helplessness and dehumanization; they collect around the body, reducing people to objects, becoming the agents of reverse autochthony (as Joe disappears into a field of goldenrod) and the wrappings of death:

> As [Henry] came around the corner of the house, Joe stepped down on the porch.
>
> "Joe," Henry said, "Less go possum hunting one night soon."
>
> Joe did not answer. He stood there a second, then he jumped off the porch and ran toward the field. He ran, crouching like a dog, until he got to the edge of the field. He straightened up then and dived into the tall weeds. The goldenrod rippled where he made his way. Henry watched the yellow ripple spread slowly across the field. When the whole field was still he turned around. The cabin door was open. He could see Sarah lying on a pallet on the floor. The white cloths that were about her head and neck were stained with blood. Her eyes were wide open. He took one look at her, then he ran as fast as he could to the house" (83)

With her wide-open eyes, her body stuffed and surrounded by death rags, Sarah becomes a fleshly counterpart to Zoraïde's rag baby, an icon of soul murder. Nell Irvin Painter defines *soul murder* as "the violation of one's inner being, the extinguishing of one's identity," a state of psychic, economic, or physical atrophy induced by the conditions of slavery and its aftermath. The "sexual abuse, emotional deprivation, and physical and mental torture" enforced by white ownership created within its victims "feelings of degradation and humiliation, impaired identity formation, suppression of vitality and creativity, deadening of feeling of self, anger, hatred, and self-hatred on the individual level and violence on the social level" (1995, 128).

Painter distinguishes her work from that of Stanley Elkins by emphasizing the network of communal support slaves created to resist irreparable psychic damage and by outlining the ways in which this system inflicted terrible burdens on both *owner and owned.* I want to add to her paradigm by suggesting that, in Gordon's 1930 story, the post-emancipation plantation world is also the site of soul murder for African Americans and, at times, for white children. In saying this, I have no desire to efface Joe's suffering or Sarah's death by shifting our attention to the fate of a little white boy. What I do want to register is the complexity of what Gordon is trying to see: the underanalyzed attachments in the postbellum South between a well-to-do white child and an impoverished black man who becomes his designated sidekick and baby-sitter. The story uses the terror wrought by Sarah's corpse and the bloody rags piled around her, first, to describe the crisis of immobility and poverty that leads this black couple to violence and death. Second, these rags enact a shift in perspective—the text veers from Sarah's death to a little boy's first dose of white panic.

In "Soul Murder" Painter explores white fathers' roles in "inculcating manhood" in the antebellum South, "which included snuffing out children's identification with slaves." When a Virginian named John M. Nelson tried in his childhood to stop slave children from being beaten, when he mingled "my cries with theirs" and felt "almost willing to take a part of the punishment," he felt the full weight of his father's retribution. In response, the child "became so blunted that I could not only witness their stripes with composure, but *myself* inflict them, and that without remorse" (143). For the white boy in Gordon's story the bloody rags defining Sarah's dead body represent a sadistic site of transformation; they enforce his separation, his nausea, his return to the big house, his flight from identification with African Americans who have been damaged to make his privilege possible. This is a story in which rags have a double valence, in which a white child makes a customary journey; he learns to see African Americans not as people but as throwaways.

Mihaly Csikszentmihalyi argues that things "demonstrate the owner's power, vital erotic energy, and place in the social hierarchy," revealing the self's continuity over time and giving solid "evidence of one's place in a social network" (1993, 23). But rags suggest more than social status; rags covered with blood carry multiple messages of mortality. As Julia Kristeva describes the body's excretions: "Such wastes drop so that I might live, until, from loss to loss, nothing remains in me and my entire body falls beyond the limit—*cadere,* cadaver" (1982, 3). If the body's embarrassing fluids describe the border between living bodies and dead ones, if body and waste are never separable since flesh is always immersed in its own dead skin, perspiration, and waste, then the flight from the decaying body can also be conveyed via rags, or clothing in the position of decay—by something falling off or beyond the body. Bodies in rags are closer to the limits of the human, closer to the body itself as rubbish or waste. Faulkner seizes on the power of this metaphor in *Absalom, Absalom!:* "[Clytie] lay on the bare floor of the scaling and empty hall like a small shapeless bundle of quiet clean rags. When he reached her he saw that she was quite conscious, her eyes wide open and calm; he stood above her, thinking, 'Yes. She is the one who owns the terror.' When he raised her it was like picking up a handful of sticks concealed in a rag bundle, so light she was" (1972, 370–71).

We have begun to see the power of cloth remnants, dirty or clean, for gathering up a constellation of social problems, for calling up an atmosphere of neglect, desuetude, or dehumanization—foregrounding the background of a society that throws people away, that treats them as objects. But as Sutpen's never-acknowledged black daughter, what exactly is it that Clytie owns? The lightness of her being glosses over what should be most heavy—not only the long line of neglected, disowned, never-acknowledged children but the marginalized acts of neglected, disowned, never-acknowledged laborers—the naked black men who "tear" Sutpen's Hundred out of the earth, the never-mentioned being of Clytie's never-mentioned mother, the way the white architect clings to his mildewing vestments to separate himself from black men who are never quite acknowledged as men. Clytie may be a Haitian rebel who burns down the House of Sutpen, but she is reduced, by the end of *Absalom, Absalom!,* to "a rag bundle," to fuel for the fire, grist for the mill. In Faulkner's novel the white female characters, Rosa and Judith, make things out of rags, but Clytie becomes the thing itself. The quick transition from

Clytie as rag to her possession of "the horror" suggests the horrors Faulkner doesn't explore, the trauma of loss and grief he transposes from Sutpen's black daughter onto the white Wash Jones and his daughter, who move away from Clytie's melancholic position to become a felt source of tragedy. In the death of Milly and her baby the reader is pressed toward tears, is invited to grieve over Jones's moving effort to prevent his granddaughter and her baby from becoming Sutpen's throwaways. ("They just heard him moving inside the dark house, then they heard the granddaughter's voice, fretful and querulous: 'Who is it? Light the lamp, Grandpaw' then his voice: 'Hit wont need no light, honey. Hit wont take but a minute,'" 291.) The primary characteristic of the throwaway, in life as in literature, is the absence of this climate of mourning. (In *A Lesson Before Dying* and *Song of Solomon* Jefferson's and Hagar's deaths receive extensive attention, I would argue, in order to resurrect the possibility of literary mourning for black characters, to say, as Pilate says of Hagar, "And she was *loved*!" [1977, 323]). But elsewhere rags or cloth remnants convey the state of being uncared for, of a landscape of ungrieved grief, a state of pollution beyond pollution. One hardly expects cloth to have this powerful, overlooked resonance.[11]

Of course, clothing offers a potent emblem across a wide spectrum of histories and cultures, providing marks of station and the evolution (or devolution) of hierarchy. In southern writing the problems of sumptuary status are hardly limited to African Americans, for in numerous texts blacks are better dressed than whites. Grace Elizabeth Hale points to a scene in "The Artificial Nigger" in which a poor white kid from the country is amazed at the sartorial splendor of a "huge coffee-colored man . . . in a light suit and a yellow satin tie with a ruby pin" (O'Connor 1971, 254) but fails to recognize that this man is black. In Faulkner's "Delta Autumn" the nameless black woman who wants Cass MacCaslin to acknowledge that he has fathered her child is better dressed than Isaac McCaslin. But cloth continues to separate the races. In "The Artificial Nigger," when the white boy and his grandfather go to inspect the dining car where they cannot afford to eat, the coffee-colored man dines with his companions behind a "saffron-colored curtain." Both Faulkner's and O'Connor's nicely clothed African Americans receive their comeuppance—as the grandfather gleefully explains: "they rope them off (256)"

In *Their Eyes Were Watching God* clothing takes on a similar intensity within the black community: "Everybody was coming sort of fixed up, and he didn't mean for nobody else's wife to rank with her. She must look on herself as the bell-cow, the other women were the gang. So she put on one of her bought dresses and went up the new-cut road all dressed in wine-colored red. Her silken ruffles rustled and muttered about her. The other women had on percale and calico with here and there a headrag among the older ones" (1990b, 39). Headrags recall an earlier period of poverty ("the other women were the gang"); when Jody wants to repress Janie's sexuality he insists that she keep her head under wraps ("This business of the headrag irked her endlessly. But Jody was set on it. Her hair was NOT going to show in the store," 51).

In text after text cloth becomes interfused with the power of status and interdiction. James Agee dedicates more than twenty pages of *Let Us Now Praise Famous Men* to a description of the clothes that poor white tenant families wear:

> The shirt is home made out of a fertilizer sack. The cloth, by use and washing, is of a heavy and delicious look: as if pure cream were pressed into a fabric an eighth of an inch thick, and were cut and sewn into a garment. The faded lettering and branding is still visible, upside down, in red and blue and black. It is made in earnest imitation of store shirts but in part by heaviness of cloth and still more by lack of skill is enlarged in details such as the collar, and . . . is sewn with tough hand stitches, and is in fact a much more handsome shirt than might ever be bought: but socially and economically, it is of like but less significance with Ricketts' cornshuck hat. (1966, 248–49)

With its "pure cream" surfaces and delicious upside-down writing this fabric spells out a universe of meaning for the writer, but such universals seem unavailable to the owner of this shirt. Agee constructs a dignity for this clothing that only *he* can describe; this shirt loses its aesthetic power when he shifts to the perspective of the poverty-stricken, class-bound white subjects he wants so desperately to anatomize and venerate (249). But even in *Let Us Now Praise Famous Men* rags suggest a deeper pollution; they describe a world drifting away from the human. In Agee's opening citation (as the bookend to his citation of Marx's "workers of the world, unite") Lear confronts the "poor naked wretches" of the heath; seeing their "loop'd and window'd raggedness," he cries, "O! I have ta'en / Too little care of this." Throughout Agee's text rags become emblems of social injustice. He devotes pages to bedding and "patchwork quilts . . . in various degrees of raggedness, age, discoloration, dirt absorption, and a sense-of-vermin, stuffed with cotton and giving off a strong odor" (157).[12] Rags represent humanity immersed in dirt: the body in extremis, in crisis.

Finally, however, rags work differently in fictions by black and white writers; they mark another space where southern writers share regional preoccupations but also part ways. That is, Chopin, Gordon, Hurston, and Walker each surround black characters with rags to quarry the trauma of soul murder or to assess the status of the throwaway, but white writers such as Gordon and Chopin use rags as their text's climacteric, as an image that reveals final trauma. In contrast, Hurston, Walker, and Morrison position rags (and their depiction of throwaway bodies) close to their novels' beginnings. These black writers' texts begin with the revelation of soul murder and then deepen this insight or work toward emanicipation.

For instance, in *Jonah's Gourd Vine* John is angered by his brutal working conditions. As he works in the cotton fields, sweat drips into his eyes and he abandons both cotton and stepfather: "'Confound yuh, gee! John Buddy, whar you gwine?' 'Ahm goin' tuh git me uh sweat-rag wipe mah face wid. Ahm tired uh sweat runnin' intuh mah eyes'" (1962, 78). Seizing this rag marks John's exit from sharecropping and new grasp of agency. In Hurston's novel rags connote crisis, but they are not turned toward the burden of the throwaway; "Heah de rag yuh wanted, John. Go 'long back to work and Ah'll give Ned uh straightenin'" (80). In this scene Hurston asks who possesses—who owns the right to—the cloth that sharecroppers help produce but do not profit from. She also connects the ethic of care running from mother to son to the epiphanic plush of the train seats that cause John to marvel.

In Alice Walker's *Third Life of Grange Copeland* rags are once more connected with soul murder and bodily fluids. Brownfield's impoverished mother is not allowed to take him to work; she pulls baits for a living, and when her baby screams at the nightcrawlers' blind wriggling, Margaret is forced to leave him alone:

> At first she left him home in a basket, with his sugartit pressed against his face. He sucked on it all day until it was nothing but a tasteless rag. Then, when he could walk, she left him on the porch steps. In moments of idle sitting he shared the steps with their lean mangy dog. And as the flies buzzed around the whiskered snout of the dog they buzzed around his face. No one was there to shoo them away, or to change the sodden rag that attracted them, and which he wore brownish and damp around his distended waist. For hours he was lost in a dull, weak stupor. His hunger made him move in a daze, his heavy eyes unnaturally bright.
>
> When he was four he was covered with sores. Tetter sores covered his head, eating out his hair in patches the size of quarters. Tomato sores covered his legs up to the knee. (1988, 256)

The text moves from the comforting sugartit to the sore-covered body as rag. Since emancipation what has changed? We find too much continuity between the lives of modern black sharecroppers and those of "slave children, particularly those whose mothers worked in the fields, [who] were also very likely to suffer physical and emotional neglect, because their mothers were rarely allowed much time off the job to spend with their children. Child care by people other than mothers could be adequate, as in the case of the young Frederick Douglass, who began life in the custody of his maternal grandmother. But in other situations, the caretakers of children might be too old, too young, or too infirm to provide adequate supervision" (Painter, 1995, 134). In depriving Brownfield of his *right* to a caretaker, Walker is following the narrative path set by ex-slave tales showing "child-rearing patterns that forced hardworking parents to neglect their children and that, as a consequence, often denied babies the opportunity to attach to a parent or parental figure securely" (134). Once again, the sugartit that becomes a "tasteless rag" reveals his young vulnerability to child abuse that is inexcusable yet necessary. The rags that begin this novel and reveal the human cost of southern sharecropping and factory economies find another symbolic counterpart in an event that Walker names as her novel's origin: the death of Mrs. Walker, a neighbor woman, no kin to Walker herself, killed by a belligerent husband. In her afterword Alice Walker describes the horror of seeing this dead woman's body when her sister, who worked for the local undertaker, "invited me into the room where Mrs. Walker . . . lay stretched on a white enamel table with her head on an iron pillow. I describe her in the novel exactly as she appeared to me then. . . . Still, I see it; not so much the shattered face—time has helped to erase the vividness of that sight—but always and always the one callused foot, the worn, run-over shoe with a ragged hole, covered with newspaper, in its bottom" (343). Once again trash or refuse gathers around a body that has been cast away—the face erased, but not the rag, the conscripted newspaper.

The point of Walker's novel is not simply to remember these conditions but to suggest a point of exit—as Ruth does in the scene where a civil rights protest and the redemption of whole cloth come together: "Although she had seen marchers before on television she was amazed to see real blacks and whites marching together in her home town! There were trim white girls in jeans and sneakers with clean flowered blouses marching next to intense black girls in high heels and somber Sunday dresses. . . . 'Are they for real?' she wondered" (323–24). If rags become limit-signs stopping the evidence of African American's humanity—a space where personal power can only be dispersed, where it cannot be encapsulated—then the advent of a new identity can also be signaled by a new economy of cloth. We will return to this point again in chapter 7 when we examine Sethe's wedding dress—also made out of rags:

> Well, I made up my mind to have at the least a dress that wasn't the sacking I worked in. So I took to stealing fabric, and wound up with a dress you wouldn't believe. The top was from two pillow cases in her mending basket. The front of the skirt was a dresser scarf a candle fell on and burnt a hole in, and one of her old sashes we used to test the flatiron on. Now the back was a problem for the longest time. Seem like I couldn't find a thing that wouldn't be missed right away. Because I had to take it apart afterwards and put all the pieces back where they were. (1987, 59)

Zoraïde, Sarah, Mrs. Walker, Sethe—it is remarkable how often in southern literature rags move out of a background or blind field to achieve the status of emblem.

At the same time, rags are so very disposable, so invisibly there, that they come to represent what is undistinguished or unremarkable in people's day-to-day lives. Why haven't we placed rags at the center of our analysis of these texts before? Precisely because they mark people or things that can be overlooked. As Jules Prown has said, "A culture's most fundamental beliefs are often so widely understood, so generally shared and accepted, that they never need to be stated. They are therefore invisible to outsiders. Indeed, they may be beliefs of which the culture itself is not aware" (1993, 3). These texts foreground rubbish that remains unexamined but still carries within it the seeds of soul murder, seeds that flourish in a culture so casual about its throwaways that it fails to repress them.

The rag becomes, then, another emblem of the body as rubbish, the body as abject or throwaway: an emblem so well established by the late 1940s that Flannery O'Connor can parody its effects in *Wise Blood* when a mummified man attracts Enoch Emory in his visit to the local museum. "There were three bowls and a row of blunt weapons and a man in the case. He was about three feet long. He was naked and a dried yellow color and his eyes were drawn almost shut as if a giant block of steel were falling down on top of him" (1949, 98). Enoch Emory steals the mummy, worships it for a while, and then "negrifies" it: "He couldn't understand at all why he had let himself risk his skin for a dead shriveled-up part-nigger dwarf that had never done anything but get himself embalmed" (176). As he gives the mummy to Hazel Motes and Sabbath Lily Hawks to become their "new jesus," the mummy gets trashier and trashier: "Two days out of the glass case had not improved the new jesus' condition. One side of his face had been partly mashed in and on the other side, his eyelid had split and a pale dust was seeping out of it" (184). But Sabbath Lily Hawks adopts the ragman with affection; she insists on playing house:

> Haze stood motionless. . . .
>
> The hand that had been arrested in the air moved forward and plucked at the squinting face but without touching it; it reached again, slowly, and plucked at nothing and then it lunged and snatched the shriveled body and threw it against the wall. The head popped and the trash inside sprayed out in a little cloud of dust.
>
> "You've broken him!" Sabbath shouted, "and he was mine!"
>
> Haze snatched the skin off the floor . . . and flung out what he had in his hand. The rain blew in his face and he jumped back and stood with a cautious look, as if he were bracing himself for a blow.
>
> "You didn't have to throw him out," she yelled. "I could have fixed him!" (187–88)

Who owns the terror now? As in *Absalom, Absalom!* a son turns into trash and is discovered to be dust all the way down. In this simulacrum of the throwaway child, O'Connor parodies white culture's fetishes and retells the story of its compulsive will-to-neglect.

I have tried, in this chapter, to make a distinction between things that are thrown away because they are horrifying and can't be confronted and things (or subjects) that are disposable, of no account, and can be safely thrown away. *Wise Blood*'s Hazel Motes is terrified by the new jesus—it represents righteous needs that obsess him—but when Walker or Chopin uses rags to connote the enormity of soul murder, they are also exposing an ethos of disposability, conveying the weightlessness of acts of neglect in a society where "neglect was routine, abuse was rampant, and anger was to be suppressed" (Painter 1995, 134). Finally, rags become such crucial emblems of throwaway bodies because only an emblem low down on the social scale can do such strange work across both black and white texts—defining an act, or the remains of a human being who becomes central not as pollution or waste but as nothing.[13]

This is the odd fate of Chopin's Zoraïde. For "La Belle Zoraïde" does not end with the mulatto heroine's revelatory embracing of her little rag child. Instead, we turn back to Manna-Loulou and her mistress, back to the narrative frame:

> "Are you asleep, Ma'zelle Titite?"
> "No, I am not asleep; I was thinking. Ah, the poor little one, Man Loulou, the poor little one! better had she died." (1991, 107)

The mistress has heard the tale, but she has already thrown away its moral; all she remembers is the sorrow of the child, and all she wishes for is the repeated trauma of the child's easy death. Once again we encounter the thoughtless pleasure—for the powerful—of the throwaway. For the white mistress this is only a bedtime story; it evokes pity for the child but invisibility for Zoraïde, for Mezor, and perhaps even for Manna-Loulou, the storyteller, as dark-skinned and cannily restless as Mezor himself. As handmaid and servant, is Manna-Loulou also a stand-in for Zoraïde, does she practice a clarifying insanity? Does she want to imagine that her mistress is also disposable—a thing made of rags? Chopin wants us to hover at a point of uncertainty. Not content to tell this ending once, she tells it again:

> But this is the way Madam Delisle and Manna-Loulou really talked to each other:—"Vou pré droumi, Ma'zélle Titite?"
> "Non, pa pré droumi; mo yapré zongler. Ah, la pauv' piti, Man Loulou. La pauv' piti! Mieux li mouri!" (107)

Hearing these words in another language, estranged, defamiliarized, leaves the reader suspended. Does Chopin repeat Creole speech as a way of emphasizing the reader's own inability to recognize what she hears, leaving us in a perpetual state of misrecognition?

At the least, this story suggests the strange preoccupations that need to be excavated in thinking about southern literature. In this story about a black heroine who throws away the very thing she loves but recaptures this love in its "true" cultural form, in a bundle of rags, Chopin reminds us that southern culture is riddled with throwaways, with people and things that get dismissed or forgotten, that don't matter enough to be repressed. As Suzanne Raitt has suggested, there is a major difference between things that are casually thrown away and other categories of pollution. Rubbish is something people look at all the time without onus or shame or desire, whereas waste is something that must be secreted away, hidden, a matter of attraction and shame.[14] *Dirt and Desire* describes a literature still in need of translation: stories and novels searching for metaphors to describe *this* indifference: "'Vou pré droumi, Ma'zélle Titite?' 'Non, pa pré droumi; mo yapré zongler. Ah, la pauv' piti, Man Loulou. La pauv' piti! Mieux li mouri!'"

Chapter Four

Race and the Cloud of Unknowing

Nineteen fifty-seven saw the making of a very bad movie set in Indiana but obsessed with a racially traumatized South. Made in the midst of the civil rights movement, *Raintree County* focuses on the 1860s and the advent of the Civil War. It dramatizes the ascent into fatherhood and midwestern nobility of Johnnie—a local hero, played by Montgomery Clift, who falls in love with his schoolmate, a vacuously blonde girl Friday played with exquisite pallor by Eva Marie Sainte. But instead of pursuing this girl or fulfilling his dream (to write the Great Hoosier Novel), he is forced to marry Susanna, a heroine played to mad imperfection by Elizabeth Taylor. Susanna carries within her an awful secret. She is, or she thinks that she is, black, mixed-race, mulatto, a half-breed, a colored girl. What drives my fascination with this rather stereotypical drama is that every time it bumps into Susanna's "secret," it starts to go haywire. Its narrative drive falters or implodes—the plot loses its linearity and goes into overdrive, laying on too much aesthetic affect.

For example, the movie heats up when, on the night of Lincoln's election, the glamorous, dark-haired character played by Taylor announces the emancipation of her house slaves. The camera scans quickly past these freedwomen's expressions of surprise to settle on two white politicians who go berserk; they adopt bizarre forms of blackface in a frenzy of theatricalized white panic. Although this film seems to be about miscegenation, the "horror" of race mixing, like the "horror" of black emancipation, simply offers another site for staging white panic.

White panic is a moment of spectacular terror when racial boundaries that had seemed impermeable become unexpectedly porous; it is a contagious emotion that spreads too quickly, creating bodies whose fear begins to permeate other bodies. In *Raintree County* this contagion spreads to Susanna herself; she takes one look at these blackened white men and screams; when Montgomery Clift rushes upstairs to care for her she agrees, in her agitation, to destroy her weird and cinematically surreal doll collection. Against a background of seesawing gothic music, Clift and Taylor begin throwing china dolls against their bedroom wall: the air is filled with shattered white bodies.

White panic, white detritus, the shattered white body: these images fill this film with ennui, and yet their presence in the southern literary tradition they are drawn from has yet to be systematically studied. We have seen that an atmosphere heavy with flour dust, cotton lint, shredded white garments, particulate white bodies, or unexpected snow recurs throughout southern literature—suggesting a dissipated, unthematized, barely visible whiteness piercing everything but noticed only by those forced to clean up its remains. For example, the effect provided by the fiction of Taylor's blackness intensifies every time she clutches her defining fetish or talisman—a disfigured doll, half white, half charred or blackened—its face partially burned in a fire that destroyed her parents' plantation, her parents themselves, and the slave woman who served as her surrogate mother, her "mammy." The doll provides the movie with its scintilla of the grotesque (something viewers in 1957 might automatically have associated with the South) in its wry vision of a racially divided face melting back into soil or earth. But also, right at the surface of this film we find what I have called the film's "fantasmatic supplement"—a high degree of repetitive, unthought, castaway material that remains both visible and inchoate.

The film tries hard to manufacture for its audience, in scene after scene, the horror of miscegenation. The doll recalls not only the fire that killed Susanna's white and black "mothers" but the fact that in death the two women have become indistinguishable; it is impossible to know who was sleeping with Susanna's father when the fire occurred, impossible to give either woman her "proper" burial in the South's segregated graveyards, impossible to know who really gave birth to Susanna. Throughout the film Taylor's character is horrified by the thought that she may be black. The doubt about her parentage sends her north to look for a spouse and drives her mad; the film underscores her self-hatred in scenes heavy with phantasmagoria: mirrors, windows, shattered dolls, heaving music, and insane asylums.

Why is miscegenation coupled so frequently with hyperbole? Annette Gordon-Reed cautions Americans about genuflecting too solemnly before the mystification of miscegenation, especially the variety of race-mixing that involves white southern patriarchs who have fathered "black" children. As she says about Thomas Jefferson's relationship with Sally Hemmings:

> Of all the Founding Fathers, Jefferson is the one who makes the strongest connection to our times. He is a man who can be quoted to support opposite arguments, and so he is portrayed as a man of mystery. There are so many ways to approach him—politics, architecture, gardening—and, of course, the history of slavery. The whole Hemmings business makes him interesting to lots of people. I find much to admire in Jefferson, but I suspect that while he is called "unfathomable" by the predominantly white historians who write about him, I can't imagine that he would seem particularly puzzling to black Americans. Rather, he appears completely predictable and depressingly familiar. (1998, 24)

The man of mystery versus the man who is completely predictable; the man who is depressingly familiar yet is read as unfathomable: epistemology is a problem at the heart of American race-thinking. This chapter makes three assumptions: first, that the problems defining southern knowledge change as we shift our attention from white to black culture; second, that the question of what and how one knows is central to thinking about southern women's fiction; and third, that this fiction presents very complex and differentiated portraits of "the mind of the South."

In *Raintree County* Hollywood's vision of southernness legislates one way of knowing the South; the film's gothic machinery promises the emergence of some terrible secret from the depths of Taylor's celebrity and despair—a secret that will resolve the tedium of Susanna's combustible melancholy. But what's arresting about this film is not its depth but what's most on its surface: white panic, shattered whiteness, and the countenance of a ravaged black doll. We've already examined the scene where Susanna simpers sweetly about her sudden desire to have "no slaves in this house," inspiring Johnnie's chief political rival to give his best Al Jolson imitation (he widens his eyes, spreads his palms wide, and sings, in a bad southern accent, "Yes, we're all sisters under the skin"). His pantomime is contagious. Another politico lurches toward the fireplace and covers his hands with soot; his face smeared with ashes, he staggers toward the laughing, screaming guests, looking, for all the world, like the black villain-outcast in *Birth of a Nation*.

It's as if the movie is sorting through old racial stereotypes, trying them on for size and then rejecting them. For what the film explores next is neither a shadowy rape nor a scene of black victimization but a white hysteria that culminates in the destruction of Jemmy, Taylor's badly sutured, racially bifurcated childhood doll. My interest in the movie lies in the way it recycles a series of filmic stereotypes and then displaces these stereotypes with a doll with a damaged face.

In 1955, after Emmett Till's brutal lynching and the disposal of his body in the Pearl River, his mother brought his body home to Chicago and, in her grief and outrage, decided to have an open casket funeral. "Television cameras captured the mass of black mourners who filed with the deliberate slowness of a dirge past Till's corpse to emerge hysterical or grimly determined on the side. . . . Mamie Bradley allowed *Jet* magazine to publish a closeup of her boy's face. The image depicted a misshapen head all the more horrible for the coroner's efforts to make the mangled corpse back into the boy." As Grace Elizabeth Hale explains, "Americans across the nation thus watched the trial haunted by the horror of the dead boy's face. They saw the bragging and confident defendants, the segregated courtroom, and the all-white male jury" as well as the mistreatment of Till's mother. "Americans saw a local white southern performance, naked and stripped of the niceties of New South boosterism" (1998, 290–92).

Raintree County's close-ups of the doll's body have an uncanny resonance with Emmett Till's death and funeral; the film puts a simulacrum of Till's face up front, on the surface, and yet leaves this contemporary event out of the film's epistemology, its obsessions with "southern" race secrets, suggesting that there can be a high degree (even in a bad aesthetic object) of unthought, castaway material trying to find figuration; the film presents a surface obsessed with an event that keeps being repeated but cannot be seen, that needs to be worked over and yet cannot come through. To say this is not to make the image progressive in any way but to suggest a complicated aesthetic, a supercoding, or supersaturation, of the images that come out of South's response to race and the nation's response to South. A major thesis of this book is that we lack categories complex enough to analyze the bizarre figures this produces, either in southern writing—or even, in this case, in the most trite films and novels about the South.

In keeping with themes we've examined in earlier chapters, *Raintree County* turns from this damaged doll to the story of the throwaway. Perpetually confused about her identity, Taylor's Susanna gives birth to a light-skinned baby. Her husband is delighted, but Susanna is terrified; she is sure that this white child has displaced a darker child who is missing:

Susanna: It's a boy.
Johnnie: It's a boy.
Susanna: Where's the other, Johnnie?
Johnnie: What other one?
Susanna: There was another, but it wasn't right.
Johnnie: Dear, it's your imagination.
Susanna: No, there was another one . . . that was dark. Did they throw it away, Johnnie?
Johnnie: No, dear.
Susanna: Are you absolutely sure?
Johnnie: Absolutely.

Instead of connecting this dialogue with earlier arguments about disposable subjects, I want to change gears, to turn to Susanna's quest for cultural and historical knowledge: to *ideas* as well as children that have been overlooked or thrown away.

Americans' ways of "knowing" Till's death were wildly divergent. The *Jackson Daily News* invoked pity not for the murdered black youth but for the two white men who stood accused: "It is best for all concerned that the Bryant-Milam case be forgotten as quickly as possible."[1] Faulkner, in contrast, commented prodigiously on Till's death. He questioned whether "the purpose of this sorry and tragic error committed in my native Mississippi by two white adults on an afflicted colored child is to prove to us whether or not we deserve to survive" (Dittmer 1995, 56). This attempt at compassion and outrage is bone-chilling (the murder is an "error," the black child "afflicted"). But even Faulkner returned to the question of responsible nurturing: "if we in America have reached that point in our desperate culture when we must murder children, no matter for what reason or what color, we don't deserve to survive, and probably won't." Is this the Nobel Prize talking, or is Faulkner bearing witness to the fact that the media coverage of Till's death—including the open-casket funeral in Chicago, the pictures of Till's ravaged, unsuturable face in *Jet* magazine, and the national television coverage of the wake—brought the national legacy of Jim Crow and the violent aftermath of slavery to the forefront of American life, mobilizing many Americans, including some white southerners, against a region-crossing racism and tyranny?

While the *Jackson Daily News* prescribes forgetting and Faulkner is worried about survival, we find a third response to Till's death in black southern communities. Black teenagers from Mississippi, Sam Block and Joyce and Dorie Ladner, identified with "this boy our age, who could have been one of our brothers." Viewing the picture of his body in *Jet* magazine, "we asked each other, 'How could they do that to him? He's only a boy'" (Dittmer 1995, 58).

Here we find three different ideas about how to handle violent racial knowledge within the confines of the segregated South: (1) a South best preserved by "forgetting," (2) a South that remains both racist and shamefaced, whose social mores and members may not deserve to survive, and (3) a South that demands new modes of action but also sees whites' violent agency as uncanny, unthinkable, unfeasible: as both strange and impossible. Each of these ways of thinking about race (and thinking about thinking) gets taken up obsessively, kaleidoscopically, in southern women's writing.

In Gordon's "One Against Thebes" a white child breaks a code when she says "yes ma'am" to a black woman who has no authority within the small compass of her plantation community. The child can suddenly feel

> Son's and Olivia's eyes on her face. Son's skin is only a little darker than the dust of the road they have been walking on. . . . Son can look at you a long time and you will not know what he is thinking. . . . He is not looking at her now but before he looked away a change come over his eyes, as if something as bright and quick as a snake had flashed up from a deep pool, shimmered for a second over its surface, and then, before you could be certain of what you had seen, flashed back again into the depths. (1990, 126)

The mind of the South, the idea of the South, rethinking the South: women writers have been charged with taking too little interest in these things, with failing to place "the region at the center of their imaginative visions." But instead of contemplating "the" mind or "the" idea of the South, I want to argue that these writers are interested in the problem of how knowledge about race and gender is controlled, with how such knowledge is disseminated.[2]

In *Jonah's Gourd Vine,* when John Pearson admits to adultery during his divorce trial, he feels publicly shamed, but he will not accuse his wife: "Ah didn't want de white folks tuh hear 'bout nothin' lak dat. Dey knows too much 'bout us as it is, but dey some things dey ain't tuh know. Dey's some strings on our harp fuh us tuh play on and sing all tuh ourselves. Dey thinks wese all ignorant as it is, and dey think wese all alike, and dat dey knows us inside and out, but you know better. Dey wouldn't make no great 'miration if you had uh tole 'em Hattie had all dem mens. Dey spectin' dat" (1962, 261). From the white narrator's sense of Son's hidden depths in "One Against Thebes" ("You will not know what he is thinking") to Pearson's insistence that "dey think wese all alike" is an enormous leap. To span this distance I want to explore several theorems suggesting the rich epistemological fields explored in modern southern women's writing.

First, to know "the" mind of the South is to know that there is an abyss between white and black ways of knowing, between two kinds of information about unequally shared southern worlds. White southerners who think at all about these differences frequently describe them in incredibly condescending terms. In *A Southerner Discovers the South* Daniels reminisces that "my first guide was Harriet, yellow and wise, who could look all that the conventional Mammy was supposed to be but who possessed knowledges and interests which made childhood under her guiding a dark excitement of endless variety" (1938, 2). Black writers are constantly probing this abyss for its dangers; white writers like Gordon recognize the edges of this abyss but genuflect or stop at its margins.

Second, to know "the" mind of the South is to know *what it refuses to think*. In constructing this theorem I am not invoking Wilbur Cash's bold, primitive portrait of the white southern mind as sensuous, impulsive hedonism, as all "primary process" ("Strictly the Southerner had no mind; he had temperament . . . he could not analyze an idea, and he could not even conceive of admitting two" [1941, 102]). Instead, I want to focus on ideas that are present but unacknowledged—on thought itself as an act of refusal. For example, when Linda Barron, a black domestic worker, describes her repetitive journey to the white neighborhood where she works, she explains that white people think about her all the time; in fact, they depend on her presence, but they refuse to probe what her journey means:

> When you get off that bus, there're a lot of people set their clocks by you. They know you're going to come along. . . . When they don't see you, they say, "Well, I haven't seen you in a long time." They set their clocks by you, but they don't know what it's like, how to walk back and forth from that bus.
>
> There is a city bus company. Everybody on that board don't ride the bus. They're professional people—never had to stand out in the rain or the sunshine. Why in the hell they don't put some domestic

person on there? I would like to be on that board. I been riding the bus when you had to sit in the back, when it was cold and you couldn't close the windows, when the dust blowing in your eyes. I know what needs to go on. (Tucker 1988, 260–61)

Baron's assertions suggest a third postulate. To know "the" mind of the South is to recognize the myriad information systems (some known to men and women of color, some to white women, some to children and underclass white men) that have been subjugated or surrogated to so-called higher ways of knowing. If these patterns abound, if they emerge and reemerge in the subsemantic palaver of women's writing, what has kept us from seeing and systematizing this complexity?

Morrison's arguments about American literature in *Playing in the Dark* are decidedly epistemological; she describes the vulnerability of the "assumptions conventionally accepted among literary historians and critics and circulated as 'knowledge.' This knowledge holds that traditional, canonical American literature is free of, uninformed [by], and unshaped by the four-hundred-year-old presence of, first, Africans and then African Americans in the United States" (1992, 4–5); it assumes that this presence had little "consequence in the origin and development of that culture's literature" (5). I have begun to argue that southern women's writing tries, with varying degrees of success, to thematize these misrecognitions. When Welty's central character in "Keela the Outcast Indian Maid" is unmasked as a crippled black man who has been enslaved in a circus sideshow, Steve, the sideshow's white barker, starts to roam; he becomes obsessed because he has failed to recognize Keela's race and gender or to rescue "her" from a fate that seems worse than death.

"Been feelin' bad ever since. Can't hold on to a job or stay in one place for nothin' in the world. They made it stay in jail to see if it could talk or not, and the first night it wouldn't say nothin'. Some time it cried. And they undressed it an' found out it wasn't no outcast Indian woman a-tall. It was a little clubfooted nigger man." . . .

"Seemed like that man just studied it out an' knowed it was somethin' wrong," he said presently, his voice coming more remotely than ever. "But I didn't know. I can't look at nothin' an' be sure what it is. Then afterwards I know. Then I see how it was."

"Yeh, but you're nuts," said Max affably.

"You wouldn't of knowed it either!" cried Steve. . . .

"Bet I could tell a man from a woman and an Indian from a nigger though," said Max. (1979, 42–45)

This ability to "know" the difference has been one mainstay of white, masculinist American fiction. If fiction by southern women spits out these archaic national themes, why has it been marginalized as postmodern Americanists march toward a more "multicultural" vision of American studies? Before charting women writers' multiple mapping of the minds of the South, I want to examine some of the dominant ways of "knowing" southern literature.

In a famous aside, Flannery O'Connor described the difficulty of writing good fiction when the Dixie Limited—the prose produced by William Faulkner—is roaring past. It is equally hard to write about the complex epistemologies driving southern women's fiction when the dominant critical machinery enshrines William Faulkner as *the* literary icon of southern studies. At issue is the fact that Faulkner is always defined not only at but *as* the nexus of southern literary history. As Eric Sundquist suggests in his powerful *Faulkner: The House Divided*: "*Light in August* . . . appeared approximately at the crest of a forty-year wave of Jim Crow laws that grew in part out of a threatened economy, in part out of increasingly vocal demands for black equality during and after World War I, and in greater part out of reawakened racist fears that had, at least in contrast, simmered restlessly for a generation between Reconstruction and the twentieth century" (1983, 68).[3] Why do critics celebrate Faulkner's historicism but overlook the way that McCullers's *The Ballad of the Sad Café* describes, say, the impoverished life of a mill town in images that eerily resemble the atmosphere that Hall and others have resurrected in *Like a Family: The Making of a Southern Cotton Mill World* (1987)? The mythifying energy of Faulkner studies takes my breath away. The endless, gorgeous machinery of Faulkner studies is cleansing, satisfying, in the same way that Joyce studies is satisfying—it provides an impressive oeuvre with codes to crack, scholars who can cite chapter and verse, and disciples who know every nook and cranny. But Faulkner's fiction also beats out the rhythms that invite us to read American letters as an epic, gargantuan, blissfully earth-shattering ballad of partisan struggle.

Even the numerology and morphology employed by some Faulkner critics can be astonishing. As Thomas Daniel Young says in *The History of Southern Literature* (1985), Faulkner's epics overshadow the "secondary" writings of Welty and O'Connor: "What one misses in the fictions of this period . . . is the all-pervasive, dominating presence of William Faulkner" (466–67). In Young's introduction this "second" generation of southern writers is defined by negation; they are not concerned with world-sweeping topics such as the "meaning of memory and history" but with shallower modernisms: with existentialism and the death of God, with "trying to find their place in an apparently meaningless and absurd universe." Young associates southern "grotesquerie" with the development in the thirties and forties of "a disturbing picture of a society whose citizens had lost all their respect for traditions, rituals, rites, and ceremonies" (468). The female grotesque is, quite simply, a degenerate form.

I want to take issue with these ongoing metaphors of gigantism and the pursuit of the epic past by suggesting that when Faulkner is said to ride the crest of the most important economic and social events in American history, his writings also tend to become *the* definition of "Southern history," dispensing the things we must attend to as "the historical" writ large. But what is most missing from Faulkner's fiction and most present in southern women writers such as Walker and Welty is a sense of the ways in which racial knowledge functions in the everyday. In *Dirt and Desire* I have begun to explore a set of formal structures utterly different from those that Faulkner discovered in masterworks such as *Absalom, Absalom!,* where his mystifications of oedipal angst and miscegenation have become bywords defining the ways in which race functions in America, making race-mixing the only game in town, *the* epic, underlying structure driving the whiteness of the American dream. The fascination with transracial sexuality, the blank terror of miscegenation, is certainly a frightening force in white American life, but in focusing obsessively on its psycho-cryptic power we miss a great deal.[4]

I'm arguing that we are accustomed to reading race as crisis—but to read race as nonentity, remainder, residue, as a set of formulae that exist automatically, unthinkingly, outside white consciousness: this hits too close to home. To think about the blood ties created and ignored in acts of transracial sexuality creates fiction that is romantic, sexy, dramatic, and recognizably patriarchal and tragic. But how do we think about the nonconsanguineal bonds created and ignored by the conditions of southern labor? What about the non-kin affiliations created in the twentieth century when a white family purchases a black woman's labor power or when this same family furnishes their house and larder with surplus labor appropriated from factory or field? And yet one can argue that these relationships are as important as the abjured kin affiliations between "black" and "white" families that resulted from slavery and its aftermath. As Mildred, a black domestic, comments in *Like One of the Family . . . Conversations from a Domestic's Life,* "it's a rare thing for anybody to find a colored family in this land that can't trace a domestic worker somewhere in their history" (Childress 1956, 3).

We can take one measure of this marginalized drama about the "secret" of unacknowledged labor in *Delta Wedding,* a novel set amidst Mississippi's wealthy cotton plantations in 1923. Here a little white girl sits down to dinner with her dead mother's family ("sighing, eating cake, drinking coffee") and discovers a series of precise vibrations. It is "the throb of the compress [that] had never stopped. Laura could feel it now in the handle of her cup, the noiseless vibration that trembled in the best china, was within it" (1946, 20). This is a splendid, prosaic indictment of commodity fetishism. What is vibrating in this china is not just the cotton compress, ceaselessly at work binding the just-picked cotton into bales, but the ceaseless vibrations of the pickers and the house servants, a vibration that trembles through the silverware and the best linens and every other expensive item in this house. What trembles in the china is the simultaneous awakening and repressing of commodity creation, of the productive labor that makes the leisured life possible, providing the capital that underwrites the most trivial acts of consumption. And the goods that decorate this wedding *are* trivial: "Papa said any kind of wedding I wanted I could have, if I had to get married at all, so I'm going to have shepherdess crooks and horsehair ruffled hats" (54). Meanwhile, at the horizon of the novel we catch the voice of the cook: "inside the house the light, tinkling sounds went on; Roxie's high laugh, like a dove cry, rose softly and hung over the yard. And from farther away the sigh of the compress reminded her of Dabney" (96). Pastoral always happens at someone's expense: "the songs of the cotton pickers were far away, so were the hoofbeats of the horse the overseer rode (and once again, listening for them in spite of the quiet, she felt as if the cotton fields so solid to the sight had opened up and swallowed her daughter)" (89). This dangerous, ghost-making world is portrayed as absolutely ordinary—filled with girls who don't see, or who always see past, the archival whiteness of cotton.

In the scene with the trembling teacup, Laura McRaven experiences—without consciousness—all the vestiges of labor power that have accumulated in the objects she holds; Welty's prose gives us the hidden genealogy of this labor. The teacup—an object of use, an object of beauty—is filled with but also hiding the machine's vibrations, which are in turn filled with the labor of the cotton pickers. But what I want most to emphasize is the epistemology, the way of knowing, that also resides in this teacup. What this object of everyday use brings to mind is a story *omnipresent but not heard;*

the vibrations in the teacup represent something that registers below the level of white self-consciousness but gets taken for granted.

If Faulkner's version of Dixie creates an endless echolalia in which it is possible to come to terms with miscegenation but to miss these laborious vibrations that are felt but not heard, the South memorialized in the differently canonized *Gone with the Wind* offers another set of distractions: another map for misreading southern women writers' preoccupations. Wanting to invent a new lexicon for reading southern women's fiction, I face a series of obstacles, including two powerful blocking texts that predispose us *not* to invent an archive detailing throwaway bodies or southern women's dramatization of "the unseen everyday." Whereas Faulkner's oeuvre has been given over to reading southern history as epic horror, Mitchell's story encourages a reading of history as epic nostalgia: both shut out a deal of light.

In spite of these shortcomings, I want to use Mitchell's novel to sharpen our sense of the epistemologies driving black and white southern women's fiction, its odd ways of knowing the South. That is, I want to dramatize the ways in which Mitchell's fiction examines "the" South's ideas of itself and to set forth one or two theorems in which southern racism looks less like an Eleusinian mystery and more like a repetitive, everyday terror—a set of practices so incessantly, so boringly enacted within the everyday that they seem to be hiding in plain sight.[5]

In *Playing in the Dark* Toni Morrison not only tells the story of the white canon; she describes a handful of white texts that struggle to rearticulate race, even as they succumb to racist conventions. She argues that novels such as *Sapphira and the Slave Girl* are deliriously retrograde in their portraits of slave women. By trying to find aesthetic forms equal to telling the story of slave-owning women's dependency on and abuse of African American servants, Cather both fails and succeeds; she stretches to the breaking point her own narrative coherence (Morrison 1992, 18–28). Morrison is eloquent about the racist complexities of Cather's writing, her failure to see the parameters of the narrative problems that haunt her. But even Morrison's eloquence cannot mend the bigotry of *Gone with the Wind*, a story that drives through slavery and Reconstruction like the Energizer bunny—its racism just keeps going and going. As Ashley comments wistfully to Melanie:

> I see Twelve Oaks and remember how the moonlight slants across the white columns, and the unearthly way the magnolias look, opening

> under the moon, and how the climbing roses make the side porch shady even at the hottest noon. And I see Mother, sewing there, as she did when I was a little boy. And I hear the darkies coming home across the fields at dusk, tired and singing and ready for supper, and the sound of the windlass as the bucket goes down into the cool well. And there's the long view down the road to the river, across the cotton fields, and the mist rising from the bottom lands in the twilight. And that is why I'm here who have no love or death or misery or glory and no hatred for anyone. Perhaps that is what is called patriotism, love of home and country." (1973, 210)

Notice the ways in which African Americans become atmosphere, but without the anxiety this produces in *Delta Wedding. Gone with the Wind* wears its racism on its sleeve; Mitchell is rarely disturbed when she catches her white characters in the act of making her black characters disappear.

Why traffic with *Gone with the Wind?* In part because of the bizarre power it exerts over so many white female readers' ideas of the South, in part because of its intriguing structures of thought: it forgets, on the level of plot, what it struggles to remember on the level of images. In fact, *Gone with the Wind* creates multiple modes of forgetting. It is a very long book with print so tiny that it makes me squint, a book whose racial politics are absolutely abhorrent, and yet in spanning its pages I find myself at odds with my own position as a libertine academic—empathizing with the Klan after they've brutalized the inhabitants of a shantytown, identifying with Scarlett as she abuses convict labor, admiring Melanie Wilkes, who is afraid to go north because her son might have to go to school with "pickaninnies." My black students do not share this sense of velocity and pleasure when reading Mitchell's book; her racism and white egotism, the erasure of the horrors of slavery, and the bigoted depictions of Reconstruction create outright anger.

How is it possible, then, to become so embroiled, so whitely forgetful, as I reread a story whose politics (and, for that matter, whose writing style) drives me over the brink? Granted, it is a brilliant stroke on Mitchell's part to make her heroine a villain, to invent a plot that moves swiftly from crisis to crisis, and to provide a classic dénouement—a reversal of fortune that, unlike all the novel's other reversals, depends on a discovery that is meant to feel, in the novel's terms, as earth-shattering as Oedipus's. Scarlett takes off her blinders, discovers she doesn't love Ashley but has desired Rhett all along—just at the moment when (as with Oedipus) such a discovery salves nothing.

I want to use the blindness driving *Gone with the Wind* to help shape the epistemological questions driving this chapter. We've explored the drama of jettisoned bodies that become a melancholy undercurrent of southern commodity culture—not as alluring ghosts but as trash or debris. Now I want to explore the omnipresence of ideas that are *known* but not *acknowledged*, the importance of what Christopher Bollas (1987) has called "the unthought known." Take the case of Eleanor Roosevelt in 1913, during her first sojourn in Washington under the "southern" administration of Woodrow Wilson.

> Wilson was the darling of what would later be called the Dixiecrats. But northern progressives such as FDR allied to him with equal fervor. For them, race was simply not an issue. Indeed, among whites race had become an issue only for the very few progressives who had founded the National Association for the Advancement of Colored People in 1909. . . .
>
> Among Washingtonians, the subject of race was rarely discussed. There was one tense moment when Josephus Daniels expressed horror that Eleanor Roosevelt brought four white servants, and a nurse and governess, to Washington. He practically ordered her to fire them: Only Negroes, he felt, should do servile work. She was stunned by what she considered the "brutality" of his prejudice and subsequently referred to it as a "shocking" moment.
>
> At the time, however, ER was largely undisturbed by the racism of prewar Washington. (Cook 1992, 204)

Can this biographical detail be accurate? What does it mean to register something as "shocking" but to remain "largely undisturbed"? What does it mean to register horrendous facts without thinking about them? For Bollas the "unthought known" is a residue of childhood imprinting us with expectations about the way the world will shape itself (or fail to shape itself) about us. These early experiences are lodged in the sensorium but not available to consciousness—hence known but unthought or unacknowledged. I want to wrest this idea from its psychological context and use it as a cognitive and political category for thinking about the South.

To see this idea in motion, we will need to examine *Gone with the Wind*'s misrecognitions, the way this novel's stereotypes jangle with its peculiar use of color, its unthinking substitution of white characters for black and vice versa. For all her moral ineptitude and repugnant stereotyping of the races, Mitchell can drive us closer to tracing the racial shape of the world that many white southern women writers of the thirties struggled to reconstellate. Scarlett's misrecognition of her love for Rhett Butler is not just a romantic convention but a mood deeply implicated in the novel's racial blindness.

This double structure of misrecognition mirrors a crucial argument Drew Faust makes about what goes wrong with Mitchell's project. She sees *Gone with the Wind* foundering upon a blindness about race and a misrecognition of the connections between race and gender:

> Mitchell lacks the critical vision of the South that gives [*Absalom, Absalom!*] its moral and literary power. Unable herself to understand the cruelties of white racism, Mitchell is incapable of translating any such insight into her fiction or into her portrayal of Scarlett O'Hara. Thus, for all her ability to see through and to challenge certain basic assumptions of southern life, Scarlett, like Mitchell, remains blind to the most fundamental reality of all: that southern civilization rested on the oppression of four million African Americans whose labor made southern wealth, gentility, and even ladyhood possible. (1999, 13)

Here we approach the problem within white southern epistemology we need to take up next. Mitchell is blind not only to racial oppression but to the inseparability of race and gender that drives *Gone with the Wind*'s definitions of ladyhood. But we also need to see that the romantic structure that allows Scarlett to make her way to one recognition (the discovery of her own "erotic truth") is also a structure primed to ward off another set of political recognitions about race as the very ground that makes Scarlett's infatuation with whiteness possible. In other words, misrecognition is not just the heroine's fatal flaw but the author's problem as well. What does this do to habitual readings of *Gone With the Wind?* What happens when we read through the lens provided by this double plot—this need to read the novel by seeing double acts of not seeing: the most popular romance of the twentieth century spawned by a monstrous twinning in which erotic misrecognition and political misrecognition go hand in hand?

The questions of misrecognition, arrested symbol systems, sequestered centers of thought (or nonthought), and the motif of throwaway knowledge (of what is over- or underlooked) are dominant, underrecognized concerns in twentieth-century southern literature. *Gone with the Wind* offers an unwitting anatomy of *the spectacle of unknowing* built into very structures of white southern life.

For example, in Tucker's *Telling Memories Among Southern Women,* the author-interviewer is struck by this repetition. She meets a series of white women who launch into stories about their black domestic workers, speaking eagerly until

> halfway through, I could tell from their slowed voices that they were not quite sure they should have begun. . . . The taboo against discussing race and a fear of saying something inappropriate (a fear born of changed attitudes toward race) made two reasons for caution.
>
> For these reasons, a number of white women would not sign release forms. They had told stories that they had heard all their lives. . . . Yet they heard these stories anew when they realized they would be written down. . . . Our unedited words are often those that are most familiar and also those that tell us more than we want to know about the culture we live in. (1988, 139)

Tucker describes a world brimming with arrested systems of knowledge, a culture that depends on the nonconceptualized, on that which hasn't been visited by a concept. I'm referring here to the nature of everyday southern thought, to what can be consumed by modern, interwar southern culture as knowledge and what cannot—a refusal to think about what one already knows.

Another spectacle of unknowing emerges from an anecdote about the Commission on Interracial Cooperation, an organization formed in 1919, in the decade just before *Gone with the Wind* was written, to promote dialogue among leaders of black and white communities as a first step to renovated race relations. This was a group that proceeded too cautiously: its goal, as Patricia Sullivan puts it in *Days of Hope,* was simply "to move beyond mutual ignorance." Clark Foreman, secretary of the Georgia CIC, was especially shocked by whites' lack of knowledge of the struggles of blacks to make a livelihood, stay healthy, or gain even minimal literacy, so in the 1920s he convened a group of prominent black and white citizens in Augusta for the purpose of mutual education. "During the first meeting, the white participants appeared genuinely shocked to learn that municipal services and paved roads did not extend to the black sections of town." The whites' feeble gestures toward change represented the merest of panaceas—and Foreman eventually turned to other modes of organizing (1996, 32).

We need to focus on these white citizens' "genuine shock" at encountering a world that they see every day—suggesting, once again, a deliberate sequestration of knowledge. It seems remarkable, even laughable, that white families who drive maids home, ride through this section of town to get to church or go to the country, act as if they are blind to the conditions they see all the time. But one of my hypotheses about southern women's writing is that it invents structures to get at this everyday world of white unseeing. We tend to think that the surface of things is less hidden than their depth. But I want to offer this crucial idea: the things at the surface are hidden in plain sight. Their very repetition is what conceals them. What these writers explore in their fiction is the structure of what is known but not thought, a misrecognized or fading epistemology—a cloud of unknowing that extends over everyday racial interactions.

White and black literatures about the South present this cloud of unknowing very differently. In *Dessa Rose* Sherley Anne Williams makes a white woman's discoveries about her own race-thinking both central and climactic. Taunted by Dessa, accused of not knowing "her" own mammy's given name (even as Rufel, the coming-into-knowledge white woman, is nursing Dessa's black child), Rufel sees the light. She begins to recognize the cost of her broken knowledge of the mammy she has "known" since childhood: "Rufel sniffed again and nodded. 'She treated me just like, just like'—She stuttered and could have wept again, seeing with an almost palpable lucidity how absurd it was to think of her self as Mammy's child, a darky's child. And shuddered. A pickaninny. Like the ragged, big-bellied urchins she had seen now and then about the streets of Mobile, running errands, cutting capers" (1986, 132). Once this riddle is imposed, Rufel can't stop contemplating the deficits in her everyday acts of unknowing: "I don't *think* I ever *thought* a *thought* during all that time that I didn't tell Ma—Dor—that I didn't tell her. . . . As if darkies could ever *know* the life she spoke of. . . . Had Mammy had children, Rufel *wondered* . . . it bothered Rufel that *she did not know*" (133–136, emphasis added). In contrast, in *Delta Wedding* this common lack of knowledge is never stated extrinsically, never climactic. As Welty says of Laura McRaven, "She could hear nothing, except for the sounds of the Negroes, and the slow ceiling fan turning in the hall" (1946, 69). This vanishing point, where blacks become atmospheric, where they vaporize into "nothing," becomes a repetitive litany: "There was no one there," except, that is, for "Vi'let, leaning on a stepladder . . . very slowly taking down the velvet curtains" (71). Finally, this leisured madness plays out very differently in the fiction of Faulkner, who, in a blaze of glory, conjures up race as an epic structure built on the foundations of guilt, giant torment, and oedipal drives that make miscegenation more culpable than incest. Fictions by Walker, Hurston, Welty, Cather, Porter, and McCullers ask us to think about how race and gender cohabit in the non-epic everyday, where African Americans who are defined as "others" become the site of neglect, of the overlooked, the throwaway: the site of ungrieved grief that never bothers to come to white consciousness—a "nothing" omnipresent and utterly obvious and yet quite difficult to see.

To fathom this focus on surfaces, we can turn to Willa Cather, who comes back to her southern roots in her final novel, *Sapphira and the Slave Girl.* The surfaces of this novel are utterly bizarre, especially in relation to the novel's racist plot and character structures: "The miller's furniture was whitewashed, so to speak, day by day, by the flour-dust which sifted down from overhead, and through every crack and crevice in the doors and walls. Each morning Till's Nancy swept and dusted the flour away" (1968, 47). This brand of whiteness, produced, of course, by black millhands, is unwanted but cannot be brushed off; it becomes a form of pollution, of whiteness as dirt, that coagulates where it is least desired. "Colbert changed his old leather jacket for a black coat, brushed the flour-dust off his broad hat, and walked up through the cold spring drizzle which was making the grass green" (49). After complaining about Bluebell's housekeeping, he "said no more, but went out into the hall and took up his wide-brimmed hat—this morning white with two days' flour-dust" (64).

This strange figure of thought, this whiteness that floats about like detachable pieces of the body, or part-objects, and settles everywhere, is utterly unlike the icon of the throwaway.[6] First, it drifts through the air to cover everyone, blacks and whites alike. Second, these vagrant signs never coalesce into a taut symbol or image; that is, Cather never converts this polluting flour from nonce detail into symbol.

My suggestion is that this whiteness—which is so very much there and yet so "natural" a part of this environment that it is nearly invisible as a signifier—serves as the "glue" of the real; it is essential to the realistic surface of Cather's novel and yet uncanny or obsessive as a symbolic site. This floating whiteness becomes a haunting signifier *of what cannot be thought or organized,* either in the nineteenth-century historyscape of the novel or in the white landscape of the 1930s from which Cather is writing. Whiteness functions as a form of detritus that floats like so much dead skin in the cold southern air. These floating particles coalesce into an almost present *structure of feeling* that has not yet emerged as a *structure of thought*—a site of uncanny, unassimilable emotions, of an "epistemological disarray" (Bersani 1977, 60) that fails to organize the underanalyzed structures of race and racial oppression that drive Cather's novel.[7]

If this allusion feels like coy, overtheorized, literary-critical sleight of hand, then why does this shredded whiteness recur so incessantly in stories and novels by white women from the 1920s to the 1980s? "A creature in a blousy white overall with ruffles . . . with bone-white skull and chalk-white face" (1972, 433) terrifies Katherine Anne Porter's Miranda with his inhumanity. *Delta Wedding* describes a world covered with lint from the cotton gin—a terror to clean, sticking to ceilings and lampshades "like a present from the fairies that made Vi'let moan" (1946, 8). McCullers and Douglas create similar scenes focusing on polluting, dislocating, unrecognizable figures and fields of whiteness that create another set of figures for the "unthought known."

How do these surfaces of fractured whiteness and ambient blackness play themselves out in *Gone with the Wind*? As we have seen, blacks are caricatured unmercifully in this novel as not fully human. And yet Mitchell's novel is also driven by textual quirks that seem to outrun the author's control. For example, the way color works in Mitchell's novel is decidedly weird. In the first paragraph we learn that "Scarlett O'Hara was not beautiful, but men seldom realized it." Her face is a composite—part Irish, part French, but also part white and part black: "her thick black brows slanted upward, cutting a startling oblique line in her magnolia white skin." Lest we think this perforated whiteness is an accident, when Scarlett slaps Ashley at Twelve Oaks, his face is oddly colored, incised—"the red mark of her hand showed plainly on his white, tired face." These lineaments are reversed in the description of Rhett Butler, whose dark face is all blackness and bristle, but with a slash of white teeth.

Mitchell is hardly an apt deconstructor of her own brand of whiteness, for elsewhere in the novel white is the color of comfort, of big houses, genteel women: the proper pallor for aristocratic anxiety. It is also the color of money, as in the milky reassurance of cotton bolls dancing above the red and green earth. But by the end of the novel these constantly, cheerfully iterated references to whiteness almost disappear, to be replaced with a dangerous festival of darkness and blackness: not just the surging presence of groups of freedmen who so terrify unreconstructed whites, but Rhett Butler himself gets darker and darker, Bonnie Blue Butler is afraid of the dark and because of this cannot be buried in the earth, and in making love Rhett and Scarlett are swallowed by blackness, while at the novel's end Scarlett thinks not about Rhett but about Mammy:

> She stood for a moment remembering small things, the avenue of *dark* cedars leading to Tara, the banks of cape jessamine bushes, vivid green against the *white* walls, the fluttering *white* curtains. And Mammy would be there. Suddenly she wanted mammy desperately,

> as she had wanted her when she was a little girl, wanted the broad bosom on which to lay her head, the gnarled *black* hand on her hair. Mammy, the last link with the old days. (1024, emphasis added)

This rhythmic play of black and white is astonishing. But the point is not that Mitchell is a protointegrationist; segregationist principles lacerate the novel to the end.

What this novel shares with some other texts by white southern women is a sense of writing from a rich and troubled field: a site of overwhelming narrative desire to talk about whiteness and blackness even while refusing, on the level of plot, to recognize the difficulty of their relationship.

Not only is Rhett exchanged for Mammy, but from the very beginning there is a surprising fluidity between black and white positions. Brent and Stuart Tarleton accuse Jeems, their slave and former "playmate," of eavesdropping and then refuse to recognize that he knows more than they know about Scarlett. Then Rhett takes his place as eavesdropper as he pops up at the end of Scarlett's and Ashley's quarrel at Twelve Oaks. We first meet Scarlett's child, Wade, struggling in Prissie's arms, miserable with her bad mothering, but Scarlett quickly takes her place as bad mother, suggesting, again, an odd interchangeability.[8] In addition, Gerald O'Hara's funeral service is nearly a scandal to the neighborhood because the Catholic service is so short; then Ashley saves the day by "reciting from memory the Episcopal burial service which he had often read over slaves buried at twelve Oaks" (701), setting up a site of exchange between the Wilkes's nameless slaves and the dead Mr. O'Hara (and bringing us back, with a start, to Gerald's initial status as a lower-class immigrant and outsider). But more startling, these invocations offer a supplement to the burial sites that mark the beginning of the novel, when we visit the graves of *three* Gerald O'Hara juniors (a repetition equal in its absurdity to Toni Morrison's deliberately ironic characters, the three deweys). As Ashley recites the invocation of the Anglican burial service he memorized while burying (how many?) slaves, the novel drifts toward a wider landscape of mourning and melancholia, of ungrieved grief for the thrown-away bodies of the black slaves who created Twelve Oaks itself.

Finally, Scarlett possesses an unlikely fluidity in the scene where Rhett ravishes her and she seems to love it. Critics have described this scene both as a rape and as the ecstasy of surrender, suggesting that Scarlett welcomes her own subordination. In fact, the color of this encounter is "dark . . . dark . . . she was darkness and he was darkness and there had never been anything before this time, only darkness and his lips upon her" (929). On the level of plot, Drew Faust has argued that Scarlett's sexuality, her liberated power as a capitalist woman, is limited when the instigation of the standard rape-lynching plot curtails Scarlett's freedom. That is, the race-terror of Scarlett's world trumps her new mastery of male roles by imposing on Scarlett the ideological fragility of the white lady and creates the conditions that demand her retreat. But while the legends of gender and race can be pried apart on the level of story, as imagery they become more and more imbricated, until Scarlett winds up in the regressively, oppressively homosocial bliss of Mammy's arms. Is Mitchell blocked, ensnared, unable (as Faust argues) to imagine freedom for blacks and therefore unable to imagine it for women? Or, does the novel manage to appeal to some readers because it touches so precisely on a world (the white southern world of the 1920s and 1930s) that refuses to think what it knows about race—and therefore keeps reenacting the bizarre double structure of a character-driven plot that caricatures and dehumanizes blacks and an image-driven plot that makes black the color that one wants to become (in the service of recovering early object relations and desires) and makes white the most fractured, witless, and monstrous of surfaces?

I'm not trying to celebrate Mitchell's (or the narrator's or Scarlett's or the white reader's) confused, dehumanizing relation to blackness at the novel's end but simply to suggest that this relation is as confused as it is racist and that this confusion is both productive and normative in the creation of white southern fiction. So, although *Gone with the Wind* calls fixities such as patriarchy into question, compelling new recognition of the forces connecting the struggle for freedom and the negotiation of self (Faust 1999, 18), my argument would also suggest that *Gone with the Wind* grows out of a world that is compelled by misrecognition. Mitchell's novel dramatizes how compelling and necessary these misrecognitions are to the white South's economy of unknowing. Or, as the pious and by now slave-free Ashley says to Scarlett after the war:

> "I can't make money from the enforced labor and misery of others."
>
> "But you owned slaves."
>
> "They weren't miserable. And besides, I'd have freed them all when Father died if the war hadn't already freed them." (967)

Gone with the Wind explores—without quite intending to—the cult of fetishized, never-seen surfaces, what is hiding in plain sight, the preoccupation not with "under" or "beneath" or "depth," but with the cult of "besides," of what is proximate, next-to, and therefore invisible. Thus Scarlett's misrecognition of her love for Rhett Butler is not just a romance convention but a mood deeply implicated in the novel's racial blindness. Or, as Ellen Gilchrist says in *The Land of Dreamy Dreams:* "No matter how many husbands Alisha has, she always keeps the same old maid" (1981, 38).

Before devoting more space to defining the unthought known as an underrecognized component of white southern political life, I need to pause, to supplement the importance of this concept with its status as ideological luxury. In Gaines's *A Lesson Before Dying* another mode of knowledge is set in motion. Jefferson, a black man present at the killing of a white liquor store owner, is arrested, charged with the man's death, and sentenced to electrocution. "She knew, as we all knew, what the outcome would be. A white man had been killed during the robbery . . . he, too, would have to die" (1993, 4). This black man's death is a form of absolute knowledge. It is a hard fact, a concept that cannot be unthought or unknown by any African American man, woman, or child in this Louisiana community.

For whites the knowledge of Jefferson's death is also absolute, but Gaines goes to great lengths to suggest that the illogic of this absolute can be glimpsed even by white people. In a scene that is as crazy as the mad hatter's tea party, Jefferson's godmother, Miss Emma, visits the sheriff's wife to plead for visiting privileges in a more dignified room outside Jefferson's prison cell. "The sheriff's wife was stunned. She nearly spilled her coffee. What was wrong with the cell? Wasn't it big enough? Yes, but they couldn't all sit down. Was it necessary that they all sit down at the same time? Couldn't they take turns?" (133). The sense of Miss Emma's proposal, and the nonsense with which it is met, creates a resurgence of white panic. The sheriff's wife admits, euphemistically, that she longs for Jefferson's death:

> She told Miss Emma she would see what she could do. . . .
>
> "Just speak to him, if you don't mind," Miss Emma said. "I done a lot for you and your family over these years."
>
> "Oh, Lord, do I know," the sheriff's wife said. "Do I know, do I know, do I know. I'll speak to the sheriff. Lord, I'll be glad when all this is over."
>
> Miss Emma dropped her coffee cup on the floor and started calling on God.
>
> "I didn't mean it that way," the sheriff's wife said. "God in heaven know I didn't mean it that way. Lou, Reverend Ambrose—can't y'all do something? The Lord knows I didn't mean it that way." (133–34)

Regardless of what she means, even "the Lord knows" how little consequence these hard facts have for her—except in this moment when her everyday, taken-for-granted, strictly-for-white-people talk spills over into the black community. Her speech loses the sheen of the quotidian and shows forth in its monstrosity.

Gaines counters the *absolute knowledge* that always attends white supremacy with still another portrait of "the" mind of the South. In the moment of the white liquor store owner's death, Jefferson cannot think straight; he is trapped within a form of knowing that can only be limited, contingent, conditional: "'They made me come with them. You got to tell the law that, Mr. Gropé.' . . . But he was talking to a dead man. Still he did not run. *He didn't know what to do . . . . He didn't know whether* he had come there with Brother and Bear, or whether he had walked in and seen all this after it had happened. . . . *He didn't know whether* he should call someone on the telephone or run . . . . *He didn't know what to do*" (6, emphasis added). Jefferson is caught between multiple wrong answers—like Richard Wright's black characters in *Uncle Tom's Children*. Like Gaines, Wright portrays the impossibility of thinking within and against this system of absolute knowledge, where every answer is fallible; he portrays the pressure of thinking at all in a southern world where the ascendant solution, the dominant way of knowing, is white-on-black violence: "She did not want to decide alone; she must make no mistake about this" (Wright 1965, 200); "he thought with despair" about whether to cross the white neighborhood without a shirt after he had been beaten (166); "his body grew taut with indecision. Yes, now, he would swing that axe and they would never tell and he had his gun" (92); "she tried to think just how it had happened" (106). Faced with two wrong answers, thinking is a terrible labor. In Wright's stories the mind-numbing work of survival is so exhausting that characters sometimes sink out of thought into some other revery: "She was thinking of nothing now; her hands followed a life-long ritual of toil. Spreading a sleeve, she ran the hot iron to and fro until the wet cloth became stiff. She was deep in the midst of her work when a song rose up out of the far off days of her childhood and broke through half-parted lips" (182). Each of these characters enacts the hardship of thinking in a world laced with too many wrong answers. This state of in-betweenness is the precondition of multiple moments of southern knowing—from the metaphysically impacted opening of Gaines's novel ("I was not there, yet I was there," 3) to the sheriff's wife's deeply ridiculous "Oh, Lord, do I know. . . . Do I know, do I know, do I know."

In this chapter I have suggested three related postulates: (1) southern literature often probes or reflects an abyss between white and black ways of knowing, (2) to know the mind of the (white) South is to know what it refuses to think, and (3) to know this abyss as it is met by the vacuum of the "unthought known" (of white ways of not knowing) is to admit a third knowledge system into our lexicon—the importance of exploring unofficial information systems that have been subjugated to nominally "higher" ways of knowing. Now we must add two more postulates: (4) that aspect of the mind of the South that is shaped by white supremacy and gives blacks the status of sacrificial nonentities also creates *an absolute knowledge* about the direction of violence in any given moment of racial crisis within the Jim Crow South, and (5) the result of this absolute knowledge can be *an absolute unknowing,* a desire not to think at all in a world where any challenge to the "fact" of white supremacy can transform an African American subject into a sacrificial nonperson, a scapegoat.

But even these theorems are hardly exhaustive, suggesting a sixth. To know the mind of the South is to recognize the weirdness and illogic that pertains in each of the first five theorems. To couple white society's absolute knowledge about violent racial practices with a portrait of white people skating on surfaces, oblivious to the weight of the unthought known—this seems absurd. To couple the importance of excavating African Americans' unofficial knowledge with moments of crisis in which no knowledge seems possible—this also seems counterintuitive. But the need to think counterintuitively is exactly what Annette Gordon-Reed seizes on in her comments about southern race-thinking as an American phenomenon. From an African American perspective, Thomas Jefferson is simply

> a fairly garden-variety version of a white man, struggling (not too hard) to come to grips with this ultimately weird relationship with black people. His slaves labored for him, they evoked responses in him. Emotionally and practically, he could not *ignore* them. I don't see how we can *begin to know* him without knowing something of the black people who attended him from birth to death. His struggle with racial issues, to the extent that he was struggling, seems very modern . . . a large percentage of the American population still hold comparable views, believing as Jefferson did that blacks are less intelligent than whites, that whites look better than blacks, that there should be no wholesale mixing of the races. This is why most black Americans can think of Jefferson as an average white person, while whites—at least those who write about him—*claim not to be able to recognize* him. To settle for the cult of Jefferson the mystery man strikes me as a distancing mechanism by those who *refuse to recognize* how commonplace his attitudes about blacks are today. (1998, 24, emphasis added)

Gordon-Reed makes several amazing points. First, she notes the impossibility of knowing Jefferson without knowing both what he knew and what the slaves around him knew. Second, she describes the unthought known as a habit of mind practiced by every scholar who mystifies Jefferson, who claims "not to be able to recognize him." Finally, she argues that the details that are least recognized, least available to intellection, are part of the commonplace, the everyday—what's most on the surface. In the next chapter I will argue that the epic status of the everyday is what southern women's writing is most about.

Chapter Five

Beyond the Hummingbird: Southern Gargantuas

Why southern gargantuas? It should be clear from the previous chapters that I want southern women writers to take up more space. But I will also argue that there is something intrinsically interesting in the question of scale in southern history and literature. What is the place of the epic? What is the place of the miniature in descriptions of both literary and material history? A newspaper in Georgia responded to the Association of Southern Women for the Prevention of Lynching's campaign in an editorial that characterized the delegates who attended the first annual meeting as "all fat and forty. . . . We cannot imagine an association of twenty prize fighters and wrestlers, more independent or able to protect themselves than the group picture indicates these women to be. But they forget that all women are not endowed with such a formidable line, and if attacked, would be helpless" (*Macon Evening News,* 4 December 1930). But attention to scale is not simply a matter of attending to gender. The task of creating southern capital also yields strategies of scale. As an example of the monumental task of creating southern capital, I want to begin with a complex story: that of the black mule skinners who built the Mississippi levee and left in their wake an immense wall of earth "higher and longer than the Great Wall of China, very likely the biggest thing that man has ever made," stretching all the way from a point south of New Orleans to Cairo, Illinois. This wall was "more than a thousand miles as the crow flies, but immeasurably longer as its thirty- to forty-foot-high embankments, one on each side, follow the endless winding of the stream" (Lomax 1993, 212). In *The Land Where the*

Blues Begins Alan Lomax describes the way in which this laborious feat, so unobtrusive and so immense, begins to loom larger and larger in his own imagination, "until now I see the levee as the most distinctive spiritual and cultural feature of the Delta landscape." Lomax thinks of the levee on two different scales. The levee is "the principal human response to the titanic power of the great river. The century of labor it cost, the shelter it provided, and the rich and cruel system it fostered shaped the history of the region" (212). But Lomax also spent his time on the delta exploring the quotidian effects of this gigantic system, collecting blues tunes about "Mr. Charlie," the legendary white foreman, and about the hard love and hard labor that made the levee world possible:

> I ax Mister Cholly what time of day,
> What time of day.
> And he looked at me, good pardner,
> Throwed his watch away,
> Oh-oh-oh-oh, throwed his watch away.
>
> Mister Cholly, Mister Cholly,
> Did the money come?"
> He say, "The river too foggy,
> And the boat don't run,
> Oh-oh-oh-oh, the boat don't run." (225)

This oscillation between the monumental and the miniature (here, an oscillation between the epic scale of the levee and the everyday deprivations of the men who built it and carried this muddy work into their songs) is the subject of this chapter.

Why start with the transition from monumental to miniature, with such manic transformations of scale? As Godzilla has taught us, size does matter. The breadth of the levee, the pittance its workers earned, the enormous wealth their labor produced for other people, and the invisibility of this back-breaking work suggest that examining matters of scale and morphology will be crucial to rethinking southern literature. In this chapter I want to investigate another overlooked issue of scale that also veers between the monumental and the everyday: southern women writers' simultaneous interest in the everyday and their inventions of gargantuan women. In "The Displaced Person" Flannery O'Connor describes a woman who looks like a mountain and acts like an earth-moving machine: "Her arms were folded and as she mounted the prominence, she might have been the giant wife of the countryside, come out at some sign of danger to see what the trouble was. She stood on two tremendous legs, with the grand self-confidence of a mountain, and rose, up narrowing bulges of granite, to two icy blue points of light that pierced forward, surveying everything" (1971, 194). We will see that the South's gargantuan women also lay claim to a dense materiality, even as they refuse the dimension of "earth mother." Instead, these figures crawl out of the earth to claim territory; they are mountainous women who take on the role of un-domesticating southern fiction, claiming vast physical as well as literary-historical space.[1]

Giant Bodies

In this chapter I want to map the bizarre psychological and political effects of grotesque bodies in southern women's fiction, since it is my conviction that this fiction (a) has a politics and (b) needs to be reread along the axis of women writers' amazing inventiveness—their daunting grotesques, their mingling of dirt and desire, their tragic invention of throwaway bodies and "old" southern children. Given the scope of this fiction, why has writing by southern women taken a back seat to writing by southern men? In 1980, Richard King helped set the scene when he published *A Southern Renaissance: The Cultural Awakening of the American South, 1930–1955*. Feminists were stunned at the race and gender bias of his study; women were excluded from *A Southern Renaissance,* as were African Americans. Their fiction may have been important, but it did not measure up to King's great themes: "I will generally focus on works which take the South and its tradition as problematic. For this reason I do not deal with black writers such as Richard Wright or Ralph Ellison or with women writers such as Eudora Welty, Carson McCullers, Flannery O'Connor, and Katherine Anne Porter" (8). To "take the South and its tradition as problematic" meant to write about the southern family romance with its mythy fathers, pithy sons, its dim wives and daughters—as these characters were conceived by white males. According to King, southern women did not, for the most part, write with the same "historical consciousness" that inspired male writers. Even when their prose imitated the grandeur of a William Faulkner or a Robert Penn Warren, southern women seemed incapable of devoting themselves to "the tortuous process of dealing with the past of the region" (8).

Of course, King is neither an artless reader nor a simple chauvinist. He argues that "all of these writers would demand extensive treatment in a complete history of the Renaissance. Black writers are not taken up because for them the Southern family romance was hardly problematic. It could be and was rejected out of hand. . . . The case with the women writers is more difficult, but my reading of them indicates that whatever the merits of their work—and they are considerable—they were not concerned primarily with the larger cultural, racial, and political themes that I take as my focus" (8–9). It has been my argument that "the larger cultural, racial, and political themes" of southern life are precisely the issues that drive southern women's writing. If critics have been blind to these themes, it is because we still have not learned to read this writing in all of its power and intricacy, nor have we discovered the ways in which it exposes the deforming effects of the southern political tradition on women, men, and children of color, on white women and children, and even on white men. If we fail to acknowledge this "larger" dimension in southern women's writing, we are missing a great deal, indeed.

Southern women's lack of thematic, stylistic, or political "largeness" has been a frequent reprise in criticism of southern fiction. In *The Faraway Country: Writers of the Modern South* Louis Rubin admits a single woman into his southern pantheon, and although he intends his chapter on Eudora Welty to be an eloquent defense of her writing, the chapter is flavored with odd diminutions of Welty's abilities. While Faulkner's Mississippi contains combatants "larger than life," Welty's Mississippi is a "tidy, protected little world." While Faulkner flings "whole dynasties of families" into space, while he writes tribal fugues about giant men who "rage at their human limitations," Welty proffers a smaller world "in which people go about their affairs, living, marrying, getting children, diverting themselves, dying, all in tranquil, pastoral fashion" (1963, 131). For Rubin, Welty may possess a "muscularity" that pushes her beyond those mere "local colorists," Katherine Anne Porter and Marjorie Kinnan Rawlings, but she is not quite Faulkner, not so big, nor so bold: "I am not proposing that her work is *as* important as Faulkner's, but I am maintaining that in scope and insight her two novels deserve to be compared *with* Faulkner's. She is no lightweight; she is not merely picturesque; she is a serious writer" (133). And yet "the most startling quality of Eudora Welty's art is her style: shimmering, hovering, elusive, fanciful, fastening on little things. Entirely feminine, it moves lightly, capriciously, mirroring the bemused, diverted quality of the people whom it describes. Like the hummingbirds that appear frequently in her stories, it darts here and there, never quite coming to rest, tirelessly invoking light, color, the variety of experience" (133–34). I want to formulate habits of reading that will take us beyond the hummingbird, beyond Faulkner's shadow, and into the hot southern day. My hope is to recover the political intrigue and bravura, the largeness and largesse, of fiction by southern women.

Let me start with an example from Welty's fiction. In her first collection of short stories, *A Curtain of Green,* we find a puzzling story titled "A Memory." The story seems to go nowhere—its plot line and its sense of character development are almost nil. And yet "A Memory" is Welty's own "spot of time"; the story seems entirely southern in setting and voice but resembles Wordsworthian autobiography in its side glances into the numinous terrors of the everyday. Although nothing happens, a little girl's secure southern world comes crashing down around her. In this moment the child's imaginative or writerly character is formed, and the results are the highly rebellious and political stories in *A Curtain of Green.*

The focus of this story is a young southern girl with a photographic obsession: she looks at everything through a frame made by her fingers. What she sees on the day of the story is a gargantuan woman, a ragged colossus in an old bathing suit. It is this gargantua who will inundate any notion that southern women writers are primarily concerned with "little things":

> Fat hung upon her upper arms like an arrested earthslide on a hill. With the first motion she might make, I was afraid that she would slide down upon herself into a terrifying heap. Her breasts hung heavy and widening like pears into her bathing suit. Her legs lay prone one on the other like shadowed bulwarks, uneven and deserted, upon which, from the man's hand, the sand piled higher like the teasing threat of oblivion. A slow, repetitious sound I had been hearing for a long time unconsciously, I identified as a continuous laugh which came through the motionless open pouched mouth of the woman. (1979, 153)

Her crossed legs "like shadowed bulwarks" among the sands, this is woman as Ozymandias; like Ozymandias, she is vulnerable to "the teasing threat of oblivion," to visions of horror and ruin. In surveying her vast, ungainly body, Welty refuses stereotypical portraits of southern women: she refuses to replicate their preoccupation with "little things." How does this human earthquake initiate a new politics of southern women's writing?

The first thing to notice about Welty's earthquake woman is her gigantism. Traditionally giants—as opposed to the intensely private, palm-sized scale of the miniature—are associated with epics and monuments, with governments as they rise and fall, with the sacerdotal moments of public life. In her marvelous book *On Longing: Narratives of the Miniature, the*

Gigantic, the Souvenir, the Collection, Susan Stewart argues that gigantism is often used to augur social change:

> The giant is represented through movement, through being in time. Even in the ascription of the still landscape to the giant, it is the activities of the giant, his or her legendary actions, that have resulted in the observable trace. In contrast to the still and perfect universe of the miniature, the gigantic represents the order and disorder of historical forces. The consumerism of the miniature is the consumerism of the classic; it is only fitting that consumer culture appropriates the gigantic whenever change is desired. (1984, 86)

Welty's giantess is the terrible harbinger of change for a demure southern girl. Why is her body potent? How might it be political?

When Louis Rubin describes Welty's prose as "shimmering, hovering, elusive, fanciful, fastening on little things," he is touching on a fragility and a miniaturization that haunt southern women's bodies as well. In Katherine Anne Porter's "Old Mortality," Miranda's father insists that his female relatives were all slender as sylphs:

> He sometimes glanced at the photograph and said, "It's not very good. . . . She was much slimmer than that, too. There were never any fat women in the family, thank God."
>
> When they heard their father say things like that, Maria and Miranda simply wondered, without criticism, what he meant. . . . What about great aunt Keziah, in Kentucky. Her husband, great-uncle John Jacob, had refused to allow her to ride his good horses after she had achieved two hundred and twenty pounds. . . . "Female vanity will recover," said great-uncle John Jacob, callously, "but what about my horses' backs? And if she had the proper female vanity in the first place, she would never have got into such shape." Well, great-aunt Keziah was famous for her heft, and wasn't she in the family? But something seemed to happen to their father's memory when he thought of the girls he had known in the family of his youth, and he declared steadfastly they had all been, in every generation without exception, as slim as reeds and graceful as sylphs. (1972, 174)

This willful miniaturization of the female body may seem comical, but it is also quite dangerous. "What is, in fact, lost in this idealized miniaturization of the body," as Stewart says, "is . . . the danger of power" (1984, 124). We see this loss most poignantly in the confinement of Miranda's Aunt Amy, who is reduced to "a motionless image in her dark walnut frame."

Estranged by a body that is caught "forever in the pose of being photographed," her nieces wonder "why every older person who looked at the picture said, 'How lovely.' . . . The whole affair was associated, in the minds of the little girls, with dead things. . . . The woman in the picture had been Aunt Amy, but she was only a ghost in a frame, and a sad, pretty story from old times. She had been beautiful, much loved, unhappy, and she had died young" (1972, 173). These young girls recognize implicitly that miniaturization insures loss of power and provides no protection against the process of time. And yet the need to miniaturize the white southern female body also works paradoxically. It not only keeps some women off horseback and out of public life; it also embroils them in southern history in the most contorted of ways. For the miniaturized female torso does not exist in simple opposition to gigantism and history—instead, the purified, rarefied, "transcendent" female body offers a site for political labor, a place for uncoding and recoding the epic disasters of the southern body politic.

How should we characterize this politicization of the intense privacy of white women's flesh? In "Identity: Skin Blood Heart" Minnie Bruce Pratt describes the ways in which public desires and private self-interest were flagrantly mapped onto her own girlish frame. In the 1960s the white female body could still serve as a fulcrum for white power politics—becoming its rallying cry and absurd rationale. At the height of the civil rights movement Pratt's father terrorized his children by lodging his own race-terrors—his flimsy belief in white supremacy—in his daughter's wayward, uncertain flesh:

> The entombment of the lady was my "protection": the physical, spiritual, sexual containment which men of my culture have used to keep "their women" pure. . . .
>
> It was this protection that I felt one evening during the height of the civil rights demonstrations in Alabama, as the walls that had contained so many were cracking, when my father called me to his chair in the living room. He showed me a newspaper clipping . . . about Martin Luther King, Jr., and told me that the article was about how King had sexually abused, used, young Black teen-aged girls. I believe he asked me what I thought of this; I can only guess that he wanted me to feel that my danger, my physical, sexual danger, would be the result of the release of others from containment. I felt frightened and profoundly endangered, by King, by my father: I could not answer him. (1984, 37)

It is crucial to examine the ways in which writing by modern southern women both adheres to and rebels against this ideological mask. As Anne

Goodwyn Jones explains, "the image wearing Dixie's Diadem" has offered, historically, a spectacular cartography for racist fears. This image

> is not a human being but a marble statue, beautiful and silent, eternally inspiring and eternally still.
>
> In that, southern womanhood is not alone. It has much in common with the ideas of the British Victorian lady and of American true womanhood. All deny to women authentic selfhood; all enjoin that women suffer and be still; all show women sexually pure, pious, deferent to external authority, and content with their place in the home. Yet southern womanhood differs in several ways from other nineteenth-century images of womanhood. Unlike them, the southern lady is at the core of a region's self-definition; the identity of the South is contingent in part upon the persistence of its tradition of the lady. (1981, 4)

We need to delve further into this tradition and what it might mean to have one's body "at the core" of the South's self-definition.

Bryan Turner suggests four different tasks that bodies create for the social systems trying to control them: "(1) the reproduction of populations in time, (2) the regulation of bodies in space, (3) the restraint of the 'interior' body through disciplines, and (4) the representation of the 'exterior' body in social space" (1997, 133). What's intriguing about the fourth category, here enacted via the socially mandated miniaturization of the white southern woman's irregularly shaped frame, is that this reification of femininity—this representation of the white woman's exterior, racialized body in social space—also has stunning repercussions for the first three categories of public discipline. The racially pure and diminutive female body in need of protection becomes the motive force, the purported source for the taboo against race-mixing. As southern myth, this fragile white body helps motivate (1) southern modes of population control, reproducing black and white populations as separate, (2) the regulated segregation of these racial bodies in space, and (3) the need for deeply interiorized categories of racism that will do the work of segregation. In other words, the small compass of the ideal white woman's body is oddly at war with its epic stature in minds of white men. This fragile white body, slim as a reed and graceful as a sylph, becomes pivotal in each crucial task of bodily discipline.

What is most remarkable about southern women's fiction is the way it refuses such discipline. When the grotesque body marches onto the page, the ideology that controls southern bodies becomes hypervisible in the most unexpected of ways. Southern women's writing is filled with bizarre somatic images that seem unnecessarily cruel or out of control, and yet this cruelty has a function: it tears at the social fabric and tries to leave it in shreds: "I have felt the destructive effects of personal race and class privilege first through [my mother's] life: her skin allergies that made her scratch her own white skin raw. The *her* in *me* feels the trap of that whiteness, the need to claw out. The times I have realized my own racism most, this image has come to mind: I am sitting in a white porcelain bathtub scraping my skin with Brillo pads; there is blood in rivulets in the tub" (1985, 167). This is from Mab Segrest's *My Mama's Dead Squirrel,* a book of essays arguing that the grotesque is a neurotic, disreputable form for southern writers. And yet when Segrest wants to contemplate the terrible effects of racism—and the work of domination that the white female body performs on behalf of this racism—she resorts to a grotesque tropology. Her mother's bloody white body reveals the social agon hidden beneath the happy surfaces of feminine charisma and cleanliness. In Segrest's memoir, women's open, wounded bodies become political intensifiers, spaces for mapping an entire region's social and psychic neuroses.

This is to argue that the bodies in southern women's fiction can be intensely political; they are often concerned with "larger cultural, racial, and political themes" simply because southern bodies have had to endure such themes in daily life. As Lillian Smith recalls her childhood in *Killers of the Dream,* its lessons revolved around her body's sexual and racial markers: "Now . . . though your body is a thing of shame and mystery, and curiosity about it is not good; your skin is your glory and the source of your strength and pride. It is white. And, as you have heard, whiteness is a symbol of purity and excellence. Remember this: your white skin proves that you are better than all other people on this earth. Yes, it does that. And does it simply because it is white—which, in a way, is a kind of miracle. But the Bible is full of miracles and it should not be too difficult for us to accept one more" (1978, 89). Southern women's fiction works with a similar irony; it abrades the surface of this purified body to bring the daily contradictions of "miraculous" whiteness to the surface. The stories we will examine work toward a massive category confusion in which the common classifications of southern life no longer make sense, in which the condensation and displacement of political contradictions onto the white female body no longer take place in secret but get held up to scrutiny.

To exemplify the female body's gargantuan labors, I want to tell the tale of another giant woman, Miss Eckhart, the foreign piano teacher in Welty's "June Recital." We have already seen that Rubin's association of Welty with the miniature evokes a world of diminished associations in which Welty's style ("entirely feminine," moving "lightly, capriciously") mirrors the charming world that good southern women were supposed to inhabit. But when we recast our image of Welty to reflect the awkward grandiosity of characters such as Miss Eckhart, Powerhouse (the enormous black jazzman), or the slovenly fat woman who stalks through "A Memory," these giant bodies invoke the messiness and hubris of Chronos himself. While Miss Eckhart's body invokes a world of gender asymmetry and the gargantua of "A Memory" draws attention to southern fantasies about class, what gets magnified through Powerhouse's fantasies and awkward frame is the debacle of segregation. This stupendous man, "so monstrous he sends everybody into oblivion," entertains white audiences, but he is refused the right to congregate with them (1979, 254–55). During intermission Powerhouse turns his "African feet of the greatest size" and his mouth "vast and obscene" toward "Negrotown" to have a drink, and then makes his way back through the pouring rain, "his mouth . . . nothing but a volcano" (273). When Welty's critics read Powerhouse as the epitome of Welty's improvisatory glee (as a sign of her ability to write jazzy fiction that competes with the best boogie-woogie), they miss this story's hidden script: the fact that even the jazzman's improvisations are restricted by segregation. Although Powerhouse mounts symbolic protests—avoiding his own sense of peril by telling thunderous tales about his wife's imagined infidelity and suicide—his powerful body still has to succumb to the illogic of Jim Crow. The merry misogyny of the stories he tells may carry the day, but they are also quite sad. His power and vastness contrast with his obsessive riffing on faithlessness and death; Powerhouse's huge frame and constricted fantasies emphasize the power and vastness of a system that still restricts this massive man's locomotion.

In the case of Miss Eckhart, we witness the oppression of a female pianist whose talent is denied because of her sex. On the thunderous summer day when she gives her concert in "June Recital," Miss Eckhart's body swells to enormous proportions; she represents new and frightening parameters for southern women's lives: "Miss Eckhart played as if it were Beethoven; she struck the music open midway and it was in soft yellow tatters like old satin. The thunder rolled and Miss Eckhart frowned and bent forward or she leaned back to play; at moments her solid body swayed from side to side like a tree trunk" (1949, 56). What is this burgeoning female body doing in the demure alcoves of white southern women's fiction?

Mary Jacobus, Evelyn Fox Keller, and Sally Shuttleworth have argued that "the body, whether masculine or feminine, is imbricated in the matrices of power at all levels" (1990, 2). It is my contention that the bodies in southern women's fiction make this imbrication visible. The grotesque bodies occupying stories by Porter, Hurston, Welty, McCullers, O'Connor, Gilchrist, and Walker become premier sites for exploring the work of a southern polity in which women are barred from public power but become central players in its symbolic scripts. Miss Eckhart is a case in point. Her giant body becomes a symbol of female artistry and self-empowerment threatening beyond words, but her gigantism also becomes a battlefield for the social violence that is ordinarily scripted onto the body of the romantic white girl. When she sits down to play for her pupils,

> the piece was so hard that she made mistakes and repeated to correct them, so long and stirring that it soon seemed longer than the day itself had been, and in playing it, Miss Eckhart assumed an entirely different face. Her skin flattened and drew across her cheeks, her lips changed. The face could have belonged to someone else—not even to a woman, necessarily. It was the face a mountain could have, or what might be seen behind the veil of a waterfall. There in the rainy light it was a sightless face, one for music only—though the fingers kept slipping and making mistakes they had to correct. And if the sonata had an origin in a place on earth, it was the place where Virgie, even, had never been and was not likely to go. (56)

When Miss Eckhart's face blends with the huge forms of nature, she is usurping a power reserved for white males.[2] Ironically, it is Cassie Morrison, a child in need of giant reveries, who brings Miss Eckhart back to earth. She reimagines her piano teacher as a fallen woman, an untouchable, and reveals the policing mechanisms of the southern economy at its worst. Stunned by her piano teacher's arpeggios, Cassie protects herself by mapping communal stereotypes of race and rape onto Miss Eckhart's great body:

> She began to think of an incident that had happened to Miss Eckhart instead of about the music she was playing; that was one way.
>
> One time, at nine o'clock at night, a crazy nigger had jumped out of the school hedge and got Miss Eckhart, had pulled her down and threatened to kill her. That was long ago. She had been walking by herself after dark; nobody had told her any better. When Dr. Loomis made her well, people were surprised that she and her mother did not move away. They wished she had moved away, everybody but poor Miss Snowdie; then they wouldn't always have to remember that a terrible

> thing once happened to her. But Miss Eckhart stayed, as though she considered one thing not so much more terrifying than another.(57)

If Miss Eckhart gives us giant dreams, her listeners know how to resist them. Caught inside during an electrical storm, her pupils have listened to her music reluctantly—for like the storm itself, Miss Eckhart's playing is abusive and grand. Terrified of her newfound power and of Miss Eckhart's refusal to bend her artistic talents toward the designated role of spinster-teacher, her pupils convert her harrowing body to its "proper" size.

Miss Eckhart's body is threatening because it becomes the locus for two different kinds of transgressions. First, instead of a "hummingbird" style that fastens on "little things," her incredible music evokes all the elements of sublimity, transcendence, and violence that critics in search of "larger themes" could desire:

> The music came with greater volume—with fewer halts—and Jinny Love tiptoed forward and began turning the music. Miss Eckhart did not even see her—her arm struck the child, making a run. Coming from Miss Eckhart, the music made all the pupils uneasy, almost alarmed; something had burst out, unwanted, exciting, from the wrong person's life. This was some brilliant thing too splendid for Miss Eckhart, piercing and striking the air around her the way a Christmas firework might almost jump out of the hand that was, each year, inexperienced anew. (56)

Second, Miss Eckhart refuses the stereotypes of white southern femininity. Her arm strikes a child; she wields too much creative power. But, as the editors of *Body/Politics* note, "the feminine body . . . is peculiarly the battlefield on which quite other struggles than women's own have been waged" (Jacobus, Keller, and Shuttleworth 1990, 2). What other battle is raging in Miss Eckhart's body?

We have already seen the displacement of racial politics onto the white female frame in Minnie Bruce Pratt's frightened memories of Martin Luther King. What brings Pratt's and Miss Eckhart's stories together is an act of displacement in which white patriarchs and little white girls are so threatened by change (by the advent of black or female empowerment) that they regroup and recommit themselves to the white female's vulnerability. What's curious about this act of fetishism is that in each case the feminine body becomes symbolically prominent—it shifts from background to battleground. As Stallybrass and White have suggested: "discourses about the body have a privileged role, for transcodings between different levels and sectors of social and psychic reality are effected through the intensifying grid of the body. It is no accident . . . that transgressions and the attempt to control them obsessively return to somatic symbols, for these are the ultimate elements of social classification itself" (1986, 26). The "intensifying grid" of Miss Eckhart's body startles these children because her playing, with its brilliance and fireworks, escapes its classification and establishes a carnival moment, a temporary liberation from the established southern order. To diminish her body's grandeur, these children, well socialized by their habitus, go on the attack; they surround Miss Eckhart with a scary set of somatic symbols, with a communal story about rape to control her unwanted unruliness. When Miss Eckhart raises herself to great heights, revealing a musical brilliance reserved for great men, her pupils find a way to restore her abjection and lowliness.

Why do they impose this terrible discipline on her body? There is, of course, a regional pattern to this discipline. When Cassie converts her teacher's tempestuous playing into racial terror, she is rehearsing the perennial story that Jacquelyn Dowd Hall calls the "southern rape complex." Hall argues that this complex, with its triumphant protection of white women, its calculated fear of black men, its ignorance of the abuses of black women, is an instrument of sexual and racial suppression, scapegoating players in the southern game who challenge the established order. Just as "lynching served to dramatize hierarchies among men," so stories of female victimization encourage white women to depend on white men. Hall reminds us that the southern rape complex is extraindividual, a "dramatization of cultural themes, a story [white southerners] told themselves about the social arrangements and psychological strivings that lay beneath the surface of everyday life" (1983, 332, 335). She explains:

> A woman who had just been raped, or who had been apprehended in a clandestine affair, or whose male relatives were pretending that she had been raped, stood on display before the whole community. Here was the quintessential Woman as Victim: polluted, "ruined for life," the object of fantasy and secret contempt. Humiliation, however, mingled with heightened worth as she played for a moment the role of Fair Maiden violated and avenged. For this privilege—if the alleged assault had in fact taken place—she might pay with suffering in the extreme. In any case, she would pay with a lifetime of subjugation to the men gathered in her behalf. (335)

It is this culturally sanctioned form of "heightened worth" that Miss Eckhart tries to avoid. Even as scapegoat the pianist has maintained a public stance; she continues to teach, to take in pupils. To adapt to the trauma of rape when female honor is still a southern rallying cry means to challenge the political order at its roots—to acknowledge rape as an ordinary, terrible crime that should result in neither racial hysteria nor ostracism for its victims. And yet, like Powerhouse, Miss Eckhart is caught in her community's drama. Willy-nilly, her body becomes "the battleground on which quite other struggles" are waged. This means there is no need to rape this woman in fact to make her conform: she is raped repeatedly in the communal imagination. And this communal rape is not just the subject of adult brutality. In Welty's story Miss Eckhart is attacked, her rape reenacted, among the community's children, who have internalized a model of female powerlessness and continue to enforce this model on each other and within themselves.

This is Miss Eckhart's designated story, and yet, to end on this note could make us forget the scene in which she plays the piano and sways in treelike ecstasy. Miss Eckhart threatens her pupils because her body suggests a different world order in which women are allowed to be noisy and grand. The gargantuan body both maps its own limits and refuses to stay within bounds, to serve asked-for ends. What resounds throughout this awkward female frame are the very power plays that the petite white female body tries to mask. If, as Louise Westling suggests, the southern white woman as "representative of Christian virtues was lauded in public to divert attention from the problems of slavery and racism," as Westling also notes, this diversion has physical consequences: "the scope of her activities was severely limited" (1985, 8). The gargantuan body exceeds these limits and attests to the pleasures of inventing extraordinary human beings whose bodies don't follow the rules. The grotesque body is the focus for a "free play with the human body and with its organs" not permitted by southern demands for conformity.

This giant female body offers itself as a totem, then, for remapping southern women's fiction—a totem that teaches two things. First, if the private bodies of white southern women are asked to become smooth public surfaces—if white women have been compelled to inhabit pleasant, undifferentiated, fragile bodies in search of protection—Miss Eckhart's gigantism transgresses this role and renders it unstable.[3] She ushers a panoply of female giants into this study, from Carson McCullers's Amelia and Frankie to Flannery O'Connor's irate redneck matrons. We may even trace a ghostly gigantism in Kate Chopin's Edna Pontellier: "She turned her face seaward to gather in an impression of space and solitude, which the vast expanse of water, meeting and melting with the moonlit sky, conveyed to her excited fancy. As she swam she seemed to be reaching out for the unlimited in which to lose herself" (1976, 29).

At the same time, each of these giant bodies serves quasi-political ends; they give us hyperbolic visions of the systemic crises within each heroine's social milieu. How do we define a systemic crisis within this context? In looking at emblems of female monstrosity we have seen that when the social hierarchy is threatened, when the margins of power start to shift, the body not only becomes prominent, it becomes a site for mapping social change. By invoking the concept of systemic crisis I want to expand on this suggestion. Not only are female bodies used as symbolic sites to demarcate undesired social change, but this symbolism has diurnal power; it offers a fetish of constancy in an inconstant world of crisis and change.

Southern bodies are caught in a daily, formulaic round of hostility, tension, and emergency: in crises that are ongoing, habitual, and monitored by white civilians and law enforcement alike. As Robin Kelley describes the pre–civil rights skirmishes that broke out on segregated southern buses in the 1940s and 1950s: "all oppositional and transgressive acts took place in a context of extreme repression. The occupants sitting in the rear who witnessed or were part of the daily guerrilla skirmishes learned that punishment was inevitable" (1994, 72). While white citizens were deputized to police the color boards, black men were denied citizenship on a daily basis. In "The Ritual of Survival" Robert Fleming testifies about this daily policing of southern race culture—an incessant round of racial and sexual emergency: "if a black man was to survive, he had to know his place, to step off the curb when a white person approached, and to lower his eyes whenever he spoke to a white woman. It seemed that daily lynchings of blacks were the meat-and-potatoes stories for the various Southern newspapers in those days, complete with graphic details of the grisly deed and the alleged crime for which the person of color lost his or her life" (1993, 33).[4] Julius Lester summarizes these structural perversions, this state of perpetual emergency when he remembers the terror of southern life during the protest movements of the 1960s, when death became an atmospheric: "to live in an atmosphere where the presence of death is as palpable as the smell of honeysuckle lacerated the soul in ways one dared not stop to know" (1991, 30).

In the face of these repeated, systematic assaults on African Americans' humanity, we will see that the fantasy of the gargantuan woman becomes equally important in African American women's writing.[5] Alice Walker's Feather Mae advances this story, as does Janie, in her reach for the horizon at the end of *Their Eyes Were Watching God:* "She pulled in her horizon like a great fish-net. Pulled it from around the waist of the world and draped it over her shoulder. So much of life in its meshes! She called in her soul to come and see" (1978, 286). The gargantuan Janie sends a promissory note. By throwing off her burdens she refuses the parameters of a racially constricted life, even as Tea Cake's lost, prancing body acknowledges the crises bred by racial hierarchy within a white-dominated culture all too careless of death.

In this context of race and gender crisis, Miss Eckhart's refusal to be miniaturized, to fit within the confines of the rape-lynching system, should also remind us of the relative difficulty—for people of color, for white women—of such public refusals. The stereotype of the "little" woman inheres so strictly in Miss Eckhart's habitus that it is always already in circulation: the southern rape complex requires the erasure of black women as victims and white women's repeated miniaturization.[6] But southern women's fiction also contests the boundaries of these expectations, even when it gives in. When the gigantic, well-muscled Amelia, the white heroine of *The Ballad of the Sad Café,* starts winning the fight with Marvin Macey fair and square, her six-foot, two-inch frame is slick with body grease and the odor of victory, and we long for her success. But when Cousin Lymon comes to Macey's support, when he flies through the air and clutches "at her neck with his clawed little fingers" so that Amelia falls flat on her back, "her arms flung outward and motionless," her body also records a larger battle scene in which southern women submit to "higher" laws (1971, 68). The exaggeration of her bodily boundaries reveals their exact location. The gargantuan woman becomes a political intensifier for mapping the gigantism of southern social derangements.

Miniature Bodies

In depicting the explosive body of a giant woman, Eudora Welty is exposing a southern power structure and its pervasive influence—the ways in which sexual and racial boundaries are enforced by white children as well as white men. Although King accuses southern women of writing without a sense of "historical consciousness," in "June Recital" this consciousness is all too acute. Miss Eckhart's lumbering frame exposes the quotidian social controls that keep African Americans and white women in their place.

It is this sense of the dailiness of history, this focus on diurnal politics, that I want to address next. In reworking the image of the southern lady—in creating her grotesque or giant antitype—white women writers do more than protest the burdens of ladyhood. Their grotesque heroines help bring the hard facts of southern racism and sexism into focus. Similarly, in revising the stereotypes of powerful (read tirelessly working and undamageable) black women, African American women writers bring the hard facts of domestic labor into crisis. But as we will see, these hard facts don't always operate through epic forms.

I've suggested that, in its outlandishness and strangeness, the giant body becomes a formal property of southern women's texts that gathers our attention and enlarges the scope of our vision so that the vagaries of southern politics (here, the southern rape complex) come to light in the sudden telescoping and shrinking of Miss Eckhart's body. We will see a similar pattern at work in Welty's "A Memory" when a fat woman's frightening body provides a moment of transformation for a staid southern child: "I saw the man lift his hand filled with crumbling sand, shaking it as the woman laughed, and pour it down inside her bathing suit between her bulbous descending breasts" (1979, 154). While the controlling body of the middle-class child promotes hierarchy, the grotesque body of this trashy white woman protests verticality. Against classicism and classism, this fat woman's sandy flesh is disturbing, excessive; her gigantism insists on the bodily equality of bowels, blood, and breasts. This excess will move us toward a rereading of class and gender hardship, toward an exploration of the excesses of a southern political system that inhabits little white girls as well as white men.

We have reached a crucial turn in the metaphors—the morphological scale—guiding my argument, for if the giant female body relays these "larger" issues, it is only insofar as she makes us pay attention to the miniature, the microcosmic, the quotidian. It is, after all, the quotidian details that express the hardest facts of southern life. Lillian Smith details these hard facts in *Killers of the Dream* as she talks with one of her students about the daily struggles of the past:

> "Your parents and I lived our babyhood in those days of wrath. But always the violence was distant, the words vague and terrible for we were protected children. A lynching could happen in our county and we wouldn't know it. Yet we did know because of faces, whispers, a tightening of the whole town."
>
> I did not say more for I was caught in those old days, remembering: Sometimes it was your nurse who made you know. You loved her, and suddenly she was frightened, and you knew it. Her eyes saw things your eyes did not see. As the two of you sat in the sand playing your

> baby games, she'd whisper, "Lawd Jesus, when you going to help us!" And suddenly the play would leave the game and you would creep close to her begging her to shield you from her trouble. . . . Sometimes it would be your father, explaining a race incident to the older children. Even now I can feel that hush, the changed voices when they saw you listening, the talking down to the little one in false and cheerful words, saying, "Sugar, what you been playing today?" (1949, 70)

Killers of the Dream describes the vanishing world of Jasper, Florida, at the turn of the century. And yet when Julius Lester describes the South of the 1940s and 1950s from the other side of the racial divide, the details are much the same.

> It is almost impossible to describe that world the civil rights movement destroyed, that world of my childhood and adolescence ruled by signs decreeing where I was and was not allowed to go, what door I had to enter at the bus station and train station, where I had to sit on the bus. How do I explain what it is to live with the absurd and pretend to its ordinariness without becoming insane? How do I explain that I cannot be sure that my sanity was not hopelessly compromised because I grew up in a world where the insane was as ordinary as margarine? (1991, 30)

To say that the large issues of southern history come down to bus stations and baby games is not to trivialize these issues but to acknowledge the banality of history. Racism may be epic in reach and scope, but its horror lives on in the particular. In looking at "A Memory" I want to address the intersections between the giant female body and civic life, to explore the particularity of the gargantuan body as it becomes a site of transaction for the South's "ordinary" economic insanities.

Welty's "A Memory" is particularly eloquent about the politics of the everyday. Like Miss Eckhart, Welty's earthquake woman does not become a public colossus or politician. Instead, we glimpse a middle-class girl watching a lower-class family playing at the beach. The girl, an avatar for Welty herself, is a snob; she is offended by this unsavory family's "tasteless" high jinks. In mapping her own childish aversions and offering them as an index to an entire social milieu, Welty gives us politics of a different order from that of the male writers of the southern renaissance, but she gives us politics all the same.[7]

David Held has argued that political theory has a special purpose; it "aims to offer a systematic analysis of politics and of the ways in which it is always bounded by, among other things, unacknowledged conditions of action. It can, thereby, fracture existing forms of understanding and reform the practically generated accounts of the political in everyday life" (1989, 4). Welty's fiction may not be exhausted by the limits of political theory, but her stories do break new ground; they help us reformulate women's relation to "the practically generated accounts of the political" in everyday southern life.

This is worth stressing because studies of southern fiction focusing on political systems have, for the most part, limited their analyses to southern politics as monument and myth.[8] When Richard King gives his definition of the southern renaissance, he values the ways in which male writers deal with the three *p*'s of southern studies: plantations, patriarchy, and the past.

> Put briefly: the writers and intellectuals of the South after the late 1920s were engaged in an attempt to come to terms not only with the inherited values of the Southern tradition but also with a certain way of perceiving and dealing with the past, what Nietzsche called "monumental" historical consciousness. It was vitally important for them to decide whether the past was of any use at all in the present. . . . The "object" of their historical consciousness was a tradition whose essential figures were the father and the grandfather and whose essential structure was the literal and symbolic family. In sum, the Renaissance writers sought to come to terms with what I call the "Southern family romance." (1980, 7)

Are there other ways to come to terms with the legitimation crises of twentieth-century southern life? First, we need to recognize that any struggle with the use-value of the past must also be construed as a struggle within the present. It is this daily loss of legitimation, the inability of traditional or established patterns to make sense of the ebb and flow of everyday life, that southern women writers address in their obsession with the southern grotesque. We need not look to "monumental" historical consciousness—not to fathers or grandfathers or even large women—to understand the complexities that the weight of tradition brings to bear upon the diurnal round of southern life. Thus short stories, cookbooks, girlish fantasies, and personal vignettes can become sites for measuring a political crisis in the making. These private narrative forms have public dimensions implicated in the apportionment of power.[9] Welty's story also demonstrates that within the class politics mapped in this story, what a child thinks at the beach may be as telling as a trip to the statehouse; she may give us access to the ordinary dominations, the insane politics of everyday southern life.

In fact, it is just such frivolous techniques of the body that the earthquake woman engages in Welty's autobiographical story from *A Curtain of Green*. Like the little girls in "June Recital," the child who narrates "A Memory" is preoccupied with the apportionment of social space, with the division of the work of domination. All her energy goes into framing and judging her world. But as this frame breaks apart, what comes into the foreground is the "unacknowledged condition of action" that dominates this child's caste-obsessed world, namely, her position within a white middle class that bases its Whiggish sense of superiority on warding off redneck threats to an established order.[10] Here the grotesque bodies in Welty's fiction give special access to these barely acknowledged conditions of middle-class self-construction.

When "A Memory" opens Welty's heroine is lying on the beach "looking at a rectangle bright lit, actually glaring at me, with sun, sand, water, a little pavilion, a few solitary people in fixed attitudes, and around it all a border of dark rounded oak trees, like the engraved thunderclouds surrounding illustrations in the Bible" (147). The frame that she makes with her fingers mimics her social heritage; this child's middle-class Protestantism helps her frame judgments about the merits of those around her.[11] As she solemnly tells us, she sees no one at the lake but children or "those older people whose lives are obscure, irregular, and consciously of no worth to anything" (147). This dismissive tone becomes ironic for the narrator, but it is deadly serious for the child, who wants to establish her aesthetic superiority. The artistic frame offers a system of stratification, a rectangle that designates who's in and who's out, who's valuable and who's not.

For Welty's little girl these schemes are intricately tied up with romance. She is in love with love itself and dreams endlessly of a secret beau, meditating obsessively on the day she touched his wrist in the stairwell at school. "It was possible during that entire year for me to think endlessly on this minute and brief encounter which we endured on the stairs, until it would swell with a sudden and overwhelming beauty, like a rose forced into premature bloom for a great occasion" (149). Ironically, "A Memory" begins in the miniature world that Louis Rubin describes as typical of Welty's fiction. We see a sensitive child on her way to heterosexual stardom, preparing for the blinkered wisdom of middle-class courtship where women relinquish their claim to the public world for summer cotillions where every nerve strains toward the opposite sex.

The first hint that something is amiss in this white girl's romance plot is signaled with blood: "I remember with exact clarity the day in Latin class when the boy I loved (whom I watched constantly) bent suddenly over and brought his handkerchief to his face. I saw red—vermilion—blood flow over the handkerchief and his square-shaped hand; his nose had begun to bleed. I remember the very moment: several of the older girls laughed at the confusion and distraction" (150). The narrator's response is stereotypically feminine—she faints dead away. Her motive seems clear; she is terrified at this splitting open of the male body, afraid of its dirtiness, its democratizing blood. Might the threat of menstruation or mortality inhere in a boy's body as well as a girl's? The older girls feel the incongruity of this reversal and laugh, but the young narrator finds her momentary superiority unbearable; when she faints, she restores her gender to its pristine passivity.

What this moment brings home is this culture's incredible anxiety about sexual difference; the heroine needs to believe that this boy is other, superior, remote from herself. But Welty details status anxiety in a way that is equally compelling. The girl's position within a rigid class hierarchy is the most predatory worry confronting her small sense of self. The narrator tells us that her ignorance about her beau's family or background "occasioned during the year of my love a constant uneasiness in me. It was unbearable to think that his house might be slovenly and unpainted, hidden by tall trees, that his mother and father might be shabby—dishonest—crippled—dead. I speculated endlessly on the dangers of his home" (151).

The "danger" of other people's homes—and the fact of class struggle—is the squalid little secret this story sets out to expose. As Pierre Bourdieu suggests, the bourgeois elite invent for themselves an "eternal sociodicy" in which "all forms of 'levelling,' 'trivialization,' or 'massification'" seem to threaten at once, and the decline of modern society is associated with apocalyptic threats to the middle-class home. Welty's child, embroiled in this sociodicy, seems particularly vulnerable to her caste's obsessive fears; she worries helplessly that her beau lives among the "undifferentiated hordes" of the underclass who threaten "to submerge the private spaces of bourgeois exclusiveness" (1984, 469).[12]

Moreover, her obsession with squalor has the exaggerated tone of a fairy tale or gothic romance, and this suggests two of the gifts that Welty's story bestows. First, the romance plot is traditionally a place where class anxiety or turmoil can be repressed. The romance usually offers (as in *Jane Eyre*) a story of assimilation, or (as in most fairy tales) a discovery that the poor little goose girl is really a queen, or (as in *Mary Barton*) a genre where love scuttles class rebellion. "A Memory" refuses these terms. Romance becomes Welty's vehicle for exploring class consciousness; for her heroine an unexpected encounter with the other generates real terror about the flimsiness of social boundaries. This breaking of boundaries is an enduring characteristic of southern women's fiction. Even a novella such as *Member of the Wedding* questions the race and gender confines of white heterosexual southern myths. Frankie may become "Frances," a budding belle, but only after McCullers asks us to mourn the sacrifice of her family's African American housekeeper, Berenice, and the death of her androgynous cousin, John Henry.

Second, like McCullers, Welty explores the odd shapes of southern class consciousness by warping our vision of the southern child. At least since Rousseau the child has functioned to circumvent rumors of "sexuality and social inequality" in the West. According to Jacqueline Rose, the storybook child "is rendered innocent of all the contradictions which flaw our interaction with the world" (1984, 8–9). But Welty's preadolescent offers a social fulcrum, an entrance to cultural monstrosities staged for children as well as adults. Why does the grown-up Eudora Welty take such pleasure in staging scurrilous scenes for her own childish double? As her heroine lies on the beach, "squaring" the world with her fingers and dreaming about her bleeding beau, this little girl's careful framework is disrupted by a family that acts out her worst social fears. This family's distinction is its slovenliness: "Sprawled close to where I was lying . . . appeared a group of loud, squirming, ill-assorted people who seemed thrown together only by the most confused accident, and who seemed driven by a foolish intent to insult each other, all of which they enjoyed with a hilarity which astonished my heart . . . when I was a child such people were called 'common'" (152). Their commonness attracts and repels the little girl: "Lying in leglike confusion together were the rest of the group, the man and the two women. The man seemed completely given over to the heat and glare of the sun; his relaxed eyes sometimes squinted with faint amusement over the brilliant water and the hot sand. His arms were flabby and at rest. He lay turned on his side, now and then scooping sand in a loose pile about the legs of the older woman" (152–53). Welty reminds us that our cognitive structures, the ways we divide up the world, are not innocent schema but "internalized, 'embodied' social structures" that are chaotic and culpable; they help enforce the most unsavory oppositions between dominant and dominated: "All the agents in a given social formation share a set of basic perceptual schemes, which receive the beginnings of objectification in the pairs of antagonistic adjectives commonly used to classify and qualify persons or objects. The network of oppositions between high . . . and low . . . fine . . . and coarse . . . unique . . . and common . . . is the matrix of all the commonplaces which find such ready acceptance because behind them lies the whole social order" (Bourdieu 1984, 468–69). This schema is central to Welty's story. The oppositions between male and female, upperclass and underclass, are the commonplaces, the building blocks of a southern class system that we may overlook because they are so ordinary. But beyond these prosaic categories of trashy white others lies an entire social order. These distinctions are its foundations, and "A Memory" describes a child who is working hard to master these categories for herself.

This process is disrupted by an unsavory fat woman who will not take her place amidst these "antagonistic adjectives." Her body is filthy; it is covered with sand, but she refuses to accept a role of abjection: "Once when I looked up, the fat woman was standing opposite the smiling man. She bent over and in a condescending way pulled down the front of her bathing suit, turning it outward, so that the lumps of mashed and folded sand came emptying out. I felt a peak of horror, as though her breasts themselves had turned to sand, as though they were of no importance at all and she did not care" (156). This fat woman is bad taste incarnate, and her bad taste, her indecent exposure, her emptying breasts have the exhilarating ability to wreck the child narrator's delimiting frame. As sand pours out of her body, we experience the emptying out of a little girl's romance plot as well. This woman's pearlike breasts are suddenly artifactual, lightened of female allure. Her anger matters; it shakes up a little girl's sense of privilege and hierarchy, as if Welty means to give notice that the class-and-sex dramas excluded from middle-class life can return in the most ungainly forms to haunt the power structure with its guilts and desires.[13]

Have I gone too far? Can a southern female child really represent the power structure? The little girl in Welty's story is obsessed with evaluating her social world. While the earthquake woman is, for her, an untouchable, a pariah, this woman's body also works to disrupt this little girl's leisured superiority, her ease with the " work of domination" that these categorical modes of otherness instill. That is, this gargantuan southern body undoes the oppressive pleasantries of middle class "taste" by imploding this child's hoped-for conformities: "I felt a necessity for absolute conformity to my ideas in any happening I witnessed. As a result, all day long in school I sat perpetually alert, fearing for the untoward to happen. The dreariness and regularity of the school day were a protection for me" (149–50). This is an amazing statement from the childish avatar of one of the foremost inventors of the southern grotesque. Within this atmosphere of anxious conformity, the gargantuan female's "untoward" explosion of the child's precarious frame seems entirely just. At the same time, the child narrator is herself a victim of her culture's fantasies, and in perusing her role in the story we must come full circle, returning, via the child's diminutive and minoritized body, to the interactive politics of a gargantuan woman who can disrupt the miniaturizing framework of a haunted little girl.

Children play a double role in southern women's writing. Marginal to mainstream culture but caught up in its process of indoctrination, the child may question her society's values and provide a narrative space for challenging its beliefs. But children also become a tragic center for exploring the effects of race and class politics in everyday life. As the focus of adult rules and regulations, the child is a victim as well as a seismologist who registers the costs of a classist or a sexist ethic; she becomes a vivid, painful pressure point, a site of strain and unrest within an unjust social system. What the child is busy learning, along with fractions and table manners, is an order, a framework, a set of ideological desires and constraints. And ideologies carry their own political freight; they are symbolic systems that are continually "mobilized to sustain asymmetrical power relations in the interests of dominant or hegemonic groups" (Held 1989, 4). The effect of the earthquake woman's family on the young Welty is to break up this assurance of hegemony:

> It seemed to me that I could hear also the thud and the fat impact of all their ugly bodies upon one another. I tried to withdraw to my most inner dream, that of touching the wrist of the boy I loved on the stair . . . but the memory itself did not come to me.
>
> . . . I sank into familiarity; but the story of my love, the long narrative of the incident on the stairs, had vanished. I did not know, any longer, the meaning of my happiness; it held me unexplained. (155–56)

At this moment Welty's story offers the specter of a southern legitimation crisis made flesh. As we watch a young child learning her culture's norms, trying to live inside them, we also see these norms breaking apart.[14] As she moves from the superiority of a high romantic framework to an altered perceptual state that admits the grotesque body in all its "untoward" irregularity, she recognizes a world outside her habitus that remains unexplained. That is, we see in this child the glimmer of the grown-up narrator, a speaker who is increasingly unable to inhabit the undemocratic certainties that both discipline and support her.

Unable to withdraw into her "most inner dream," this child is experiencing a diminutive version of a southern legitimation crisis. A culture comes to a crisis in legitimation when normative structures start to change and there is a gap, a dissonance, between the demands or framework of an older social apparatus and people's current expectations and needs (Habermas 1975). As old norms are pushed aside, new norms are invented that lack the force of motivation and belief. Louis Rubin has argued that this dissonance is a pivotal experience in the twentieth-century South, where old sources of certitude and belief remained entrenched but failed to offer "an adequate basis for daily experience." For Rubin this becomes a world doomed to fall apart. "In attempting to hold onto its traditional modes of thought and behavior so far as the Negro is concerned, the South seeks to retain a social structure doomed in and by time. In so doing, it fights a losing battle, in which racial segregation is but the immediate issue" (Rubin and Jacobs 1961, 15). The dangerous potential inherent in angry women and their redneck consorts suggests another site of conflict. Welty's story reenacts the demise of a rose-tinted southern worldview that is no longer serviceable but seems quite irreplaceable. "A Memory" reenacts that catastrophic moment when a social formation starts to break down and the cracks or gaps in its systems of classification seem more powerful than the system itself.

Welty has inscribed the miniature catastrophes of "A Memory" in the cusp of a full-blown southern crisis. Her story comes at the center of *A Curtain of Green,* a book set in the Great Depression that dramatizes the defamiliarization of the American dream as it is mapped onto depressed southern bodies. The regional devastation of this depression, with its displacements of entire populations, its exaggeration of the already aggravated chasm between the North's (relative) wealth and the South's greater penury, its acceleration of the breakdown of a closed agrarian world, could only drive home the object lessons (and utter inadequacy) of an impoverished worldview whose demise is half-mourned and half-celebrated in "A Memory." Unlike most of the characters in *Curtain of Green* (mainly idiots, half-wits, deaf-mutes, sideshow or plantation relics, and con men), the heroine of "A Memory" seems out of place, for she is solidly middle-class and hopelessly lyrical. But by placing a formative moment from this white girl's uneventful past at the center of her story, Welty transforms the definition of an epic event; she insists that history is made by children, too. By suggesting that this story's narrator may be Welty herself, by dramatizing a moment from a southern female life when the rage for class demarcation and lyricism breaks down, Welty also suggests a mode of psychic transformation. It is this child's youthful penchant for accurate vision, for seeing the socially unspeakable, that works to produce an adult writer who will not turn away from the grotesque but writes unflinchingly about Miss Eckhart or Powerhouse or the tenant farmers in "A Whistle." By questioning the values of a child who is at first repelled but finally feels eroticized by the grotesque world around her, "A Memory" offers the beginnings of an epistemic break, a new era in one writer's consciousness: a suggestive description of that moment in Welty's own life when the feminine obsession with the romance ethos shatters, to be replaced with a passion for the ordinary power plays of southern life.

This ongoing crisis is played out in "The Power and the Glory," Robb Foreman Dew's autobiographical essay about Baton Rouge in the 1950s. As Dew describes the glory of inhabiting a white female body with the power to attract southern men—a body that also symbolizes women's supposed transcendence of class and race politics—she also describes a world where this symbolism inevitably breaks down:

> We worked so hard at being appealing! We had bedrooms that looked like beauty parlors, with storklike hair dryers, cosmetics of every variety, fashion magazines on our bedside tables. We slept miserably with enormous, bristly rollers wound into our hair and got up at six in the morning to unwind them so that we could painstakingly backcomb and construct our pageboys. . . . We applied makeup base, eyeliner, mascara, lipstick, and a final dusting of loose powder. . . . This was in order for us to go to school! For me each day was like a premiere, and, in fact, I went to school as little as possible, because putting in an appearance required more energy than I could muster.
>
> One morning I couldn't find my eyelash curler, and so positive was I that without curled eyelashes I would be remarkable, that I would look grotesque, that I claimed illness and did not leave the house. . . . I no longer felt certain of my grasp of reality. If I was elected to one thing or another I began to suspect that it was because there was something terribly wrong with me—a physical deformity or perhaps some sort of obvious mental illness . . . that elicited enormous sympathy from my schoolmates. I could no longer manage all the secrets of my own life in the face of the image I tried to sustain in public. (1987, 122)

The fear of looking hideous, the description of southern charm as "a crippling thing that entailed turning one's whole intelligence toward an effort to be pleasing to other people" (121), reinvokes the southern grotesque. While Mab Segrest argues that southern "women who refuse to stay in their place—who refuse to be grotesque, to stay fallen—upset the whole shebang," my own thesis is exactly the opposite. Following Porter's and Welty's lead, white southern women writers who appropriate the grotesque are at work constructing a female tradition that refuses the genteel obsession with writing (or inhabiting) the beautiful body, in exchange for something more politically active and vehement: for the angry sex- and class-conscious writing of the southern gargantua.

In Welty's story, the violence unfolding from the earthquake woman's grotesque body is threefold. First, this lower-class woman possesses a vitality that shatters the complacency of the prim narrator; her body language is so squalid and damning that it breaks the frame of the little girl's story altogether.[15] We encounter a second variety of violence in the patriarchal hand that piles sand higher and higher on this woman's body, "like the teasing threat of oblivion" (153)—smashing this girl's delusions about an idealized division of sexual labor. Here we confront the rigid divisions of autocracy and the work of domination that marks southern gender relations. But this woman also responds to her consort's violence with a violence of her own. ("A slow, repetitious sound I had been hearing for a long time unconsciously, I identified as a continuous laugh which came through the motionless open pouched mouth of the woman" [153].) If her slovenly body, her sandy disarray, seems threatening, it is because she mouths a new world where the beautiful body fails to keep at bay the heterogeneity and injustice that southern manners are designed to hide.

Finally, Welty's story gathers power from the fact that this earthquake woman is not the ideal southern lady but her antitype, her mocking double. With a mirroring violence, this woman's daughter hurls herself up and down the beach. Angry and wild, she is curled in her "green bathing suit like a bottle from which she might, I felt, burst in a rage of churning smoke" (153). When this young girl explodes, she comes "running toward the bench as though she would destroy it, and with a fierceness which took my breath away, she dragged herself through the air and jumped over the bench. But no one seemed to notice" (155). Welty invents the grotesque bodies in *A Curtain of Green* to expose the small, angry dramas of southern life that everyone experiences but no one acknowledges. And smack in the center of this volume of stories, we encounter a new female vastness: the earthquake woman's excessive body opens up the excesses of a caste system that inhabits little girls as well as great men.[16]

In story after story, Welty explores a southern world that fails to support its bodies, a comical culture whose comedy evaporates when its subjects wither, die, commit suicide, choose between the insane asylum and marriage, or endure crippling pain. This pain is not just the fate of a laboring class in the midst of national depression (the world Welty depicts in "The Whistle," "Flowers for Marjorie," or "A Worn Path") but that of a southern aristocratic class as well. Southern high culture, for all its seeming power, also lacks a working thesis, a mode of synthesis, a place to sustain the body. We feel this lack most sharply in the well-born Clytie, who sees a repulsive reflection of her face and drowns, her legs sticking out of the rainwater barrel "like a pair of tongs" (Welty 1979, 178). This is a frightening image of the body made mechanical and robbed of its being, an immobilized body that will fit neither the feminine nor the aristocratic frame invented by high southern culture.[17]

Bourdieu suggests that "the schemes of the habitus, the primary forms of classification, owe their specific efficacy to the fact that they function below the level of consciousness and language, beyond the reach of introspective scrutiny or control by the will" (1984, 466). The framing metaphor in "A Memory" brings some of these "primary forms of classification" into prominence. I have suggested that Welty's grotesque bodies have the uncanny ability to shift our focus even farther, so that the invisible schemes of the white southern habitus move closer to consciousness, become achingly visible. Perhaps it is no accident that Welty's earthquake woman is huge and ungainly. Her body has a great weight to bear, a weight made greater because southern women writers have worked so hard and so successfully to decode their region's political unconscious via the bodies of their gargantuas.

African American Writing and Scale

This chapter has focused on white fiction's inventions of female gargantuas who attack the class and race politics splintering the pallid bodies of white women and children. But what about African American gargantuas? In "Everything That Rises Must Converge" a plump white dowager meets her match in a black "giant of a woman. Her face was set not only to meet opposition but to seek it out. The downward tilt of her large lower lip was like a warning sign: don't tamper with me" (O'Connor 1971, 415). Perhaps one of the reasons Alice Walker likes Flannery O'Connor's fiction so much is that O'Connor's black giants do not provide blissed-out racial landscapes for white incorporation but the proportions of a gargantuan anger that grows as the civil rights movement grows. Black women writers deploy shifts in bodily scale too, but for different ends. Hurston's gargantuan Janie and Walker's Feather Mae share an acorporeality, or transcendence, that diffuses the energy of Welty's or O'Connor's hyperfleshy characters; Janie and Feather Mae retrieve the monumentality of earth; they conjure a past that wells up in the lost bodies of the Indian mound or in Lake Okeechobee's power to swallow black workers whose labor has been usurped by white landowners or settlers.

If white writers deploy giant white women to fend off the fragrance of the shrinking magnolia, for black women, gigantism—the myth of expansive size or strength—can carry the sting of oppression: "She was fully five feet ten inches tall—at least seven inches taller than Anna—and loomed above the heads of the little group on the levee like an amiable golden giantess, her feet set wide apart to support the weight that fleshed her big frame" (E. Douglas 1988, 374). In stories such as Douglas's "On the Lake" the black giantess is a domestic worker who is asked to support the weight of her employer's white family as well as her own.[18] As Susan Tucker explains, "the black domestic in literature is . . . frequently shown as a physically strong and robust woman, particularly by white authors. . . . Black writers . . . show more of the toll that such emotional and physical strength took" (1988, 107). Or, as Lillian Hellman recounts a conversation with her African American housekeeper, Helen: "Black women get old fast," said Helen. "Yes," Hellman replied, "watching white women stay young" (Hellman 1960, 242).

Many southern whites entertained crueler fantasies. In the Jim Crow South blacks were imagined to age more slowly than white people, a belief that allowed whites to employ aged domestics with little concern for their welfare. By proclaiming a gargantuan strength "in black women no matter what the circumstance, white women could ignore the fact that low pay and social injustices worked to keep these blacks at subsistence level" (108). Tucker explains how these stereotypes worked. "The strength of black women was often established by comparing black women with weak white women. The stereotype of the southern white woman suggested that she was a person of almost hysterical weakness" (108) desperately in need of someone else's labor.

When black women are abused in this way, underpaid and overworked in order to augment white women's imagined physical powerlessness, the black gargantua can become a cipher for anonymity, for the erasure of black subjectivity. "Did I tell you about when Mother died?" asked Anne

Robertson, one of Tucker's white informants. "Well, we didn't have time to set up nurses, and I called Sarah Sells . . . [to be] in the hospital room when we couldn't be there." After several nights, Robertson was restive; she left her mother in the care of her youngest daughter, Lillian, and Sarah Sells, her mother's black employee: "Sarah said the minute my sister and I walked out of the room, Mother closed her eyes and died. And of course, Lillian was the only one from the family with her. I said, 'Lilly, what did you do?' And Lilly said, 'Mother, if I'm ever in the room with anybody that dies again, I hope a great big black woman is there to hold me.' She said, 'Sarah just grabbed me and held me and held me and held me and patted me, and held me, held me, and held me'" (133). These repeated verbs and direct objects ("and held me and held me") take us farther from the sentence's ostensible subject (Sarah Sells) and suggest that what's really gargantuan here is an unexamined white narcissism. But this exploitation is so habitual that I want to examine the underlying sense of scale that makes this delusive sense of entitlement possible.

We have already examined the concept of the "unthought known" as a way to think about the ideological limits of white knowledge in a South divided between Anglo and African American ways of knowing. Now I want to return this concept to its psychoanalytic origins in order to think about the morphology of white southern fantasies about black domestic workers. In *The Shadow of the Object* Bollas (1987) invents the concept of the unthought known to dramatize the power of the child's early holding environment in creating the adult's somatic sense of the world. Every child must be physically cared for; the infant's body senses (but does not learn to conceptualize) the contours of its early holding environment. The comforts or deprivations of this early world help to shape adult anticipations—the sense of how the world will answer the ego's needs. Bollas swerves from object relations theory to an examination of the child's caretakers as "transformational objects"; the phrase is awkwardly abstract, but it tries to capture a shape-changing world designed to meet a child's animal-poetic needs. That is, instead of describing the importance of transitional objects such as blankets or teddy bears that allow a child to separate from its parent, Bollas explores the importance for the child of connecting to mothers and nannies as human prostheses who create a holding environment that bolsters the infant's felt but unexamined sense of her own powers of transformation.

For many white southerners, African American women created this necessary holding environment, and with it the white child's future sense of

self. In other words, African American caretakers provided a bizarrely scaled map of white self-renewal that persisted deep into adult life. Why "bizarrely scaled"? Because in taking up the vast political and economic entitlement of white supremacy, white grown-ups maintained, deep into adult life, an infantile fantasy: the wish to be a miniature white child in the care of a gigantic black woman. Thus white grown-ups could prolong a fantasy in which black domestics were caught in amber, stuck in the reservoir of unthought inner space—orbiting endlessly in the role of psychic prosthesis or "transformational object." What results is the complete evisceration—in the white imagination—of African American subjectivity. Although Robertson insists that "these maids . . . [were] really a very important part of the network of life in this part of the country" and that we were "taught that they were our friends," her narrative obviates any recognition of Sarah Sells as a human being. Instead, the domestic worker, in her vast and enviable scale, becomes a generic ambience, a category or condition of white narcissism and self-affection, as in, "I hope a great big black woman is there to hold me."

Not surprisingly, the heroines of *The Third Life of Grange Copeland* and *Jonah's Gourd Vine* are antitypes to this stereotype: fragile black women with enormous inner strength—their bodies worn out by their economic marginalization and their husbands' neglect or violence. These heroines' small size makes them vulnerable, and their formidable intellects are slowly diminished by continued physical compression: "Lucy was crumpled in a little dark ball in the center of the deep mound of feathers" (Hurston 1962, 148); Mem becomes "a haggard automatous witch, beside whom even Josie looked well preserved" (Walker 1988, 80). This pollution and miniaturization finally stand in for the loss of emotional and economic stability.

Black women writers ask gargantuas and their antitypes—these incredibly shrinking women—to perform a political work very different from the white gargantua's. In the case of Mem or Lucy, diminished scale or body size suggests an initial refinement (imitating the immaculate bodyscape defined by the white belle), but these physically impoverished women also enact the slow diminution of selfhood in an endless round of housekeeping, sharecropping, birthing, and sustaining a family. Although white women writers such as Welty or Porter portray black workers such as Old Nannie or Old Phoenix as women whose bodies are shrinking away, and although Welty and Porter also criticize the polity that thrives on these women's exploitation, these writers restrict their exploration of black women's lives to

textual margins, to beseeching vignettes. In her most sustained fictional outpourings Welty dwells with the gargantuan Miss Eckhart, the immigrant outsider, while Porter focuses on the miniatures of Miranda's childhood or Aunt Amy's adventures. Do gargantuan female bodies represent, then, another locus where black and white women southern writers part ways? Yes and no. To answer this question fully we need to examine three different settings from which African American women fling their heroines into space—inventing a universe filled with dark-skinned gargantuas but emptied of the "amiable golden giantesses" that white people see in their dreams.

Amplitude in Space

In her narrative *Incidents in the Life of a Slave Girl* the ex-slave Linda Brent captures the severe restriction of slavery when she disappears into her small "loophole of retreat" for seven years to hide from her rapacious white master. All around her slave women are hounded and diminished, and even in death Linda's aunt Nancy loses all geographic prerogative; she is destined for her white mistress's graveyard because, as Brent imagines that she hears the mistress opine sentimentally: "I was so long used to sleep with her lying near me, on the entry floor" (Jacobs 1973, 150). Escaping to the North, Brent delights in the appearance of wide-open space: "I called Fanny to see the sunrise, for the first time in our lives, on free soil; for such I then believed it to be. We watched the reddening sky, and saw the great orb come up slowly out of the water, as it seemed. Soon the waves began to sparkle, and every thing caught the beautiful glow" (163). Celestial gigantism or amplitude in space offers one strategy for constructing a black female epic.

Lucille Clifton also captures this "great orb" of the self in "ca'line's prayer." Writing about her great-great-grandmother Caroline, a once-enslaved southern ancestress, Clifton explores themes we have plumbed before: a white culture marked by its neglect, by its carelessness about making African American subjects into throwaway bodies:

> i have got old
> in a desert country
> i am dry
> and black as drought
> don't make water
> only acid
> even dogs won't drink

But Clifton ends her poem with an explosion of scale. The small "i," the desiccation and painful diminishment of this ancient woman's body, opens onto a limitless memoryscape:

> remember me from wydah
> remember the child running across dahomey
> black as ripe papaya
> juicy as sweet berries
> and set me in the rivers of your glory
> Ye Ma Jah (1980, 33)

The gigantism of Africa, with its Dahomey warriors and its giant orishas (invoked in Ye Ma Jah—the goddess of vanity and the sea, of pomp and fertility), suggests the hope of the African name, the gargantuan reworking of an absent past.[19] Clifton avoids white myths constricting either African or African American scale; she refuses the violence wreaked on "comforting" black domestics by shifting her text's gigantism from body to landscape, something Morrison repeats in invoking the breath-stealing tree that scars Sethe's great back.

The Avenging Domestic

Domestic caregivers like those imagined by Anne Robertson and her children are, in white fantasy, always available, always on call. In response, Alice Walker invents, in Sofia, a large black woman who uses her iron as a weapon. Miss Sofia enters *The Color Purple* as a middle-weight giant: "Harpo so black he think she bright, but she ain't that bright. Clear medium brown skin, gleam on it like on good furniture. Hair notty but a lot of it. . . . She not quite as tall as Harpo but much bigger, and strong and ruddy looking, like her mama brought her up on pork" (1983a, 38). But when Sofia defies the power of a local white family, she is forced into prison, maimed, and then released in order to care for the white woman who incarcerated her. As Sofia's defeated body retreats, as she stops scraping the world with her eyes, she becomes a potent stand-in for the southern grotesque—her body mapping the very codes that have broken and betrayed her. But once Sofia stops nursing these white folks and gets to come home, her gigantism is slowly resurrected. When she is visited by "Miss" Eleanor Jane, the finally-grown-up white child whom she cared for, Eleanor Jane's toddler (a boy with his own giant name, Reynolds Stanley Earl) rummages through Sofia's house, sacking the laundry she has just ironed and pillaging the outlying rooms. As this polluting white child grows bold and destructive, Eleanor Jane pleads with Sofia to say that she loves him.

> No ma'am, say Sofia. I do not love Reynolds Stanley Earl. Now. That's what you been trying to find out ever since he was born. Now you know.
>
> Me and Henrietta look up. Miss Eleanor Jane just that quick done put Reynolds Stanley on the floor where he crawling round knocking stuff over. Head straight for Sofia's stack of ironed clothes and pull it down on his head. Sofia take up the clothes, straighten them out, stand by the ironing board with her hand on the iron. Sofia the kind of woman no matter what she have in her hand it look like a weapon. (232–33)

In this fine scene of truth-telling Sofia refuses to play the role of "a great big black woman" who is only there to hold white people.[20] "I got my own troubles, say Sofia, and when Reynolds Stanley grow up, he's gon be one of them. But he won't, say Miss Eleanor Jane. I'm his mama and I won't let him be mean to colored. You and whose army? say Sofia. The first word he likely to say won't be nothing he learn from you" (234). To be an African American in this armed southern society is already to be part of an epic, to be fighting hard on the losing side.

In Rita Dove's "The Great Palace of Versailles" domestic implements turn, once again, into weapons:

> *Nothing nastier than a white person!*
> She mutters as she irons alterations
> in the backroom of Charlotte's Dress Shoppe.
> The steam rising from a cranberry wool
> comes alive with perspiration
> and stale Evening of Paris.
> Swamp she born from, swamp
> she swallow, swamp she got to sink again. (1986, 63)

The figure of the avenging black worker merges with the dream of consuming space as Beulah appropriates all of Versailles for her fantasies. Ironing a white woman's dress with a vengeance, her own skirt "flashes crimson"; Beulah's imagination, her worldwide ownership, is vast. Even caught in the small "shoppes" of the Midwest, she contains multitudes.

African American Gargantuas

Is there room in this analysis for capacious black gargantuas, for characters whose sense of scale enlarges our sense of the black South's "cultural, racial, and political themes"? In characters who have migrated from the South to the North in *Song of Solomon,* Morrison demonstrates that the ability to take up space is always political. When Milkman and Pilate are hauled off by a white policeman simply because of the color of their skin, the humiliations of Michigan's jailhouses linger: "His eyes traveled up his body. The touch of the policeman's hand was still there—a touch that made his flesh jump like the tremor of a horse's flank when flies light on it. And something more. Something like shame stuck to his skin. Shame at being spread-eagled, fingered" (1977, 210).

To restore Milkman's humanity, Pilate changes shape; she shrinks in order to free his tremor-struck flesh. Milkman and Guitar recall her "raggedy" shuffle into the police station: "Louise Beaver and Butterfly McQueen all rolled up in one, 'Yassuh boss. Yassuh boss.' . . . She didn't even look the same. She looked short, short and pitiful" (206–207). Humiliated by the loss of their manhood, neither Milkman nor Guitar will recognize her political sacrifice, her willingness to forego her own body to get them out of jail. "As she stood there in the receiving room of the jail, she didn't even come up to the sergeant's shoulder—and the sergeant's head barely reached Milkman's own chin. But Pilate was as tall as he was" (208). Once the two men have been freed, "Pilate was tall again. The top of her head, wrapped in a silk rag, almost touched the roof of the car, as did theirs. And her own voice was back" (209). Size does matter. And yet when an African American woman shrinks so that these young men won't have to, they refuse to recognize her sacrifice: "I told you she was a snake. Drop her skin in a split second" (206). In Pilate, Morrison invents a magical character who changes shape at will. And yet in giving Pilate these mythic dimensions, Morrison comments not only on her capaciousness but on lessons learned in the South about the shape-changing necessary to survive white supremacy. She deploys Ovid's magic to show how unmagical it is to live inside the myth of America.

To shrink and then expand at will—"to slip into them all—to change. To change for a moment into Gertrude, into Mrs. Gruenwald, into Twosie—into a boy. To *have been* an orphan" (Welty 1949, 139): in *The Golden Apples* the twelve-year-old Nina Carmichael wants to inhabit every class, race, and gender that surrounds her. But at the end of the novel she is becomes passive, bloated: "Mrs. Junior Nesbitt, heavy with child, was seated where he could see her, head fine and indifferent, one puffed white arm stretched along the sewing machine" (139). To take up space is to shrink into a role; her "puffed white arm" can reach no farther than the implements of her "indifferent" domesticity. In contrast, Alice Walker begins *In Search of Our Mothers' Gardens* with an epigraph from Bernice Reagon's *Black Women and Liberation Movements:*

> I come out of a tradition where those things are valued; where you talk about a woman with big legs and big hips and black skin. I come out of a black community where it was all right to have hips and be heavy. You didn't feel that people didn't like you. The values that [imply] you must be skinny come from another culture. . . . Those are not the values that I was given by the women who served as my models. I refuse to be judged by the values of another culture. I am a black woman, and I will stand as best I can in that imagery. (1983, xi)

To stand "in that imagery" suggests the importance of reaching out to other African American women with the goal of shared size and power. But to stand in that imagery also means taking comfort in one's size, claiming the space one already inhabits.

Once again, African and Anglo American women writers part ways. Janie, Feather Mae, Morrison's Pilate: these are women who take up space of their own, but their magnitude is never directed toward white needs, nor toward the demands of a black bourgeoisie:

> And when she stood up, he all but gasped. She was as tall as his father, head and shoulders taller than himself. Her dress wasn't as long as he had thought; it came to just below her calf and now he could see her unlaced men's shoes and the silvery brown skin of her ankles.
>
> She held the peelings precisely as they had fallen in her lap, and as she walked up the steps she looked as though she were holding her crotch. (1977, 38)

Morrison's Pilate is, like McCullers's Amelia, androgynous, larger than life, and immensely, heroically capable. But while McCullers's character ends her career and her fistfight lying flat on her back (undone, disauthored, in tragic capitulation to the worst of white patriarchy), Pilate's life ends in tragedy and largesse.

> "Pilate? You okay?" He couldn't make out her eyes. His hand under her head was sweating like a fountain. "Pilate?"
>
> She sighed. "Watch Reba for me." And then, "I wish I'd a knowed more people. I would of loved 'em all. If I'd a knowed more, I would a loved more."
>
> Milkman bent low to see her face and saw darkness staining his

> hand. Not sweat, but blood oozing from her neck down into his cupped hand. (349)

Morrison may redeploy Miss Amelia's great dimensions when she invents Pilate, but she rejects the abject ending of McCullers's white giantess. Milkman's cupped hand captures Pilate's generosity to others—a generosity that is not a dispersal of her person or her body but an expansion.[21] Pilate's goal is to pass her strength and her subjectivity on to her people: a power that the white gargantua—in her isolation and loneliness—has never been able to summon.[22]

Chapter Six

Politics in the Kitchen: Roosevelt, McCullers, and Surrealist History

In 1938 Eleanor Roosevelt attended a conference in Birmingham, Alabama, organized to address the broad range of economic and racial problems facing the South. This conference was organized by Joseph Gelders, a former professor and labor organizer who had testified in 1937 before the La Folette Committee on Civil Liberties about antilabor violence in the South. This was a period of extraordinary antiunion violence within the South, and soon after his testimony Gelders was assaulted and left to die by guards employed by the Tennessee Coal and Iron Company.

As Patricia Sullivan tells the story in *Days of Hope,* the conference Gelders helped initiate after his ordeal resulted in what was arguably the most diverse group of southerners to gather under one roof, including congressmen, sharecroppers, newspaper editors, students, and business leaders.[1] These varied constituencies made several radical endorsements—including support for federal antilynching legislation and equal salaries for black and white teachers. Justice Hugo Black, University of North Carolina president Frank Gordon, and Eleanor Roosevelt addressed the plenary sessions. But most stirring of all, a fifth of the participants were black, and, as Virginia Durr reported, it was "a wonderful sort of love feast because it was the first time that all these various elements from the South had gotten together. And we were not segregated" (Sullivan 1996, 99).

On the second day Bull Connor, the Birmingham chief of police, ended this festival. He ordered the resegregation of the municipal auditorium where the conference was taking place. At his word a chalk line bisected the auditorium; blacks went to one side and whites to the other. Arriving late in the day, Mrs. Roosevelt sat down with the conference's black participants. By 1938 she was, of course, no stranger to controversy. As Sullivan explains:

> The *Rosslyn Chronicle* reported that in a speech Mrs. Roosevelt delivered to a black gathering in 1936, she used the word *equality* twelve times and *equal* six times. The paper referred to a photograph of the First Lady sitting beside a black woman at a welfare gathering "so close their bodies touched." That same year an issue of the *Georgia Women's World* had a cover photograph of Eleanor Roosevelt being escorted by a black professor at Howard University. An article attacking Mrs. Roosevelt charged: "Surely no other roamed the country at will as she does. . . . Walter White and the other Negro boys who ran the streets of Atlanta a quarter of a century ago seemed to find special favor in the eyes of Madam Roosevelt." (1996, 159)

Cornered by a white policeman at the Birmingham conference and ordered to move, she responded by picking up her chair and setting it down smack in the middle of the line dividing blacks from whites, where she stayed for the remainder of the afternoon.

Testimony is a form of action in which speech reaches toward deed. Here Roosevelt's body, divided by a little chalk line, gave testimony in a way that her speech did not. After this fierce public gesture, Roosevelt's response to reporters seemed oddly understated: "In the section of the country where I come from [segregation] is a procedure that is not followed. But I would not presume to tell the people of Alabama what they should do" (Sullivan 1996, 100). Still, this breach between word and body, Roosevelt's insistence on practicing a bodily form of witnessing, was noted in the black press. *The Afro-American* observed that "if the [white] people of the South do not grasp this gesture, we must. Sometimes actions speak louder than words" (Sullivan 1996, 100).

Several things interest me about this incident. First, Roosevelt became, in this moment of protest, a hybrid body—a person divided in half by the brutal constraints of Jim Crow. Second, this is another example of the southern uncanny—an eloquent action that is also an improbable sideshow event in which the nation's first lady is cut in half in Birmingham, Alabama, neatly bisected by the laws of her own country. Third, this anecdote raises the question of where "the political" or "the historical" resides. For a number of southern critics the capacity to participate in (or to write about) local institutions and the regulatory principles guiding the public realm marks the central difference between twentieth-century southern women writers and their male contemporaries.

Although *The Member of the Wedding* seems very far from the political crises of the Southern Conference on Human Welfare in Birmingham in 1938, in this chapter we will see that McCullers's novel struggles to make its own version of history. *Member of the Wedding* has a humble setting; much of it takes place in the tame domestic space of the kitchen. But I will argue that this novel not only mimics, it also reworks the proportions of Roosevelt's actions at the Birmingham conference. This novel reunites bodies but also bisects them, investigates utopian social goals, and explores southern African Americans' and white children's access to the public sphere. Finally, by focusing so obsessively on divided characters, it provides a space for exploring the political divisions of the 1940s and for deepening our sense of the everyday forces driving Eleanor Roosevelt's political hybridity.

Let's begin with the story of another haunted southern child. "John Henry did not play with the dough; he worked on the biscuit man as though it were a very serious business." The kitchen is the place for serious political work in McCullers's novel, but is this biscuit man part of it? John Henry gives his homunculus a detailed nose and "a little grinning raisin mouth . . . separate fingers, a hat on, and even a walking stick." This is a painstaking self-replica, the perfect image of John Henry's own tiny body, but the result of his labor brings us, once more, to the southern grotesque. The little doughboy comes out of the oven so misshapen and bloated that it seems to repeat, in demure biscuit form, the painful transformation we witness at the beginning of *Uncle Tom's Cabin,* when a slave child changes into a deformed old man. "It had swelled so that all the work of John Henry had been cooked out, the fingers were run together, and the walking stick resembled a sort of tail." This description looks, at first, like an example of literary testimony. Perhaps this little boy is at risk from the hot political atmosphere of the South of the 1940s (both John Henry and Honey Brown are queer individuals who would also have been at risk during this period in Nazi Europe). Does this bloated doughboy also predict that John Henry is fated to fall apart? But instead of developing a thematics of imminent danger, McCullers dispenses with horror and delights in the trivial: "John Henry just looked at it through his glasses, wiped it with his napkin, and buttered the left foot" (1975, 8).

Is it any wonder that so many critics insist that a political abyss divides southern male writers from their female counterparts? To distance the girls from the men, in his book on *The Southern Writer in the Postmodern World,* Fred Hobson seizes on the grand scale of men's writing, its talent for pondering history, for contemplating the sweep of the social.

> I have spoken earlier of the southern novel of ideas and conscious social commentary as having been principally a male domain. . . . And it might be added that the "big novel" to which I alluded in the beginning—the ambitious novel, that work concerned with the sweep of history or with the public arena or both—has also in the South generally (with an exception such as *Gone with the Wind*) been undertaken by male authors: Faulkner, Wolfe, Warren, Ellison, and Styron. Whether this is because the male, particularly in southern society, was usually conditioned to think more ambitiously, that is, to ponder history and politics in which *he,* after all, could more easily participate—or whether it is because the vision of the male writer has tended for other reasons to be more abstract, less attentive to everyday truths and concrete details than that of most women writers—is debatable. I tend to think it is something of both. (1991, 78)

Whereas canonized writers like Warren and Faulkner write toward the panoramic view, the big picture, women like Porter, Welty, or O'Connor seem more intrigued by that slice of life, the short story, with its shrewd, half-made torsos, its bodies in shreds. But I have been arguing that these shredded torsos register not only "the sweep of history" but the complex connections between the body's intimacies and its civic demands. This habitual separation of the public arena from life's "everyday truths and concrete details" requires at least three sorts of critique.

The first is epistemological. What would happen to southern literary criticism if we reevaluated southern women writers' preoccupations with the trivial, the everyday? Might large-scale consequences accrue to our bodies, might we begin to transform the precincts of political knowledge? In a recent essay Ross Chambers suggests that we ignore the world's trivia at our peril. Why is there no place in our vast analytic for the elfin pleasures of fugue states (including "napping in class, calling in sick, walking the dog" [1994, 766])? Attention to these moments opens a spate of unsung political and philosophical issues: "What kind of narrative treats the trivial as significant? How does it go about establishing the importance of the supposedly trivial? What modifications does this suppose in conceptions of knowledge, and in the evaluations on which our recognition of knowledge rests? Is there something like an epistemological 'time out' that might have philosophical, educational or critical interest?" (766). We might ask the same of southern fictions: do the narrative fugues, the minor pleasures to be gleaned from stories by Eudora Welty or Katherine Anne Porter, also have the capacity to reconfigure crucial knowledge systems—such as our ways of knowing the South? Might there be something appropriately ambitious about establishing the importance of "trivial" events (such as cookbooks or cotton harvests) within the vast sweep of southern political life?

Second, the language separating the trivial from the "historical" in itself is delusive. "It would be mistaken," as Henri Lefebvre writes in *The Production of Space,* "to picture a hierarchical scale stretching between two poles, with the unified will of political power at one extreme and the actual dispersion of differentiated elements at the other. For everything (the 'whole') weighs down on the lower or 'micro' level, on the local and the localizable—in short, on the sphere of everyday life. Everything (the 'whole') also depends on this level: exploitation and domination, protection and—inseparably—repression" (1991, 151–52).[2] The pressures connecting everyday life with large-scale economies suggest another register for negotiating a traditional separation of "history" from everyday truths. Everything—especially the ambitious sweep of politics and history—has already invaded the trivial world and helped to shape it. At the same time, while this micro level supports and replenishes the power structure, it is also a source of social change, of a thousand daily resistances.[3] We need to reenvision, from within the confines and rebellions of this "lower" southern world, the eccentric work that women's writing performs on behalf of the dailiness of southern history. The grotesque bodies that Welty, McCullers, Walker, and O'Connor invent may reflect the miniature blandishments of the private arena; they may rattle us with their casual openness and multiple wounds; but these bodies also connect us with the mess, indelicacy, and legislated insensitivity of the public domains in which the multitudes operate.

Third, and perhaps most important, in southern women's writing the "microeconomy" of the body rains down on the "macroeconomy" with splendor and vengeance. At the end of Ellen Gilchrist's "Rich" a failed banker kills himself and his adopted daughter—splattering their bodies all over the expensive consumer goods that catalogue his place among a New Orleans elite:

> The inside of the camp was casually furnished with old leather office furniture, hand-me-down tables and lamps, and a walnut poker table from Neiman-Marcus. . . .
>
> The bullet entered her head from the back. Her thick body rolled across the hardwood floor and lodged against a hat rack from Jody

> Mellon's old office in the Hibernia Bank Building. One of her arms landed on a pile of old *Penthouse* magazines and her disordered brain flung its roses north and east and south and west and rejoined the order from which it casually arose. (1981, 22–23)

Gilchrist opens her text to the wounded, processional bodies of grotesque realism with a huge dose of sadism and glee. She refuses to write a retronarrative separating bodies from the objects that make up their history; she insists on establishing a grid in which *bios* and *polis* are intensely interconnected.[4]

In pursuit of these ideas I want to propose two different topics for this chapter. The first will be a reading of *Member of the Wedding* that spells out its preoccupations with hybrid bodies and the public sphere. But I also want to use these concerns to ponder the literary uses of southern "history"—especially the ways in which women writers make this history more readable and perhaps more responsible than critics have recognized. Why is this case so hard to make? The answer is surprising, for even when the critic shoves the "trivial" and the "historical" close together, it is southern women themselves who set the terms for their texts' official separation from "history."

"I Don't Write Historically or Anything"

In one of her interviews, Eudora Welty pops right out and says to William F. Buckley, "I was just thinking from the workmanship point of view of the novelist—I mean, I am not a bit interested in preserving the home of Jefferson Davis. . . . That Jefferson Davis doesn't have much to do with it is what I am trying to say" (1984, 104–5). This is, of course, rather delightful. But in another interview Welty falters, suggesting ways in which she might be eclipsed by "the historical" when she writes outside—or beyond—the collective penumbra of race-thinking and southern-history-as-tragedy that marks the fiction of William Faulkner.

> *Brans:* In one of your essays you talk about Faulkner, and you say that Faulkner has this sense of blood guilt about the Indians and then about the blacks. In your own work you don't have that.
>
> *Welty:* Well, it's not my theme. You know his work encompassed so much and so many books and so many generations and so much history, that that was an integral part of it. I don't write historically or anything. Most of the things that I write about can be translated into personal relationships. I've never gone into such things as guilt over the Indians or—it just hasn't been my subject. My stories, I think, re-

> flect the racial relationships—guilt is just one aspect of that. Certainly I think any writer is aware of the complicated relationship between the races. It comes out in so many even domestic situations.
>
> *Brans:* Very few of your stories deal directly with blacks, though. And those that do, I've wondered if the blackness is a necessary part of the character. For example, old Phoenix. Why is she black?
>
> *Welty:* It's not a deliberate thing, like, "I am now going to write about the black race." I write about all people. I think my characters are about half white and half black. (1984, 299)

This is a very weird thing for any southern writer to say; in fact, it's not even close to an accurate accounting of Welty's treatment of race in her fiction. To come to terms with Welty's bizarre invocation of the hybrid, bisected southern body, I want to turn to her story about Old Phoenix and the ways in which this story gives the lie to Welty's assertion that "I don't write historically or anything."

As Welty thinks further about the accuracy of what she's said to Brans (as well as the accuracy of his suggestion that she doesn't write about race), she begins to have second thoughts.

> What started me writing it was the sight of a figure like Phoenix Jackson. I never got close to her, just saw her crossing a distant field early one afternoon in the fall. Just her figure. I couldn't see her up close, but you could tell it was an old woman going somewhere, and I thought, she is bent on an errand. And I know it isn't for herself. . . . When I got home I wrote that story that she had made me think of. She was a black woman. But then I suppose it would be more likely to be a black woman who would be in such desperate need and live so remotely away from help and who would have so far to go. I don't think that story would be the same story with a white person. The white person could have the same character, of course, and do the same thing, but it wouldn't have the same urgency about it." (1984, 299–300)

Which framework is right? Is "A Worn Path" about a character who is "half white and half black," or is there something historically accurate about the figure of a single black woman risking this lonely path?

In the last story in *A Curtain of Green,* Phoenix Jackson tries against overwhelming odds to repeat her yearly pilgrimage from country to town to get the medicine her injured grandson—his throat opened from drinking lye—needs to stay alive. Although this story participates so obviously in the genres of magical realism and sentimentality, "A Worn Path" is often anthologized because it offers a unique combination: it is a heroic narrative (that is, a story archetypal and deindividualizing) about a black woman who conforms quite magnificently to American expectations about rugged individualism.[5]

But if we look closely we can see that, for all the hypothetical romance of Phoenix's journey, her story refigures a set of frightening facts. In *The Promise of the New South* Edward Ayers's description of African American migrant practices adds a layer of qualification to these "American" themes (the orphan's journey to success or self-discovery, survival of the hyperindividual against all odds). Ayers suggests that the mobility of this period—the very mobility that forces Old Phoenix to care for her grandchild alone—came at great cost to black families. Men found their best work on plantations and in mills, while women found their best-paying jobs in towns as domestics, creating a division of labor that pulled black men and women "in strongly divergent directions by the hope of a decent living" (1992, 151–52). "Not only were relatively young families thus prematurely divided" (including half-grown children, who were often hired out as this damaged child could not be), but "older people sometimes found themselves without nearby kin to care for them" (152). This detail gives us a way to unbind the world that drives Welty's story. The mythic structure that seems to celebrate female individualism and endurance is perhaps better read as an elegy for a culture that demands excessive individuality from those least able to provide it.[6]

"It was the sight of a figure . . . just her figure." How much history can be wrung from a figure? Welty stumbles on a little-analyzed fact about the burdens white labor practices imposed on African Americans, as well as the costs to children and the elderly of the very freedoms celebrated during the Great Migration: "I suppose it would be more likely to be a black woman who would be in such desperate need and live so remotely away from help and who would have so far to go," Welty says, apologetically, only half-recognizing that this desperate need has been, until recently, erased from the map of southern history. Welty and her cohorts are constantly remaking these maps.

We see, then, the first connections between women's writing and the provenance of southern history. Welty and her cohorts catalogue histories that have been subsemantic, unspoken, out of use. In another story from *Curtain of Green,* "Keela: The Outcast Indian Maid," a crippled black man named Little Lee Roy is captured by white men who come upon him "like a cyclone." Little Lee Roy is put in a cage at the circus and forced to change both his race and gender and to act the part of a crazy, live-chicken eating

Native American woman. "It wasn't nothin' it could do. It was just took up," Steve, the carnival barker, says, in his futile quest to find "Keela" and make reparation (1979, 84).

In *The Land Where the Blues Began* Lomax tells several stories about black enslavement that survived well into the twentieth century. The old-timers he interviews describe what it means to be "just took up":

> *Alan Lomax:* How old were you when you went on the levee camp?
> *Bill Gordon:* About eleven.
> *Walter Brown:* Me and him went out there bout the same time.
> *Bill Gordon:* I was about eleven. I was too small for to put the harness on my mule—I could put the collar on, but I couldn't put on the harness. The mens would put my harnesses on for me an I'd push the collar, bottom upwards, and then push it up on the small part of the mule's neck.
> *William Hart:* Well, when I come round the levee camp, I's a little kid. Nineteen nineteen—a fella out of Memphis called a "man catcher." Catchin boys, carryin em down to the camps . . .
> *Alan Lomax:* Tell us what a man catcher was.
> *William Hart:* Well a man catcher is just like a . . . getting up labor for the levee camps, you know.
> *Bill Gordon:* You want some men, right? He'll get um for you. (1993, 244)

Peonage, or forced labor, was a common practice in the South in the opening decades of the twentieth century, and the work of levee-building accomplished by men like Bill Gordon and Walter Brown presented a monumental, dangerous task. One of the levee workers, George Adams, directed Lomax to the plantation of one of the better-known overseers, the now-wealthy "Mister Cholly" Idaho: "In my days on the levee, I worked so many of them," he said quietly, "I just couldn't say how many. But I'm proud of this—I never crippled a nigger in my life. . . . Yes, I've handled labor in here for forty-six years and I've never crippled one. And that's a good record. Some of these foremen would beat um up just to act smart, but I didn't whip a nigger until it was necessary and then I'd made a good job of it" (227). Welty does not give us the details of Little Lee Roy's crippling. But all around the edges of his story we can read the "blood guilt" of man catchers, as well as the "history" imposed on Native and African Americans in the circus of U.S. civic life.

How much history can be wrung from one figure? A second function of "history" in southern women's writing is the exploration of the unseen everyday—practices known but unthought, hiding in plain sight, a field that we've explored in each of the preceding chapters. But in this chapter I want to take on a third provenance of "history" in these women's texts. Let's call it, for the moment, "fantasmatic history," a history written with a surrealist edge.

We find an example in McCullers's description of the kitchen, with its weirdly morphing walls; this is the place where Berenice, the black housekeeper, spends most of her time:

> After the darkening yard the kitchen was hot and bright and queer. The walls of the kitchen bothered Frankie—the queer drawings of Christmas trees, airplanes, freak soldiers, flowers. John Henry had started the first pictures one long afternoon in June, and having already ruined the wall, he went on and drew whenever he wished. Sometimes Frankie had drawn also. At first her father had been furious about the walls, but later he said for them to draw all the pictures out of their systems, and he would have the kitchen painted in the fall. But as the summer lasted, and would not end, the walls had begun to bother Frankie. That evening the kitchen looked strange to her, and she was afraid. (1975, 7)

These bizarre pictures serve multiple purposes in McCullers's narrative. First, they bring the war right into twelve-year-old Frankie's home, crucial for a novella set in Georgia in the mid-1940s that wants to wrangle with southern politics, with the war's potential for infinite chaos and disturbance and change, not in Europe, but on the home front. Second, these walls become the site of Berenice's political alphabet, of the lessons in black history she gives the children. In the end these walls also recast her tragedy; when she loses her job these pictures are calcimined over, whitened, like Frankie herself at the end of the novella. Third, these drawings are surrealistic. They change our vision of the enclosed parameters of the white southern home and suggest the passel of mischief McCullers is up to.

In *The Predicament of Culture* James Clifford uses the term *surrealism* "to circumscribe an aesthetic that values fragments, curious collections, unexpected juxtapositions—that works to provoke the manifestation of extraordinary realities drawn from the domains of the erotic, the exotic, and the unconscious" (1988, 118). This is a wonderfully exact description of John Henry's aesthetic practices:

> Sometimes his mind was like the pictures he drew with crayons on tablet paper. The other day he had drawn such a one and showed it to

> her. It was a picture of a telephone man on a telephone pole. . . . It was a careful picture, but after she had looked at it uneasiness had lingered in her mind. She looked at the picture again until she realized what was wrong. The telephone man was drawn in a side-view profile, yet this profile had two eyes—one eye just above the nose bridge and another drawn just below. And it was no hurried mistake; both eyes had careful lashes, pupils, and lids. Those two eyes drawn in a side-view face gave her a funny feeling. (131)

I want to argue that McCullers is trying to give the reader this funny feeling too. But how does a child's drawing, a telephone man with a Picasso-like mask, probe the special insanities that constructed southern lives in the 1940s?

Surrealist or fantasmatic history strives for three effects. First, it makes us encounter the strangeness of a particular historical moment, attacking the familiar, provoking eruptions of the unanticipated otherness of the everyday. What does it mean to make the everyday marvelous or filled with the uncanny? "Frankie lived in the ugliest house in town. . . . The house was empty, dark. Frankie turned and walked to the end of the block, and around the corner, and down the sidewalk to the Wests'. John Henry was leaning against the banisters of this front porch, with a lighted window behind him, so that he looked like a little black paper doll on a piece of yellow paper" (38). If the walls in this novella morph into strange designs, so do the people. John Henry becomes "a little black paper doll"; Uncle Charles, in his death, looks "like an old man carved in brown wood and covered with a sheet" (71). At its margins the novella is testing the limits of segregation, putting the South's racist reality "deeply in question" by "blackening" its characters and experimenting, as does surrealist art, with the possibilities of "putting the pieces of culture together in new ways" (Clifford 1988, 120).

Second, surrealist history grabs hold of the reader, impinging on quotidian reading practices with a force that Roland Barthes calls the "punctum." Barthes invented this term to account for the spell-binding effects of perfectly ordinary photographs. These photographs have, at their base, a sense of anonymous acceptability, a capacity to evoke mass appeal in their conformity to a commonplace world that makes images recognizable: "John Henry was leaning against the banisters of this front porch, with a lighted window behind him". But for Barthes, this recognizability is interrupted by the punctum—an energy that breaks or punctuates commonplace reality, shooting out like an arrow and piercing the reader(1981, 49–55), a peculiar, unaccountable detail that makes contact, that stings or pierces—"he looked like a little black paper doll on a piece of yellow paper."

We encounter this "shock of the unintelligible" again and again in McCullers's prose. In surrealist art, collage is used to break up the conventional and attack the veneer of the real in order to gain access to the unconscious and attack the deceptive surfaces of normalcy. The figures in *Member of the Wedding* are always breaking up or breaking into conventional codes: "she could feel Berenice's soft big ninnas against her back, and her soft wide stomach, her warm solid legs. She had been breathing very fast, but after a minute her breath slowed down so that she breathed in time with Berenice: the two of them were close together as one body, and Berenice's stiffened hands were clasped around F. Jasmine's chest" (113). In *Member of the Wedding* Frankie, a white preadolescent girl, and Berenice, the black housekeeper who cares for her, make a very strange figure, indeed. Clearly McCullers feels a compulsion, like Welty, like Roosevelt, to imagine figures half white and half black. But is there something hallucinatory or surreal about this making of two bodies into one that we need to pursue? What gets written into—or out of—this body?

We know that domestic labor was one of the few occupations open to black women in the South.[7] The displacement of Frankie's and Berenice's body into the space of "visual dislocation" foregrounds Berenice's occupation and gives it, like John Henry's portrait, a bizarre side-view profile. Like surrealist painters, McCullers refuses the parameters of the natural body in order to tap powerful unconscious desires to merge with other human beings. But she also describes the results of this longing in the South; this hybrid body punctuates the boundaries of ordinary racial practices (a black woman nestles a needy white girl in her arms) to critique the unexamined object relations driving this need. Like surrealist art, this bizarre somagram suggests that the body is "not a continuous whole but an assemblage of conventional symbols and codes" (Clifford 1988, 133).

In other words, McCullers pushes two very different aspects of Berenice's occupation into prominence. In interviews with white employers of African American domestic workers, Susan Tucker discovered that

> domestics were usually much in evidence at white gatherings—parties, weddings, Christmas dinners—and yet, most of the white women to whom I spoke told me they did not recall the existence of photographs of domestics at these functions. Many of them nevertheless gave me consent to look through family scrapbooks, and in them, again and again, I found many more pictures of domestics than I had

> been led to expect. In such photographs the domestics are often obscured and in the background. (1988, 273)

But McCullers makes a curious choice in her story: Berenice stays in the foreground; she maintains an incredibly charged *presence* throughout the novella. (We can say that, for once in white woman's fiction, she is portrayed as figure, not ground.)[8] "It seemed to F. Jasmine that Berenice resembled a strange queen, if a queen can be colored and sitting at a kitchen table. She unwound the story of her and Ludie like a colored queen unwinding a bolt of cloth of gold" (96).

Berenice's stories are frankly emancipatory. "We all of us somehow caught," she says to Frankie, as the two of them breathe together. "I don't want to be caught," Frankie replies. "'Me neither,' said Berenice. 'Don't none of us. I'm caught worse than you is' . . . it was John Henry who asked in his child voice: 'why?' 'Because I am black. Because I am colored.'" In the South, Berenice explains to John Henry, African Americans suffer randomly; they are "caught that first way I was telling you, as all human beings is caught," but "we caught as colored people also. Sometimes a boy like Honey feel like he just can't breathe no more. He feel like he got to break something or break himself. Sometimes it just about more than we can stand" (113–14).

If Frankie's blending with Berenice suggests political lessons white children should take in with their crackers and milk, it also represents the way Berenice herself is "caught," her body captured by the need to care for Frankie, her stiffened hands hardened by a life of overwork. This double-bodied figure pushes us toward a clearer understanding of African Americans' place in the white southern home. In *Telling Memories* Tucker interviews a self-designated "domestic engineer" named Linda Barron, who argues that myths about whites' closeness to black domestic workers are just that—myths:

> Course, when you've worked for the same people for twenty-four years, there are people who say you are part of the family. Well, you're *not* part of the family. As long as you work, you have access to the house, the food, the secrets, the stormy life, the fun life. And sometimes you also experience the same things that these people you are working for experience. But so far as you're part of the family, I can't see that, because you're different than they are.
>
> Like my political differences. They know I'm politically motivated and they're not, and they don't think like I do. (1988, 258)

Frankie and Berenice share incredible political dreams in the kitchen. Later in this chapter it will be crucial to talk about the fate as well as the content of these politics, but for now, we should note that any reading of progressive intimacy between Berenice and Frankie needs to be mitigated by a sense of limitation, by Barron's descriptions not only of the politics and economies separating southern blacks from whites but of her sense that African American workers are forgotten in the midst of their enormous centrality to white people's lives.[9]

The third function of the surrealist history we find in *Member of the Wedding* is the introduction of heterogeneity and the potential for change within cultural maps that seem fixed or static. Berenice is the ultimate hallucinatory artist; her stories resemble the automatic writing that allowed footprints of the unconscious to travel slowly across the page:

> And when she had begun this way, on a long and serious subject, the words flowed one into the other and her voice began to sing. In the gray of the kitchen on summer afternoons the tone of her voice was golden and quiet, and you could listen to the color and the singing of her voice and not follow the words. F. Jasmine let the long tones linger and spin inside her ears, but her mind did not stamp the voice with sense or sentences. She sat there listening at the table, and now and then she thought of a fact that all her life had seemed to her most curious: Berenice always thought of herself as though she was somebody very beautiful. Almost on this one subject, Berenice was really not in her right mind. (79)

Like Cassie Morrison and her fascinated remembrance of a rape during Miss Eckhart's majestic recital, Frankie will not let Berenice's power wander too far from home; she censors Berenice's majesty, even though Frankie has already absorbed her regal bearing ("she walked the streets entitled as a queen and mingled everywhere," 44). To be in one's right mind in *The Member of the Wedding* is always to be in the wrong. As its plot sweeps through Frankie's growth from an aberrant tomboy into her candidacy for "Little Miss White Southern Culture" the novella describes the need to deform the self to stay within social bounds. The hyperkinetic techniques McCullers uses to pierce this town's cultural verities suggest that the "normal" self Frankie establishes by the novella's end is, at its deepest core, an accession to deformity. So although Berenice's unconventional convictions—about freedom, about her own beauty, about the importance of everyone's participation in the public sphere—frighten Frankie, they are finally more promising as a site of psychosocial identity.

Not only does Frankie's determination to walk the streets "entitled as a queen" anticipate her admiration of Berenice as "a strange queen" but John Henry also traces Berenice's uncomfortable shadow: "after the bath he had put on Berenice's high-heeled shoes. Again he asked a question by which he meant nothing. 'Why?' he asked. 'Why what, Baby?' said Berenice" (107). Again, McCullers's use of children's and domestic servants' voices to create a break in "the real" (that is, in the stories validated by the dominant culture) has a powerful effect. *Member of the Wedding* tries to introduce the possibility of change into a southern history already building toward the civil rights movement of the 1950s. The seeds of this change lie in its shifting perspectives, its foregrounding of the demons of childhood, its mirrorings of grown-up ruthlessness and violence.

Given this focus on formal economies of disruption and emergence, it is hardly surprising that Berenice's kitchen becomes a hallucinatory space where all sorts of things travel from background to foreground. In a climate where one hallucinatory body is simultaneously occupied by a white child and a black woman (suggesting a dangerous, attractive, parasitic, expansive, claustrophobic merger between the two), the walls of the kitchen also become another site of "juxtaposition or collage":[10] "They sat together in the kitchen, and the kitchen was a sad and ugly room. John Henry had covered the walls with queer, child drawings, as far up as his arm would reach. This gave the kitchen a crazy look, like that of a room in the crazy-house. And now the old kitchen made Frankie sick. The name for what had happened to her Frankie did not know, but she could feel her squeezed heart beating against the table edge" (4). *The Member of the Wedding* supplies its readers with dozens of weird hieroglyphs. Not only does Berenice supply the children with forbidden political names, but these walls themselves recall African American spiritual practices. As George Lipsitz says of the visual artist Renée Stout's search for an African aesthetic: "once she knew what to look for, African items and icons appeared all around her. On a visit to California in 1986, she noticed newspapers covering the interior walls of a black woman's home and recognized their connection to African 'protective print' and 'spirit writing.' The Mande people in Africa, among others, placed religious writing inside leather charms . . . throughout the southern United States, black people often placed newsprint on walls and in shoes, or left the Bible open at night as a continuation of African ways in America" (1995, 14). This protective writing is incorporated in Stout's own work, while in *Member of the Wedding* John Henry is the artist of the peculiar. But these paintings remain in Berenice's jurisdiction and suggest, once again, the limits of Frankie's reality testing, surrounded as she is by hallucinatory haloes.

Curiously, American whites at this time also began to experience a series of hallucinations about domestic workers, and these political fears about black power bring us back to Eleanor Roosevelt's practical hybridity. During the war Roosevelt argued vehemently for equal citizenship rights across racial lines, using the dangers of battle to attest to the bravery of African and Anglo American men fighting on Pacific and European fronts. Angered by her rhetoric, many white southerners held her responsible for a new spirit of rebelliousness among American blacks. "The most fantastic expression of this charge," Sullivan argues, "was the 'Eleanor Clubs,' allegedly organized by black domestics at the behest of the First Lady for more pay, more privileges, less hours, and less work." Rumors about these clubs "flooded the South during 1942 and 1943. . . . Several investigations, including one by the Federal Bureau of Investigation, found no evidence that any such clubs existed. The rumors were fed by a shortage of domestic help due to better-paying opportunities in defense industries and to the organization of black women into clubs and branches of organized labor" (1988, 160). That the FBI should be involved in such an investigation suggests that fantasmatic history is simply another version of American history writ in water. In repeating these stories, the "fabric of reality" tears open and something frightening that drives American society rears its head.[11]

The Member of the Wedding is set in the midst of this climate of rumor, resistance, and anxious reform. As we have seen, this novella provides ambiguously progressive roles for Berenice, the African American domestic worker (whose hybrid body replicates Roosevelt's own), and for Frankie (a young girl whose global ambitions and aspirations for public recognition—not to mention her name—replicate FDR's own), as well as a new space for investigating the problem of repetition—of the endless renegotiations of racist conventions that absorbed southerners in the thirties, forties, and civil rights decades. To explore these variegated issues, we need to investigate the metaphysical and political parameters associated with the "unhomeliness" of the American home.

There's No Place Like Home

Entranced since his boyhood by *The Wizard of Oz,* the novelist Salman Rushdie encounters a paradox in the film's finale. Remembering Dorothy's insistence that "there's no place like home, there's no place like home" as she clicks her Technicolor heels and zings back to the black-and-white world of Kansas, Rushdie suggests that the film's primary message, its sentimental knowledge that home is best (as if Kansas could compare to the razzle-dazzle of Oz), masks a nightmarish truth. For Dorothy, for Rushdie, home is a no-place—a site without safety or comfort—a place marked by migrancy and impossible longing.[12]

This nightmarish sense of home inheres even more violently in a cultural icon filmed the same year: the movie version of *Gone with the Wind.* This movie's most memorable moment (ignoring the scene where Rhett sweeps Scarlett up those Grand Guignol stairs) focuses on Scarlett's covenant with her dead father. Just before intermission, grabbing a fistful of dirt, Scarlet recalls her father's vow to cleave to the land. As the camera closes in, she expostulates: "I'll never be hungry again." The movie tugs at filial heartstrings; it plumbs the sentimental side of dirt—its gritty touch, its connection to the dead. But in the novel this scene does not tug at one's heartstrings; the novel's vision of Scarlett's plantation home is remarkably unsentimental:

> As from another world she remembered a conversation with her father about the land . . . when he said that the land was the one thing in the world worth fighting for.
>
> "For 'tis the only thing in the world that lasts . . . and to anyone with a drop of Irish blood in them the land they live on is like their mother. . . . 'Tis the only thing worth working for, fighting for, dying for."
>
> Yes, Tara was worth fighting for, and she accepted simply and without question the fight. No one was going to get Tara away from her. No one was going to set her and her people adrift on the charity of relatives. She would hold Tara, if she had to break the back of every person on it. (1973, 428)

Scarlett's fantasy points *Dirt and Desire* in at least two directions. First, it evokes the tragic history of dirt in the South, the way that dirt as property, as money-making machine, is mingled not only with desire but with blood. Second, these bodies point to the genesis of the southern grotesque within a particular locality—the back-breaking labor needed to establish the white southern home.

The special claustrophobia, the grotesque genesis of the white home in the segregated South, is also the focus of *Member of the Wedding,* published a decade after *Gone with the Wind.* More than any story we've examined, McCullers's novella is filled with grotesques, from Berenice's particolored eyes, to Frankie's gigantism, to John Henry's cross-dressing and his freakish desires to imitate the little pinhead girls in the circus or to consume doppelgänger biscuit men in which John Henry's own work is so thoroughly "cooked out" that even "the walking stick resembled a sort of tail" (8). Despite these saturnine details, *The Member of the Wedding* is a story very much tamed by its readers, touted as a tale for young adults about young adults—an economical way to learn about the pangs of growing up.

There are good reasons for this sentimental reputation. First, one finds scenes of real sweetness in McCullers's novella. Although Frankie's knife zings through the air and the kitchen wall heaves with children's drawings and the sighs of an ongoing world war (airplanes and "freak soldiers" mingling with Christmas trees and child-drawn flowers), although Frankie feels lonesome and afraid, she is also uplifted by the novel's nostalgia for the oddments of childhood. John Henry talks frankly about Frankie's smell; he finds her perfume-soaked body dizzying, odorous: "'I can smell you the minute you walk in the house without even looking to see if it is you. Like a hundred flowers.' 'I don't care,' she said. 'I just don't care.' 'Like a thousand flowers,' said John Henry, and still he was patting his sticky hand on the back of her neck" (11).

The child-entranced riffs of McCullers's prose seems both daring and saccharine:

> Already John Henry was asleep. She heard him breathe in the darkness, and now she had what she had wanted so many nights that summer; there was somebody sleeping in the bed with her. She lay in the dark and listened to him breathe, then after a while she raised herself on her elbow. He lay freckled and small in the moonlight, his chest white and naked, and one foot hanging from the edge of the bed. Carefully she put her hand on his stomach and moved closer; it felt as though a little clock was ticking inside him and he smelled of sweat and Sweet Serenade. He smelled like a sour little rose. Frankie leaned down and licked him behind the ear. Then she breathed deeply, settled herself with her chin on his sharp damp shoulder, and closed her eyes: for now, with somebody sleeping in the dark with her, she was not so much afraid. (13)

This passage wavers delicately between infantile and adult sexuality. At first, like any young animal, Frankie feels comforted to have someone else in her bed. And then the scene threatens to veer out of control. John Henry is small and vulnerable, his chest deliciously naked: her hand is on his stomach—where else will it roam? But instead of sexual experimentation, Frankie licks John Henry's ear and settles her chin "on his sharp damp shoulder." Even though the passage works through a principle of gender reversal (he is a sweet rose, she is libidinal; she is the aggressor-protector, he is the sleeping beauty), McCullers makes this reversal seem ordinary rather than transgressive. Passages like these, evoking Frankie's perfume or the pseudo-danger of an encounter in bed, have given this novella its reputation for nostalgia and poetry.

Examined closely, however, this work exceeds its putative source–the pimply sorrows of a young girl's trying adolescence. Frankie grows up surrounded by the static of World War II, the racial complexities of black disenfranchisement, and the fight for lost voting rights; McCullers's novella struggles against the trauma of living in the Jim Crow South—not only by exploring its black characters' experience of segregation but by enumerating the woefully unequal working conditions for black men and women in the 1940s South. McCullers also explores the violently abrogated desires that drove the Great Migration a decade earlier, and not just as a strong historical background that swirls through and troubles her text. Instead, *The Member of the Wedding* scrabbles toward the center of these problems, suggesting that such world-historical moments start in the kitchen and become even more momentous as they infect the everyday.

We have begun to excavate *The Member of the Wedding*'s weird sense of history, its queering of the southern child, its chill rendering of southern politics, its odd narrative strategies, in order to get a vision of the strange world McCullers is struggling to articulate. We sense this strangeness from the novel's beginning, with the rambling conversations that echo endlessly in Berenice's kitchen: "The three of them sat at the kitchen table, saying the same things over and over, so that by August the words began to rhyme with each other and sound strange. The world seemed to die each afternoon and nothing moved any longer. At last the summer was like a green sick dream, or like a silent crazy jungle under glass. And then, on the last Friday in August, all this was changed" (1). This sense of talking in a loop, of "saying the same things over and over," gives an accurate sense of quotidian conversation, of a world of slow southern small talk.[13] But this repetition also seems dangerous. These characters are stuck in a world that dies "each afternoon" until "nothing move[s] any longer." This feeling of being caught in a loop of senselessly scripted recitations needs to be read thematically and persistently, as one of southern literature's identifying features.

Faulkner captures this rhythm in "Dry September" when, in the space of three pages, a group of barely differentiated white men work themselves into paroxysms of aggression and worry as they make plans to lynch an innocent man: "Believe, hell! . . . Wont you take a white woman's word before a nigger's? . . . You don't? . . . Do you accuse a white woman of lying? . . . You're a fine white man. . . . To think that a white man in this town— . . . Do you mean to tell me you are a white man and you'll stand for it?. . . . You mean to tell me . . . that you'd take a nigger's word before a white woman's? Why you damn niggerloving—" (1950, 169–72). In southern literature, most of these repetitive loops involve race. Sometimes they are shared among texts, as in the obligatory moment when a white women sees a black person in an inappropriate place and seems to know immediately how and where to scream, an act taken to almost parodic extremes when Kate Chopin's Désirée realizes that her own baby is black, or when the strapping mother in Gilchrist's "President of the Louisiana Live Oak Society" sees a tiny black teenager wearing one of her fluffy new bath towels and falls apart. In the next chapter I will add to this sense of the repetitions that occur at points of racial transition by describing the literary habits surrounding southern objects—the obsessions about who gets to own them, what kinds of fantasies white people have about black people's hypothetical covetousness, and what kind of stories African Americans tell about acquiring their own objects within an economy of scarcity.

For the moment, however, I want to associate *Member of the Wedding* with another kind of loop—with a sense of what it means to be up against the automaton of the law—to be caught in racial practices that cycle over and over, as a form of endless, cruel social stutterance. In *The Land Where the Blues Began* Lomax describes a habitual exchange between himself and a local Mississippi sheriff in the 1940s, a man who threatens him with jail just for consorting with black musicians:

> "Now we come to something I can't really believe, now that you tell me that you were raised in the South. I heard you shook hands with a nigger! Is that so or not?"
>
> "Oh, no sir, you know I'd never do a thing like that," I assured him. Why, if my family were to hear of my doing that, I reckon they'd disown me."
>
> "And they'd be right, wouldn't they son? . . . You say we've got some talented niggers here in Tunica? . . . What're their names?"
>
> "Well, Mister Son House is the—" I knew I'd made a mistake before the words were out of my mouth. . . .
>
> "You call a nigger Mister," he snapped. "I don't believe you're from Texas at all. . . . You're a fake. You're probably an agitator. Maybe even a spy. And I'm gonna hold you till we can check with the FBI."

> A big steel jail door opened right off the sheriff's office. Cold, dank air crept in my shirt collar. (1993, 23)

Padgett Powell tells a similar story from his memories of Florida in the 1950s:

> Now take the photo of me, my mother, and a beagle named Gyp. . . . An interesting thing happens one day in this yard. There is no photo of it. That there is no photo tells more than if there were. This yard is cared for by a colored man, a term I will use for its historical accuracy. I recall him vaguely: Khaki pants, easy moves, keeping quiet. One day, upon some odd occasion that I got into a conversation with him, I did two things in the presence of my mother which represented the very cornerstones of the good manners my parents were insistent one display: I addressed the yardman as *Mister,* and I responded to him *Yes, sir.* These are two simple but powerful tools one can use even today with startling good results, and I am fond of using them when in the presence of elders who regard the world as one of irremediable decline, and I might even have been selfishly expecting some subtle profit to come from so addressing a yardman in 1957. But only moments after this exchange I was told by my mother that the *Mr.* and the *sir* were not correct. At this abrogation of absolutes I can honestly report being mystified: Why not? You just don't. (1987, 18)

I'm repeating these stories to re-create the sense of vertigo, of being caught in a historical stutterance that happens again and again—in Mississippi, in Florida, in Louisiana. If you're not feeling groggy or dizzy, you should be, for Ernest J. Gaines tells the same story, but from the other side of the racial divide, in *A Lesson Before Dying,* a novel set in Louisiana during late 1940s. An elderly black woman shows up at the house of her white employer to talk about her son, now in prison and under a death sentence.

> "I done done a lot for this family and this place, Mr. Henri. . . . All I'm asking you talk to the sheriff for me. . . ."
>
> "I can't promise anything," he said, and sipped his drink.
>
> "You can speak to your brother-in-law."
>
> "And say what?"
>
> "I want the teacher talk to my boy for me."
>
> He looked over her head at me, standing back by the door. I was too educated for Henri Pichot; he had no use for me at all anymore. But just as Miss Emma had given so much of herself to that family, so had my aunt. So Henri Pichot, who cared nothing in the world for me, tolerated me because of my aunt.

> "And what do you plan to do?" he asked me.
>
> I shook my head. "I have no idea." He stared at me, and I realized that I had not answered him in the proper manner. "Sir," I added. (1993, 21)

Repetition is characteristic of most cultural practices, but these crises over the appellation of "sir" or "mister" not only suggest a South stuck, across regions, in a repetitive loop; these texts also ask us to fathom the irrationality of these practices for those who do not feel their logic. The commands—of sheriff, mother, employer—are experienced as senseless, monotonous affairs, demanding obedience to traumatic laws that cannot be internalized. As a result, these laws seem uncanny, unheimlich, impossible. That is, the demands white culture makes are completely habitual and familiar, and yet, from the perspective of the traumatized, continue to seem impossible, unfamiliar—even in the moment that they are repeatedly reenacted. The experience of saying "sir" creates a patchwork of hallucination, a block of ongoing "acausality" in which someone rediscovers that an inescapable reality "has been absurdly given as such"—creating a moment when, as Carl Einstein has said of his own art, "the uninterrupted fabric of reality is torn, and one inhabits the tension of dualisms" (1929, 95).

How is this relevant to McCullers's novella? First, this sense of habitual strangeness is a predominant feature of *The Member of the Wedding*. From the beginning, every habit seems uncanny, every story, custom, ritual, or verbal act begins to sound peculiar, inexplicable, nonhabitual. "By August the words began to rhyme with each other and sound strange. The world seemed to die each afternoon and nothing moved any longer." This is a community that runs on loops of senselessly repeated injunctions. Frankie has to marry a little white beau; she feels the compulsion, when angry, to call Berenice "nigger"; she cannot go to the Freak Pavilion since "Mrs. Littlejohn said it was morbid to gaze at Freaks" (152). And yet these injunctions can only be experienced as staged schizophrenia. One cannot exit from the victor's speech, and yet, caught at its margins, such speech can only be felt as repetition or stutterance.

In addition, McCullers's novella is caught up in the question of "the Law," as the local police are described with a surrealist's eye: "At last she was staring at the Law and finally he looked into her eyes. He looked at her with eyes as china as a doll's, and in them there was only the reflection of her own lost face" (149). Is this meant to be uncanny or comic? Frankie's fascination with law enforcement often seems sophomoric, as in her overidentification with local inmates, as well as her fear that she will be put in jail for "braining" a sailor. But the law comes under scrutiny in two other ways. First, there is Frankie's middle-class sense of certainty, her absolute ease with authority. When she notifies the police to find her lost cat, Berenice chides her, "'I can't see how it is such a wise Idea to trifle around with the Law. No matter for what reason.' 'I'm not trifling with the Law.' 'You just now set there and spelled them out your name and your house number. Where they can lay hold of you if ever they take the notion'" (29–30).

Berenice is only half teasing. At the end of the novella her brother Honey is sentenced to eight years on the chain gang for a minor infraction. He "was out on the road now with a sentence of eight years" (149). His disappearance is linked to John Henry's death, for a similar hush comes over Berenice and Frankie when either name is mentioned. In the same moment that Honey gets locked away for breaking into the drugstore owned by the local white marijuana dealer, John Henry sickens and dies:

> He was locked in the jail, awaiting trial, and Berenice rushed back and forth, canvassing money, seeing a lawyer, and trying to get admission to the jail. She came in on the third day, worn out, and with the red curdled glare already in the eye. A headache, she said she had, and John Henry West put his head down on the table and said he had a headache, also. But nobody paid any mind to him, thinking he copied Berenice. "Run along," she said, "for I don't have the patience to fool with you." Those were the last words spoken to him in the kitchen, and later Berenice recalled them as judgment on her from the Lord. John Henry had meningitis and after ten days he was dead. (151–52)

The Member of the Wedding sets up a direct link between Honey's incarceration and John Henry's death to foreground a connection between the "consequential" death of a white boy and the senseless injunctions of racism—returning us to this text's interest in exposing the grotesque genesis of the southern white home, but also to its focus on hybridity, its unwillingness to separate the experiences of black and white characters, whose identities are so distinct that they necessarily overlap or impinge on each other.

Hybrid Bodies

For example, every character in this book breaches uncrossable boundaries. While Frankie crosses her society's unseen line of segregation with impunity and adopts the trappings of boyishness ("she wore a pair of blue black shorts, a B.V.D. undervest. . . . Her hair had been cut like a boy's,"

2), Berenice is more tortuously divided: "She was very black and broad-shouldered and short. She always said that she was thirty-five years old, but she had been saying that at least three years. Her hair was parted, plaited, and greased close to the skull, and she had a flat and quiet face. There was only one thing wrong about Berenice—her left eye was bright blue glass. It stared out fixed and wild from her quiet, colored face, and why she had wanted a blue eye nobody human would ever know. Her right eye was dark and sad" (3). McCullers has trouble making her black heroines desirable; her fiction is, to say the least, unevenly progressive. But what we're exploring now is another kind of progress in McCullers's text, her exploration of a society that refuses to acknowledge the strains created by segregation.

In search of a new identity, Frankie begins her journey by touring familiar white neighborhoods and then veering toward the center of town. But in keeping with this novella's take on "the Law," the center is tortuous: "the sun burned like an iron lid on her head and her slip was stuck wet to her chest and even the organdie dress was wet and clinging in spots" (58). This image of the white habitus as torture chamber echoes Richard Wright's and Alice Walker's descriptions of white people's homes. Frankie passes the "gray choked streets of the [white] section" with its "dust and sad gray rotten shacks" and then crosses the boundary dividing whites from blacks: "From the sad alleys and crooked streets of the mill section she crossed *the unseen line* dividing Sugarville from the white people's town. Here were the same two-room shacks and rotted privies, as in the mill section, but round thick chinaberry trees cast solid shade and often cool ferns grew in pots upon the porches. This was a part of town well known to her" (58, emphasis added). As with Eleanor Roosevelt's line-straddling, this passage opens in only one direction: Frankie can travel and dream but Honey cannot. Frankie identifies with Honey as someone who is bounded by his society and yet incomplete; his relatives describe him as a "half-boy" whom "God had not finished," someone who will never become a man in a culture fixated on heterosexuality and on black men as "boys" or "uncles." From her position of relative authority, Frankie tries to formulate a global solution for his woes:

> "I know what you ought to do. You ought to go to Cuba or Mexico. . . . You are so light-skinned and you even have a kind of Cuban expression. You could go there and change into a Cuban. You could learn to speak the foreign language and none of those Cubans would ever know you are a colored boy. Don't you see what I mean?"

> Honey was still as a dark statue, and as silent. . . . With a jerk [he] turned and went on down the lane. “It is fantastic.” (125)

For Honey’s wrongs and her private pain, Frankie’s answer is emigration. This story is set, after all, on the far side of the South’s Great Migration, a pattern of escape that also fills Frankie’s dreams of the North. She imagines her brother and his bride “going away . . . and as they traveled to the North, a coolness came into the air and dark was falling like the evening dark of wintertime” as they pass dainty chocolates wrapped in “pleated shells” (30).

Frankie’s identification with the paths African Americans forged on the Underground Railroad and during the Great Migration is of a piece with McCullers’s compulsion to create bodies that are half white and half black. Berenice’s mother, Big Mama “was an old colored woman, shriveled and with bones like broomsticks; on the left side of her face and neck the skin was the color of tallow, so that part of her face was almost white and the rest copper-colored. The old Frankie used to think that Big Mama was slowly turning to a white person, but Berenice had said it was a skin disease that sometimes happened to colored people” (119). McCullers and her characters share an incredible preoccupation with whether things can turn toward or into each other. Even the radio tunes into “a mixture of many stations: a war voice crossed with the gabble of an advertiser, and underneath there was the sleazy music of a sweet band. The radio had stayed on all the summer long, so finally it was a sound that as a rule they did not notice. . . . Music and voices came and went and crossed and twisted with each other, and by August they did not listen any more” (8). This passage suggests a growing inability to distinguish foreground from background; things, people, and ideas that have been oppressed begin moving outward and upward. In addition, McCullers registers the schizzy effect of these changes—an inability to differentiate between what is important and what is unimportant—a problem of strained epistemology, of a hybrid music so irritating that its mixed messages go unheard. As with the deaf heroine of *Can’t Quit You, Baby,* no one wants to encounter this chaos, to think fully about change. But the strength of McCullers’s novella is that it keeps re-creating, parading, needling the reader with transformation. “The geography book at school was out of date; the countries of the world had changed. Frankie read the war news in the paper, but there were so many foreign places, and the war was happening so fast, that sometimes she didn’t understand it” (21).

Last in this list of hybrids, John Henry is not only racially but sexually double. He looks like "a little old woman dwarf, wearing the pink hat with the plume, and the high-heel shoes" (117). This need to construct figures who are half black and half white, half female and half male, half old and half new, brings us back to Eleanor Roosevelt, to the question of public time, and the social forces that resist the blending of two races into "one body."

Public Time

In *Days of Hope* Sullivan explains that by the early 1940s "racial repression began to take on an overtly political cast. Shortly after Elbert Williams, a founder of the NAACP in Brownsville, Tennessee, launched a voter-registration campaign in 1940, he was lynched. That same year the Mississippi legislature enacted a law requiring that textbooks used in black schools exclude all references to voting, elections, civic responsibility, and democracy" (1996, 137). At the same time, a number of antisegregationist institutions were busy organizing to defeat the poll tax—a debate that came before the Congress in the Soldiers Vote Bill of 1942, a piece of legislation "which aimed to provide absentee ballots for federal elections to men and women serving in the armed forces. It was 'the most volatile measure dropped in the hopper since Pearl Harbor,' reported *The New York Times*" (6 September 1942, 7). The racial implications of this amendment were dazzling. The bill contained an amendment to suspend all poll-tax requirements for members of the armed forces for the rest of the war. Since the armed services employed almost four hundred thousand African American personnel from the South alone, huge numbers of blacks would suddenly gain new authority by acquiring equal access to the vote. While this patriotic bill passed with only minor demur, the South prepared itself for larger battles to come. As Virginia Durr's father wrote from Birmingham: "All white people in Alabama are buying pistols and other ammunition in preparation for the race war that is coming" (Sullivan 1996, 117). It is within this background of violence that Berenice holds Frankie in her arms and educates her—half-way—in the politics of race. "They were talking about whether to vote for C. P. MacDonald. And Jarvis said: 'Why, I wouldn't vote for that scoundrel if he was running to be the dog-catcher. I never heard anything so witty in my life.' Berenice did not laugh. Her dark eye glanced down in a corner, quickly saw the joke, and then looked back at Frankie" (30). This quip becomes one of the repetitive loops that dominate McCullers's novella:

> "I don't want to go back in that dark old ugly house all by myself."
>
> She stood on the sidewalk, looking at John Henry, and the smart political remark came back to her. She hooked her thumb in the pockets of her pants and asked: "If you were going to vote in an election, who would you vote for?"
>
> John Henry's voice was bright and high in the summer night. "I don't know," he said.
>
> "For instance, would you cast your vote for C. P. MacDonald to be mayor of this town?"
>
> John Henry did not answer. . . .
>
> So she had to remark without an argument behind her, and all by herself like that it did not sound so very smart: "Why, I wouldn't vote for him if he was running to be dog-catcher."
>
> The darkening town was very quiet. (38–39)

Something is clearly amiss. Berenice fails to laugh; Frankie searches for John Henry's laughter in the "darkening town." It is high time to move off the plateau that suggests that a southern book about children and domestic workers is more limited in its aesthetics or insights than, say, a book about race and incest.

How do we define political agency? David Held suggests that politics, as practical activity, is "the discourse and the struggle over the organization of human possibilities. As such, it is about power; that is to say, it is about the *capacity* of social agents . . . to maintain or transform their environment, social or physical. It is about the resources which underpin this capacity" (1989, 1). Berenice cannot vote, but she has a strong sense of her own ideology and of the ideological restraints imposed by others. The talks in the kitchen, those repetitive loops, often consist of utopian politics:

> They would sometimes begin to criticize the Creator. They would judge the work of God, and mention the ways how they would improve the world. And Holy Lord God John Henry's voice would rise up happy and high and strange, and his world was a mixture of delicious and freak. . . .
>
> But the world of the Holy Lord God Berenice Sadie Brown was a different world, and it was round and just and reasonable. First, there would be no separate colored people in the world, but all human beings would be light brown color with blue eyes and black hair. There would be no colored people and no white people to make the colored people feel cheap and sorry all through their lives. No colored people, but all human men and ladies and children as one loving family on the

> earth. And when Berenice spoke of this first principle her voice was a strong deep song that soared and sang in beautiful dark tones leaving an echo in the corners of the room that trembled for a long time until silence. (91)

If this seems too fancifully far from the legislative realm to be political, imagine that, although *politics* and *history* are words said with bated breath, in the South at this time brilliant men were engaged in doddering strategies of racial containment. Speaking not only about the cruelty of these gestures but about the imbecilic state of pre- and postwar southern politics, Walker Percy celebrates the fact that, in the 1980s, for the first time in 150 years, the South had not only become more progressive but shared so many racist traits with the rest of the nation that it was no longer on the defensive about race, either about "this peculiar institution or what followed it. . . . I don't think we realize how much Southern talent and Southern brains went to defending this. I remember growing up when the best brains in the Senate and the House from the South were devoted to defending against the anti-lynch bill. That to me is a poor way to spend your time and energy" (1984, 105).

With this intransigence in mind, might one describe even Berenice as a political theorist? As David Held suggests,

> The aim of political theory as the critique of ideology is to enlighten those to whom it is addressed about the political system in which they live and in so doing, to open up and elaborate alternative possible political worlds. . . . What distinguishes it as a theoretical enterprise is the attempt to elaborate and project a conception of politics based on a 'thought experiment'—an experiment into how people would interpret their needs and abilities, and which rules, laws, systems they would consider justified if they had access to a fuller account of their position in the political system. (1989, 5)

This is precisely the role Berenice plays in McCullers's novella. She encourages countless thought experiments and provides both Frankie and John Henry with a "fuller account" of the unequal positions that drive southern political systems. But in order to grow up to be free, white, and thirteen, Frankie must create an identity separate from this knowledge. For her, growing up means finding a way to fit in, to accommodate the social, to become part of this unequal culture. In addition to its riffs on hybridity, then, *The Member of the Wedding* tells the story of a little girl desperate to join "public time," to invent a set of workable tenets that might give her a coherent identity.

At first she tries to keep up with the transformations of World War II: "It was the year when Frankie thought about the world. And she did not see it as a round school globe, with the countries neat and different-colored. She thought of the world as huge and cracked and loose and turning a thousand miles an hour" (20). When the allied forces fail to win the war in two months, "she wanted to be a boy and go to the war as a marine" or to give blood. But she was afraid—not of the war or the soldiers, but "because the war did not include her, and because the world seemed somehow separate from herself" (20–21).[14] This sense of separation begins to displace (even as it grows out of) her anxiety about the segregated South of the 1940s.

Frankie's solution to her dilemma is both silly and eccentric. She decides to join her brother within the institutional framework of his wedding, since so many other routes to community are blocked. Marriage was among the few public institutions open to southern women;[15] Frankie imagines joining it with wonderful verve. She wants to marry both bride and groom and to be elevated into the elegant, icy coolness of the adult world:

> Sitting across from the soldier at that booth in the Blue Moon, she suddenly saw the three of them—herself, her brother, and the bride—walking beneath a cold Alaskan sky, along the sea where green ice waves lay frozen and folded on the shore; they climbed a sunny glacier shot through with pale cold colors and a rope tied the three of them together, and friends from another glacier called in Alaskan their J A names. She saw them next in Africa where, with a crowd of sheeted Arabs, they galloped on camels in the sandy wind. Burma was jungle-dark, and she had seen pictures in *Life* magazine. Because of the wedding, these distant lands, the world, seemed altogether possible and near: as close to Winter Hill as Winter Hill was to the town. It was the actual present, in fact, that seemed to F. Jasmine a little bit unreal. (66–67)

These notions are wonderfully foolish, and yet they also allow Frankie to create a surrealist's geography in which she acquires the virtues of public speaking and joins in a zany drive toward globalization that has already begun to heat up during this world war. What fascinates me most about Frankie's adventures, however, is how close they come—as parody and as desire—to the most conservative estimations of what civic individuals need, of what citizens strive to earn within the framework of public time.

The historian J. G. A. Pocock has argued that history ("in all but a few, rather esoteric, senses of the term") is always about "public time": it is "past politics," that is, "time [that has been] experienced by the individual as public being, conscious of a framework of public institutions in and through which events, processes and changes" happen (1985, 91). For Pocock, an appropriately historical sense of public being can only occur in the civic realm, in those crowded thoroughfares of society in which an individual feels a sense of participation or belonging. This public realm, unlike the social realm, "must be conceived as institutionalized and formalized, since otherwise the distinction between public and private cannot be maintained" (91). This realm, in turn, bestows the categories one uses to think about the private. "The institutionalization of the public realm leads to the institutionalization of social experience and modes of apprehending it" (71). From the exciting viewpoint of recent social history this seems rather tiresome: it presents a very limited way of looking at history through the lenses of those who are dominant, through the victors' frames. And yet I want to foreground this picture of how reality should work because it comes so close to Frankie's sense of reality: it is a replica of a twelve-year-old's portrait of how the world works.

For Frankie–F. Jasmine, joining her brother's marriage would mean recasting her chaotic private experience as an ordered and public affair, to be valued for her blood and yet to practice public forms of race-mixing. Thus, in a wry way that we should also take seriously, Frankie invents a new, communal landscape where everything is cool and iridescent, where chaos is frozen or "folded" and everything is in order; she invents a new public discourse (the chanting of the J A names) that connects people rather than severing them, and she goes international, her world neatly captured in the dangerous colors of *Life* magazine. "F. Jasmine," her new persona, longs for a new public self (or, in Pocock's terms, for a way of apprehending her self publicly). In her painful need to grow up she wants to be part of a community, to be represented to herself and for herself, as being-toward-the-world. She also seeks a way of apprehending time that will escape the cruelties of the present.

The problem is that, in the terms of the novella, the only community available for her is straight, white, and segregated. This means dispensing with or throwing away the only two people who really matter to her—John Henry, her queer little cousin, and Berenice. Let's return, then, to the question of surrealist history—and to what McCullers's fiction achieves on the huge stage of southern history. I've suggested that this book achieves a lucidity best summarized by the surrealists. McCullers's prose tries to "shake what is called reality by means of nonadapted hallucinations so as to alter the value hierarchies of the real" (Einstein 1929, 95). The meaning of the "value hierarchies of the real" seems clear, but what are "nonadapted hallucinations"? We gain a greater sense of this bizarre notion in the barbarity of John Henry's death—a death that seems both hallucinatory and sadistic.

When Frankie asks for him, "the words of Berenice became so terrible that she would listen in a spell of horror, but a part of her could not believe. John Henry had been screaming for three days and his eyeballs were walled up in a corner stuck and blind. He lay there finally with his head drawn back in a buckled way, and he had lost the strength to scream. He died the Tuesday after the Fair was gone, a golden morning of the most butterflies, the clearest sky" (152). In surrealist art, hallucination has the effect of breaking with the smooth machinations of culture and introducing "blocks of 'a-causality'"—alternatively speeding up and slowing down our access to realities that have been "absurdly given as such." This art introduces oscillations at the surface of things; the pattern of the real is torn. John Henry's death represents such a tearing. As Frankie plunges toward a more conventional identity, John Henry and Berenice are caught in these very blocks of a-causality where culture's absurdity becomes visible. Although his death seems unmotivated, uncalled for, and without cause, it is also acausally overdetermined.

Berenice is certain that John Henry's death from meningitis is linked to her neglect, but within the novel's logic a more primal cause is Honey's incarceration and Berenice's inability to claim the same forms of justice for him that operate for white culture. What these twin "deaths" reveal is a system of linkages invisible to the eye but utterly powerful, in which the lives of blacks and whites, women and men are so intertwined that any disturbance within one quadrant sets up a reaction in another. The novella's hallucinatory plot twists and its strange hybrid images suggest a political system driven by "radically different principles of classification and order"—a sublunary world of the scary and marvelous that neither "the Law" nor Frankie's father nor any God-fearing white citizen suspects.

I'm not arguing that the rigidities and proprieties of this small southern town are hallucinatory, but that these practices *create so many boundaries* that almost anyone can step out of their "right mind" into the condition of hallucination. In addition, these rigidities promulgate an inability to see how deeply people's lives are interconnected. White parents leave a child in a black woman's care. The white cop down the street and his schoolmate, the local D.A., put this woman's brother away under penal conditions so harsh that they are hardly believable. The white child gets sick. Meanwhile, the nightmare that African American citizens experience remains unperceived, or uncared-for, by these clean-faced white citizens. The child dies; his death was inevitable—it was meningitis. (A disease designated particularly for white southern boys who don't want to grow up to be white southern men?) But he is also killed by the avenging angels of a political unconscious that, in McCullers's novella, stays so close to the surface that you could stick out your tongue and lick it, like demon ice that's melted into thin air.

John Henry's death is also connected to Frankie's need to grow up. She gets a new name and new preoccupations; she does away with her earlier category confusion and gets beyond the need at every crisis to run to the refrigerator for spoonfuls of sweet condensed milk. But McCullers refuses to let this growth into a unified, coherent human being happen without revealing its cost. Frankie learns to sublimate her desire for John Henry's quirkiness within the ordinary high jinks of Mary *Littlejohn,* her new-minted friend. Kept from a long-lasting friendship with Berenice, Frankie moves to the white suburbs and is instructed to find a nice white beau her own age. Frankie's job as a southern grown-up is to take her proper place in a narrow identity quadrant—a grid dividing men from women and blacks from whites—with divisions so rigid that they separate people, absolutely, along the axes of gender and race. These invisible lines are present everywhere in McCullers' novella, and Frankie must learn *not* to cross them.

Still, John Henry reappears in her dreams. "He came to her once or twice in nightmare dreams, like an escaped child dummy from the window of a department store, the wax legs moving stiffly only at joints, and the wax face wizened and faintly painted, coming toward her until terror snatched her awake" (153). He is like a part of the soul or psyche tortured by the superstructure. Like the doll Lily Belle, like the cooked biscuit man, like the freaks who can't escape their place at the fair, John Henry is an emblem of humanity tortured into a form it cannot bear. Thus, while everything at the end seems tranquil as Frankie progresses toward marriage with that nice little white beau, John Henry's death is, of course, the book's emblem of that white boy and that marriage. His death reveals that everything is not tranquil but in a state of emergency; the South itself is in crisis, anxious about the end of the war and the advent of racial catastrophe, and its children are caught within a racial, homosocial ideology that demands terrible conformity to its norms. Through these final, uncanny images McCullers is protesting the safe, protected boundaries of northern and southern homes, boundaries that repress the sweet child voices, the wild serenades that leap forth when children discover that there's really no place like home.

Roosevelt's History

The Member of the Wedding tells two stories at once. First, McCullers give us the lush and painful tale of a little white girl's growing up—a story of self-naming, self-expansion, and self-censorship. But as wry counterpoint McCullers foregrounds the story of the environment the little girl must grow into—a world that ignores its own habits of oppression, that forgets that propriety is also the site of structural violence—that is, southern characters can only find their identities in a site where the self is deeply, irremediably violated. To grow up means to adopt these deformities, and although childhood represents, at least for McCullers's characters, the only site where one can resist the madness of the grown-up habitus, it is also a temporary, provisional site, a place marked by its own loss, by death and lamentation.

I've suggested that McCullers's version of surrealist history has three dimensions. First, it renders the familiar strange, so that events that had seemed obvious or matter-of-fact are suddenly causeless and incomprehensible. Second, it impales the reader with the force of the unexpected, creating a series of luminously irrational found objects and images that result in the precipitate of untoward desires. That is, it makes us want *this* history, not *that* one, the unofficial histories of children and chain gangs, not the official stories of legislatures and watchmakers. It opens windows, provokes a perturbation in the usual categories and an eruption of otherness where it's least wanted. Third, it provides an avenue for exploring the heterogeneity of the very systems that seem most homogeneous. "'Those butterflies,' he said. 'They are trying to get in'" (11). "Already the moths were at the window, flattening their wings against the screen" (117). This is a culture where only half the inhabitants are allowed to come in, but already the other half are hovering. By 1946 (*The Member of the Wedding*'s date of publication) African Americans are in the courts, on buses, in the streets, creating institutions that will support both present and future protest.

We need to examine a fourth dimension of McCullers's excursus into history, for, as Adorno suggests, the strongest art is not always conscious of its own historicity:

> It is the historical moment that is in the work of art constitutive: the most authentic works are those that give themselves over to their historical raw material without reservation and without any pretense to floating above it somewhere. Works of art are in this sense unconsciously the historiography of their own epoch; history is not the least form of knowledge they mediate. That is precisely why they are in-

> commensurable with historicism, which seeks to reduce them to a history external to them, rather than to pursue their genuine historical content. (261)

In making history monumental, what is lost is a sense of its unintelligibility in the flux of experience: its rawness, its presentness. Such writing is not about the act of reflecting history; instead, it is of it and in it.

In this sense Eleanor Roosevelt's body, which from the beginning of this chapter supported our understanding of *Member of the Wedding*'s obsessions, can now be surrounded by McCullers's own aesthetic act. What Roosevelt provides is a living example of collage that breaks down a conventional body into multiple parts, sending the South's political not-so-unconscious into overdrive, putting pieces of this culture together, publicly, in new ways. McCullers's compulsions to echo this hybridity help us name the historicity of Roosevelt's act, not as an "event" that explains other events and texts to come but as a hallucinatory form of self-splitting that had to be enacted again and again before it could move from testimony into law and finally into everyday praxis.

While chapter 5 sought lenses to magnify the presence of southern literature's mammoth women, in this chapter we have turned from archetype to chronotype, from giant women to the hollows of history. In order to transform the long-canonized misperception that women writers lack interest in the chronicled South, I have proposed several antidotes. First, we can unearth the historical records that women's texts embrace, recovering the hybrid bodies in *The Member of the Wedding* as well as the figures of the southern gargantua as literary symptoms for a series of large-scale historical movements sweeping the modern South. Thus when Flannery O'Connor invents a black giantess to bring down an inanimate white aristocracy in "Everything That Rises Must Converge" (1961) this character, who rides on a newly integrated bus carrying "a mammoth red pocketbook that bulged throughout as if it were stuffed with rocks" (415), enacts a violent politics opposing the nonviolent strategies of groups such as the Student Nonviolent Coordinating Committee (SNCC) in the early sixties.[16] That is, in order to challenge assertions about southern women's noncompliance with the grand issues of civic life, we could explore the ways in which their gargantuan figures are always historically grounded. We would see that the white gargantuas of the 1930s not only challenged the ideal of the diminutive southern lady but reshaped an era in which the ASWPL sought to overturn entrenched southern visions of white female fragility in order to dissociate this imagined fragility from the need for the retaliatory violence of lynching (Hall 1993, 194). In contrast, the black gargantuas of the 1930s could be said to emerge from a decade in which black women first began to encounter—in the promise of Roosevelt's New Deal—new public support for resisting injustice.

True enough. But for the purposes of this study it seems more useful to continue to challenge the stereotypical terrain of southern studies by exploring southern women's reluctance to write either monumental or empirical histories. In casting Eleanor Roosevelt as an artist of the surreal and McCullers's novella as a history-making continuation of her hybridity, my goal is to supplant C. Vann Woodward's reading of southern history as epic or tragedy with the revisionary histories of black and white southern women who deploy an archive of surrealist, subsemantic, and everyday histories to refigure the public sphere.

In this chapter I have argued that historicism is always more complicated. These writers also deploy the minutiae of social history in intricate ways, inventing surrealist techniques to unearth what is most forgotten about daily life, especially the peculiarity of the quotidian. As de Certeau suggests, "the everyday has a certain strangeness that does not surface, or whose surface is only its upper limit" (1984, 93). We have seen multiple examples of this strangeness in McCullers's novella. It surfaces again in *Delta Wedding* in the kitchen scene where Roxie, a black domestic, and Ellen, her white employer, seem utterly at home with one another, baking and talking, until

> finally, people began to come out in the halls or downstairs dressed. "Orrin! You look like a man!" cried Ellen. "Oh, the idea!"
>
> "Mr. Ranny growin' up too, in case nobody know it," said Roxie. "Miss Ellen, did you know? That little booger every mornin' befo' six o'clock holler out de window fo' me. 'Roxie! I need my coffee!' and make me come right up."
>
> "The idea!" said Ellen. (274)

As inflected by Welty, Ellen's exclamation is blithely ironic. "The idea! . . . The idea!" she continues to gabble, even as she refuses to have any idea at all about how oppressive Roxie's working conditions are. Given this deliberate ignorance of the costs of servitude, Ellen's lack of anxiety about the system of labor driving her family's plantation system may be expected, but Welty's ironic frame defamiliarizes this thoughtlessness, making it visible, unfamiliar, remarkable. Her portrait of a modern plantation's dependence on invisible labor offers a trenchant example of the unthought known. Roxie's services are taken for granted; the objects in this world (like the people who own them) are ceaseless in their cries for maintenance—they are, as Marx suggests, roused "from their death sleep" only when they are "bathed in the fire" of African American labor (1977, 459). The presence of this labor is longed for, even cherished, but the *people* performing this labor receive neither adequate compensation nor acknowledgment.

I am suggesting that southern women's writing pulses with history's atmosphere as well as with its facticity. As Jules Prown comments in "The Truth of Material Culture," "History can never completely retrieve the past with all its rich complexity, not only of events, but of emotions and sensations and spirit. We retrieve only the facts of what transpired; we can not retrieve the feel, the affective totality of what it was like to be alive in the past" (1993, 6). In the next chapter we will turn to the objects that give this "affective totality" its ballast.

Chapter Seven

White Objects, Black Ownership: Object Politics in Southern Fiction

In *Dirt and Desire* I have set about reorganizing a series of categories for analyzing southern women's fiction—tracing an uneasy journey that includes works by black and white writers. We see how uneven the parameters of this journey can be in a conversation between Alice Walker and Eudora Welty that took place in 1973. Recounting this conversation, Walker describes her deep sympathy with Welty but also explains that, as writers, she and Welty are worlds apart in their consciousness of race, the politics of writing, and feminism:

> *AW:* Over the years have you known any black women? Really known them?
>
> *EW:* I think I have. Better in Jackson than anywhere, though only as you'd expect, within the framework of the home. That's the only way I'd have had a chance, in Jackson up until now. Which doesn't take away from the reality of the knowledge, or its depth of affection. (Walker 1984, 136–37)

Although Welty describes an ongoing relationship with the black woman who nursed her mother through her last illness, as well as a young woman who was her maid for a decade and has gone on to invent a powerful professional life, it is impossible not to hear in these limited friendships the echoes of Flannery O'Connor saying, albeit from the still crueler world of the 1950s, "No I can't see James Baldwin in Georgia. It would cause the greatest trouble and disturbance and disunion. In New York it would be nice to meet him; here it would not" (O'Connor 1979b, 329), or the narrator of Ellen Douglas's *Can't Quit You, Baby* insisting that there would be no getting around the fact that her black and white characters know each other only because the white woman is the black woman's employer. "There would have been no way in that time and place . . . for them to get acquainted, except across the kitchen table from each other, shelling peas, peeling apples, polishing silver" (1988, 4–5). Douglas adds that the only other venue for friendship would have been through participation in local politics—and that such friendships were dangerous and rare.

Walker redoubles our sense of the distance between southern white women and women of color:

> When we face each other, talking at first in starts, I think how odd it is that I feel entirely relaxed, entirely comfortable. Considering how different we are—in age, color, in the directions we have had to take in this life, I wonder if my relaxation means something terrible. For this is Mississippi, U.S.A., and black, white, old, young, Southern black and Southern white—all these labels have meaning for a very good reason: they have effectively kept us apart, sometimes brutally. So that, although we live in the same town, we inhabit different worlds. This interview itself is an accidental meeting. Though we are both writers, writing in some cases from similar experiences, and certainly from the same territory, we are more strangers, because the past will always separate us, and because she is white and not young, and I am black and not old. Still, I am undaunted, unafraid of discovering whatever I can.
>
> She is modest, shy, quiet, and strong as the oak tree out in the yard. Life has made a face for her that concentrates a beauty in her eyes. They light with directness, and will not be moved downward or to the side. (131–32)

Despite Walker's clear-sightedness about Welty's falcon eye, she raises a crucial question. Is it possible to consider both black women who write about the South and southern white women under the rubric of "southern writers"? What does it mean to write from the same gender and territory but from different races?[1]

From the perspective of Tucker's *Telling Memories Among Southern Women,* a book that describes the relationships between black domestic servants and white employers in the segregated South, the differences seem vast and insurmountable. In the early decades of the twentieth century a majority of black women labored in white homes, their children's lives punctured by absence.[2] Many white women enjoyed—and took for granted—black women's assistance in cleaning, cooking, and raising their children. This created a series of "mercenary" extended families, "kinlike" affiliations that were not created by miscegenation or bonds of blood, but by the white purchase of acts of maternal surrogacy, by the appropriation of maternal labor. These extended nonkin groups, semisurrogate families that operated outside the constraints and freedoms shared by blood kin, created relations of unmitigated complexity. In a conversation about the role of black domestic workers in the South, a white woman named Ellen Owens explains her diffident attachment to her black caregiver's daughter, starting with their strained interactions at "Mama Lou's" funeral: "I remember Amelia—her daughter who I had known when I was little—Amelia was standing by the grave. And they had lowered the coffin, and she was just . . . sobbing. Her older sister . . . Adele said, 'Come on, Amelia, we've got to go.' And Amelia wouldn't leave. That stands out in my mind—that she just stayed there and sobbed. I was standing a little behind her, and I didn't know how to help" (Tucker 1988, 140). These two grown children bear a complex relation to each other and to the woman who parented them so differently. As Owens insists:

> She was always like my mother. That's why I called her Mama Lou. . . . She came every day but Thursday. She came at seven in the morning and left sometimes as late as nine or ten. She was always with us. And even when we'd go on vacation . . . for like a month at a time . . . she always went with us—everywhere. And so she was really a member of the family. . . .
>
> No, I don't remember her missing her girls or sending postcards to them or anything on these trips. I guess they stayed with their daddy, and maybe Adele, the older one, watched out for Amelia. I don't remember that it was ever discussed.
>
> I couldn't be without her! And many, many a Thursday, I'd go over to her house. You know, since I didn't want to be away from her, I'd go spend the day over there and be part of their family. (140)

If Mama Lou becomes Owens's second mother, what is Owens's relation to Mama Lou's daughters?

> I wasn't the nicest child in the world. We were friends, but I probably had the upper hand, knowing she was my maid's daughter. . . . No one stopped me or heard me, I guess. We never talked about race in my family—never. We never talked about me having more than

> Amelia, either, materially. The one thing I can remember, even remotely related to the topic was that Lou was our housekeeper—she wasn't our "maid," according to my mother. So I always worry, still, if the word *maid* has bad connotations. (141)

There is a great deal to condemn in this history. Owens claims a mother but not a sister. She worries about the proper word to use but uses it anyway to distance herself from Amelia. She thinks about her own difficult behavior as a child but not about the conditions of her surrogate mother's employment. She repeats the unending stories of white southern silence, of the deliberate noncirculation of words and ideas about race in homes that depended on underpaid African American labor.

The moral seems clear enough. This is a story about inequality and exploitation: about a black mother who is forced by her mode of employment to leave her children not just during the day but for lengthy "vacations," who does not receive the privilege of a day off, since the white child she cares for haunts even her home. This is a story about a white girl who "couldn't be without her" but never considers the needs of Mama Lou's own children: their names are omens that cloud neither her speech nor her future.

Although this moral seems clear, it should not distract us from another crucial pattern: the problem of living in a world of merged or crossover objects, of working out relations among people and things that are shared, appropriated, or partitioned across racial lines—but within radically different semiotic and emotional systems. Missing this, we miss a great deal that brings writings by black and white women together—and sets them apart.[3]

For the moment, I want to move from the charged world where children pass back and forth among women (with its overtones of owning other people—"She was always like my mother . . . I couldn't be without her") to what would *seem* to be a less tempestuous, psychologically distorted domain—that of crossover objects, of a world of unevenly shared things. We find a curious example of these crossover objects in a story about sea grass baskets made in the South Carolina low country. Coiled baskets for winnowing rice have been produced up and down the Carolina coast for more than two centuries, using techniques for basketry and rice harvesting imported from Africa. Louise White, a devoted basket sewer, "explained that while she was keeping house for a certain family she would examine a set of sweetgrass placemats her mother had made many years before. If she found a place that needed repair she would 'carry a palm from home in my pocketbook' and mend the break, 'just to see how long Mama's basket will be there'" (Rosegarten 1987, n.p.). White not only expresses a family pride in objects beautifully made but responds to the desire to preserve these objects over time, even in white peoples' homes (or perhaps especially in white homes, where they were liable to meet with the ancestral fate of becoming throwaways). These objects possess very different meanings for the white family who owns them and the black women who care for them, but I'm suggesting that this shared history also creates a bizarre space of mediation that needs to be explored.

For example, in *Sapphira and the Slave Girl* Willa Cather describes the bare, grassless yards that graced African American dwellings (the clean-swept yard was a another custom carried from Africa): "The 'back yard' was hard-beaten clay earth, yellow in the sun, orderly only on Sundays . . . the ground . . . was littered with old brooms, spades and hoes, and the rag dolls and home-made toy wagons of the negro children. Except in a downpour of rain, the children were always playing there, in company with kittens, puppies, chickens, ducks that waddle up from the millpond, turkey gobblers which terrorized the little darkies and sometimes bit their naked black legs" (1968, 21–22). This is a landscape of pleasure that the white narrator views with displeasure; for her it seems filled with part-objects and punitive objects. The room presided over by Till, the African American woman who is the source of the white narrator's stories, is also brimming with discards. Her chest contains her dead master's old books, "the woolly green shawl he had worn as an overcoat, some of Miss Sapphy's lace caps and fichus, and odd bits of finery such as velvet slippers with buckles. Her chief treasure was a brooch, set in pale gold, and under the crystal was a lock of Mr. Henry's black hair and Miss Sapphy's brown hair, at the time of their marriage. . . . The miller himself had given it to her, she said" (291–93). By adding the emphatic "she said," the grown-up narrator (a fictionalized version of Cather herself) adds undertones of suspicion: Did Till take the brooch, or was it given to her? The text raises this question of petty larceny but never explores it. What stops this white narrator from recognizing the complex transmission of these objects across cultures? Why is she unable to see value in the Africanist features in either these laborers' yards or their homes? The only objects she recognizes as useful are those that have been owned by white folks; it is her fantasy that African Americans center their lives around these valued things. As we will see, this is a recurrent fantasy in white women's depictions of black populations in the South. With one or two exceptions, these writers have difficulty seeing any object relations that are not mediated by whiteness.[4]

Writing thirty years later with more knowledge and considerably more respect, Alice Walker describes the traditional swept yard with delight in "Everyday Use": "I will wait for her in the yard that Maggie and I made so clean and wavy yesterday afternoon. A yard like this is more comfortable than most people know. It is not just a yard. It is like an extended living room. When the hard clay is swept clean as a floor and the fine sand around the edges lined with tiny, irregular grooves, anyone can come and sit and look up into the elm tree and wait for the breezes that never come inside the house" (1991, 520). While Cather imagines the migration of objects from big house to yard, Walker imagines migration in the opposite direction; she sees African-inspired artifacts—hand-stitched quilts—going from country to city, where quilt-making has suddenly been revalued as a rare form of folk culture. The story's suspense revolves around a mother's decision about whether to give her quilts to the daughter who covets them as art or the daughter who intends to use them.

Again, the moral weight of the comparisons between Walker and Cather seems painfully obvious.[5] But the surprise (and the very thing I want to stress) is not so much the different microcosms these women writers inhabit *but that so much drama revolves around things in southern literature*—who owns them and what this ownership means. Why does this drama remain so important, not only post-emancipation, but deep into the twentieth century?

The prospect of writing a chapter focused on the objects hovering in the background of southern literature seems daunting, especially in the shadow of discursive theory—Foucault's demands in *The Archaeology of Knowledge* (1972) that we turn our eyes away from the dazzle of objects to a world apportioned by language, where things take on a strange and nonglittery appearance.

> What . . . we wish to do is to dispense with "things." To "depresentify" them. To conjure up their rich, heavy, immediate plenitude, which we usually regard as the primitive law of a discourse that has become divorced from it through error, oblivion, illusion, ignorance, or the inertia of beliefs and traditions, or even the perhaps unconscious desire not to see and not to speak. To substitute for the enigmatic treasure of "things" anterior to discourse, the regular formation of objects that emerge only in discourse. (47)

Foucault has helped initiate an academic practice in which it *is* crucial to see past things, to dissolve a world of "thereness" and historical inertia in order to look at the formative powers of discourse: linguistic habits "that systematically form the objects of which they speak" (49). This loosening of word from referent has been fundamental. How else to make sense of the following scene from *Dessa Rose,* where two women battle over the meaning of *mammy?*

> The white woman gaped, like a fish, Dessa thought contemptuously, just like a fish out of water. Anybody could make this white woman's wits go gathering.
>
> "My, my—*My* Mammy—" the white woman sputtered.
>
> . . . "Your 'mammy'!" No *white* girl could ever have taken *her* place in mammy's bosom; no one. "You ain't got no 'mammy,'" she snapped. . . . "You don't even know 'mammy's' name. Mammy have a name, have children."
>
> "She didn't." The white woman, finger stabbing toward her own heart, finally rose. "She just had me! I was like her child."
>
> "What was her name then?" Dessa taunted. "Child don't even know its own mammy's name. What was mammy's name? What—"
>
> "Mammy," the white woman yelled. "That was her name."
>
> "Her name was Rose," Dessa shouted back. (1986,124–25)

Sherley Anne Williams dramatizes the confusion of a white woman who was raised by a slave and now nurses a black woman's baby because the black woman's milk has dried up. Dessa's thighs are covered with scars; she has lost her mother and husband and been brutalized in slavery, and she finds it unbearable listening to the white woman simper on and on about her "Mammy"—even though this woman acts as wet nurse to Dessa's own infant. In fact, Dessa and the white woman happen to be talking about two different women (Dessa's biological mother, Rose, from whom she's been sold away, and the white woman's caretaker, Dorcas), but the real point of this bitter exchange is that, although blacks and whites share objects in southern culture, they do so from the perspective of radically different semioses.

This difference stretches from South to North in Rita Dove's *Thomas and Beulah* in a poem describing Beulah's job in a white-owned dress shop in Ohio. As Beulah "irons alterations / in the backroom of Charlotte's Dress Shoppe," the air fills with white women's odors, the iron awakening "perspiration / and stale Evening of Paris." Dove's language captures the different worlds that gather around these objects when she contrasts the pretentiousness of the white "Shoppe" with Beulah's angry "*Swamp she born from, swamp / she swallow, swamp she got to sink again.*" She limns the different ways that Beulah and these white girls think about whites' clothing: "Beyond / the curtain, the white girls are all / wearing shoulder pads to make their faces / delicate. That laugh would be Autumn, / tossing her hair in imitation of Bacall" (1986, 63). Beulah, in contrast, has commandeered red silk from the shop to line her dress. This pilfered object saved "against all rules" from a "botched coat" creates a stir; when she lifts a knee, "she flashes crimson." Again, the poem focuses on an object that travels, defining the connections and borders between cultures.

Dove gives us three things to consider. First, she foregrounds the extent to which black and white worlds interpenetrate within an economy of black servitude, so that a single set of objects shares two different interpretive fields. Second, she describes the intimacies of appropriation as Beulah identifies—briefly—with Autumn:

> A hanger clatters in the front of the shoppe.
> Beulah remembers how
> even Autumn could lean into a settee
> with her ankles crossed, sighing
> *I need a man who'll protect me*
> while smoking her cigarette down to the very end.

Third, Dove describes the ways in which an object owned by one culture can—phenomenologically—be split in two. But in parsing these "discursive" intricacies, what do we miss? What happens to the weight of the iron, the odor and texture of the object's resistance? "The iron shoves gently / into a gusset, waits until / the puckers bloom away."

Contrary to Foucault, I will argue that we still must struggle to intuit the "treasure of 'things' anterior to discourse," for by focusing on things only as language we may miss the rich, heavy plenitude of objects that have had to be *lifted* by African Americans. "Dabney and India loaded him up" (47), Welty says, describing Little Matthew's fate in *Delta Wedding,* as his play is interrupted by a flurry of arriving guests. When Battle, the father of the bride, roars down the hallway, he is "followed by four Negroes, all of them carrying big boxes. 'Here's Dabney's doin's,' he said. 'All creations coming out of Memphis. What must I do with it, throw it out the back door?'" (126). Is this weight a discursive formation? George "was alone now—except, that is, for Vi'let, leaning from a stepladder with one knee on a bookcase, very slowly taking down the velvet curtains" (71). Why is Vi'let's body off kilter, if not with the very heft and value of *things* dispensing her body's activities? Not to mention the wedding cake, that "tall white thing, shining before God in the light of day. It was a real fantasy! Only God knew if it was digestible" (263). This fantasmatic whiteness is neither nourishing nor especially edible, but still it requires someone's labor. "'You watch that cake, Howard! Do you know what'll happen to you if you drop that?' 'Yes ma'am. *Dis* cake not goin' drop—no'm.' 'That's what you *say.* You have to *carry* it straight up, too'" (264). And what about the rich, heavy plenitude of the cargo carried by roustabouts in "The Little Convent Girl"?

> And the roustabout throwing the rope from the perilous end of the dangling gang-plank! And the dangling roustabouts hanging like drops of water from it—dropping sometimes twenty feet to the land, and not infrequently into the river itself. And then what a rolling of barrels, and shouldering of sacks, and singing of Jim Crow songs, and pacing of Jim Crow steps; and black skins glistening through torn shirts, and white teeth gleaming through red lips, and laughing, and talking and—bewildering! entrancing! Surely the little convent girl in her convent walls never dreamed of so much unpunished noise and movement in the world! (King 1995, 172)

Lomax describes the particular rolling pace of these cargo handlers—not only their singing but the style of movement imported from Africa that permitted the massive transfer of heavy goods from land to water and back again. Oddly, these men become "drops of water" at the very moment King's story invites us, for the first and last time, into the mind of this very staid child—"bewildering! entrancing!" she seems to say, as if the little convent girl identifies not only with the music but with this lifting of objects, this constant carrying of white men's burdens. In a world where African Americans are so responsible for the fate of these objects—for "their rich, heavy, immediate plenitude"—but not allowed to possess this plenitude, how do we dismiss things and look only to their discursive formations?

White Objects

What were slaves allowed to own? Very little, Elizabeth Fox-Genovese tells us in her book on black and white women in the Old South. "Slaves normally received their basic support in kind: rations, clothing, lodging. . . . Most slaveholders were likely to buy shoes and some clothing for their slaves, although many bought cloth and made clothing from it, and some even produced cloth. . . . But all goods belonged to the master" (1988, 95).

Although most slaves retained limited power of possession, most of the goods in the plantation household passed through African American hands.[6] The tools for production, crops harvested, household objects cleaned, polished, and mended suggest an extraordinarily intimate relation to the implements that made up the antebellum southern world. This intimacy must have been experienced as contradiction; since supplies were purchased in bulk on most plantations, the sheer mass of these objects "required the constant assistance of slaves," and yet, for white masters, "the presence of slaves required that the supplies be kept under lock and key" (119).

Privation, surveillance: under these standards the New World plantation was, at best, a site of limited plenty in which a white mistress's access to larder or smokehouse and her intermittent distribution of supplies underscored enslaved Africans' participation in an economy of scarcity in which the goods needed for comfort and sustenance were often present but secreted away.[7]

Morrison dramatizes this economy of dearth in *Beloved,* when Sethe responds to Beloved's beseeching "Tell me, . . . tell me your diamonds" (1987, 58). This luminous request cries out for translation: "Tell me your valuable stories which will also become my treasures," Beloved seems to say. But to make "diamonds" into such a translatable metaphor doesn't get at the thing's weight, its shining. This is also a request, plain and simple, to talk about things: "Tell me about the treasures you did and did not get to possess; tell me why you did not wear those earrings until you were free; tell me how you survived in the miserly economy of Sweet Home."

The objects that obsess Sethe most from her early life are those needed for her wedding to Halle. "I never saw a wedding, but I saw Mrs. Garner's wedding gown in the press, and heard her go on about what it was like. Two pounds of currants in the cake, she said, and four whole sheep." The numerate weight of these things creates hunger for the objects that make life good and possible, that have allowed Mrs. Garner to "go on": "But it wasn't going to be nothing. They said it was all right for us to be husband and wife and that was it. All of it" (58–59). This "all" as "nothing" becomes something when Sethe collects—cautiously, surreptitiously—the picked-over items she turns into a dress:

> Well, I made up my mind to have at the least a dress that wasn't the sacking I worked in. So I took to stealing fabric, and wound up with a dress you wouldn't believe. The top was from two pillow cases in her mending basket. The front of the skirt was a dresser scarf a candle fell

> on and burnt a hole in, and one of her old sashes we used to test the flatiron on. Now the back was a problem for the longest time. Seem like I couldn't find a thing that wouldn't be missed right away. Because I had to take it apart afterwards and put all the pieces back where they were. (59)

The sting of this passage resides in the fact that these things are waste, detritus, leftovers—soiled by someone else's desire. But these leftovers are also testimony to Sethe's wonderful bricolage, to the fact that she manages to wear anything other than slave cloth or osnabriggs to her wedding: putting together something from whole cloth, wresting meaning from meaninglessness. But even this proud act is braced with pain; Sethe has to put everything back when she's done. Her lack of ownership in things is parallel to her lack of ownership in self.

What I want to emphasize in this moving story is not only the economy of scarcity but the velocity with which things move back and forth between cultures, and the radically different meanings objects acquire in each context. These traveling objects are a continuous, overlooked theme in literature about the South—a preoccupation shared by southern blacks and whites alike. Even the advertisements for runaway slaves contain an obsessive cataloguing of the items of clothing the slaves are wearing, as well as the objects they are thought to have stolen.[8]

This velocity—the availability of things for translation across cultures—is equally important in black writers' stories about African American time, money, or labor that has been stolen by whites. In *Incidents in the Life of a Slave Girl* Linda Brent's grandmother is granted a degree of freedom only at night, "after all the household work was done." She is allowed to bake crackers to buy her freedom—provided she also uses the profits to clothe herself and her children. After years of baking, her small stock of wealth is countermanded, given in loan to a mistress, who promises "to repay her soon." Brent explains that this loan was never repaid and that the objects bought with this loan, including a silver candlestick, stayed in the white household after the mistress's death. "The reader probably knows that no promise or writing given to a slave is legally binding; for, according to Southern laws, a slave, *being* property, can *hold* no property" (Jacobs 1973, 4). We've come full circle, to the world Fox-Genovese outlines and one of its central traumas. To be property, not to have property, in a world increasingly defined according to Lockean principles of self-definition through property, creates both identity trauma and a site of incredible animus between white and black culture.

This story of racialized property relations is repeated again and again in southern literature. It functions most glaringly in literature from or about the antebellum South. Linda Brent explains that, in her early life in a comfortable home, "I was so fondly shielded that I never dreamed I was a piece of merchandise" (4). To describe the horror of her grandmother's five children being sold, Brent uses the language of things: "These God-breathing machines are no more, in the sight of their masters, than the cotton they plant, or the horses they tend" (6). She deepens this outrage by describing her own inability, at her father's death, to go to his house for the laying out. Instead, "I was ordered to go for flowers, that my mistress's house might be decorated for an evening party." (8). Spending the day making garlands to decorate her mistress's house "while the dead body of my father was lying within a mile of me" was extraordinarily painful. "What cared my owners for that? He was a mere piece of property" (8).

To focus on the relations among persons, races, and objects suggests an important, overlooked category for reading southern literature. But this is also a complex category to rethink. So far, this has been a book about *subjects*—easy enough to theorize given the critical arsenals for describing selfhood and subjectivity at our fingertips. But I'd like to give an example of why we need to think about things by noting how quickly the story of traumatized subjectivity can flip, in southern literature, from a drama about subjects to a drama about things. In Charles Chesnutt's "Po' Sandy," a tale from *The Conjure Woman,* Sandy is a hard-working slave who has to work even harder because he is so popular among his master's friends. "I wisht I wuz a tree, er a stump, er a rock, er sump'n w'at could stay on de plantation fer a w'ile," Sandy says. His wife Tenie is a conjure woman who obligingly turns him into a tree, but his body still bears the marks of local ordinances. A woodpecker pecks at his branches, so that when Sandy returns to his human form to talk to Tenie, "he had a little roun' hole in his arm, des lack a sharp stick be'n stuck in it" (1969, 49). Clearly, Chesnutt changes Sandy from subject to object and back again to express Sandy's ambiguous status in the southern world he inhabits. We witness a continuing litany of assaults on his objectified body. Turpentine pours out of his bark for the master's profit, creating another set of scars. So, Sandy and Tenie decide to turn into foxes and run away, but on the eve of this transformation, Tenie visits the woods and finds the stump of Sandy's body moldering in the woods. His trunk has been cut down to provide lumber for the master's new kitchen:

> W'en she seed de stump standin' dere, wid de sap runnin' out'n it, en de limbs layin' scattered roun', she nigh 'bout went out'n her min'. She run ter her cabin, en got her goopher mixtry, en den follered de tracker er de timber waggin ter de sawmill. She knowed Sandy could n' lib mo' d'n a minute er so ef she turnt him back, fer he wuz all chop' up so he'd 'a' be'n bleedst ter die. But she wanted ter turn 'im back long ernuff fer ter 'splain ter 'im dat she had n' went off a-purpose, en lef' 'im ter be chop' down en sawed up. She did n' want Sandy ter die wid no hard feelin's to'ds her. (54)

Sandy's object status seems inescapable. As we have seen, split subjects litter the southern fiction of this period; we find bodies that have been broken open or put upon by the law, people who discover African American ascendants and disappear, with Désirée or the little convent girl, into water or earth. In "Po' Sandy" we also encounter a body that becomes an environment, as well as the tormented features of the southern grotesque. Sandy experiences a mode of self-shattering far more traumatic than bourgeois neurotics dream about in their philosophies.

But Chesnutt's story takes a curious trajectory when this splintered *subject* turns into a split or splintered *object*. All at once the environment starts to talk back. Sandy's boards are fashioned into a kitchen whose constant moaning and groaning demands its abandonment. Although Sandy's desire for self-ownership leads to a deadly objectification, he also becomes an object too frightening to possess, and eventually this kitchen migrates back to the black community. The African American narrator of Sandy's story wants to use the old kitchen for a church, and he tells this ghost story to the property's new owners for the express purpose of making this object travel once again. That is, Chesnutt creates a crossover object that crosses back.

This story has an additional historical edge, for Julie Saville's book on Reconstruction in South Carolina suggests greater hardships for blacks after emancipation than before. For all the restrictions Fox-Genovese describes, slaves at least enjoyed limited rights of usage: *not property in, but access to* a portion of their master's things. Post-Reconstruction, African Americans knew hypothetical freedom but were subject to even severer restrictions. So, although postbellum literature does not struggle with a contemporary history of self as property, after emancipation blacks faced an even more object-poor economy: a diminished relation to both territory and things.[9]

This diminished relation continued well into the twentieth century. At the beginning of Elizabeth Spenser's "First Dark," Frances Harvey describes her childhood memories of the ghost stories that fascinated both her white relations and her family's black servants:

> "We'd lie all night like two sticks in bed, and shiver. Papa finally had to take a hand. He called us in and sat us down and said that the whole thing was easy to explain—it was all automobiles. What their headlights did with the dust and shadows out on the Jackson road. 'Oh, but Sammie and Jerry!'" we said with our great big eyes . . .
>
> "Who were Sammie and Jerry?" asked Tom Beavers.
>
> "Sammie was our cook. Jerry was her son, or husband, or something. Anyway, they certainly didn't have cars." (1991, 355–56)

The ghosts thought to be the effect of headlights seem, by the end of the story, to be the effect of the gap between those who own headlights and those who do not. One of the ghosts, a light-skinned black man, appears twice to ask white people who are blocking the road to move their bulldozers or cars out of his way so he can take a sick girl to town in his wagon. After he appears to Frances Harvey, she is convinced of his reality: "reading late in bed . . . I thought, I could have given her a ride into town. No wonder they talk about us up North! A mile into town in a wagon! She might have been having a baby" (366). By the end of the story, Frances Harvey gets possession of herself—and a desirable lover—by abandoning her worldly possessions (especially her mother's expensive, famous clothes, in hat boxes "big as crates," and her family's beautiful, historical house "that would have been on a Pilgrimage [house tour] if Richton had had one" 354)—as if these ghosts can be exorcised when the economy that failed to support them is also exorcised. The extrinsic theme of "First Dark" is hardly surprising, involving the usual rehearsal of the ghostliness of southern history, summed up in the final look of the house—"All unconscious of its rejection by so mere a person as Tom Beavers, it seemed, instead, to have got rid of what did not fit it, to be free, at last, to enter with abandon the land of mourning and shadows and memory" (370). What is surprising is the fact that this story "houses" so much of its drama in racially specified objects.

We find a reprise of this preoccupation in Welty's "The Wanderers," in which on the day of her mother's laying out, Virgie Rainey feels suffocated by her neighbors. As women bring food and beautify her mother's corpse for its laying out, as rooms spill over with folks garrulous and unfamiliar, Virgie recoils.

> The ladies tiptoed forward and could be seen bending over the bed as they would bend over the crib of a little kicking baby. They came out again.
>
> "Come see your mother."
>
> They pulled harder, still smiling but in silence, and Virgie pulled back. Her hair fell over her eyes. She shook it back. "Don't touch me."
>
> "Honey, you just don't know what you lost, that's all."
>
> They were all people who had never touched her before who tried now to struggle with her, their faces hurt. She was hurting them all, shocking them. They leaned over her, agonized, pleading with the pull of their hands. It was a Mrs. Flewellyn, pulling the hardest, who had caught the last breath of her husband in a toy balloon, by his wish, and had it at home still—most of it, until a Negro stole it. (1949, 240–41)

What a strange portrait of a "southern" thing, this tiny, insignificant toy: its contents, a white man's breath, imagined to be so desirable that it has been stolen by a Negro. Again we meet this preoccupation with things that are not racially marked but acquire the veneer of race as they pass between cultures. With an eye toward comedy, Welty uses this detail to characterize an entire community—one that, in its oddity, accepts Mrs. Flewellyn's macabre need but refuses to tolerate Virgie's desire for privacy, her wanting not to be touched. Here white desire is grotesquely parsed. The reference to the balloon is risible, excessive, but isn't it also a bit self-indulgent? How typical *is* this weird locution? And how is it southern?

Julia Reed argues that contemporary southern literature can be characterized by a specialization in tacky objects, that it is *too* replete with things, with lurid, half-baked atmosphere. "The current literary South doesn't have much to do with the real South, which is a rather more complicated place," she says. The South of today's fiction "is a place where people speak in simple sentences and sing-songy rhythms. . . . Reading this stuff is like going to Wal-Mart. It's got everything . . . pimento cheese sandwiches, good silver . . . weddings in which everybody wears baby blue including the bride and groom, lots of iced tea and Cokes and Salem cigarettes, casseroles made from canned cream of mushroom soup." Describing a recent collection of Lee Smith's short stories (and cruelly titling them "the Bubba Stories"), Reed says that Smith writes books "for people who want to read what they think of as 'Southern' fiction" (1997, 23).

The literature we've been examining is filled with a litany of objects that, in their exoticism, localism, and eccentricity, seem designed to provide just such a southern "reality" effect. When the about-to-be-murdered family in "A Good Man Is Hard to Find" stops at Red Sammy Butts's barbecue for lunch, Red Sammy's stomach hangs over his trousers "like a sack of meal swaying under his shirt" (1971, 121). When McCullers wants to give *The Member of the Wedding* just the right touch of the local, she invokes Frankie's love of hoppin' john. When Alice Walker wants to characterize the southern town that stops Brownfield Copeland on his way north, she describes advertisements for "Brown Mule tobacco, Red Cherry snuff and laxatives . . . Cajun whiskey, Old Joe and Grape Beer" (1988, 46). When Ellen Gilchrist wants to evoke the aura of New Orleans, she lists, with a touch of irony, "confederate jasmine, honeysuckle, sweet alyssum, magnolia, every stereotyped southern flower you can imagine" (1981, 24). Each object gives a sweet jolt, a glance into a particular world. Seized, like surrealists, by these "found" objects, each author attempts to precipitate a particularly local desire. At the same time, it is difficult to think about these objects in a manner that does not trivialize them.

But let's look at the passage from Welty's "The Wanderers" again, for there is nothing trivial about the fantasy that drives Welty's story. First, Welty parodies the strange animation of Katie Rainey's body in death (the logic of exposing the corpse to all eyes like "a little kicking baby"), as if parodying the idea that Katie's new-minted face could offer Virgie some compensation for her loss. Second, the notion of using a balloon to catch a dying man's breath suggests the lineaments of a culture that is very busy consuming trauma—that feeds on the most bizarre and bodily of crises. Third, this funny story repeats the sad drama of a person who turns into an object and, when this object is stolen, "experiences" a loss of property in self, mimicking the genesis of black enslavement. And yet, when a white man is defined in this way—his life retold as the theft of a balloon's empty whiteness—his family is actually conserving, preserving the special provenance of white identity.

What's going on? Why fantasize so hard about this insignificant object? Why does Mrs. Flewellyn need to imagine its traveling across the boundaries of race and culture? It is as if she imagines that all objects associated with white people are, and must be, desirable, as if African Americans are out there, by the dozens, coveting the spittle in a white man's balloon. Cather's descriptions of the slave cabins in *Sapphira,* published nine years before Welty's story, repeat this fantasy in "historical" form. On the south side of the slave cabins Cather envisions gourd vines "which grew faster than any other creeper and bore flowers and fruits at the same time." The purpose of this plantscape is the incorporation of bits and pieces of the big house, for the gourds are cut into bowls for holding "meal, butter, lard, gravy, or any tidbit that might be spirited away from the big kitchen to one of the cabins. . . . The gourd vessels were invisible to good manners" (1968, 21). Cather never mentions the conditions that made the migration of food and goods to the cabin so necessary.[10] Why do twentieth-century white fictions still reproduce so much anxiety about blacks owning objects?

Black Ownership

The first hypothesis of this chapter should already be clear: there is an overlooked, underanalyzed story involving southern objects that extends backward in time to slave narratives and forward in time to the fictions of contemporary black women who write about the South, including Alice Walker, Sherley Anne Williams, Rita Dove, and Toni Morrison. This drama of object possession presents two patterns that are unexpected. First, we've seen a set of anxieties or stories about traveling or "shared" objects in the radically unequal worlds of black and white culture. Second, these anxieties are reconstructed by black and white writers alike.

But the focus on objects that travel between worlds (even those that do not move but inhabit different semiotic "discourses" within a single geography) suggests at least two more effects. In the second half of this chapter I will argue that while African American literature traces the costs of caring for white bourgeois objects—for white people's things—this literature also describes the need to generate a set of objects that have not been marked or soiled by whiteness. For example, in "generations: a memoir," Lucille Clifton traces her "southern" parents' migration to a small town in New York, where "the closest big city was Buffalo, twelve miles away. One time daddy walked there to buy a dining room set. He was the first colored man in Depew to have a dining room set. And he walked to Buffalo to get it. He got it on credit from Peoples', a store where they gave colored people credit back then." (Clifton repeats a story we've already heard as a *southern* story. She explains that she hated the Peoples' man who came by to collect money each week because "Daddy called him Mr. Pitterman but he called Daddy Sam. And his name was Samuel too, Samuel Pitterman, and if Daddy could be called Sam so could he. But he never was.") "Anyway, my Daddy wanted to have this dining room set and he walked to Buffalo to get it and when he got to Peoples' the salesman there told him he didn't need a dining room set. And Daddy told that man that his great-grandmother was a Dahomey woman and he could have anything he wanted. And so he got it. And walked back home, and they delivered the set. First colored man to own a dining room set in Depew New York" (1980, 266). Later we will explore Clifton's use of family legend—the fact of an African place name—as capital. But for now I want to note the contrast between her repeated pride in her father's possessions and the deprivations conjured up so easily by the white salesman who tries to talk her father out of his desire.

If African American writers depict the trauma of dispossession and invent a counter-rhetoric of possessive individualism marked by African American names, my second hypothesis is that white southern writers have great difficulty bestowing independent object relations on their black characters:

> "And Partheny," Shelley said, "Mama is so sad, she missed her garnet pin. It was Papa's present."
>
> "Mr. Battle's present!" Partheny said dramatically.
>
> "Yes, and, Partheny, Mama wondered if maybe while you were cooking for Papa's birthday barbecue, if maybe you might have just seen it floating around somewhere—if maybe you could send word to her where you think it might be. Where to look." . . .
>
> "Step inside—don't set your heels down, I've been mindless four and a half days. But let me just look around in parts of the house. Don't suppose that pin could have flown down *here* anywhere, do you?" (Welty 1946, 168)

In this barely covert struggle over ownership, is Partheny sought out for her voudoun powers, or is she being accused? She makes her way around the house, patting the quilt, tapping the fireplace, and then, in the next room, "making little sympathetic, sorrowful noises, and a noise like looking under the dishpan" (169). Partheny comes back into the room with a love charm for the girls' uncle and the request that the children tell their mother that she "ransacked even de chicken house—felt under de hens, tell your mama. . . . I don't know what could have become of Miss Ellen's pretty li'l garnet present, and her comin' down agin, cravin' it, who knows. Sorry as I can be for her" (171).

In this violently partitioned landscape, things flow back and forth with incredible speed and vehemence and with various degrees of transgression. But even when the thing itself has not flown, it becomes a pretext for conversation, the source—for black and white writers—of exploring the ways in which objects become crucial sites for both cultures as they mediate their uneven relationship.

For example, in Hurston's "The Gilded Six-Bits" (1933), Joe's beloved wife, Missie May, has an affair—for a fake gold piece—with "Mister Otis D. Slemmons of spots and places" (1989, 226). The early days of Joe's and Missie May's marriage are blissful, and the reader discovers this bliss in their elaborate rituals for exchanging objects. Joe throws his pay—nine sterling dollars—in a silvery shower through the open door while Missie May searches for him in mock alarm, only to lock with him "in a rough and tumble . . . a furious mass of male and female energy" (226). Laughing, she seeks out the sack of candy kisses in his pocket, as well as a batch of other gifts—chewing gum, "sweet soap," handkerchiefs. After her tryst with Slemmons, the couple recovers remnants of this bliss only after Missie May gives birth to a son that is Joe's "spittin' image," reinitiating their playful barter (233). Tentatively in love again, Joe takes the tainted gold piece to a white merchant's store, where this exchange of objects becomes a pretext for white definitions of blackness:

> "Fifty cents buys a mighty lot of candy kisses, Joe. Why don't you split it up and take some chocolate bars, too. They eat good, too."
>
> "Yessuh, dey do, but Ah wants all dat in kisses. Ah got a lil boy chile home now. Tain't a week old yet, but he kin suck a sugar tit and maybe eat one of them kisses hiself."
>
> Joe got his candy and left the store. The clerk turned to the next customer. "Wisht I could be like these darkies. Laughin' all the time. Nothin' worries em." (234)[11]

Hurston sets the complexities of Joe's and Missie May's love for one another against these white folks' simple view of black folks. Once again these complexities are partly mediated by the couple's relations to the objects they possess:

> There was something happy about the place. The front yard was parted in the middle by a sidewalk from gate to door-step, a sidewalk edged on either side by quart bottles driven neck down into the ground on a slant.
>
> . . . It was Saturday. Everything clean from the front gate to the privy house. Yard raked so that the strokes of the rake would make a pattern. . . .
>
> Joe splashed in the bedroom and Missie May fanned around in the kitchen. A fresh red and white checked cloth on the table. Big pitcher

> of buttermilk beaded with pale drops of butter from the churn. Hot fried mullet, crackling bread, ham hock atop a mound of string beans . . . (224, 226)

The need to imagine African Americans' desire for "white" objects is not just white people's fantasy about their race's desirability, nor is it simply a reflection of an enduring economy of scarcity. Instead, I want to argue, these facts and fantasies fulfill political and economic needs—specifically, that personhood be reflected in acts of property-owning (not only of land but of portable property as well). Hence the white shopkeeper's need, at the point of transaction, to slap a definition on Joe, to define blacks as "simple"—especially within an economy in which his own livelihood depends on an African American clientele; hence Hurston's need to describe the objects in Missie May's and Joe's world with such loving precision.[12]

Given the plenitude of the world Hurston portrays—*a world rich in things*—is it any wonder that Richard Wright objected to Hurston's fiction, given his parallel portrait of a family of Mississippi sharecroppers after the devastating flood depicted in "Silt" (1937)?

> "Le's see the kitchen," said Tom.
>
> The stove-pipe was gone. But the stove stood in the same place.
>
> "The stove's still good. We kin clean it."
>
> "Yeah."
>
> "But where's the table?"
>
> "Lawd knows."
>
> They opened the back door and looked out. They missed the barn, the hen house, and the pig pen. . . .
>
> [May] turned to Tom. "Now, whutcha gonna do, Tom?"
>
> He stood looking at the mud-filled fields. . . .
>
> "Lawd, but Ah sho hate t start all over wid tha white man. Ah'd leave here ef Ah could. Ah owes im nigh eight hundred dollahs. N we needs a hoss, grub, seed, n a lot mo other things." (512–13)

Wright uses this bleak portrait of muddy, absent things to show how very little circulates between white landowner and black tenant. In contrast, Hurston uses the plenitude that Missie May and Joe share to reveal the intricacy of their lives, including the vestiges of Africanist spiritual practices that pattern their yard, as well as the great distance between this couple and the white world that constructs self-serving fantasies about them. That is, Hurston is after something else—not just the delineation of an unfair economy but the self-defining act of black consumption, the appropriation of white objects into an African American economy, as well as the white fantasies that drive southern class politics. In this she resembles white writers such as Porter, Welty, and Douglas, who use object dramas to similar effect. But Hurston supersedes these white writers in her understanding of the role objects play in the everyday exchanges among southern blacks, as well as the importance of objects in claiming self-ownership.

To see how this elaborate depiction of objects works differently in black and white southern fiction, I want to suggest several ways to reorganize our thoughts about literary objects. I will also explore the underlying hypothesis of this chapter: things acquire such an aura in southern literature because they are shadowed by a world where people have been defined as things.

In *Virtue, Commerce, and History* Pocock suggests that new relations between self and property emerged at the beginning of the modern era: "property, without losing any of its significance to personality, was defined less as that which makes you what you are than as that to which you have a right. With this interpretation we enter upon that fascinating and elusive relationship between the notions of right and ownership, and upon that world of language in which 'property'—that which you owned—and 'propriety'—that which pertained or was proper to a person or situation—were interchangeable terms" (1985, 104). This relation becomes even more vexed for southern whites and blacks because of the way the southern caste system depended on a racial distribution of persons and property until deep into the twentieth century. As Alice Walker says of Brownfield Copeland, the deranged sharecropper of *The Third Life of Grange Copeland:* "He was expected to raise himself up on air, which was all that was left over after his work for others. Others who were always within their rights to pay him practically nothing for his labor. He was never able to do more than exist on air; he was never able to build on it, and was never able to have any land of his own; and was never able to set his woman up in style, which more than anything else he wanted to do" (1988, 79). What does it mean to view such moments not only as critique but as a continued attempt to reread the unintelligibility of race in the everyday South? We need to reorganize our thinking about the objects portrayed in southern fiction to encounter (1) the material weight of these objects, (2) their elusiveness or lightness for black consumers ("he was expected to raise himself up on air"), and (3) the discursive patterns that legislate property distribution in order to construct racial differences. But first I want to explore the roles that objects play in the theories of Arendt, Marx, and Freud in order to understand the impact of the materials that pass back and forth between black and white southern cultures.

The Object Bestows Stability

In Wright's "Silt" Tom is ecstatic about the discovery of his flood-buried plow: "Tom called from around the cabin. 'May, look! Ah done foun mah plow!' Proudly he dragged the silt-caked plow to the pump. 'I'll wash it n it'll be awright'" (1989, 512). The recovered object represents a restoration of dignity; it attests to Tom's ability to make a living and to the potential for some constancy in this unsteady world. As Arendt argues in *The Human Condition,* objects are important because they give one's life solidity and permanence. "The sudden, spectacular rise of labor from the lowest, most despised position to the highest rank, as the most esteemed of all human activities, began when Locke discovered that labor is the source of all property" (1958, 101). For Arendt, "work and its product, the human artifact, bestow a measure of permanence and durability upon the futility of mortal life and the fleeting character of human time" (8). Wright uses Tom's and May's recovered objects to suggest an economy of deprivation—the ways in which, for African American families on the Mississippi Delta, the river colludes with the white man's economy to deprive them of table, crop, food, "n a lot mo other things"—but he also conveys the self-esteem that worked-for things create. Even though this family is prevented by the sharecropping economy from marshaling their valuable labor to create the property in objects and land their hard work merits, Wright suggests that the objects they do possess bestow an unexpected measure of "permanence and durability" on lives that are all but impossible.

Commodity Fetishism or, the Object as a Container for Work

If Arendt suggests the object's solidity, Marx's vision dissolves this solidity into two vertiginous frames: the first involving the work necessary for the object's creation (and the hiding of this labor in "commodity fetishism"), the second involving its monetary form—the abstraction of the work the commodity has absorbed into the impudent world of capital. Marx's analysis goes a long way toward explaining the complexities of Hurston's "Gilded Six-Bits": her creation of a black family that lives both in and out of a white capitalist system. Silver dollars are erotic love tokens one moment, abstractions permitting the purchase of staples, "meat and lard, meal and flour, soap and starch . . . . bananas and apples" (1989, 233) the next. What's fascinating about Hurston's story is her reinvention of Joe's silver dollars as objects that have an erotic use-value (apart from their sliding spectrality as capital) in this marriage—as if the game between Missie May and Joe recovers, in its reinvention of these playful coins, the "masses of crystallized labor time" Joe has expended on the night shift at the G and G Fertilizer works. At the same time, this money binds the couple more tightly to the white company's economy ("the yellow coin in his trousers was like a monster hiding in the cave of his pockets to destroy her" 230), and also becomes the site where Joe is most vulnerable to the condescending mercantilism of the white shopkeeper. Whereas Wright uses ordinary objects to describe his characters' exclusion from a white economy—even as these characters provide its foundation—both Hurston and Clifton (in her memoir about her southern ancestors) want to parse the slippery relation between African and Anglo American economies. This slipperiness suggests a third pattern for thinking about the objects that pass back and forth between cultures—one that also involves a dissolution of the object's solidity.

The Object as the Royal Road to the (Political) Unconscious

In Marx's model the object—insofar as it is politicized or theorized—dissolves back into the fire of its labor. For Freud, in contrast, the object provides a compass within the sea of the unconscious where "things" are never what they seem. We've seen the ways in which things conjure up the weight of the material world that African Americans created, cared for, and carried in the deep South. Now we need to think in more depth about the imaginary properties of these objects. In *Marxism and Form* Fredric Jameson suggests that

> for Freud there is no such thing as an instinct or drive in its pure or physical state: all drives are mediated through images of fantasies, through their object language or "Vorstellungrepräsentenz." . . . So it is that some chance contact with an external object may "remind" us of ourselves more profoundly than anything that takes place in the impoverished life of our conscious will. For unbeknownst to us, the objects around us lead lives of their own in our unconscious fantasies, where, vibrant with mana or taboo, with symbolic fascination or repulsion, they stand as the words or hieroglyphs of the immense rebus of desire. (1972, 99)

We've already encountered this "object language" in Ellen Fairchild's fantasies about her brooch's disappearance and in Mrs. Flewellyns's notion that an African American ran away with her husband's last breath. The objects that are imagined to move back and forth between cultures give us a powerful look at whites' fantasies about black culture. Porter captures the way this phantasm of ownership contaminates even the most intimate relationships between whites and blacks. In "The Old Order" she tells the story of Nannie's exodus to a cabin of her own: "They fixed Nannie up with a good bed and a fairly good carpet and allowed her to take all sorts of odds and ends from the house. It was astonishing to discover that Nannie had always liked and hoped to own certain things, she had seemed so contented and wantless" (1972, 349). Why shouldn't Nannie hope to own "certain things"? Because in the fantasy life of her white employers, Nannie herself becomes an object in the "immense rebus of desire"; she is visited, these white children are surprised to learn, even by those who did not "own" her. "Her grandchildren and her white family visited her, and all kinds of white persons who had never owned a soul related to Nannie, went to see her, to buy her rugs or leave little presents with her" (349). But even Porter's story is contaminated by what it hopes to critique. When Nannie returns to the big house to work, "to show their gratitude, and their hope that she would come again, they would heap upon her baskets and bales of the precious rubbish she loved, and one of her great grandsons Skid or Hasty would push them away beside her on a wheelbarrow" (350). We return to the continued association of African American characters with waste, rubbish, the throwaway, to white fantasies about black propertylessness that cast African Americans into the realm of detritus, reeling in the shallows and shadows of whiteness.

Finally, neither Arendt's, nor Marx's, nor Freud's model of objectivity is adequate to explain the force of object relations in southern literature. How do we account for whites' repetitive desire to withhold things from blacks, or their need to redefine the meaning of the objects blacks do possess as rubbish? Paradoxically, this withholding of objects reflects a withholding of personhood from African Americans in an economy in which blacks are still half-defined not as persons but as property.

The Object as Persona and Property

Pocock suggests that in the modern period "the distinction between persons and things gained in prominence; and instead of being the mere prerequisite to political relations between persons, property became a system of legally defined relations between persons and things, or between persons through things" (1985, 104). In this context Porter's insistence that Nannie's white employers were astonished to discover that Nannie had always liked and hoped to own certain things is especially startling. As Mem Copeland says so vehemently in *The Third Life of Grange Copeland:* "Me and these children got a *right* to live in a house where it don't rain and there's no holes in the floor" (1988, 119). Even while the South lingered on the threshold of a fully commercial, mercantile economy, the ideological bonds defining personhood were already in place, defining selfhood in terms of the right to be nurtured by things that proved one's status (and offered more than a modicum of comfort) within the precincts of possessive individualism.

As Pocock suggests, modernizing societies have reinvented the notion of property, which comes to be seen "less as that which makes you what you are than as that to which you have a right" (104). And yet within the South, the right to bestow or withhold both land and commodities was severely restricted; it was seen as a "whites only" privilege. That is, even as African Americans like Joe and Missie Mae began to acquire and display their own forms of mobile (and territorial) goods, whites were unwilling to see this display in its complexity, as a statement not only of the right to possess things but of the right to possess personhood: "Wisht I could be like these darkies. Laughin' all the time. Nothin' worries em."

This defensive sense of privilege, of whites' exclusive right to bestow personhood and property on nonwhites, still echoes in postmodern texts about the post–civil rights South. In *Can't Quit You, Baby* Tweet's stroke forces Cornelia, her white, hard-of-hearing employer, into Tweet's home, where the white woman discovers an object stolen from her house:

> Finally Tweet says, Yeah, it's yours. Belong to you. Yeah.
>
> I know.
>
> I know you know. But you never missed it, did you?
>
> No.
>
> You got four, five them gold barrettes. Naturally, you wouldn't have missed one.
>
> I would have given it to you, Cornelia says.
>
> Yeah. Didn't I say you wouldn't have missed it? Why not give it to me?
>
> Why? Cornelia says. Why did you steal my gold barrette?(1988, 253–54)

Cornelia invokes her right, as lord of the manor, to distribute objects at will: "I would have given it to you." But Tweet responds with a very different reading of this event—she describes a white home filled with unused objects, catalogues her own violated "rights," and suggests that Cornelia's objects are not desirable because of their intrinsic value but because they open thresholds for Africanist magic:

> Tweet laughs. Evil, she says. I'm evil. Then, Right is right, yeah. Uh huh, and wrong is wrong. People don't do *bad* by accident.
>
> Why did you do it?
>
> Maybe your hair was caught in it? You think maybe I took your hair? Make a mojo? Fingernail clippings? Blood, too, like blood from old used Tampax, Kotex? I throwed out enough in my day. From your panties when you—when you—fff-flooded? Washed enough of them. Shit? Cleaned enough of your toilets.
>
> Cornelia moans. She feels as if her joints are being pulled apart, as if a jackhammer is sending its vibrations all through her body. (254)

Along with Nannie's former employers, Cornelia has only seen her possessions through a cloud of assumptions about her exclusive right to possessive individualism. But while Porter depicts Nannie's eagerness for white leftovers ("to show their gratitude, and their hope that she would come again, they would heap upon her baskets and bales of the precious rubbish she loved"), Tweet responds with a catalogue of white detritus: a description of the waste she has had to handle, reversing the spectrum of personhood by defining a world filled with white pollution.

We've come back to the start, to the discovery that southern fiction invests so much drama in *things* because, in southern definitions of race, even the most trivial objects can mark the border between black and white. But Tweet's anger also reveals that, in a world where having things contributes to the ideology of personhood, objects also provide access to political being (here, quite nakedly, to the fantasy of power or domination over another). As Pocock suggests: "The century that followed the Financial Revolution witnessed the rise in Western thought (something not dissimilar may have been occurring in contemporary Japan) of an ideology and a perception of history which depicted political society and social personality as founded upon commerce: upon the exchange of forms of mobile property and upon modes of consciousness suited to a world of moving objects" (109). We've been exploring the world of moving objects in southern women's fiction in order to understand (1) how these objects become a crucial site of identity and (2) the fact that any redistribution of property can imply a redistribution of personal and political power.

My point is simple. The reifications of slavery have continued to exert a residual effect, contaminating perceptions about who is and who gets to possess property. As Spillers suggests in "Mama's Baby, Papa's Maybe," under slavery genetic reproduction was not "an elaboration of the life-principle" but a way of extending the boundaries "of proliferating properties." This blurring of kin group and property still has bizarre effects. Formerly, if kinship were possible between those who were considered to be either the possessor or the possessed, then property relations themselves were eroded, since children would "belong" to both mother and father (1994, 471). In this system, Spillers reasons, enslaved offspring could not be orphaned, and kinship itself loses meaning, "*since it can be invaded at any given and arbitrary moment by the property relations*" (469). In this chapter I have argued that the social residue of these older economies and beliefs continues to disrupt the dispersal of personhood, even post-integration.

In conclusion, I want to examine the uncanny ways in which kinship, property, and language start to blur in Lucille Clifton's memoir about her family's southern history. In "generations: a memoir" the crisis over ownership between white and black cultures acquires an eerie linguistic spin: words become objects to be exchanged in the battle for propriety:

> She said
>
> I saw your notice in the Bedford newspaper and I thought isn't this interesting, so I figured I would call you and tell you that I am a Sale and I have compiled and privately printed a history of the Sale/Sayle family of Bedford County Virginia and I would be glad to send it to you. But why are you interested in the Sayles? (1980, 227)

Clifton's memoir (in which her southern family becomes free and solvent enough "to walk in the North and see some things," 254) begins with a conversation between a voluble white woman who has labored to collect her family's genealogy and a black poet who is tracing her own southern lineage. Clifton is related to this white lady through ties of slavery and blood labor and wants to remobilize these ties in order to create her own counter-genealogy. But to renew this relationship to the past puts her in danger of reinitiating her relatives' depersonification or muting at the hands of white culture. The white woman's magisterial "she said," a phrase that is set apart typographically and opens the memoir, suggests her assumed ownership of speech and of a "family of names." But as we will see, names can also become "moving objects" that construct a "royal road" to political being.

First, Clifton's advertisement appears in a newspaper; it takes up public space, announces entrance into a domain "founded upon commerce" (109). Moreover, Sale is a homonym for Clifton's maiden name, Sayles, announcing a mode of capitalist exchange. But from the beginning of this memoir a woman descended from Africans who once belonged to the Sales enters the marketplace on her own terms.

> Her voice is sweet and white over the wires. What shall I say to this white lady? What does it matter now that Daddy is dead and I am a Clifton?
>
> Have you ever heard of a man named John F. Sale? I ask.
>
> Why yes, he was a great-uncle of mine, I believe. She is happy and excited.
>
> Well, my maiden name was Sayles, I say.
>
> What was you father's name? she asks. She is jumping through the wires.
>
> Samuel, I say.
>
> She is puzzled. I don't remember that name, she says.
>
> Who remembers the names of the slaves? Only the children of slaves. The names are Caroline and Lucy and Samuel, I say. Slave names.
>
> Ooooh, she cries. Oh that's just awful. And there is silence. (227)

We turn to the rediscovery of throwaway bodies, the lurking presence of the unthought known. We return to the question: How do you write a story everyone knows and nobody hears?

Clifton's answer is: orthographically. Her family has long practiced a history of linguistic resistance. During Reconstruction they stayed "close to the Sale place and all the slaves had stayed there after emancipation because they said the Sales was good people, but they had just changed their last name to Sayle so people would know the difference" (244).[13] Although Clifton's father left school in second or third grade and could barely write his name, he was an avid reader who loved books, and he "changed his name to Sayles (instead of Sayle) after finding a part of a textbook in which the plural was explained. There will be more than one of me, my father thought, and he added the s to his name" (243).

Clifton wants to draw our attention to the power of speech as self-ownership. The white woman who calls to say "I am a Sale and I have compiled and privately printed a history" is not just claiming a genetic family but a field of force: the white privilege of constructing and grounding an epic history in a minor family of names. (We could also say that her language lies. She is not just a "Sale," but a "seller"; just as her family bought and sold slaves, so she will exchange her family of names with all "respectable" [that is, white] bidders.) It should come as no surprise that even when this white woman motions toward an egalitarian dialogue with Clifton—"I will be glad to send it to you"—she also counters with hierarchy: "why are you interested in the Sayles?" That is, "What family of names do you own or claim?"—a question that also implies, in the context of Clifton's past, "What right have you to question "the sales," that is, our traffic in African Americans?"

> Then she tells me that the slave cabins are still there at the Sale home where she lives, and the graves of the slaves are there, unmarked. The graves of my family.
>
> She remembers the name Caroline, she says, her parents were delivered by the midwife, Mammy Caroline. The midwife Mammy Caroline. (227)

We return to the persons as well as the objects that cross racial lines in the postbellum South. I have argued that it is crucial to recognize the extraordinary, worrisome presence of these crossover persons and objects in southern fiction—to capture a sense of these shared surfaces as well as of their radically different semiotics across cultures. In a sense, we're moving back to Foucault's discursive model of things, since the same objects emerge differently for different cultures. But to jump from object to discourse is to miss the struggle created by the very fact of unequal sharing:

> Is the Nichols house still there? I ask.
>
> Still with the family in it, she says. I hear the trouble in her voice.
>
> And I rush to reassure her. Why? Is it in my blood to reassure this thin-voiced white lady? I am a Clifton now, I say. I only wanted to find out about these things. I am only curious, I say.
>
> I can help you, she sighs. I can help you.
>
> But I never hear her voice again. . . .
>
> Yet she sends the history she has compiled and in it are her family's names. And our family names are thick in her family like an omen. I see that she is the last of her line. Old and not married, left with a house and a name. I look at my husband and our six children and I feel the Dahomey women gathering in my bones. (227–28)

If the power of an alien white language now resides in a dying lady, it becomes unclear just who this language belongs to. "Our family names" become "thick in her family like an omen." We suddenly have to ask, which language is figure, and which ground? which language is dominant, and which muted? And what about the referents Clifton possesses that Miss Sayle does not? "I feel the Dahomey women gathering in my bones."

These Dahomey women open Clifton's text to something unexpected; by hitting on a phrase outside the normal purview of white American speech, Clifton tantalizes her readers with a spectrum of meaning that seems beyond the control of the dominant culture; she widens the scope of her memoir with a word that is not bounded as, say, Miss Sayle's white genealogy is bounded. She also recognizes that to own objects, land, houses, a genealogy, a history, is to own a site for claiming selfhood—a site for claiming rights. "The person is not primarily separable from his or her objects; exchange consolidates or threatens social bonds" (Pocock 1985, 106). As the "privately printed history of the Sale/Sayle family of Bedford County Virginia" makes its way into Clifton's possession, there are two simultaneous flowerings—the reinvention of "Dahomey" as an unfinished name, the site for both culminating and reinitiating an unfinished history, and the invention of a counter-genealogy in Clifton's memoir—one that is *publicly* printed and has heft in the reader's hand. The genealogy stretches back to "the generations of Caroline Donald born in Afrika in 1823 and Sam Lois Sale born in America in 1777" and forward to Clifton's children

> Sidney
> Frederica
> Gillian
> Alexia four daughter and
> Channing
> Graham two sons,
> and the line goes on.
> "Don't you worry, mister, don't you worry."

Why are names so crucial here, and why does Clifton give them such material weight? Spillers describes a ledger from the Middle Passage in which entries carefully enumerate "the names of ships and the private traders in Barbados who will receive the stipulated goods, but 'No. Negroes' and 'Sum sold for per head' are so exactly arithmetical that it is as if these additions and multiplications belong to the other side of an equation." The accountant who labored so precisely over these details includes everything but *the names* of these African captives. This omission is staggering, since "a narrative, or story, is always implied by a man or woman's *name:* 'Wm. Webster,' 'John Dunn,' 'Thos. Brownbill.' . . . But the 'other' side of the page . . . equally precise, throws no face in view . . . the destruction of the African name, of kin, of linguistic, and ritual connections is so obvious in the vital stats sheet that we tend to overlook it. Quite naturally, the trader is not interested, in any *semantic* sense, in this 'baggage' that he must deliver" (1994, 467–68). To own things, to have a name, to seize the prerogative of naming oneself when deprived of one's indigenous name or land: these are powerful ways to create property in oneself, to disrupt "the proper."

In this chapter I've juxtaposed "white object panic" (the terror that blacks might use the moving objects that have become the calling cards of capitalist and late capitalist society as a route to self-possession) with symbolic monuments to black ownership in which property does, in fact, offer a new route to propriety in self. I've also suggested that the racialization of hybrid or crossover objects becomes an obsession for black women and white. Finally, as Clifton's "northern" memoir of her "southern" ancestors suggests, this drama is not restricted to region. Clifton describes trips with her mother in upstate New York to white neighborhoods where objects refuse to cross over: "Some Sundays in the summertime me and her used to go for walks over to the white folks section to look in their windows and I would tell her when I grew up I was going to take her to a new place and buy her all those things" (272). In Rita Dove's "Wingfoot Lake" things are more tractable. Beulah, the poem's protagonist, focuses on the South's segregated swimming pools and then turns to the seemingly liberated space of a Goodyear company picnic in the post-sixties Midwest: "Now this *act of mercy:* four daughters dragging her to their husbands' company picnic, / white families on one side and them / on the other, unpacking the same / squeeze bottles of Heinz, the same / waxy beef patties and Salem potato chip bags" (1986, 72). Finally, African Americans have attained the right to acts of possessive individualism, but the objects they possess remain separate but equal. Is it any wonder Beulah begins to long for "Thomas' Great Mississippi / with its sullen silks?" And yet, reading white and black fictions side by side, one must always temper such nostalgia with memories of the throwaway bodies that falter among such sullen silks.

To stage a final contrast between the interplay of objects and names in black and white texts, in *The Member of the Wedding* Frankie's ultimate fantasy of self-possession involves repairing watches in her father's thing-laden shop. She longs to sit at the bench fixing time, making it run smoothly. In her fantasy, "sometimes a crowd of sidewalk lazies would collect to watch her from the street and she would imagine how they said: 'Frankie

Addams works for her father and makes fifteen dollars a week. She fixes the hardest watches in the store and goes to the Woodmen of the World Club with her father. Look at her. She is a credit to the family and a big credit to the whole town'" (1975, 60). In contrast, when Clifton imagines her ancestress's accession to public time, it is via the grim vehicle of a public hanging. When her great-grandmother, Lucy, killed the white father of her mixed-race child, Lucy stood at the crossroad "with the rifle in her hand" waiting for the consequences. The amazing fact handed down via family legend is that "they didn't lynch her" but permitted a legal trial—Lucy's only access to civil space. Clifton imagines Mammy Caroline at the hanging, watching over her daughter. Where Frankie dreams of repairing watches, Clifton watches over the drama of the past: "the lady whose name they gave me like a gift had her neck pulled up by a rope until the neck broke and I can see Mammy Ca'line standing straight as a soldier in green Virginia apart from the crowd of silent Black folk and white folk watching them and not the wooden frame swinging her child" (245).

This is a story about being, for once, inside the spectacle of the law, about the grim possibility of self-representation ("Mammy Ca'line got one of the lawyer Sale family to defend her daughter. . . . They had a legal trial and Lucy was found guilty, and hanged," 244). And yet, within this public sense of an ending, Clifton's response is a profoundly private body language. Speaking of Mammy Ca'line, her great-grandmother Lucy, and herself, Clifton focuses on the unsaid, the throwaway body, the unthought known: "And I know she made no sound but her mind closed around the picture like a frame and I know that her child made no sound and I turn in my chair and arch my back and make this sound for my two mothers and for all Dahomey women" (245). Literature about the South turns repetitively, gorgeously, and endlessly to the body that bears such witness. How can so much pain create such an aesthetic? The other way to ask this question is—how can it not? What Clifton adds to this aesthetic is a sense of objects that cannot cross over, that will not cross back. At the same time the place name "Dahomey" crosses continents, generations, and economic systems, creating a new object politics for those willing to "Get what you want, you from Dahomey women" (232).

Chapter Eight

The Body as Testimony

I want to channel surf. Watching the cartoon network with my daughter, I feel ditzy and mad about the range of toys she's learned to desire. Fascinated by the neat little rooms demonstrated in the Barbie Fold'n Fun House, she puts them on her holiday list, until I'm bored and appalled beyond tears. Incarcerating Barbie in a plasticine version of that old pumpkin shell or glass coffin seems so tedious now, so old hat. But here's my daughter clamoring for more, longing for the shrunken world of Polly Pocket and her dwarfish sisters, or for the de-eroticized zoophilia of Mattel's latest petting zoo.

The boys' commercials are more exciting but just as stereotypical, citing the sublime instead of the beautiful as the way to cultural power. I'm almost asleep and inured to this violence—but as I watch this bizarre array of transformers, X-men, cyborgs, and tentacled teratomas, I'm stung awake: these commercials offer the mirror image of one of my own academic obsessions; they enact a violent traffic in the grotesque.

Working on a chapter about how the grotesque functions in fictions by southern women, I've become habituated to these images; I forget that these hypertrophied grotesques are most often the playthings of men, who discover as a birthright their privileged ability, their publicly bestowed right to reassemble the fragmented body. Given this masculine traffic in the grotesque (in a world where any woman can *be* the grotesque, but only men can rescript its boundaries), what caused an amorphous group of southern women, widely dispersed in space and time, to seize upon the grotesque as their leitmotif—to snatch this body image away from masculine culture and bend it to their own cultural purposes? To answer this question we have already entered a strange and marvelous world. Southern women writers pack their fictions with characters whose bodies and minds refuse to be average—characters extraordinary because they are witless or limbless, crippled, deaf, or blind, hermaphroditic or filled with same-sex desire, Lilliputian or gigantic—hybrid characters with bodies and minds that refuse, or fail to comprehend, the norm. These southern freaks and eccentrics—from Carson McCullers's moony adolescents to Eudora Welty's gargantuan musicians—reawaken the tipsy magic of carnival; southern women's fictions dance with pinhead people, with the microcephalics who were the ornaments of turn-of-the century circuses; they tremble with the fierce body language of bearded ladies and murderous misfits, with giant southern matrons whose girth exceeds their desires. In the midst of this charade we also find childish characters deformed by the South's dreamy dreams, kids who are physically traumatized, bent out of shape by racist and sexist southern ideologies: ancient children, old before their time, or their bizarre, grown-up counterparts—adults forever silly and young, grown-ups who can only be described as psychosocial grotesques.

This panoply of bodies in process or bodies in pain, this parade of beings on the rim, the painful margins of southern society, appear without ceasing in stories by southern women. One of the problems I've set out to answer in *Dirt and Desire* is—why? What causes this obsessive presence in southern literature? What is the source of this impressive display of misfits, dimwits, giant women, and lunatics? One answer is the need to invent new forms for thinking about the unthought known and to circumvent the rigid systems of race and gender, the "normal" deformities of southern culture.

But first, in order to dramatize the collective impact of so many bizarre bodies, I want to turn to the contrasting mystery of the postmodern grotesque. In "The Morphing of the American Mind" Tom Engelhardt describes the political limits of cyborg culture; he criticizes the civic usefulness of America's contemporary grotesques. While children of the fifties became masters of cold war imperialism by restaging Iwo Jima or playing endless games of Cowboys and Indians, Engelhardt suggests, this "national story of battle triumph has disappeared along with the toys that animated it" (1994, 15). Instead, in the multicultural America of the nineties, children turn to cybershopping's latest goblins, to the Red Dragon Thunderzord or the Superhuman Samurai Syber-Squad; that is, instead of reversing the complicity of white triumph by playing the old stories backwards (invoking Native Americans who triumphed over the cavalry or enslaved African

Americans who led battles against their southern masters), postmodern children escape "history" altogether. "Out here in the cybermarketplace, all history has been superseded by a new kind of story-telling. On that floor is a set of 'stories' barren of historical content, reflecting only the stripped-down global selling environment from which they arise; so insular (yet all-encompassing) as to be no stories at all" (15). In contemplating the robotic array of monsters and cyborgs in postmodern media culture, Gabrielle Schwab seconds Engelhardt's story and argues that the postmodern grotesque serves a peculiarly domesticating function. The repetitive throng of klingons, power rangers, and mutant ninjas don't incite the world to violence but help obliterate the violence of media culture; they offer a text or screen "onto which cultural fantasies, desires, fears, anxieties, hopes, and utopias are projected. Cybernetic organisms inspire such projections because they are products of a technological, or artificial manipulation of the body. A great deal of the fascination with such technological manipulations stems from the fact that the manipulated bodies are, on an unconscious level, also perceived as phantasms of the fragmented body" (1989, 194). Schwab argues that these postmodern bodies, perceived not only as fragments but as quasi-organic mixtures of machines and animals that operate with the inhuman velocity of the mechanical grotesque, do necessary cultural work. They offer a way of coping aesthetically, of "working through an uncanny and potentially dangerous fascination with bodily fragmentation" (194) that is the legacy of modern technological culture. These postmodern grotesques help to demobilize frightening social possibilities by bestowing an illusion of command or control over technology's fragmenting drives. For Schwab this becomes the central reason for the grotesque's "preeminent role" in postmodern culture. "In the grotesque body the underlying phantasms of the fragmented body are domesticated" (194).

If the postmodern, robotic grotesque involves aesthetic distance, if it functions as an unearthly defense against the pain of history and the forces of technological self-splitting, for women writing in or about the modern South these "underlying phantasms of the fragmented body" offer something else; they provide the opportunity for repelling beauty and undomesticating or estranging the down-home space their characters inhabit; they offer a disturbing way of bearing witness or giving testimony, a peculiar threshold for reconfiguring the way we think about the South's racist history.

Katherine Anne Porter's Old Nannie is a case in point. Exhausted by decades of childbirth and physical labor, she refuses to work for the white family whose lives are too intertwined with her own, asking instead for isolation and a private cabin. No longer "the faithful old servant Nannie, a freed slave," she is suddenly "an aged Bantu woman of independent means, sitting on the steps, breathing the free air" (1972, 349). But this sonorous freedom spells danger for no one; Nannie is allowed to live in peace because her body has passed out of usefulness: "The black iris of the deep, withdrawn old eyes turned a chocolate brown and seemed to spread over the whole surface of the eyeball. As her sight failed, the eyelids crinkled and drew in, so that her face was like an eyeless mask" (349).

As she withdraws from white culture, Nannie's damaged sight intensifies her body's brownness, but instead of providing a new racial aesthetic, Nannie's life flattens out. Freed from the work of bondservant, she refuses white culture's domestic order. But her body is not the exuberant site of cultural renewal that a theorist of the grotesque such as Mikhail Bakhtin might imagine. Instead, it is covered with the stigma of past work. Her masked face is eyeless, refusing the look of others, but it is also sightless, blinded by years of other-directed labor. Nannie not only loses the pleasure of sight; she is unable to return the other's gaze.

Whereas Bakhtin stresses the fertile work of the fragmented body, emphasizing its archaic contact with the outside world of growth and becoming, and Schwab and Engelhardt stress its postmodern bankruptcy—the emptying out of the grotesque's capacity to do meaningful political work—I argue that the gnarling of the southern grotesque offers another index altogether: a space for reading the way that *bios* is determined by history. Nannie's body, for all its recovered dignity, offers a frightening somatic site for measuring the intrusions of a white supremacist world and its aggressions.

We find another example in the first story from Welty's *Curtain of Green*, "Lily Daw and the Three Ladies," in which Lily becomes a quintessential southern white woman as grotesque. A dummy with a scar, an amiable half-wit like Forest Gump or Boo Radley, her body's surface has also been mangled—cut open and cut into—by her father's knife. If Lily's beauty evokes the cheerful good looks of the southern belle, by taking the belle's body and exaggerating its features (the belle's empty-headed charm become Lily's dim-wittedness, the belle's masochistic openness to patriarchy Lily's horrible scar) Welty makes Lily's body grotesque and puts its features to critical use: "'Hello,' said Lily. In a minute she gave a suck on the zinnia stem that sounded exactly like a jay bird. There she sat, wearing a petticoat for a dress, one of the things Mrs. Carson kept after her about. Her milky-yellow hair streamed freely down from under a new hat. You could see the wavy scar on her throat if you knew it was there" (1979, 8–9). Lily is headed for the Ellisville Institute for the Feeble-Minded of Mississippi, but she ends up getting married instead. Welty plays up the similarities between these two institutions, as if to argue that marriages and insane asylums offer more or less the same advantages for white southern women.

By wedding this critique to Lily's torso, Welty invents an intriguing contact zone for the reader's body: a site of disturbance, uneasiness, and pleasure that suggests a dual function for southern grotesques. First, southern women writers use the grotesque to map an array of social crises; the open, wounded, bleeding, excessive, corpulent, maimed, idiotic, or gargantuan body becomes the sign of a permanent emergency within the body politic. But to reduce the grotesque to social symptom is also to depersonalize its anarchic charm, to anaesthetize it or hold it at arm's length. Second, we must begin to explore the ways in which the grotesque disturbs the reader's passivity by creating peculiar effects of enjoyment, angst, anger, and mimetic pain. That is, the grotesque can operate symptomatically by presenting a set of disgusting or pleasurable protuberances with the power to arrest, to fixate, and to make unexpected demands on the reader's body.[1]

In this chapter I want to explore the ways in which these protuberances provide a powerful emotional fix; addictive, excessive, unreadable, all too readable they contribute to the literary body's capacity to give testimony, to bear witness to trauma. As Shoshana Felman suggests, "the specific task of the literary testimony is . . . to open up in that belated witness, which the reader now historically becomes, the imaginative capability of perceiving history—what is happening to others—in one's own body, with the power of sight (of insight) usually afforded only by one's own immediate physical involvement" (1992, 108). How does the literary grotesque invite the reader's body to "open up"? How can the other reach into one's own body? If "literature bears testimony not just to duplicate or to record events, but to make history available to the imaginative act" (108), how is this capability evoked in southern texts?

Hypertrophy

To understand the complexity of such bodily acts of witnessing we need to explore several variations on the grotesque as southern theme. First, in order to reawaken the communicative effects of the southern grotesque, we must recognize that it is inconstant, metamorphic, mutable: its uses vary, even within the same author's texts. Second, the grotesque is both a figure of speech and a state of mind. The little white girl who visits Lillian Smith's home in *Killers of the Dream* is not outwardly grotesque, but she becomes freakish, amorphous, a throwaway—in the white community's imagination. Unloved by Milkman, Morrison's Hagar also imagines that her beautiful body is grotesque: "Look at how I look. . . . I look like a ground hog. Where's the comb?" (1977, 312). She tries to resolve her imagined malformation with still more hybridity: "Lipsticks in soft white hands darted out of their sheaths like the shiny red penises of puppies" (215). Hagar goes shopping in Michigan, but her self-hatred offers an object lesson in fantasies about race and gender that thrive in the South.

Third, what the figurative grotesque adds to southern fiction is an element of the fantastic or the marvelous: a body magic that is fascinating, amorphous, and labile—a lability that swings many ways. This body magic gives the grotesque the power to titillate, threaten, or to mingle with the reader's body in unexpected ways; it pushes us to explore the ways in which every body mingles dangerously with the world. This is nowhere more evident than in Alice Walker's "The Voice of the Peacock":

> The fact that in Mississippi no one even remembers where Richard Wright lived, while Faulkner's house is maintained by a black caretaker, is painful, but not unbearable. What comes close to being unbearable is that I know how damaging to my own psyche such injustice is. In an unjust society the soul of the sensitive person is in danger of deformity from just such weights as this. For a long time I will feel Faulkner's house, O'Connor's house, crushing me. To fight back will require a certain amount of energy, energy better used doing something else. (1983b, 58)

Here "the" grotesque is neither a figure of speech nor a state of mind but something vehicular, a constant danger posed by white supremacy as it occupies ordinary space. To combat this occupation, Walker's testimonial verges on surrealism as she insists on the breakdown of conventional space and its savage assault on her own human frame.[2] She replaces the effects of a white bourgeois reality with bodily dislocation, sharing with her surrealist precursors a desire to reveal the "natural body" as a painful assemblage of someone else's codes and symbols. As Faulkner's and O'Connor's houses press on Walker's flesh with near-gothic vengeance, the solidity of everyday southern architecture is denormalized, stretched out of shape, revealed as the source of physical and spatial deformity. Crushed by these houses, Walker reminds us that bodies are never alone or unique but always double, mutual, mixed with their environments—the products of a violent hybridity.

In Walker's memoir the communication of ordinary injustice relies on this topos of the open body—a body loaded with political and emotional anagrams of the social. Walker reminds us that racial-territorial crises in the South have culminated in acts of physical violence, in terrifying bodily harm. Set against the fury of a segregated world, the figure of Walker's open, burdened flesh becomes a powerful topos for absorbing and conveying the psychological impact of random acts of racial violence.

The most crucial task for contemporary readers of southern literature (and the first variation on the grotesque as southern theme) is to acknowledge that the grotesque is a form of social protest steeped in local politics. In describing earlier incarnations of the Rabelaisian grotesque Bakhtin suggests that the open, unfinished "body of carnival is not separated from the world by clearly defined boundaries; it is blended with the world, with animals and objects" (1968, 27). But the southern grotesque gives us the frightening results of this bodily blending. The body is fetishized as the site of both self and culture—a place where culture is mapped onto subjectivity and the pain of this mapping becomes visible. We see this all too clearly when Old Nannie's estranged husband, a former slave named Uncle Jimbilly, becomes so misshapen that he can barely move. He "was so old and had spent so many years bowed over things, putting them together and taking them apart . . . he was almost bent double. His hands were closed and stiff from gripping objects tightly . . . and they could not open altogether even if a child took the thick black fingers and tried to turn them back" (Porter 1972, 340). Jimbilly's stiffening body mobilizes the static pain of caste by moving the cost of labor that is out of sight or out of mind into bodily consciousness. In chapter 1, I argued that the grotesque is a figure of speech with the volume turned up, that its bodies entice our hearing because of their anomalousness. But here anomaly is simply the norm. Stuck in the white child's restless body and invited to share her fascination with Uncle Jimbilly's stiff hands, the reader encounters the irrevocable force of a system of southern labor that, even post-emancipation, failed to heal the sufferings of former slaves. In a lower South that replaced slavery with a predatory system of sharecropping and black tenancy, Uncle Jimbilly's deformities signify an unyielding social violence. By marking the site where world is introduced into body, the grotesque offers a forum where the established order can be redoubled, troubled, made palpable.

This political edge is corroborated by the grotesque's spatial peculiarities, its representation of hyperspatialized flesh (its rending apart of normative space, its radical reopening of the field of the world). As Henri Lefebvre suggests, social space is mired in conservation and stasis: "one of the deepest conflicts immanent to space is that space as actually 'experienced' prohibits the expression of conflicts. For conflicts to be voiced, they must first be perceived, and this without subscribing to representations of space as generally conceived" (1991, 365). In other words, the spaces we inhabit seem so stolid, so inevitable, that it is hard to pierce them. Everyday space is a site of prohibition—but also of blindness and enticement. As Lillian Smith recalls of her childhood in northern Florida:

> there were nine of us who grew up freely in a rambling house of many rooms, surrounded by big lawn, back yard, gardens, fields, and barn. It was the kind of home that gathers memories like dust, a place filled with laughter and play and pain and hurt and ghosts and games . . . our world was not limited to the South, for travel to far places seemed a natural thing to us. . . .
>
> We knew we were a respected and important family of this small town but beyond this we gave little thought to status. (1978, 30–31)

We return to the unthought known, to space as an "outside" that seems neutral, natural, free of ideas. Smith suggests that the places we inhabit—however dingy or bereft—are plump with forgetting. She draws on images of conflictless community in order to contest them; she is as adamant about describing the deforming weight of segregated space as is Alice Walker. In *Killers of the Dream* everyone looks normal, but they are deeply deformed and cut apart. "[A] terrifying sense of impending disaster hung over most of us. . . . [Even] favored children of a home . . . favored by exceptional knowledge and good will could not escape the weight of taboo . . . once under it, these children . . . were squeezed by its weight, shaped by it as were all until they, like the rest, became little crooked wedges that fit into the intricately twisting serrated design on life which THEY WHO MAKE THE RULES had prepared for us in Dixie" (92). As a deliberate derangement of bodily space, these violated bodies suggest forces that shape the environment but remain hard to see. For Smith, the shaping of "favored children" into "crooked little wedges" describes an omnivorous racism elided in simple celebrations of place.

The grotesque as figure of speech, state of mind, and as hyperspatialized body becomes a somatic tool or "wedge" that points to the dangers of everyday domesticity. Although place may seem neutral, indifferent, or even user-friendly, this sense of impermeability occurs precisely because the material world forgets about or covers over its throwaways. But I've already suggested that the southern grotesque rides into town with a vehicular energy that mobilizes lost time and space. The grotesque reverses reverse autochthony; it delights in the conversion of ground into figure.

In Ellen Gilchrist's "The President of the Louisiana Live Oak Society" we are invited into an upper-class home furnished with old and new money—with Aubusson carpets and paintings by Dufy, with ancestral portraits glittering beneath sixteen-foot ceilings. The space is beautiful, the plot slender: Gus, a black child from the projects, comes home with Robert, a white boy whose parents are away. When Robert's liberal mother comes back early, she spots Gus—tiny, at leisure, sauntering across her carpets "in the baby-blue towel, black as a walnut tree in winter, draped as a tiny emperor, carrying his empty champagne glass in one hand" (1981, 35). Like the terrified white woman whose scream initiates a lynching in "Big Boy Leaves Home," Lelia lets out "an ancestral, territorial scream, she screamed her head off," and Gus jumps out the third-story window to his death. Figure once again goes to ground. But what's remarkable about this story is that Lelia's white son jumps out too. It is Robert's folly to think that Gus might be permitted—even vicariously—to share in his life of privilege, and the extent of this illusion is revealed when Robert, seeing Gus fall, envisions him flying upward again, a magic ascent tracing a drug-induced arc from the lower stories Gus inhabits as a dope pusher who plies his wares beneath the live oak trees in Audubon park, to the upper-story world of Robert and his parents. When Robert follows his friend out the window, the story ends with two grotesque, mangled bodies—their lost potential mingling with the scents of the crepe myrtle tree. Here the open bodies of two children make the unremarkable properties of "neutral" white space both outrageous and visible. Temperamentally, these children function as a hybrid body; each depends on the other; the death of one necessitates the death of the other. But spatially, ideologically, and socially these children are defined oppositionally, and Gus's fate for crossing into this "neutral" white space is his sacrifice. The boys' fractured bodies suggest the contradictions inherent in and hidden by elite southern space. Robert's parents live in a house built from and dependent on the capital and hallucinogens wrestled from the ghetto, and yet they define themselves as utterly self-reliant. The fates of their children suggest a spatial symbiosis made visible by the grotesque.[3]

By spatializing ideology and presenting its bodily impact, southern authors such as Gilchrist and Walker use the grotesque's opened bodies to trace the physiognomies of the unthought everyday. If southern children become, in Smith's language, cripples "whose legs have been cut off" (94), their bodily topography creates a secret map of their habitus. For Smith, as for Walker, the cozy ampleness of the upper-class white southern world, the comforting places its children inhabit, are clandestine and laced with oppression: "There are the signs without words: big white church on Main Street, little unpainted colored church on the rim of town; big white school, little ramshackly colored school; big white house, little unpainted cabins. . . . And there are the invisible lines that turn and bend and cut the town into segments. Invisible, but electrically charged with taboo. Places you go. Places you don't go. White town, colored town; white streets, colored streets; front door, back door" (95). How do we enact radical changes in regional politics when the regulative force of public space is so strong? By adding or subtracting excess flesh from the body, the southern grotesque has been used, over the space of half a century, to mobilize spatial unrest, challenging the homogeneity and regulative ideals of "ordinary" space. At its best the grotesque troubles these ideals by breaking up the surface of a world that had formerly seemed—at least to its white inhabitants—static, continuous, unified, proper.

But if broken, ungainly bodies can offer this earnest social geometry, how can they also evoke the somatic depth that makes southern writing so powerful? Why is the grotesque so vulgar and bodily? And how can I press its vulgarity into sentience, much less into my sentences? I have argued that the grotesque character whose body is marked with physical extravagance or otherness offers an index to the distribution of political power in southern society. But for the grotesque to shine forth, we must also recognize its slovenliness—its messy bodily capers—as they resist an overt social politics. In Porter's description of Nannie's rebirth as an aged Bantu woman, Nannie's eyes not only become emblems of the bodily harm that whites have inflicted on African American culture; her gaze refuses a leisured readability ("her face was like an eyeless mask," 349). While the grotesque offers a symbolic switchboard providing a map of the discarded bodies miring Smith's Florida or Porter's Texas, it also resists the phenomenon of reading altogether. Nannie's disappearing eyes, her viewless face, create sensations both ecstatic and nauseous, provoking bodily impressions that repudiate our analysis.

By invoking the grotesque's aura of obsession, fetishism, and fixation—its overtones of sadism and jouissance—I am suggesting that we need to dig deeper, to consider the revulsion implicit in Porter's image of Nannie's eyes, the sadism implicit in Gilchrist's dying children, and the self-flagellation implied in Smith's desire to invent public images that tear "down deep into [the] muscles and glands" (Smith 1978, 96). In order to understand a "southern" grotesque, we must tease out its connection with the risible, the archaic, the unspeakable, the obscenely unsentimental. The second formal property of the grotesque, one at odds with my earlier maps, is its brutal physicality, its propensity for somatic revulsion and rapture, its refusal to make friends with the social. The grotesque's disgusting protuberances are sticky and ecstatic, winsome and unbearable, rapturous and offensive. Gnawing at the gullet, they refuse to speak to (that is, they refuse even to refuse) the order of things. The grotesque or wounded body becomes an image that—even in its most comic incarnations—can only make disintegrating marks on the reader's flesh. As Slavoj Zizek argues, "in so far as it sticks out from the (symbolic and symbolized) reality of the body, the wound is 'a little piece of the real,' a disgusting protuberance which cannot be integrated into the totality of 'our own body'" (1991, 78).

What is the force of this fragment that cannot be impaled on culture's hooks? In Carson McCullers's *The Member of the Wedding* the grotesque appears with an amoebalike force—it teases the reader toward a gauntlet of fascinating forms:

> The Giant was more than eight feet high, with huge loose hands and a hang-jaw face. The Fat Lady sat in a chair, and the fat on her was like loose-powdered dough which she kept slapping and working with her hands. . . . The Wild Nigger came from a savage island. He squatted in his booth among the dusty bones and palm leaves and he ate raw living rats. . . . The Wild Nigger knocked the rat's head over his squatted knee and ripped off the fur and crunched and gobbled and flashed his greedy Wild Nigger eyes. Some said that he was not a genuine Wild Nigger, but a crazy colored man from Selma. Anyway, Frankie did not like to watch him very long. . . . The little Pin Head skipped and giggled and sassed around, with a shrunken head no larger than an orange, which was shaved except for one lock tied with a pink bow at the top. The last booth was always very crowded, for it was the booth of the Half-Man Half-Woman, a morphidite and a miracle ofscience. . . .
>
> "I doubt if they ever get married or go to a wedding," she said. "Those Freaks." . . .
>
> John Henry held out an imaginary skirt and, touching his finger to the top of his big head, he skipped and danced like the Pin Head around the kitchen table.

> Then he said: "She was the cutest little girl I ever saw. I never saw anything so cute in my whole life. Did you, Frankie?" (1975, 17–18)

How do we react to these body-obsessed moments?[4] McCullers's story of the Wild Nigger is sad and horrifying; his bone-crunching and rat-gobbling abjection must be politicized (that is, read through the grid of segregationist fantasies) in order to be made bearable. But what about John Henry's identification with and love for the little pinhead girl? What about my own revulsion-desire for the Fat Lady's deadpan body, her floury biscuit-flesh?[5]

Zizek argues that grotesque bodies unleash a barrage of unwanted symptoms—including a revulsion so strong that a viewer may overreact to this stimulus by reducing repulsive characters to their social or regional components, making the body a civic cipher, an infectious carrier of regional or national crisis. If a character seems excessively monstrous or diseased, an audiences may try to avoid the pleasurable or abhorrent feelings this conjures by making the abjected body allegorical, insisting that it *is* decipherable, that it represents something politically "rotten" in the protagonist's country (1981, 79). This act of allegorizing is the very operation I've performed on texts perused in this chapter, and yet the political mapping of the grotesque's physical coordinates can itself be mapped as a reaction-formation, a defense against anxieties about bodily waste and decay.

Where does this leave us? What happens if we refuse to think about the grotesque as the objective correlative for civic decay? Are there other ways to digest the sideshow wonders that could pass for a politics in McCullers's stories? What really happens to readers of southern fictions as they continue to encounter these repetitious bodies: page after page of characters who are bizarre, bloated, inundated with wounds? For Zizek the answer is a startling universalism, a refusal of any act of regional reading: "the symbolic order [and for Zizek this means *any* symbolic order] is striving for a homeostatic balance, but there is in its kernel, at its center, some strange traumatic element which cannot be symbolized, integrated into the symbolic order"—*das Ding* (1991,132). We could say that McCullers gives us a comic rendition of *das Ding* in her juxtaposition of the pinhead girl's citrus-shaped head with its incongruous bow floating on top, signifying both her status as a female object who is made for display and her status as a body on the edge, a sibyl approaching the limits of the social.

According to this model the body that "cannot be symbolized" represents something far more intolerable than our psychic discomfort in inhabiting lumpish bodies that heave and bleed. The grotesque's most notable characteristic in McCullers's sideshow prose is the massive permeability of flesh itself. The giant with his hankering hands or the Fat Lady's all-too-alienable skin may be mildly perturbing. But in this paragraph's flow (or undertow) we encounter something else that frightens: the giant's hands lose themselves in the fat lady's doughy skin, which shapes itself into a flesh-and-blood eating madman whose image vomits up the empty-headed pin-head girl and the ravaged body of the hermaphrodite. This ravaging is not just the physical work of genetic malfunction or cultural chicanery but the inevitable interweaving of bodies that is, for Zizek, the "mortifying" power of human understanding: the flesh-shaping negation inherent in all cultural-symbolic systems "before which the living substance is utterly helpless" (1992, 52). The grotesque becomes the endpoint, the unreadable mystery of the random violence visited on all human flesh. If every knowledge system "is also a social epistemology—a system that carves the world into political fictions with the daily authority to cause thousands to starve, to lose their jobs, to die in wars, or other socially sanctioned acts of violence" (52), the grotesque gestures in the direction of this violence but refuses to provide its map. In this variation on the grotesque as literary theme, the ungainly body cannot be integrated into the particulars of any regional political theory; it does not offer a threshold but repudiates the consolation of social critique.

But can this model give way to other thresholds? While noting the power of Zizek's ideas, I want to suggest that the grotesque's symbolic poverty—its somatic portrait of *das Ding* (with its emphasis on the endlessly penetrable body)—can offer a third model for interpreting the southern grotesque: the body's capacity to bear witness. As Shoshana Felman argues, witnessing is composed of bits and pieces of a memory "that has been overwhelmed by occurrences that have not settled into understanding or remembrance, acts that cannot be constructed as knowledge nor assimilated into full cognition, events in excess of our frames of reference" (1992, 5). The fractured, fragmented nature of testimony spills over into (and may sometimes depend on) the bodily sorrow and nonsense of the grotesque.

And here I want to answer a question posed by Michael O'Brien—a challenge to the idea that we can identify a peculiarly "southern" grotesque. To this I must reply "Yes," in thunder. In one sense the South's grotesques look just like the bizarre bodies of any highly somaticized literature. As O'Brien argues in a review of Bertram Wyatt-Brown's 1994 book on the house of Percy, historians err when they describe southern culture as peculiarly diseased or pathological or grotesque. When Wyatt-Brown argues that the history of the Percys displays an ample supply of doubt, anxiety, repression, disease, and betrayal, O'Brien counters: "Wyatt-Brown is impressed by the singularity of this mayhem. In fact, this is the history of any family. We all have attics stuffed with madwomen, madmen, stained wedding dresses, old photographs ripped in half. Family history is no less ordinary for being savage."[6] This is persistently true. But literature about the South turns often in the direction of deranged or deformed bodies in order to multiply the possibilities for confronting the strangeness of the South's brand of savagery, especially the ways in which racial violence or prohibition distorts ordinary bodies. This confrontation can begin quite humorously, as in Morrison's *Song of Solomon* when Milkman's father, Macon Dead, remembers eating the South's most succulent pig: "He even liked General Lee, for one spring they slaughtered him and ate the best pork outside Virginia, 'from the butt to the smoked ham to the ribs to the sausage to the jowl to the feet to the tail to the head cheese'—for eight months. And there was cracklin in November. 'General Lee was all right by me,' he told Milkman, smiling. 'Finest general I ever knew. Even his balls was tasty'" (1977, 52). This is a prime example of the ribald, raucous, and classically Bakhtinian grotesque. Here history is dismissively rolled into a pork belly, and Robert E. Lee is consumed—balls and all—by a self-empowered black farmer who owns his own land and can feed off the fat of the earth. The grotesque, piggy body has the power of carnival; it converts high to low. But like most carnival acts, eating Robert E. Lee doesn't change very much. Macon also remembers the white men who killed his father: "Had a dog run, they did. That was the big sport back then. Dog races. White people did love their dogs. Kill a nigger and comb their hair at the same time. But I've seen grown white men cry about their dogs" (52). Morrison describes ordinary black subjects who just disappear, whom the white imagination makes sub-subhuman. Carnivalization veers into degradation as black men, once again, become throwaways—ciphers defigured, depersonified, subordinated beneath the grotesque. Women writers employ the grotesque dynamically—to repersonify people and ideas who have disappeared. This results in black characters such as Morrison's Pilate (a gargantuan woman lacking a navel—her loss representing a place of noncontact with lost African earth) or white characters such as O'Connor's Mrs. Turpin. Mocked by an ugly college girl whose eyes fix on Mrs. Turpin "like two drills" (1971, 497), Mrs. Turpin becomes, in her pitiless racism, another piggy figure, "an old wart hog" (500) from hell, while her shoats become "idiot children, their little slit pig eyes searching the floor for anything left" (506). The grotesque is not an exclusively southern form. But its bizarrely opened bodies are particularly useful in bearing witness to the soul-puncturing rigidity of a culture where gender arrangements have been lacerating and racial cruelty is still taken for granted.

Body-Witnessing

In *Reconstruction* Eric Foner prints a letter written by A. D. Lewis, a black North Carolinian, to the governor of his state describing a violent encounter between himself and a white neighbor. This encounter suggests the volatility of a postbellum world in which the most ordinary events acquired political meaning with astounding rapidity.

> Please allow me to call your kine attention to a transaction which occured today between me and Dr. A. H. Jones. . . . I was in my field at my own work and this Jones came by me and drove up to a man's gate that live close by . . . and ordered my child to come there and open that gate for him . . . while there was children in the yard at the same time not more than twenty yards from him and jest because they were white and mine black he wood not call them to open the gate. . . . I spoke gently to him that [the white children] would open the gate. . . . He got out of his buggy . . . and walked nearly hundred yards rite into my field where I was at my own work and double his fist and strick me in the face three times and . . . cursed me [as] a dum old Radical. . . . Now governor I wants you to please rite to me how to bring this man to jestus. (1988, 122)

What makes this encounter so extraordinary?

First, we need to take measure of Lewis's powerful expectation that justice might be served, his spatial and bodily prerogatives defended by the state, his dignity defended. As Foner comments, this expectation could only flourish during the liminal period of Reconstruction, when one set of codes constructing black conduct had been swept away while another was still coming into being. "Only over time would the South's new system of social relations be worked out. As David L. Swain, former governor of North Carolina, remarked in 1865, 'With reference to emancipation, we are at the beginning of the war'" (123).

Second, in this time of enormous upheaval in southern manners, spatial practices were in transition; property codes had been thrown into disarray. Lefebvre insists that space deceives us because its coordinates mask power relations. Ordinarily "the space of a (social) order is hidden in the order of space," where the operating procedures of the powerful not only disguise the logic of hierarchy but appear to result from the "innocent" logic of ownership or territory. If "there are beneficiaries of space, just as there are those excluded from it" or deprived of space, this fact is ascribed to the normative properties of the everyday world (1991, 289). But in the postwar South this normalization began to fall apart, and the body's too-intimate connection to the landscape found voice as freedmen argued that past labors should entitle them to portions of their former owners' estates. As members of a black convention in Alabama urged: "the property which they hold was nearly all earned by the sweat of *our* brows," or, in the words of a freedman from Tennessee: "they should have given us part of Maser's land as us poor old slaves we made what our Masers had" (Foner 1988, 105, 164).[7] Having created the Confederacy's wealth and contoured its turf, these freedmen asked for simple justice; they sought property in the form of spatial recompense.

In Lewis's letter we see that any vestige of this longed-for redistribution of resources evokes an extraordinary white hysteria. The black man's territory, which had been either nonexistent or subject to severe regulation, becomes, at least for the moment, a hard-to-regulate place, while Lewis's children, the once-potent source of white capital, are suddenly decommodified, out of reach.[8] By penetrating this space and puncturing Lewis's flesh, the white man insists on preserving past prerogatives of penetrability: he evokes the lost possibility of his right to African Americans as property. In this violent action the unresolved political and spatial tensions of the public world are resolutely marked on the private body. At the same time Lewis claims his subjectivity as well as his bodily prerogative. That is, Lewis's letter is also an act of testimony; it bears witness to bodily trauma. At first this witnessing is buried in Lewis's necessary euphemisms, his brief formalities: "Please allow me to call your kine attention to a transaction which occured today." But this is a deliberate understatement of a "transaction" in which a man has been beaten: a fact that emerges only in the letter's cumulative physical detail, its absolute insistence on talking back.

In order to explore the profound role that southern bodies play in acts of bearing witness, we need to acknowledge the ways in which testimony departs from ordinary forms of communication, stretching the word beyond its expository limits and in the direction of the world. "To testify—to *vow* to *tell,* to *promise* and *produce* one's own speech as material evidence for truth—is to accomplish a speech act, rather than to simply formulate a statement. As a performative *speech act,* testimony . . . addresses what in history is *action* . . . and what in happenings is *impact*" (Felman and Laub 1992, 5). In writing a letter describing the wrong done to him, Lewis not only attempts to make his beating physically *present* to the governor, he asks for an active response: "Now governor I wants you to please rite to me how to bring this man to jestus."

But if testimony is the essence of speech as *act,* a site where speech reaches toward deed, it often describes experiences that erupt in *das Ding,* that seem overwhelming, unassimilable, beyond local remedy—events that are both incomprehensible and in need of a listener.[9] Those able to listen to a tale of trauma also partake "of the struggle of the victim." As Dori Laub explains, they are seized upon by "the memories and residues" of someone else's traumatic past. "The listener has to feel the victim's victories, defeats and silences, know them from within, so that they can assume the form of testimony" (Felman and Laub 1992, 58). This willingness to be vulnerable to someone else's past marks off testimony from other forms of communication. "While historical evidence to the event which constitutes the trauma may be abundant . . . the trauma—as a known event and not simply as an overwhelming shock—has not been truly witnessed yet, not been taken cognizance of. It is in the listening to the event—being listened to and heard, that the 'knowing' of the event is given birth to" (57).

This sense of testimony that tries to take place in the absence of witnesses finds an unbearable echo in Richard Wright's "The Ethics of Living Jim Crow," in which, half a century after Lewis's beating, Wright uses a grotesque tropology to revisit the silences—the unspeakability—of his past. Brutalized by his white age mates and punished by his mother for testifying against them, Wright describes the trauma of silence. He describes a child's battleground where black kids throw crumbling railroad cinders while white kids hurl broken bottles that pierce the skin. Possessing crueler weapons and better hiding places, Wright's white opponents shroud themselves "behind trees, hedges, and the sloping embankments of their lawns" (1965, 4).

Lacking the fortifications of white urbanity, the young Wright suffers a serious head wound. Frightened and bleeding, he races down the street when his mother comes home to show her his injuries, expecting her to become a participant, a sympathetic co-owner of his trauma: "I could just feel in my bones that she would understand. . . . I grabbed her hand and babbled out the whole story. She examined my wound, then slapped me." Longing to bear witness, Wright is given a thrashing that makes him delirious:

> She grabbed a barrel stave, dragged me home, stripped me naked, and beat me till I had a fever of one hundred and two. . . . She finished by telling me that I ought to be thankful to God as long as I lived that they didn't kill me.
>
> All that night I was delirious and could not sleep. Each time I closed my eyes I saw monstrous white faces suspended from the ceiling, leering at me.
>
> From that time on the charm of my cinder yard was gone. The green trees, the trimmed hedges, the cropped lawns grew very meaningful, became a symbol. Even today when I think of white folks, the hard, sharp outlines of white houses surrounded by trees, lawn, and hedges are present somewhere in the background of my mind. Through the years they grew into an overreaching symbol of fear. (5)

Unable to find a listener, Wright's dreams erupt in bodily symptoms; his psyche offers its own somatic version of testimony. Visited by nightmares, porous to cultural and familial derangements, he simulates the deforming environs described by Walker and Smith where immobile houses have the power to lacerate. In a suburban scene of ordinary white supremacy Wright dramatizes an environment of perpetual distortion where white people's domiciles cut into flesh and bone. The grotesque bodies haunting Wright's dreams not only reveal white injustice, they index Wright's own sense of spatial emergency. White pastoral is stretched and mutilated to reveal its inherent sadism.

The peculiar powers of witnessing inherent in the grotesque emerge from this repetitive blending of body and world; the grotesque is a figure that registers the body's social contamination and becomes itself a contaminant. Instead of offering a degraded form, a response to existential decay or to southern degeneracy, the obsessive use of this trope provides an incredible mimetic device—a way of transferring a version of history from the other to one's own body—in a world where such transfer has been denied.

To understand the complex machinations of this body-witnessing we need to foreground the grotesque's relation to secrecy and silence. The muteness imposed on the young Richard Wright erupts in frightening bodily images, suggesting that, in a world where testimony is denied, where children are safest when they learn *not* to bear witness, the body opens its own nightmare registers of communication. In *Promised Land* Nicholas Lemann describes this onslaught of voicelessness in his tale of the repressive southern world of the twenties and thirties that resulted in the Great Migration:

> Black Clarksdale was full of rumors and secrets, because there was so much that couldn't be expressed openly or that blacks were in no position to investigate. Everybody black in Clarksdale knew, though there was no hard proof of it, that Bessie Smith, the great singer who died after a car accident outside Clarksdale in 1937, had been refused admission to the county hospital on grounds of her race, at a time when she could still have been saved. Shortly after that, the same hospital refused admission to the wife of one of Clarksdale's two or three most prominent black citizens, a dentist named P.W. Hill, when she was in severe distress during childbirth. She and her baby died on the road to Memphis, or so the story went; it was so shrouded in mystery that even Dr. Hill's son and namesake doesn't know what really happened, because he never dared to ask his father about it. (1991, 35)

How do people live with these unspoken facts? How does the body respond to a violently diminished capacity for testimony? Psychic defenses include somatic repression and transgenerational haunting. Physical resources include violence, two-headed men and women, and migration. But the central literary response to silence and censorship is somatic hyperbole: a refusal to name can become a physical site where figurative deformities find their genesis.[10]

In addition, the most crucial observation we can make about Wright's—or Walker's, or Smith's—stories is that these writers bear witness to distortions that happen among the barely visible minutiae of daily life. The grotesque operates as a stain or wound testifying to the unsymbolized traumas of the everyday, to events that are never registered in the world and yet leave a mark on children and grown-ups—whether they are at work, out of work, or at play. What is extraordinary about each of these stories is the ordinariness, the earthliness of the realities they convey. Although the grotesque glitters with the aura of the astonishing, the out-of-the-ordinary, its associations with the fabulous or fantastic should not obscure (and may in fact be the very ground for) its capacity for bearing witness to the most unassuming human dramas.

I'm suggesting that although the grotesque body is constructed to shock, distracting the reader from self-soothing abstractions, its impact also works unevenly to accentuate the "doubleness of social being" that can become a habitual response to situations of political cruelty. In an unjust world, as Michael Taussig suggests, there are a thousand daily situations

understand these stigmata, historians must query the child's body: "Fathers have only to mistake effects for causes, believe in the reality of an 'afterlife,' or maintain the value of eternal truths, and the bodies of their children will suffer" (1977, 147). What kind of suffering does Smith find in her childhood memories?

Smith's genius in unearthing this buried incident from her early life is threefold. First, as Dori Laub demonstrates, "a witness is a witness to the truth of what happens during an event" (Felman and Laub 1992, 80), and Smith manages—in the midst of the Byzantine permutations of turn-of-the-century southern racism—to recognize what constitutes an event. By making an incident in the lives of two children so compelling, she begins to explore the gargantuan implications of small acts of racism (or, in Foner's terms, she describes "the way an everyday encounter rapidly descended into violence and acquired political meaning" [1988, 122–23]).

Second, Smith's testimony points to the paradox of publicity—to what is known in her world but rarely spoken. It seems more than ironic that an event Smith describes as scripted, collective, and histrionic never sees the light of day; it remains a bitterly private drama lacking listeners. This visibility coupled with an absence of listeners is crucial to our sense of Smith's past, for in testimony the act of bearing witness is always profoundly interactive, a form of covenant-making in which the listener becomes a co-owner or co-participant in trauma. When Smith keeps insisting, "I shall tell it," she is really insisting, "you shall hear it." What is collectively hidden will be collated and shown.

Finally, by insisting that southern culture not only is *in* her body but has created her body, become her body, Smith anticipates Pierre Bourdieu's insistence that a group's "ultimate values . . . are never anything other than the primary primitive dispositions of the body, 'visceral' tastes and distastes, in which the group's most vital interests" (1984, 474) are both hidden and embedded. Shorn of its ceremony the body is, at best, a torn, riven thing—covered with hungry orifices. Smith recollects that "we learned the dance that cripples the human spirit, step by step, we who were white and we who were colored, day by day, hour by hour, year by year, until the movements were reflexes and made for the rest of our life without thinking. . . . These ceremonials in honor of white supremacy, performed from babyhood, slip from the conscious mind down deep into muscles and glands and become difficult to tear out" (96). It is Smith's reimagining of these orifices as painful depths that gives the white southern body its potential for bearing witness. Writing not only means bearing witness to pain but finding strategies for testifying about what others have silenced, crippling the white body to make it speak.

In the South of Lillian Smith's childhood the body of the upper-class white child might be physically unharmed, but her psyche has been penetrated by horrors, perforated by everyday life in "a region that values color more than children" (75): "So we suffered the grown folks' trouble, but without understanding. Cruel things were learned casually. You would be in the buggy with your father, out near the turpentine still where the convict gang worked. . . . A foreman would come over and make his report. 'What he needs is the sweat box,' sometimes he'd say of a troublesome Negro. And you'd sit there listening while chills curled over your body and mind" (70). Although Smith's father refuses to deploy this particular brand of torture, his livelihood depends on convict labor he has leased from the state. Smith recalls confusing memories of "these same friends" who "gave you and your little sister candy and dimes and . . . presents from Savannah. Strange, how you remember a little bag of candy and a sweat box together" (70).

Smith looks without flinching at her own racist culture, which bears down on African American subjects without ceasing. In this turn-of-the-century world the potential for either white or black witnessing, for giving testimony against racist norms, is violently repressed:

> All knew that under quiet words and warmth and laughter, under the slow ease and tender concern about small matters, there was a heavy burden on all of us and as heavy a refusal to confess it. The children knew this "trouble" was bigger than they, bigger than their family, bigger than their church, so big that people turned away from its size. They had seen it flash out and shatter a town's peace, had felt it tear up all they believed in. They had measured its giant strength and felt weak when they remembered.
>
> This haunted childhood belongs to every southerner of my age. (25)

We return to the matter of scale, to the epic proportions of the everyday and a fantasmatic rearrangement of space in which "quiet words," "slow ease," and "tender concern" become burdensome, in which childhood itself is permeated with panic. I have argued that this conflation of scales, in which the public world haunts or penetrates the quotidian, is one of the defining characteristics of fiction by southern women. Southern literary children (as well as the sociological giants and miniatures haunting their lives) give us a "history of bodies" in which the disciplinary work of dominant cultures becomes intimate and visible. Political power not only penetrates local bodies, it seeps through people who seem inconsequential and suggests the public logic behind their disarray.[11] It is this seepage of power into miniature or minoritized bodies that defines the southern grotesque as a prototype for literary testimony.

I have begun to trace a pressure that is, if not unique, then at least familiar to the South: the strategy of speaking through the broken body. In the first half of the twentieth century, stories about psychic or bodily trauma, or perhaps I should say, the increasing absence of such stories, begin to pile up. As an adult Richard Wright struggles to find words forbidden to him as a child. Lacking a primary listener he conjures baby nightmares and rearticulates his childhood terror as the sign of madness in the grown-up world. We find a similar pattern in *Killers of the Dream,* where the silence of childhood erupts in scary somatic images. Once again Smith emphasizes the pressure *not* to tell:

> "But you said yourself she has nice manners. You said that," I persisted.
>
> "Yes, she is a nice child. But a colored child cannot live in our home."
>
> "Why?
>
> "You know, dear! You have always known that white and colored people do not live together."
>
> "Can she come to play?"
>
> "No."
>
> "I don't understand."
>
> "I don't either," my young sister quavered.
>
> "You're too young to understand. And don't ask me again, ever again, about this!"
>
> Mother's voice was sharp but her face was sad and there was no certainty left there. (36–37)

"Don't ask me again." Smith explains how the paradox of absolute racial knowledge can sit, side by side, with abhorrent acts that remain shamelessly known but unthought. Although Smith's story acts as a screen memory, a substitute for "buried experiences that I did not have access to," like Wright she is driven by the urgency to speak: "I believe there is one experience which pushed these doors open, a little," Smith says. "And I am going to tell it here." She begins with the story of "a little white girl" who has been "found in the colored section of our town, living with a Negro family in a broken-down shack":

> This family had moved in a few weeks before and little was known of them. One of the ladies in my mother's club, while driving over to her

> washerwoman's saw the child swinging on a gate. The shack, as she said, was hardly more than a pigsty and this white child was living with dirty and sick-looking colored folks. 'They must have kidnapped her,' she told her friends. Genuinely shocked, the club women busied themselves in an attempt to do something, for the child was very white indeed. The strange Negroes were subjected to a grueling questioning and finally grew evasive and refused to talk at all. This only increased the suspicion of the white group. The next day the club women, escorted by the town marshal, took the child from her adopted family despite their tears. (35)

This is an Ovidian tale of child-stealing and fairytale cruelty. Although Janie, the stolen child, is removed from her home by brute force, she seems happy (at least in her white family's eyes) to be thus transported. Swinging on the gate between cultures, she has sudden access to white aristocratic domesticity. In Smith's childhood home she is dazzled, caught in a shower of light, and in this ecstatic space Lillian and Janie become mirror images, doppelgängers, the world's happiest twins: "she roomed with me, sat next to me at the table . . . she wore my clothes, played with my dolls and followed me around from morning to night. . . . I was as happily dazed, for her adoration was a new thing to me; and as time passed a quick, childish, and deeply felt bond grew up between us" (35).

This "deeply felt bond" may be a rich child's fantasy, and yet it offers both Lillian and Janie a resting place amidst the attenuated violence of the Jim Crow South, for even Smith's peaceful Florida home is saturated with status anxiety and economic asymmetry. Here the distance between adjacent spaces seems immense, as children migrate between incommensurable worlds, from the "pigsty" made by dirty, "sick-looking colored folks" to the theoretically clean and communal space of Smith's household. The surrounding vicinity is deliberately schizophrenic: "Our father owned large business interests, employed hundreds of colored and white laborers, paid them the prevailing low wages, worked them the prevailing long hours, built for them mill towns (Negro and white), built for each group a church, saw to it that religion was supplied free, saw to it that commissary supplied commodities at a high price, and in general managed his affairs much as ten thousand other southern businessmen managed theirs" (33). Political hegemony depends on the ability to control people's material contexts. "If workers can be persuaded . . . that space is an open field of play for capital but a closed terrain for themselves, then a crucial advantage accrues to the capitalists" (Harvey 1990, 233). This segregated world is something other than the accidental mythos in which (as he apologizes to his children) Smith's father happens to find himself; instead, its practices support a high-stakes game in which this father arranges space to maximize his family's investments.

Having crossed these borderlands in both directions, Janie's body and history make worlds collide. In zoning Janie for whiteness the club women try to create the illusion of a level playing field among children that draws both crackers and mill owners together. By replaying the brief pastoral moment when Janie bridges hierarchical worlds, Smith tries to create a sense that even inimical racial spaces (the ghetto, the big house) have something in common: there is a safety zone, a haven for children, a place in between. But this hopefulness collapses; in trying to make Janie feel at home in their unequal world, the club women's real motive is to resurrect the boundaries between everyone. Both of these children's homes become nonplaces, sites of absence and distance that belie the possibility of even small acts of collectivity.[12]

The loss of even an imagined community becomes the central burden of Smith's story. On the surface Janie is welcomed into her new home: "I do not know why my mother consented to this plan. Perhaps because she loved children and always showed concern for them. It was easy for one more to fit into our ample household and Janie was soon at home there." But Smith is supercharging this territory to describe the pangs of Janie's deterritorialization—and it comes all too soon.

After a telephone call from a "colored" orphanage, "there was a meeting at our home. Many whispers. All afternoon the ladies went in and out of our house talking to Mother in tones too low for children to hear." These ladies feel an obsessive need to cross and recross the threshold of whiteness. "As they passed us at play, they looked at Janie and quickly looked away again, though a few stopped and stared at her as if they could not tear their eyes from her face" (35). The image of these ladies is premonitory. They have discovered that Janie is not "white" but "black," the child of mixed parentage. This failure to "tear their [own] eyes from her face" foregrounds their maenad-like rage at the mixing of body parts; they are fascinated and repulsed by the implacable category confusion Janie's being evokes. Like these ladies, Smith is also obsessed; if she tears this incident from her own life, she fears, everything else will be torn open as well. That is, Smith remembers herself neither as playmaker nor audience but as an actress: as someone complicitous in parental drama; for in order to obliterate Janie's whiteness, these motherly white women not only participate in her mutilation, they conscript their own children to help. Lillian and her sister participate in Janie's exile, just as they had earlier applauded her kidnapping. This cruelty occurs without any grown-up solace; no one steps in to alleviate Janie's suffering.

Still oblivious to the sea change that is about to occur, these little "white" girls hear their father's guffaws: "Work it out, Mame, as best you can. After all, now that you know, it is pretty simple." So much for "the mind of the South." Although the father denies it, to know (when such knowledge is forbidden—"Don't ask me again") is always to complicate. Although the gap between adult perceptions and children's feelings was already immense, the space connecting these realms now becomes an abyss as the mildest of mothers tosses her children over a precipice:

> [She] told us that in the morning Janie would return to Colored Town. . . . She asked me if I would like to give Janie one of my dolls. She seemed hurried, though Janie was not to leave until next day. . . . And in dreamlike stiffness I brought in my dolls and chose one for Janie. And then I found it possible to say "Why is she leaving? She likes us, she hardly knows them. She told me she had been with them only a month."
>
> "Because," Mother said gently, "Janie is a little colored girl." (36)

Smith presents a southern world unanchored and unmoored, where little girls slip, like Wonderland's Alice, into the interstice of this "because." In describing this nightmare plight, *Killers of the Dream* presents a world so obsessed with protecting its racial imaginary that it offers children of every color a quick trip to nowhere, a nightmare journey into a segregated void that is also the site of psychic deformity.

Smith uses the figure of the grotesque to draw us into this void. She invites us to feel how children get conscripted, how they are forced to join an uncanny theater. In its "dreamlike stiffness" the child's body is transformed into a puppet or mannequin, the absurd equivalent of the doll that will be offered as a token of sanity. There are other stage directions. Segregation is hardly a matter for gentleness, but Smith's mother enacts its by-laws in a "gentle" tone, delivering a blow to the substantiality of her children's flesh. Suddenly the body's primary attributes—its imagined wholeness, extension in space, and hoped-for impenetrability—are not absolute, but relational, theatrical, vulnerable.

To realize that the body is the only ticket to privilege and yet is nothing substantial, is, in fact, nothing like a body, is not one's own, nor one's parents', but a hollow space society carves out and arbitrarily names or disdains—this cripples children who are just learning to trust their sensual density and the seriousness of the body's claims. Shocked and hurt, the "white" children lash out at their mother, hoping to subvert this tragic loss of spatial autonomy.

> "But she's white!"
> "We were mistaken. She is colored."
> "But she looks—"
> "She is colored. Please don't argue!"
> "What does it mean?" I whispered.
> "It means," Mother said slowly, "that she has to live in Colored Town with colored people." (36)

The question is existential, but the mother can only respond in flat prose with a geography lesson. No one cares—not even Lillian Smith in writing her memoir—to think further about what Janie's proscriptive blackness means for Janie herself. Banished again, does she find love in the arms of the black family who adopted her, or is she is left to her own private sorrow, marked by stigmata as a child of neither color, to be cast out of this moneyed world into a never-ending metamorphosis from subject to abject?

Unwilling and unable to hone in on Janie, Smith uses a grotesque tropology to bear witness to what she *does* know—her own part as a monstrous initiate. A co-conspirator with her sister, she joins a community of collective malice:

> I was overcome with guilt. For three weeks I had done things that white children were not supposed to do. And now I knew these things had been wrong.
>
> I went to the piano and began to play, as I had always done when I was in trouble. I tried to play my next lesson and as I stumbled through it, the little girl came over and sat on the bench with me. Feeling lost in the deep currents sweeping through our house that night, she crept closer and put her arms around me and I shrank away as if my body had been uncovered. I had not said a word, I did not say one, but she knew, and tears slowly rolled down her little white face. (38)

As Smith's text veers toward sentimentality (with its emotional triumph and self-comforting tears), she suddenly pulls back from the reader to administer a shock—and in this moment she describes one site of genesis for the southern grotesque. In anatomizing a scene that helps generate the dominant literary figure of her generation, Smith also helps elucidate this metaphor's awkward role in bearing witness to trauma.

In Smith's hands the grotesque body is the appropriate genre for proclaiming trauma because it does not move us to tears—in fact, it disrupts the easy solipsism of an identification with Janie or Lillian. It descends like a deus ex machina with the power to rearrange the reader's perceptions of southern space. (As Ruth Padel says of the *mekhane,* the deus ex machina so popular in fourth-century Greek drama: its entrance marks the moment when "the interior opens up, something comes out from within . . . and rearranges the situation" [1990, 363].) This is the intensity Smith wants her grotesque body to have. As it enters her text with the demonic nonchalance of a social machine that seems to descend from above, it also emerges from the interiority of white victims who pretend to be helpless against the ecstatic machinery of white segregation. "I began to understand slowly at first but more clearly as the years passed, that the warped, distorted frame we have put around every Negro child from birth is around every white child also. Each is on a different side of the frame but each is pinioned there. And I knew that what cruelly shapes and cripples the personality of one is as cruelly shaping and crippling the personality of the other" (39). The simplicity of this exposition is the source of its power: The grotesque is something "we have done"; it is both a random act and a framework. It is also an action that bleaches out the acting power of the "I." This "I" becomes an "each" that is indistinguishable from the acted-on other. White transitiveness turns in on itself. After this deformation the "I" may return as a fiction—but it is haunted, reformulated, sentenced to dwell outside its own powers of consent: "I began to see that though we may, as we acquire new knowledge, live through new experiences, examine old memories, gain the strength to tear the frame from us, yet we are stunted and warped and in our lifetime cannot grow straight again any more than can a tree, put in a steel-like twisting frame when young, grow tall and straight when the frame is torn away at maturity" (39). The sturdy verbs asserting self-knowledge ("I began to understand. . . . And I knew. . . . I began to see") become strategies for declaring the "I's" power in order to deflate it—to establish its participation in acts of communal maiming. Here the self's rhetorical capacity to "begin," "acquire," "live," "examine," and "gain . . . strength" seeps away as Smith compares the experience of being southern to the anguish created by an instrument of torture that turns southern children into creatures wracked by social and psychic deformities. Her indictment may be florid, her prose hyperbolic and sweeping, but this is part of the point. For Smith, to be a white southerner is to know and be the grotesque—to overwrite, overread, and participate in an economy of cruelty, defensiveness, reaction formation, and overcompensation. Within this economy morality, maturity, or even the decision to cast off the worst forms of racism offers no shelter against the power of a self-stunting habitus.

Why belabor this point? I want to use Smith's self-dramatizing alignment with the southern grotesque to express its complexity as a figurative form of witnessing. As we have seen, testimony offers its listeners the chance to experience history—that is, events that have happened to others—within the domain of one's own body, with the perceptual power that is casually reserved for one's own body. As Felman argues in her essay on Camus, the most extraordinary property of bearing witness is its capacity to make history somatic, to make someone else's experience seem visceral (1992, 108).

In corroboration, we have encountered within the grotesque a psychosocial layering in which the jagged torso, punctured by culture, filled with empty economies, becomes a cartographic machine for reassembling knowledge about social conventions and codes. (Recall that in Alice Walker's house-deformed psyche she gives us in miniature the political topography of segregation.) At the same time, the grotesque is something more—and something less—than a map. If the grotesque body offers heterogeneous routes to southern pathologies, if its acts of surplus mutilation work emotionally and cognitively to undo normal readings of space and time, it is also a trope that bears witness to its own inadequacies. It is hyperbolic, uneven, and comic, and yet it plunges us into bizarre acts of transference. In other words, the grotesque mimics the quandary of living between an intelligible body inhabiting intelligible space and an unthinkable, unintelligible body that endures a terrible relativity. (That is, Smith uses the grotesque to give this shared relativity a regional depth. If the literary grotesque becomes a paradoxical space where the private body and the regional or national body come together, it is also, for Smith, a place of slippage where the South's regional story comes apart.)

I have suggested that the grotesque becomes, among other things, a shorthand for unwitnessed trauma, and yet southern literature is also much cannier than this—and less instrumental. Smith focuses on what happens to both black and white southern children when the open secret of race is staged without any means of bearing witness to its traumatic effects. As a dénouement she gives us another staged effect: the literary creation of the southern grotesque as a testimonial form. This bold metaphor repeats itself throughout Smith's memoir: "From the day I was born . . . I was put in a rigid frame too intricate, too twisting to describe here so briefly, but I learned to conform to its slide-rule measurements" (29). For Smith the social framework always denotes deformation; it condenses the violence Smith associates with Confederate nostalgia and her hatred of repressive evangelists: "For all are tied up with each other and have much to do with the quality of the southern conscience that is stretched so tightly on its frame of sin and punishment and God's anger" (101).[13]

In the story of Janie we see a hypothetical site for these images, and yet we also see how the grotesque is not only abrasive but inadequate. Its ornate verbal machinery is too clumsy to express very much. At the same time, even the most baroque of Smith's grotesques, even the images that draw attention to themselves as contrivances, give me the shivers. As Smith traces the distorting force of ideology in folks' daily lives, as her text rises to the limits of baroque sentimentality, she continues to show us a stain, a "mysterious detail that 'sticks out,' that does not 'fit' into the symbolic network of reality and . . . indicates that 'something is amiss'" (Zizek 1992, 116). Felman has described the failure of testimony as the listener's failure: a loss of historical imagination reflecting an inability to bear witness to another's predicament. The grotesque situates itself in this failure but also draws attention to the body as stain or spot, to the tacky, sticky somatic self that will not go away.

Finally, I want to return to the idea that the ungainly, damaged southern body calls forth an array of emotional responses, including empathy, identity, horror and comic release. The frisson of disturbance a reader encounters in the grotesque can inspire an incredible sense of pathos combined with shocked recoil, with a sense of relief that "this is not my body." This uncanny recognition is part of the grotesque's power—a recognition that is always replete with denial, since every body is riddled with holes, beset with its own incompleteness and embarrassing excess. Thus, for the reader, the body that is not-me can become anyone's approximate body: a body proximate to abjection, embarrassment, anxiety, and the trauma of an inevitable hybridity, of the body's amalgamation with its environment. This figurative body is only available as the carrier of social paradox and crisis, as a tantalizing knot or aporia. It is simultaneously the point where the self's relation to society becomes unreadable, because the body is mere corporeality; its crises are censored, hushed up, condensed and displaced as somatic symptoms. But the grotesque body is also a flagrant *overrepresentation* of the body that insists on being read. It is perforated, inconsistent, permeated with otherness: a delicious, frightening riddle, an invitation to decipher the hierarchies, the power relations, the psychic geometries of daily southern history. It is this overdetermined, mingled economy that suggests the grotesque's power in acts of southern witnessing. As readers we oscillate between the demands it makes on our somatic intellect (I may not want to be this body, but it draws me; it fascinates me: What can this body mean?) and the demands it makes on our epistemic body. (How do I ward off or disavow this knowledge; how can I allow myself to connect with the contaminating bodies of others?)

The grotesque body presents, then, a riddle that will not go away. It is not just a worn-out, "torn-away frame" but a framework that tears. Far from being domesticated, as southern women move from the twenties to the fifties and sixties, the grotesque gets wilder and less manageable; it functions as a sign of nonintegration, a signal from a world that practices segregation without reprieve. Its excess of meaning (this awkward figure that endures too much mutilation and invites comedy in its whiff of excess) functions with precise imperfection; it opens a space of permeable, ongoing disturbance and offers another way of engaging with the reader's soma: a kind of contact zone where the reader runs smack into ideology—but ideology as body and blood.

Chapter Nine

Studying the Waffle House Chain, or Dirt as Desire in *Their Eyes Were Watching God*

In the end, I have to come back to "the" South, for there is one more obstacle to finding an audience for southern women's fiction. How should we address the current minoritization of southern studies within the academy, the diminished place of the South in the academic marketplace? Why does the South sell best to the South?

This hasn't always been the case. In their heyday, southern literary and historical studies were at the center of American studies. Faulkner became America's answer to Joyce, Brooks's and Warren's Agrarian-inspired New Criticism its answer to Leavis, and a series of powerful, influential historians (as socially conscious about race as British Marxists have been about labor) answered to no one but simply redrew the districts of American history. The South was a puzzle to be solved on the way to formulating a uniquely American sense of identity. In the midst of the civil rights movement the need to solve this puzzle intensified. To understand American race-thinking, one had to understand the South; to follow American economic trends, one needed to follow the South's rise from its depression-era status as the nation's number one economic problem to its air-conditioned spree as the Sunbelt. For several decades the South seemed to have cornered the market on economic pathos, upward mobility, and racist drama. Its particolored response to the New Deal and the civil rights movement offered great political projects that fascinated national scholars well into the seventies and eighties.

The urgency is now elsewhere, as different parts of the national population become prominent in an era of massive migration and globalizatio satisfy new demographic or economic needs. In addition, American Studi has seen three crucial shifts. First, scholars of regionalism have ushered in a more sophisticated set of topographical epistemologies, making it plausible to argue that "the" South is defunct as a category because there are so many Souths. Second, the South has lost its aura as national metaphor (that is, as national scapegrace, with a dramatic edge on the study of terror) because everywhere is now the South. (This foregrounds nationwide repetitions of racial prejudice; *Brown v. Board of Education* did, after all, originate in Topeka, Kansas, and Rodney King's beating took place in California, not to mention busing riots in Boston and race rebellions everywhere). As the horrors of racism have migrated, the fascination with the South as a singular source of these stories has waned. Third, in the midst of globalization, the United States has encountered other urgent projects—rethinking colonialism, postcolonialism, the Cold War, America's relation to new monetary systems, migrant and immigrant populations (including the growing diversity not only of black but of Asian, Latino, and Native American populations), and an increasing sense of connectedness to the roller-coaster economies of developing nations in a shrink-wrapped, petroleum-drunk world. The South now participates in these issues on an equal footing with other American regions.

In any event, the grand, satisfying story, the highly plotted bifurcations of the war between North and South, the matter of slavery, the many puzzles over the sources of fractured union and reunion no longer stimulate the same appetite for knowledge. Nor do these stories evoke as much sympathy for the melancholic white southerner, that most homebound and "placed" of all Americans, who still wants to be carried back to ole Virginie—homebred but ironically still longing for home.

One decision on how to market "the" South amidst these changes has been a will to mythologize, to reinvent the South as another source for whatever's hot in the academic marketplace—meaning, for the moment, cultural studies, multiculturalism, and circum-Atlantic geography. As William R. Ferris, the editor of the *Encyclopedia of Southern Culture,* said in a 1997 *New York Times* interview: "The South is the image of Huckleberry Finn and Jim—black and white figures dependent on each other for survival. . . . The South is where the two great cultural streams from Africa and Europe converge" (*New York Times,* 29 August 1997, A9).

But to read the apartheid South as the epic site of racial intersubjectivity smacks of political opportunism at best. Two days after the Ferris interview, the *Times* converted these myths to mock epic, giving us a sense of what at least one of these cultural streams can amount to. Governor Fob James of Alabama (who appealed, in the nineties, to white voters still interested in what the *Times* reporter called "cultural issues") defined the conservative edge of one of these streams. James is notorious for revivifying the Scopes Monkey Trial halo of the South. Not only did he threaten to send out the National Guard to block a court order calling for the removal of the Ten Commandments from an Alabama courtroom, not only did he send a letter to a federal judge arguing that the Bill of Rights does not apply to the states, but he was a politician comfortable with the southern mores of the twenties and thirties, happy to live in the "Sahara of the Bozart." James used state funds to send Alabama's high-school teachers a book on the merits of creationism; he also reinvented old forms of national tragedy by reintroducing chain gangs for Alabama state inmates (*New York Times,* 29 August 1997, A1). As David G. Bronner, a prominent Alabamian, said plaintively: "Why he does some of these things is beyond me. . . . He focuses on things that, at best, the public may like to hear but in reality do not do much for a poor state. It has a lot of the same synergies of the Wallace era: get people all riled up and not accomplish anything" (*New York Times,* 29 August 1997, A10). Even Republican demagogues demurred, suggesting that James's politics "evoke all the most negative stereotypes of the Old South" (A10), as well as a chance for antisouthernists to say "see, nothing's changed." Meanwhile, offering sound bites for the national press, James recommended that "state workers study the Waffle House chain, the Governor's favorite restaurant, as a model for government efficiency and consistency. 'They're all good,' Mr. James told the state personnel board. 'That's the thing I like about it. There ain't no surprises'" (1).

With this kind of national coverage of the Stone-Age South, it is little wonder that, as Anne Jones argues, those who "speak of southern cultural studies in the same breath with gender studies, or Chicano/a studies . . . still . . . evoke surprise. More often than not the result is still polite or humorous dismissal, not curiosity or encouragement" (1997, n.p.). After sporadic and politically induced prominence spun out of the South's difference and inferiority, southern studies is now marginalized or ghettoized in the academy, and fiction by southern women is hardly the flavor of the month.[1] As Jones argues: "There is still a national climate that even today uses the South either to scratch the nation's itches or as the trash bin of its history. Ironically, some of the most insistent stereotyping of southern studies within the academy comes from the very corners where cultural diversity found its earliest champions. It is difficult still for many professors to see how spending time teaching *The Birth of a Nation* and *Gone with the Wind* does anything to further diversity. On the contrary, they feel it may subtly teach students ancient hatreds." In this climate, it is surprising to be wedded so obstinately to reanimating southern fiction. Why write about southern women writers now?

First, because there are so many of them. We now possess a powerful century and a half of women's writing coming out of the South. How do we account for the similarities among these writers, as well as their regional and historical differences? In *A Room of One's Own,* Woolf explains that we write back through our mothers if we are women. She traces a remarkable line of descent in which the advent of women's writing becomes as important a world-historical event as the War of the Roses; she describes the importance of eighteenth-century women to the emergence of great artists such as Austen, the Brontës, and George Eliot in the nineteenth century. With this history in mind, it is amazing to think about the unbroken stream of extraordinary writing by southern women stretching from the Civil War to the present.[2] It is amazing because this feat is matched by no other American region. But most remarkable is the question of what southern writing does to Woolf's theorem. If we write back through our mothers when we are women, the question we must ask in the South is—which mothers?

Many white southerners were raised by black women, while many black southerners lost the constancy of their mothers to underpaid work in white homes. What is the status, in white women's fiction, of African American women's voices, speech, writing? Why does Willa Cather locate the source of her stories about the South in Till, the former slave she portrays in *Sapphira and the Slave Girl,* rather than her own parents? Why does she enfranchise this freedwoman's speech and disenfranchise the Canadianized speech of Nancy, who is in the end this story's most progressive black woman? Similarly, what is the status, in black women's fiction, of white women's writing? What does it mean for Alice Walker not only to identify with Zora Neale Hurston but to trace her roots back to the stories of Flannery O'Connor, whose house (just down the road from her parents' sharecroppers' shack) was made with slave labor? In order to parse the connections that this century and a half of strong writing has made possible, we need to explore a broad set of variables—not only an increase in letter and journal writing among white women during the Civil War, but the growing numbers of literate black women after the war and the effect of their writing and voices on mainstream white writers such as Chopin, King, and

Glasgow, as well as the effect of white women's writing on these black contemporaries. We find in a handful of stories written in the 1890s this rarity. The white women writing these stories describe hidden black mothers who not only are literate but possess the letter, the scene of inscription, as a form of writing that both frees and imprisons the body. But these stories also raise the question: Who owns the alphabet? As "Désirée's Baby" ends, a "black" mother's letter falls into the hands of her "white" son—a man cruel to his slaves and blind to his origins. The story ends with his unspoken sensations, with feelings put into play by black writing. The shock of bodies that follow the letter of the law is met by an aftershock: the power of African Americans to rescript the meaning of that letter.

I've argued that white southern women writers are marginalized not only because of the region they come from but because the lenses that most critics use to disseminate their work make these writers seem relatively tame or mundane, whereas black women writers are rarely countenanced as "southern." I've suggested new ways to think about southern writing that should heat up this territory and spark debate about southern women's roles in the shaping of American fiction. These writers are wonderfully intemperate. As Flannery O'Connor commented after a rough social outing: "I have just got through talking to one of our honorable regional (with a vengeance) bodies. . . . After my talk, one lady shook my hand and said, 'That was such a nice dispensation you gave us, honey.' Another said, 'What's wrong with your leg, sugar?' I'll be real glad when I get too old for them to sugar me" (1979a, 119–20).

Second, scholars have yet to account for the extraordinary formal power of fiction by southern women—the ways in which their texts are politically and aesthetically loaded. These authors depict a world that is, quite literally, crazy with meaning, a craziness that includes the prevalence of throwaway bodies in an economy based on white privilege, a national epistemology of racial unknowing (of consuming trauma as a media event but not absorbing the implications for those traumatized). This literature stirs up new ways of thinking about labor and object relations, and about the ways in which commodities become magnets for labor, points of crossover, exchange, blockage, or leakage between black and white cultures. At its best, southern women's writing refuses to echo the mute, invisible whiteness characterizing canonical American literature but attempts something that is just as uneasy. In *The Member of the Wedding,* John Henry's "chest was white and wet and naked, and he wore around his neck a tiny lead donkey tied by a string. . . . [He] had a little screwed white face and he wore tiny gold-rimmed glasses. He watched all of the cards very carefully, because he was in debt; he owed Berenice more than five million dollars" (1975, 3). Whiteness and blackness are painful categories in McCullers's novella: Berenice's brown eye is fixed and sad, John Henry's white face is "screwed." Even more painful is McCullers's ironic joke about this little boy's unpaid debt. The exorbitant sum of five million dollars recalls African Americans' demands during Reconstruction to recover their full contributions to a spiraling American economy. In *Reconstruction: American's Unfinished Revolution,* Eric Foner describes the angry logic of Bayley Wyat, after his family's eviction from land that freedmen had been granted near Yorktown, Virginia: "We has a right to the land where we are located. For why? I tell you. Our wives, our children, our husbands, has been sold over and over again to purchase the lands we now locates upon. . . . And den didn't we clear the land and raise de crops ob corn, ob cotton, ob tobacco. . . . And den didn't dem large cities in de North grow up on de cotton and de sugars and de rice dat we made?" (1988, 105).

Earlier I suggested that the usual direction for characters in southern fiction is a descent from figure to ground. Like the child in *Meridian,* like Grace King's little convent girl, they fall into some local version of "that vast, hidden, dark Mississippi that flows beneath the one we see; for her body was never found" (King 1995, 176). But another formal characteristic of southern fiction is that the southern grotesque (or here its cognate, the racial sublime) offers a trope where this direction is reversed.

> Then, as Robert watched, Gus pushed off from the earth. He began to ascend back up through the broken branches like a movie played in reverse, like a wild kite rising to meet the sun, and Robert was amazed and enchanted by the beauty of this feat and jumped from the window high into the air to join Gus on his journey.
>
> And Lelia beat on the door and beat on the door and beat on the door. (Gilchrist 1981, 37)

In this unusual scene a black child who has come to earth emerges in hallucinatory splendor to claim the white child who is his twin. Gilchrist is responding to the death by drowning of the black child in *Meridian* (as well as to half a dozen other tales). In both of these stories a child is picked up and made into weird, vertiginous images. We have already examined Meridian's valiant response when a black child who has been playing in her neighborhood drowns. In a devastating scene, Meridian gathers his corpse in her arms and carries him to City Hall. In bringing the mess of the margins to the center, Walker protests the melancholic landscape of race-loathing and cruelty that surrounds her black characters. The child's lost body represents lives that have been thrown away, stories that have never happened, labor that could have supported the lives of black children, foundations never plumbed. *Meridian* uses the grotesque to transform the meaning of African Americans who have been consigned to the status of waste, rubbish, pollution. As ground becomes figure, formlessness form, the grotesque puts a face on facts and subjects who have been defaced, and the reader is showered with the fantasmatic: with the discovery that in this South, the uncanny is there every day, is the everyday.

If earlier stories by southern women portray a society cleansing itself, earth or water swallowing bodies that have become objects of attrition, stories written after the racial ferment that gathered speed during World War II break this pattern; they work past the contamination of place by dispensing pollution. Instead of recycling trauma, these stories unearth it, creating an in-your-face monstrosity crazy with meaning. Throughout *Dirt and Desire* I have argued that Walker and her cohorts excavate a series of everyday crises that describe life in the twentieth-century South—a time of enormous upheaval that includes the depression, the New Deal, World War II, the civil rights movement, and decades of postmodernization. We need to continue investigating the way these upheavals make their way into women's fiction by repeating our usual habits of opening texts to discover sociopolitical coordinates and by looking at the amazing formal properties that have responded to what is nonmonumental in southern history. In excavating the everyday traumas of some southern lives, women writers have created an extraordinary, richly aesthetic field of fiction. "'Listen and I'll tell you what Miss Nell served at the party,' Loch's mother said softly, with little waits in her voice. She was just a glimmer at the foot of her bed." In Welty's *The Golden Apples* Mrs. Morrison tells her son about the elaborate foods served at a ladies' social:

> "An orange scooped out and filled with orange juice, with the top put back on and decorated with icing leaves, a straw stuck in. A slice of pineapple with a heap of candied sweet potatoes on it, and a little handle of pastry. A cup made out of toast, filled with creamed chicken, fairly warm. A sweet peach pickle with flower petals around it of different-colored cream cheese. A swan made of a cream puff. He had whipped cream feathers, a pastry neck, green icing eyes. A pastry

> biscuit the size of a marble with a little date filling." She sighed abruptly.
>
> "Were you hungry, Mama?" he said. (1949, 94)

The list is paradoxical—appetitive and delicious—but also miniaturized, attenuated, nonnourishing. These cream puff palaces are a swan's world away from Bakhtin's celebration of food in its triumphal relation to work, from the gargantuan bodies that course through southern fiction, from the possibilities of witnessing. But in Loch Morrison's question this text takes on an intriguing formal problem. In a white world so attentive to lavish aesthetic surfaces, how does one break in and animate a subsemantic history that lacks extrinsic figuration? How does one dramatize the break between an aesthetic surface where everything is wittily artificial and one woman's growing hunger? Welty invents a lightly symbolic aside from a little boy to catch the desperate tone beneath his mother's chant. Elsewhere in southern fiction, this subsemantic history is unearthed with the help of the grotesque and the skitter of transitional objects as they pass back and forth between cultures. If this fiction hasn't disturbed us, it is because we, too, have bypassed the strange literary economy that makes the strangeness of the South's vernacular bodies so visible.

Third, although I have traced some parameters for exploring differences between black and white women's writing about the South, further explorations are paramount. Although white writers have not written—with any clear knowledge—about black culture, and black writers—with fascinating exceptions like *Seraph on the Sewanee*—are not especially interested in writing about white culture, we find some surprising similarities among African and Anglo American southern fictions (including an obsession with the throwaway body, redefining southern ways of unknowing, gargantuan bodies, the grotesque, and crossover objects, as well as a redefinition of what counts as politics), suggesting, if not a shared culture, then a weirdly shared set of preoccupations. In looking at these themes, which bifurcate regularly across the lines of race and locality, we also need to explore the toxicity of even the most progressive moments in Anglo and African American writing—the complex investments that drive any act of fiction-making.[3] Welty's most antiracist story, "Where Is the Voice Coming From?," is an unsentimental story about the murder of Medgar Evers that commands a disturbing complicity. As Welty says: "I did write a story the night it happened. I was so upset about this and I thought: I live down here where this happened and I believe that I must know what a person like that felt like—this murderer. . . . I was wrong in the social level of the man accused—that's interesting, isn't it?—but I think I still knew what the man thought. I had lived with that kind of thing" (1984, 182).

Welty describes her own sense of "place" from the bizarre double consciousness of a white southern liberal. To feel horrified for Medgar Evers but to know the mindset, the place-set, the "where" of the man who killed him drives Welty to narrate this event, not because storytelling is a southern way of life but because her author-narrator is haunted by excessive knowledge. Writing in the first person from the bone-chilling perspective of the hypothetical white hick who plans the assassination and pulls the trigger, Welty knows too well this landscape of race-loathing, knows the endless melancholia attached to throwaway bodies, to traumas so quotidian that they simply repeat themselves and in this repetition mire the earth, reproducing whiteness as an unseen surface that permeates everything—a floating, insubstantial field that even resists the white woman creating it, troping it. One wants to turn away from a writer who knows and understands this much, to disavow any connection to her. But it is important to study this fiction precisely because it keeps trying to handle, shape, and bring to life forbidden knowledge: "I believe that I must know what a person like that felt like—this murderer."

Alice Walker explores a similarly toxic knowledge about race and place, but from the perspective of an African American murderer. In *The Third Life* Brownfield describes himself as a southerner; he loves the South because it encourages systematic sadism and yet treats its sadists unsystematically: "He realized an extraordinary emotion. He loved the South. And he knew he loved it because he had never seriously considered leaving it. . . . Its ways did not mystify him in the least. It was a sweet, violent, peculiarly accommodating land. . . . One felt unique in one's punishment if not in one's crime. This appealed to Brownfield. It meant to him that one could punish one's own enemies with a torture of one's own choosing" (1988, 230–31). Among Walker's texts *Third Life* is the least read and least analyzed, perhaps for the same reasons one draws back from Welty's story. In place of Welty's knowledge of a white man's bloodthirsty psyche we encounter Walker's understanding of a black man who is equally motivated by race hatred. Both men identify themselves as southerners.

Fourth, in suggesting new categories for analyzing this literature, I've only scratched the surface. One model for this book has been *Reconstructing Womanhood: The Emergence of the Afro-American Woman Novelist*, in which Carby argues that the late nineteenth and early twentieth centuries are generally regarded as the age of great African American men, "as the Age of Washington and Du Bois, marginalizing the political contributions of black women" during a period of "intense intellectual activity and productivity" (1987, 6–7). I have moved this project into the modern South and challenged truisms celebrating this period as the Age of Faulkner, Warren, and Wolfe. We have seen that southern women's writing creates its own renaissance as it moves through the New Deal and the civil rights movement: political struggles that resurrected the hopes of postbellum Reconstruction. As Gunnar Myrdal wrote in 1944: "Not since Reconstruction has there been more reason to anticipate fundamental changes in American race relations" (xix). The changes resonating in women's writing go far beyond the categories I've begun to enumerate. What about the role class plays in constructing the throwaway body? What about the South's lesbian and bisexual writers? How do McCullers and Smith transform our sense of Katherine Anne Porter's homophobia? What about O'Connor's sexuality—how did it influence her work? From another angle, what are the regional differences that divide northern- (or western-) from southern-raised black women who write about the South? Can Ohio account for the differences between Toni Morrison and Alice Walker? What about the fictions of Elizabeth Maddox Roberts, Ellen Glasgow, or Grace Lumpkin, writers I seldom discuss because they are rarely interested in my not-so-secret obsession, the southern grotesque? Were they influenced by African American women's writing? Did they follow the Harlem Renaissance? Each of these questions needs to be multiplied and reinflected with regard to a dozen variables. For example, when the northern writer Lucille Clifton writes about the South in "ca'line's prayer," she explores themes I find in any number of "southern" texts: a white culture of neglect, the return of the throwaway body, and pollution as desuetude—a realm of loss beyond the magic of dirt. But Clifton also writes in the wake of the civil rights movement; she ends her poem with the hope of the African name, with a dreamy reworking of a distant cultural past: "remember me from wydah / . . . and set me in the rivers of your glory / Ye Ma Jah" (33). Similarly, in *Their Eyes Were Watching God,* when Hurston turns aside from Tea Cake's ruined, desiccated body to celebrate Janie's gigantism and ecstasy, in her horizon-snatching she resembles Ye Ma Jah—the Yoruba goddess of the sea. But are these gestures really so similar? Clifton's poem was published more than thirty years after Hurston's novel in *good times* (1969), a volume of poetry describing a mythical American South and a mythical Africa from an urban, racist, union-breaking North specified with greasy precision in "pork chops": "old man gould sent a train south / picking up niggers / bringing them up no stop / through the polack picket lines / into the plant / . . . oh mammy ca'line / a nigger polack ain't shit" (48). Both Hurston's and Clifton's texts suggest that African American women explore the bodies white culture has thrown away by rewriting these bodies, reinventing them in a way that white writers cannot—or at any rate have not. But in 1969 Clifton is also able to proclaim the cultural centrality of her role as African American woman writer in a way that Hurston could not, in part because Clifton has benefited from Hurston's invention of a celebratory black vernacular. *Good times* ends: "children / when they ask you / why is your mama so funny / say / she is a poet / she don't have no sense" (48).

To think at all about southern women's literature—and literature by black women who write about the South—is to unearth an incredible number of undernoticed, still-to-be analyzed, still-to-be-historicized themes. We've already noted how often southern writers use inordinate bodily descriptions to show the ordinary effects of southern racial history—that even Lyndon Johnson summons a bodily analogy to describe a political rival from Georgia. The deformation of the southern body is a surprisingly constant theme in stories and anecdotes about the South. Bodily anomaly is portrayed not in isolation from the segregated world but as a hybrid form or somagram already mixed with or imprinted by its environment. But in distinguishing women's writing I want to turn to a final matrix of ideas that has obsessed me throughout *Dirt and Desire*—the importance of dirt itself. We've examined images and characters who gather around two different sites: the making of subjects into bodies who are tossed into melancholic landscapes charged with earth, or water, or fire—characters who move from figure to ground, who become the unthought known—and a related set of figures whose absence defines a culture of neglect, whose loss does not become elemental: throwaway bodies who don't matter enough to be repressed. But in describing southern literature's death obsessions (both black writers' revelations about soul murder and white writers' attempts both to fathom and keep this murder unknown), something is missing, some keynote. We also need to explore women writers' exuberant, hyperbolic, and sensuous obsession with dirt.

Unlike the rags explored in chapter 1, dirt is a very "big" symbol in southern women's writing—redolent and ambivalent. In O'Connor's "Revelation" Mrs. Turpin cannot stop thinking about dirt: "Sometimes, at night when she couldn't go to sleep, Mrs. Turpin would occupy herself with the question of who she would have chosen to be if she couldn't be herself. If Jesus had said . . . 'There's only two places available for you. You can either be a nigger or white-trash.' . . . She would have wiggled and squirmed . . . and finally she would have said, 'All right, make me a nigger then—but that don't mean a trashy one.' And he would have made her a neat clean respectable Negro woman, herself but black" (1971, 490). In *Dessa Rose* the black heroine cannot escape from the sweatbox; she is claustrophobically immersed in her own dirt: "I had cried a long time in that box, from pain, from grief, from filth. That filth, my filth. You know, this do something to you, to have to lay up in filth. You not a baby—baby have clean skin, clean mind. He think shit is interesting. . . . But you know this dirt. Laying up there in my own foulment made me know how low I was. And I cried. I was like an animal; whipped like one; in the dirt like one" (1986, 206). Here the lowliness of one's own bodily refuse—its capacity to trouble Dessa's sense of her own humanity—seems unredeemable. And yet on the proximal page Dessa's lover values her even more for what she has endured; the sites of trauma left on her body, the places flayed and soiled, become touchstones, places of connection: "'Dessa, you know I know how they whipped you.' His head was right by my leg and he turned and lifted my dress, kissed my thigh. Where his lips touched was like fire on fire and I trembled. 'It ain't impaired you none at all,' he said and kissed my leg again. 'It only increase your value.' His face was wet; he buried his head in my lap" (208). Pollution metaphors often define what it is like to be outside human care, but they may also augur a turn toward redemption, reparation, rebirth.

Michael O'Brien suggests that there has been too much ado about the South's literary renaissance—since any ordinary culture of letters will produce many good writers, a few great ones, and one or two writers of genius (1993, 170). But we've known, at least since Virginia Woolf's invention of Judith Shakespeare, that a renaissance among women writers is something unusual. The demons of silence, disempowerment, and impeded productivity, as well as the difficulty of constructing a public voice in a world bent on women's privation, have created enormous impediments to the exercise of women's writing genius. An extended community of women writers marching out of the South seems, in this context, a remarkable feat—and one in need of more exploration. An extended community of women writing and thinking—as obsessively as Mrs. Turpin—about dirt is even more extraordinary. In fact, if we still want to entertain the hypothesis that southern literature is sometimes obsessed with community, then we must also hypothesize that it is obsessed with pollution.

We can construct a surprisingly orderly map among southern women writers of literary approaches to pollution behaviors. First, there are characters who are demented about dirt, hypersensitive about crossing pollution barriers, and adamant about the sacrosanct status of their own class or race. Mrs. Turpin's pollution anxiety reaches to her animals: "Our hogs are not dirty and they don't stink. . . . They're cleaner than some children I've seen. Their feet never touch the ground" (493). Such characters participate piously in beliefs about white supremacy or the virtues of a black middle class. When Meridian takes Wile Chile, a pregnant, garbage-eating adolescent into her dorm room, her African American housemother is enraged. "'She must not stay here. . . . Think of the influence. This is a school for young ladies.' The house mother's marcel waves shone like real sea waves, and her light-brown skin was pearly under a mask of powder." (1976, 37). These characters maintain their social power by upholding strenuously demarcated boundaries against pollution, instantly policing ideas that "confuse or contradict cherished classifications."[4]

Alongside the pollution-obsessed we encounter a second group of characters whom God-fearing citizens abhor. Unkempt, disorderly, or simply outside their designated territory, these polluting characters must be killed or ritually excluded.[5] In Welty's improvisations on the theme of Fats Waller, the white audience loves Powerhouse when he is performing, but the minute he stops he becomes a polluting agent who needs to be ostracized. In *Killers of the Dream* Lillian Smith suggests that even whiteness can become a category of pollution when it is the result of miscegenation.[6] These characters attest to the disciplinary success of a system that separates genders, races, classes, and ethnicities but can never be certain—in the midst of its absolute certitude—about where to draw the line.

But dirt obsession can also disrupt southern culture's dominant idols, exposing their unreasonable rigidity. And here we discover a new and feral southern theme: a third group of characters who consecrate filth, who adore dirt and revel in becoming pollutants.[7] Under this rubric we find a strange cross-section of characters, ranging from Dessa Rose to Porter's Miranda, McCullers's Amelia, Welty's Easter, Gilchrist's Rhoda and Lele, Walker's Wile Chile and Meridian, Morrison's Pilate and Clytie, and Hurston's Janie.

One of the many purposes of this book is to invent a new archive that will allow us to see the complicated work done by southern women's fiction: categories that both separate and draw texts together across Anglo and African American cultures. Here I will venture one more similarity. Both black and white women writers are obsessed with characters who play with or consecrate pollution. For Walker's Meridian, Welty's Virgie, or Porter's Amy, dirt promises an escape from bourgeoisification. This is hardly endemic to southern literature; play with pollution energizes a wide range of regions and cultures. But dirt works persistently and strangely in southern fiction, suggesting a route to cultural transgression, to a gendered change of worldview. For pleasure in dirt—in matter out of place—shadows a "southern" preoccupation with community precisely because dirt operates structurally—as any community's center and surface.

In Welty's "Moon Lake" the little orphan girls who are ostracized by the middle-class campers have a daily, instrumental connection with the soil; these sober children earn their keep by laboring in the fields until their hands are rough and dirty and their hair becomes bleached and pale. But the orphan Easter also brandishes a chimerical relation to dirt. To her clean, bourgeois playmates Easter's dirty body seems oracular: "Easter's hair was a withstanding gold. Around the back of her neck beneath the hair was a dark band on her skin like the mark a gold bracelet leaves on the arm. It came to the Morgana girls with a feeling of elation: the ring was pure dirt. They liked to look at it, or to remember, too late, what it was—as now, when Easter had already lain down for a drink and left the spring. They liked to walk behind her and see her back, which seemed spectacular from crested gold head to hard, tough heel" (1949, 118–19). The pleasure these little girls take in Easter's gritty necklace, in the "pure dirt" encircling her neck, depends on the transgressive potential of Easter's easy crossing of pollution barriers—her ability to risk social danger: "Easter flipped out a jack-knife and with her sawed fingernail shot out three blades. 'Do you carry that in the orphan asylum?' Jinny Love asked with some respect. Easter dropped to her scarred and coral-colored knees. They saw the dirt. 'Get down if you want to play me mumblety-peg,' was all she said, 'and watch out for your hands and faces'" (119). This obsession with dirt emerges not only from Nina's and Jinny Love's smug pleasure at Easter's low caste but from the charismatic power of a child whose body is ecstatically transgressive, who refuses to inhabit the systems of cleanliness and power that regulate pristine children's lives. The pollution that marks Easter's class status also makes her body seem luminous, powerful, golden. Although dirt signals white-trash origins, Welty also suggests that Easter has access to a social economy where authority is partly dirt-based.

This celebratory relation to dirt may seem counterintuitive. In *Purity and Danger* Mary Douglas argues that an interest in dirt runs up against society's "strongest mental habits" (1984, 36). In the twentieth century dirt avoidance becomes both a moral matter and an issue of "hygiene or aesthetics"; the discovery of the bacterial transmission of diseases made it hard to think about dirt except in terms of pathogens and pathology (35). But Douglas insists that we need to think about modern dirt avoidance anthropologically, as part of a reaction-formation against "matter out of place": "Where there is dirt there is system. Dirt is the by-product of a systematic ordering and classification of matter, in so far as ordering involves rejecting inappropriate elements" (35). If literature by southern women thrives on dirt fetishism, it is because dirt, filth, contamination, and decay become sites for condensing the social complexities that emerge from any encounter with abjection, with people—and this includes "white trash," African Americans, and women in general, characters who experiment with disorder.

Thus dirt has an intriguing double function in southern literature. First, it is a producer of systems: "You are burnt beyond recognition," Edna Pontellier's husband chastises his sun-loving wife, as she emerges from the sea in the opening pages of *The Awakening* (Chopin 1976, 4). In this strictly gendered, color-coded world, any deviation from the norm is punished with scorn or ostracism. One can be burnt or not burnt, deviant or proper, dirty or clean, but not both simultaneously. That is, the border separating filth from cleanliness operates with near-tactile authority; it becomes a rigid demarcating system separating inside from outside, high from low, man from woman, lady from prostitute, white from black. In Porter's "The Old Order"

> the horses jogged in . . . and Grandmother, calling out greetings in her feast-day voice, alighted, surrounded by her people, with the same flurry of travel that marked her journeys by train; but now with an indefinable sense of homecoming, not to the house but to the black, rich soft land and the human beings living on it. Without removing her long veiled widow's bonnet, she would walk straight through the house, observing instantly that everything was out of order. . . . Within an hour someone would have driven away in the buckboard with an order for such lime for whitewash. . . . Home-made lye soap would be produced from the washhouse, and the frenzy would begin. (1972, 322–23)

But what drives this frenzy? As "every mattress was emptied of its corn husks and boiled, every little Negro on the place was set to work picking a fresh supply of husks, every hut was thickly whitewashed . . . every filthy quilt was brought to light": the offending adjectives naturalize the need for white patronage.

While ritual cleansing establishes the "legitimacy" of the caste hierarchies portrayed in Porter's story, it does equally unsavory work in Smith's *Killers of the Dream* by bolstering ritual beliefs in racial contamination. In the scene where Janie, a light-complected child, is discovered in the segregated ghetto, the meddlesome club woman who finds her grows hysterical at finding a "white" child in the black ghetto; she deploys metaphors of contamination to convince herself that Janie must be separated from her black family: "the shack, as she said, was hardly more than a pigsty and this white child was living with dirty and sick-looking colored folks. 'They must have kidnapped her,' she told her friends" (1978, 34).

Second, although dirt becomes a rhetorical place marker for cosmos- or system-creating, a signpost that allows southern citizens to recognize a middle-class macrocosm and its underclass boundaries, it also serves as a disrupter of systems. That is, it becomes the stuff of rebellion, the foundation for play, the ground of racial protest and gender unrest, as well as the earthy basis for children's delight in sullying grown-up categories. When Tarwater consecrates an appalling new covenant in O'Connor's *The Violent Bear It Away,* he smears his face with earth. This act of consecrating what others regard as polluting or dangerous is also the central task for Walker's Meridian: "Into a tub went Wile Chile, whose body was caked with mud and dust, whose hair was matted with dust, and whose loud obscenities mocked Meridian's soothing voice. Wile Chile shouted words that were never uttered in the honors house. Meridian, splattered with soap and mud, broke down and laughed" (36). Dirt functions as a powerful source of antagonism; Meridian adopts Wile Chile's bilious strategies when she embarks on her iconoclastic quest to overturn Jim Crow justice in the post–civil rights South.

Why is there so much transgressive potential and political pleasure in dirt? Dirt is redolent with bodiliness, with the uncensored glee of childhood, the pleasures of infantile eroticism. We sense this excremental magic in a pollution-filled scene from Gilchrist's "Traveller," where a white girl watches her pale cousin bathe:

> I found her in the bathroom sitting upright in a tub of soapy water while Sirena knelt beside it slowly and intently bathing her. I had never seen a grown person being bathed before.
>
> Sirena was running her great black hand up and down Baby Gwen's white leg, soaping her with a terry-cloth washrag. The artesian well water was the color of urine and smelled of sulphur and sandalwood soap, and Sirena's dark hand was thick and strong moving

> along Baby Gwen's flawless skin. I sat down on the toilet and began to make conversation. (1981, 142)

Amidst these contraband fragrances Gilchrist imagines the mingling of self and world. That the world can be stained with the self implies—almost magically—that the self can also be stained with the world. This pleasure in incantatory imperfection intensifies:

> I lit a cigarette, trying not to look at Baby Gwen's black pubic hair. . . . "Want a drag?" I asked, handing her the cigarette. She nodded, wiped her hand on her terry-cloth turban, took a long luxurious drag, and French inhaled.
>
> The smoke left her mouth in two little rivers, curled deliciously up over the dark hairs above her lips and into her nostrils. She held it for a long moment, then exhaled slowly through her lips. The smoke mingled with the sunlight, and the steam coming from the bathwater rose in ragged circles and moved toward the open window.
>
> Baby Gwen rose from the water, her flat body festooned with blossoms of sandalwood soap, and Sirena began to dry her with a towel.(143)

When Baby Gwen's renovated torso is wreathed in soap it seems to condense the very power that resides in bodily margins. Here dirt becomes the celebratory edge where the tentative self meets the exuberant world. In other words, if dirt can define the vulnerability of the body at its margins, in "Traveller" Gilchrist also celebrates pollution as creativity, as the pleasurable potential to become something other than oneself. But is dirt-worship ever so simple? We need to contemplate the role that Sirena, as African American domestic, plays in this scene of washing in whiteness.

This is a tableau in which a dirty girl lingers in the bath while her white friend looks on—both children at leisure as a brown woman labors over the white bather's body, lathering her pallid skin. Gilchrist's story seems to offer a critique of this segregated sensuality. I've argued that the bath provides a space for play, for exploring the pleasure these white children take in matter out of place, especially their participation in adult pollutions (cigarettes and perfume versus well-water scented with urine). Gilchrist sullies the artificial boundary separating Sirena's dark hand from Baby Gwen's white one; as dirty water streams off Baby Gwen's body, as Lele glimpses her companion's black mustache and pubic hair, we sense the ambient dirtiness and arbitrariness of the novel's color-coded class system. Baby Gwen presides over a kingdom that is contradictory to its core: her fiefdom eroticizes passages between racial and economic zones in order to denaturalize (and ideologize) any act of boundary crossing.

At the same time, the conventions that equate Sirena's working body with illicit pleasure—with an expansive and sexual bodiliness—are so familiar that they are appalling. While Baby Gwen's flatness is "festooned" with soap bubbles, while her dirtiness becomes the precondition for metamorphosis, Sirena is exempted from this half-magic; as a working woman she is the source of Baby Gwen's metamorphosis but not its recipient. By making Baby into a white figure who shines radiantly against Sirena's dark body, Gilchrist teeters toward stereotype. "Slavery did not transform the black female into an embodiment of carnality at all, as the myth of the black woman would tend to convince us," Hortense Spillers argues. "She became instead the principal point of passage between the human and non-human world. Her issue became the focus of a cunning difference . . . the route by which the dominant male decided the distinction between humanity and 'other' . . . [decided that] black is vestibular to culture. In other words, the black person mirrored for the society around her . . . what a human being was *not*" (1984, 76). Neither vegetable nor animal, Sirena is associated with water, feces, fecundity, fundament—with the stuff we are made from. Her association with dirt intensifies our sense of her exile to the inhuman.[8] Or, as Henry Louis Gates Jr. says of the white man who owned the local restaurant in his home town in West Virginia: "He ran the taxi service, too, and was just as nice as he could be, even to colored people. But he did not want us sitting in his booths, eating off his plates and silverware, putting our thick greasy lips all over his glasses. He'd retire first, or die" (1995, 18). Trying on clothes that might be destined for white patrons was equally forbidden: "Mama . . . wore white pads called shields under her arms so her dress or blouse would show no sweat. We'd like to try this on, she'd say carefully, articulating her words precisely and properly. We don't buy clothes we can't try on, she'd say when they declined, as we'd walk, in Mama's dignified manner, out of the store" (17). How do African American women writers use the categories that have been used to malign them?

In *Song of Solomon* Toni Morrison invents a black character who revels in dirt. Speaking of the white woman she worked for, Circe explains this woman's reasons for suicide: "Do you hear me? She saw the work I did all her days and died, you hear me, died rather than live like me. Now, what do you suppose she thought I was?" Living in this dead woman's house, putrefying it with vermin and dog feces, Circe vows: "I will never clean it again. Never. Nothing. Not a speck of dust, will I move. Everything in this world they lived for will crumble and rot" (1977, 249). And yet—perplexingly, paradoxically—amidst Circe's dirt Milkman's quest for his family history truly begins: He asks Circe about his grandfather, murdered by the white people whose house she so justly debases: "'Did you ever know his real name?' 'Jake, I believe.' 'Jake what?' She shrugged, a Shirley Temple, little-girl-helpless shrug. . . . 'Thanks,' he called back, louder than he needed to, but he wanted his gratitude to cut through the stink that was flooding back over the humming of the dogs" (250). Where there is dirt there is not only revenge, but payoff or pleasure.

In *Their Eyes Were Watching God* we discover a similar semiotics of dirt-based pleasure when Janie returns from the muck and her dirty, nonchalant body breeds amazement in others:

> What she doin' coming back here in dem overhalls? Can't she find no dress to put on?—Where's dat blue satin dress she left here in?—Where all dat money her husband took and died and left her? . . .
>
> The men noticed her firm buttocks like she had grapefruits in her hip pockets; the great rope of black hair swinging to her waist and unraveling in the wind like a plume; then her pugnacious breasts trying to bore holes in her shirt. They, the men, were saving with the mind what they lost with the eye. The women took the faded shirt and muddy overalls and laid them away from remembrance. It was a weapon against her strength and if it turned out of no significance, still it was a hope that she might fall to their level some day. (1990b, 10–11)

Why is Janie so dangerous? She possesses ropelike hair that unravels in the wind, or is it feathered, like a giant plume? Her breasts move and change, they seem interactive, while her body is mixed with earth, her clothing muddy, covered with the world's own bodiliness. As Ann Carson suggests, in myth woman's boundaries become "pliant, porous, mutable. Her power to control them is inadequate, her concern for them unreliable. Deformation attends her. She swells, she shrinks, she leaks, she is penetrated, she suffers metamorphoses. The women of mythology regularly lose their form in monstrosity. Io turns into a heifer, Kallisto becomes a bear, Medusa sprouts snakes from her head and Skylla yelping dogs from her waist" (1990, 154). In *Their Eyes Were Watching God* dirt represents the endless power of formlessness—the threat of feminine margins, the spaces where Janie has extended herself beyond her community's norms.[9] "To Janie's strange eyes, everything in the Everglades was big and new. Big Lake Okeechobee, big beans, big cane, big weeds, big everything. Weeds that did well to grow waist high up the state were eight and often ten feet tall down there. Ground so rich that everything went wild. Volunteer cane just taking the place. Dirt roads so rich and black that a half mile of it would have fertilized a Kansas wheat field. Wild cane on either side of the road hiding the rest of the world. People wild too" (193).[10] But if we want to understand Janie's high-spirited relation to dirt, we will need to examine the geographic difficulties Hurston confronts in exploring the use-value of dirt, especially since pollution fantasies have played such a major role in white definitions of African Americanness. Writing from the far side of a southern world that already saw African Americans as pollutants, why does Hurston snatch off her shields, pour such opulent pollutants into the pages of an already risky novel?

On the muck Janie and Tea Cake plan to rent a room with a bath: "Now we got uh chance tuh git uh room at de hotel, where dey got uh bath tub. Yuh can't live on de muck 'thout yuh take uh bath every day. Do dat muck'll itch yuh lak ants" (123). The need for cleansing crops up at the story's end: "The light in her hand was like a spark of sun-stuff washing her face in the fire. Her shadow behind fell black and headlong down the stairs. . . . She closed in and sat down. Combing road-dust out of her hair. Thinking" (183). Hurston's characters are preoccupied with cleansing, but the act of washing in light produces a gorgeous superfluity of blackness. The shadows thicken, Janie's torso elongates, her body follows her up the stairs. As the room is broomed out and its staleness evacuated, Janie also banishes the road dust that covers her body. Here the proximity of meditation to dirt is quite powerful as Hurston suggests a felt similarity between the thoughts and the dust particles traversing the borders of Janie's body. The physical drifts in the direction of the metaphysical, for in combing and thinking Janie inhabits a borderland between the material and the immaterial, and dirt becomes a rich symbolic site hurrying materiality toward epistemology.

Dirt-obsession marks a difference between two ideas about play, a distinction between the ordinary and the extraordinary game. Gilles Deleuze maintains that ordinary games contain a certain number of fixed principles that preexist any game's playing and organize its execution as well as its outcome. But the extraordinary game possesses "no preexisting rules, each move invents its own rules . . . all throws affirm chance and endlessly ramify it with each throw." Instead of dividing up a closed space "between fixed results which correspond to hypotheses," we find a nomadic, nonsedentary distribution. A game "without rules, with neither winner nor loser, without responsibility, a game of innocence, a caucus-race, in which skill and chance are not longer distinguishable" clearly has no reality and would not be amusing (1990, 59). How does dirt-obsession open the way to alternative kinds of play?

In *Let Us Now Praise Famous Men* James Agee describes the rules of an ordinary southern game. He finds himself following a black man and woman to explain why he and Walker Evans have violated rules of decorum to photograph a black church; he wants to apologize. Terrified by the unexpectedness of his approach, the couple hurries away, the woman falls, the man stops, and Agee finds himself trapped in elaborate rituals he cannot transcend:

> In that country no negro safely walks away from a white man, or even appears not to listen while he is talking, and because I could not walk away abruptly, and relieve them of me, without still worse a crime against nature than the one I had committed, and the second I was committing by staying, and holding them. And so, and in this horrid grinning of faked casualness, I gave them a better reason why I had followed them . . . asked what I had followed them to ask; they said the thing it is usually safest for negroes to say, that they did not know; I thanked them very much, and was seized once more, and beyond resistance with the wish to clarify and set right, so that again, with my eyes and smile wretched and out of key with all I was able to say, I said I was awfully sorry if I had bothered them; but they only retreated still more profoundly behind their faces, their eyes watching mine as if awaiting any sudden move they must ward, and the young man said again that that was all right, and I nodded, and turned away from them, and walked down the road without looking back. (1966, 41)

Agee cannot surmount the excruciating rules that reinforce white superiority and black deference and organize this outcome: for African Americans inhabiting the Jim Crow South, danger lurks in every moment of white supremacy *and* in every moment of deviance from such supremacy.

The question of *Let Us Now Praise Famous Men* is how to get outside these scarifying rules. One of Agee's strategies is to focus, ultimately, on white rather than black sharecropper culture. Within this culture he enumerates every dirty item he can find. Dirt offers Agee this twofold difference. First, pollution ushers the aura of reality into his text. He calibrates the meaning of white people who give off an odor, who stink. But, second, Agee tries to use the fact of this refractory dirt to define their heroism in the midst of squalid embodiment. As we've already seen in *Dessa Rose,* messing with dirt can change (at least for individual characters) the districting of race and class supremacy; it offers a chance to move outside ordinary rules, to explore a world that is nomadic, nonsedentary, unexpected—in which the rules can change, or at least become unpredictable.[11] In redistricting deviance, in playing with filth or pollution, ordinary games can shift into extraordinary ones.

A final answer to the question—why dirt and desire?—must involve an exploration of pollution's charismatic properties, its capacity to carry the reader toward the limits of the local, to experiment with emancipation. In fact, dirt has a dazzling array of associations in Hurston's tale. It is, first and foremost, a place marker for the ordinary that limits or depresses the range of Janie's experience. When her granddaughter is transported by Johnny Taylor's kiss, Janie's grandmother deflates Janie's euphoria: "'Ah don't want no trashy nigger, no breath-and-britches, lak Johnny Taylor usin' yo' body to wipe his foots on'" (12). Why do Granny's words have the power to convert Janie's feelings into "a manure pile after the rain"? Not only does dirt as curse or invective stand in for "all the rejected elements of ordered systems" (M. Douglas 1984, 35), it has enormous deflationary power because it also condenses language's capacity to make traumatic cuts in our memories—mortifying pleasure until the listener complies, parsing charismatic presence into nothingness, dead matter, decay.

Dirt as death-dealer and kingmaker becomes palpable in Janie's relationship with Joe Starks. "Janie loved the conversation and sometimes she thought up good stories on the mule, but Joe had forbidden her to indulge. He didn't want her talking after such trashy people."[12] For Janie to stay in the domain of the clean is also, paradoxically, to stay out of the carnival of power and community. Rituals of cleansing are attempts "to create and maintain a particular culture, a particular set of assumptions by which experience is controlled" (M. Douglas 1984, 128). Such rituals are especially dangerous for women. When conversations about Matt Bonner's yellow mule become a central source of community bonding, Janie is kept from the pleasure of tale-telling; she is not allowed to be polluted by commoners. As a result, she is kept out of everything sweet that draws people together.

We are close to the special pleasures of dirty writing. Dirt is a community creator, the main source of exchange in stories binding townspeople and neighbors together. That is, if communities depend on the orderly impulses that separate system (a given set of accepted laws) from anomaly (everything existing outside these laws), this outside remains a tantalizing presence; it cannot be entirely eradicated by system. The "gum-grease" talk of trashy people always evokes high spirits in Jody's store; it intensifies community by moving this community toward its symbolic limits, incorporating or testing the "beyond." But Janie is forbidden this oneiric intensity. "When Lige or Sam or Walter or some of the other big picture talkers were using a side of the world for a canvas, Joe would hustle her off inside the store to sell something" (84). Dishing dirt, telling tall tales: these acts suggest a communal fascination with matter out of place and the instrumental uses of this fascination. In focusing on the mule's corpse and the folk who gather round for the dragging out and mock funeral, Hurston foregrounds the bodily element of fellowship; she suggests that the carnivalization of dirt is a central source of community as everything turns into flesh, bowels, and earth.[13] Preaching from the mule's gut (a site redolent with pleasure but already stiff with rigor mortis), Joe Starks makes the mule's supererogatory flesh into a weird emblem of achieved collectivity.[14]

We have arrived at the precipice of carnival, where language mocks or insults the deity. For Hurston each encounter with dirt, with degraded matter that lingers in the margins, opens a zone that is dreamlike, chimeric; it moves Hurston's novel to a new level of reverie. The scene accompanying the mule's funeral is among the novel's most surreal and animistic, clenching Hurston's homage to detritus as a source of creativity. We encounter in dirt its metaphysical aura, its capacity to call attention to levels of existence beyond the ordinary. As the vultures inspect their dinner, they wait for their very own "Parson" to come.

> "What killed this man?"
> "Bare, bare fat."
> "What killed this man?"
> "Bare, bare fat."
> "Who'll stand his funeral?"
> "We!!!!!"
> "Well, all right now."
>
> So he picked out the eyes in the ceremonial way and the feast went on. The yaller mule was gone from the town except for the porch talk, and the children visiting his bleaching bones now and then in the spirit of adventure. (58)

This animal chorus mimes and defamiliarizes the world that Janie and Jodie inhabit. These animal bones suggest the profundity of a world elsewhere, of a domain of possibilities in which what is rejected, useless, or edged with decay becomes charged with value: no small feat in a fictional universe where black women must struggle to transcend their debasement as the mules of the world.

We've come back to the very definitions of southern literature I promised to resist—to a literature about place and community. But on what is this strong sense of community based? In *The Promise of the New South* Ayers describes "the sense of pollution whites associated with blacks, no matter how clean, how well-dressed, how well-mannered they might be. As a New Orleans newspaper argued in 1980, . . . when the state was considering the segregation of its railroad cars, . . . 'A man that would be horrified at the idea of his wife or daughter seated by the side of a burly negro in the parlor of a hotel or at a restaurant cannot see her occupying a crowded seat in a car next to a negro without the same feeling of disgust.' Any man 'who believes that the white race should be kept pure from African taint will vote against that commingling of the races inevitable in a "mixed car" and which must have bad results'" (1992, 139–40). Why did it take the South so long to tire of this "ordinary game" played over and over again? In 1945 James Eastland, Delta planter, Mississippi senator, bigot, stood before his colleagues on the Senate floor to give a speech about the abysmal performance of black troops in Hitler's Germany. Filling the *Congressional Record* with inaccuracies that other senators had to correct, Eastland finished with a peroration on white supremacy: "I am proud of the white race. I am proud that the purest of white blood flows through my veins. I know that the white race is a superior race. . . . It is responsible for all the progress on earth" (Dittmer 1995, 18).

Pollution obsessions bind groups together. But I'm also suggesting that dirt can be used in extraordinary as well as ordinary games. To play an extraordinary game is to risk getting dirty, to soil oneself, to go out of bounds. ("Easter dropped to her scarred and coral-colored knees. They saw the dirt. 'Get down if you want to play me mumblety-peg' was all she said, 'and watch out for your hands and faces'" [Welty 1979,119].) But it also carries the threat of oppression. When Janie goes out into the muck to work instead of staying home like a good bourgeois wife, it is the "romping and playing" that make her popular and make her belong. But on the muck, dirt also takes on a frightening valence. Families come "limping in with their shoes and sore feet from walking. . . . Permanent transients with no attachments and tired looking men with their families and dogs in flivvers. People ugly from ignorance and broken from being poor" (125). These workers are bruised and hard-bitten; they move at the behest of southern Florida's capitalist overlords: "All night now the jooks clanged and clamored. Pianos living three lifetimes in one. Blues made and used right on the spot. Dancing, fighting, singing, crying, laughing, winning and losing love every hour. Work all day for money, fight all night for love. The rich black earth clinging to bodies and biting the skin like ants" (125). Edgy and overdetermined, this imagery describes the indigent situation of migrant workers and suggests one source of their pain—the sting of landscape and the sting of racism as it impinges on bodies that are precariously sheltered and fed. But dirt also becomes a medium for redefining race in Hurston's novel: the "black earth" is rich, but it is also biting—a simultaneous revaluation and desentimentalization of the white association of blackness with earth. Hurston transforms the ordinary pollution metaphors that Ayers and Gates record, for in her text blackness is everywhere deployed as a location of energy and value—a site of exaltation and power instead of detritus and soiling. Dirt is not only an apparatus for sullying the dominant culture's idols; it becomes a site for restructuring the contamination associated with race-thinking itself.

"Her shadow behind fell black and headlong down the stairs." This celebration recurs throughout *Their Eyes Were Watching God* as both bonus and afterthought: "Phoeby's hungry listening helped Janie to tell her story. So she went on thinking back to her young years and explaining them to her friend in short, easy phrases while all around the house, the night time put on flesh and blackness" (23). If dirt connotes, first, a set of exclusion-based rules that create the laws of association and, second, the pleasure or displeasure of embodiment as it connects with community, in *Their Eyes Were Watching God* we also encounter a contemplative or meditative use for pollution. Joe Starks and Janie's grandmother are convulsed by dirt—by the dusty, world-encroaching bee, by the used-up carcass of the mule, by Jody's disintegrating body and Janie's body-revealing curse. But when Janie challenges Joe Starks, hurling back the very pollution metaphors that he has used to empty her life, Joe is shattered. And finally Janie is free to adventure with Tea Cake, a pariah who also becomes a concentration of everything forbidden to Janie—open talk, open laughter, risky games—a life lived for its outrageous use-value rather than for the lubricity of exchange. Tea Cake participates in the violence that accompanies male hierarchy, but he is also the ticket to forbidden forms of female dirt and communal play. Finally, in addition to dirt's representation of infantile, libidinal pleasures, we learn from Hurston's unconstrained images that reclaiming earth's marginalia can also offer an epistemological thrill, a site for unmaking the meaning of flesh itself. As a boundary phenomenon—a site connecting being to non being, formlessness to form—"uncleanness or dirt is that which must not be included if a pattern is to be maintained" (M. Douglas 1984, 40). Thus to include it, to highlight it, to transform what counts as detritus, is one way to begin to change the soul of pattern itself, to supplement an ordinary with an extraordinary game, to take the unthought known and make it self-contemplative.

We cannot leave this spectrum of pollution behaviors without noting that white women often use dirt to explore the possibilities inherent in a fantasied self-blackening, a boundary-crossing "negrification" (safer, as Mrs. Turpin explains, than becoming white trash), whereas black women use dirt as a means of transcendence, a way of changing the meaning of blackness altogether. But this romance with dirt as a place of boundary-crossing or transcendence must finally fall back into real domestic arrangements, to the reminder that, in modern southern culture, both white and black women have been fastened to dirt—defined as its source and charged with its removal. In *Telling Memories Among Southern Women: Domestic Workers and Their Employers in the Segregated South* both African and Anglo American women remind us of the burdens of cleanliness. Sophie Stewart, a white woman in her forties, describes her childhood relation with Ernestine (the niece of her family's maid whose summer job was to baby-sit Stewart's sisters on trips). The white and the black child experience each other's skin as a form of irritating, inescapable dirt:

> On the way home [from these trips] she and I fought like cats and dogs. I remember I had black skin under my fingernails and she had white skin under hers. We scratched and fought, probably because we were the same age. And probably I should have been the one nursing those children. See, it was a detriment to have maids in a way, because a lot of us can't cope without them. It has taken us years to learn to cope with a house. So I think my generation, the transition going from being raised by them—having them, then a lot of us can't have them now—this transition has been hard. (Tucker 1988, 240–41)

In contrast, Linda Barron, a black domestic worker seven years older than Stewart, understands all too well that the skills needed to clean houses and care for children create a terrible urge for white families to "have" black domestics; she suggests that the strains of nurture and cleanliness should result in a recognition of domestic work as skilled labor: "Domestic workers . . . don't think high of themselves. At one time I looked upon domestic work as a job that was not skilled, and then I looked at the white people there, and I saw I was not really that less skilled than they were. A lot of times when the telephone rang, I would not say, 'I am the maid.' I hate that word. They'd say, 'Who is this?' I'd say: 'My name is Linda. I work here'" (258).

Their Eyes Were Watching God revels in its own dirty writing, in a new theater of pollution. But Hurston also returned, at the end of her life, to earning her living as a maid, helping a white woman "cope with a house." In juxtaposing Hurston's role as domestic worker with her exuberant novel and her nearly forgotten death, I want to note how close ecstatic ideas of pollution can come to the throwaway, to people who are reinscribed as rubbish, as castaways, as beings too easily forgotten within a culture of racist neglect.

Sophie Stewart (the white woman who longs for black "help") follows this trajectory from pollution obsession to disposal or dispossession in her relation with Hattie, a black woman who worked for her family for twenty years:

> She came to my wedding that last year she worked. Mama wanted her to wear a white uniform, but she came in her church clothes. She was very handsome when dressed up.
>
> But she never lived well. Her house—I think once you've been in a black house, you never forget it—with all the little pictures around of her family, and she had little dresser scarfs on tables. You know, I was in the third or fourth grade when I went there, and I knew that was the only thing about Hattie I didn't feel at home with—her home. She had a dirty little kitchen, and they kept pigs in the backyard. I remember they cut the tail off one pig to fatten him up. He would spray blood all around, you know, and they were going to kill this thing when it got big enough. (238)

Face to face with another culture, encountering poverty created by the less-than-living wage that her family pays Hattie, Stewart can only respond with pollution talk. She is dismayed that someone who cleans a white home and operates as a white girl's surrogate mother ("She used to say we were her children," 238) inhabits an uncanny space where middle-class white people cannot feel at home.

This is doubly odd because of Stewart's occasional clear-sightedness as a white grown-up—her empathy with blacks who were "dirt poor": "they were hardly making enough money to eat" (239). But Stewart also uses dirt remorselessly to set up "claims and counter-claims to status." Beliefs about people, spaces, or objects imagined to be polluting and therefore dangerous "also carry a symbolic load . . . some pollutions are used as analogies for expressing a general view of the social order," imposing system "on an inherently untidy experience. It is only by exaggerating the difference between within and without, above and below . . . that a semblance of order is created" (M. Douglas 1984, 3–4).

When Hattie starts hallucinating, demanding more money, and becoming (in this white family's estimate) too paranoid, she is fired, and Stewart, that once-loving child, also casts her away: "She's not in a very good condition now. She never did have any money. She still lives near where my mother lives, and I think I should do something for her, but I didn't want to be involved with her. If I sent her money, she'd be on my doorstep, and I don't want that. It would be just too hard with her mental problem" (239).

Pollution beliefs shore up social systems of political exclusion, but they are also much more slippery, more vehicular; they provide the rhetorical basis for acts of human disposal, for converting those who are described as dirty into rubbish, the disappeared, throwaways.

White southern women's writing may participate in or may try to reverse this assembly line of automatic, mechanically reproduced trauma. Sitting in the doctor's waiting room, Mrs. Turpin watches "a lank-faced woman. . . . She had on a yellow sweat shirt and wine-colored slacks, both gritty-looking, and the rims of her lips were stained with snuff. Her dirty yellow hair was tied behind with a little piece of red paper ribbon. Worse than niggers any day, Mrs. Turpin thought" (O'Connor 1971, 490). Like Jody Starks, Mrs. Turpin is obsessed with status, but by the end of "Revelation" she recognizes that she is lower, spiritually, than the "companies of white-trash . . . and bands of black niggers in white robes, and battalions of freaks and lunatics shouting and clapping and leaping like frogs" (508). Once again pollution obsession and transcendence go hand in hand. But these leaping frogs also remind me of another text obsessed with dirt: that strange moment in Porter's "The Fig Tree" when musical tree frogs help a little girl bury a melancholic weeping that comes out of the earth that, if heard too long, might simply turn into grief.

"The Fig Tree" is a story about a little white girl's fear that she has prematurely buried a chick. I have already argued that Miranda is a lyrically tense and hypersensitive child who keeps stumbling on historical crypts, on metapsychological sites of delayed or rejected mourning.[15] The grownups in "The Old Order" murmur constantly, thoughtlessly, about dead African American children, tortured slaves, and bodies that have been casually disposed of—buried in the dirt that Porter's children try so assiduously to explore. The dead chick's weeping brings Miranda smack dab against this catacomb of unthought knowledge (knowledge that never appears in "The

Fig Tree" itself but remains mired in the stories around it and in Miranda's inexplicable preoccupation with burial and dirt). But at the end of "The Fig Tree," when Miranda comes to Aunt Eliza's farm, we turn from a haunted to an empirical world, from ghosts to the fastidious music of tree frogs, shy little animals who shed and eat their own skins. Once again Porter crystallizes an epic within the miniature world of the throwaway. After asking Aunt Eliza to explain the lamentations that follow her everywhere, Miranda learns that it is neither a dead chick nor the voices of haunted slaves that she hears, but simply the music of local amphibians:

> "Just think," said Great-Aunt Eliza, in her most scientific voice, "when tree frogs shed their skins, they pull them off over their heads like little shirts, and they eat them. Can you imagine? They have the prettiest little shapes you ever saw—I'll show you one some time under the microscope."
>
> "Thank you, ma'am," Miranda remembered finally to say through her fog of bliss at hearing the tree frogs sing, "Weep weep . . . " (1972, 361–62)

The frogs' appetites are sweetly erotic and terribly disturbing: the emblem of a self-cleansing, self-devouring culture made from creatures who can only feed at the surface of things, who eat their own skins. Miranda's "scientific" knowledge is blissful because it marks a return to the conceptual fog that envelops those around her. And yet the weeping continues—echoing white culture's capacity for racial predation. These persisting sagas of transgenerational haunting do not materialize in the clanking chains of the southern Gothic but in the music, sensuality, and lost bodies of throwaway subjects still mired in earth: in dirt still too close to desire.

Notes

Prologue

1. Wright's story is set at the southernmost tip of Maryland, a peninsula just across from Newport News, Virginia. In *Reconstruction* Foner comments that Maryland was "as divided internally as any in the South. Its 87,000 slaves . . . were concentrated in the countries of southern Maryland, whose large tobacco plantations recalled the order of the deep South. The area was economically stagnant, but its political leaders dominated the state, thanks to an archaic system of legislative appointment that reduced the influence of Baltimore" (1988, 39). He also describes the involuntary "apprenticeship" of free black children in the months following emancipation: children who were once again taken from their parents to provide unpaid labor for white planters (40–41, 201). For a sense of the social and economic formations that African Americans shared not only with Tidewater Virginia but with the deep South, see Wright's own descriptions of sharecropping and black-white inequality.

2. In this project, one of my precursor texts is *Reconstructing Womanhood,* in which Carby challenges a commonplace of African American studies—that the late nineteenth and early twentieth centuries were an age of great men, of Washington and Du Bois. Carby argues that this not only marginalizes "the political contributions of black women" but gives short shrift to the writings of Frances Harper, Pauline Hopkins, Anna Julia Cooper, and Ida B. Wells. It is her aim to "reconstruct our view of this period" (1987, 6–7), just as it is my aim to displace the dominance of Faulkner, Percy, Warren, and Wolf with the voices of their brilliant female contemporaries. "Reconstructing" is crucial to this project in another way. In examining the lush world of writing that southern women produced from the New Deal through the civil rights movement and its aftermath, we will see that this is a period that reinvented the hopes for political equality glimpsed during Reconstruction. It is also a period in which southern women's writing reshaped these hopes in increasingly bizarre and refractory ways. And yet when critics examine black and white women writers in a southern context, all too frequently the litmus test for whether they qualify as good regional writers involves their conformity to

white, male-derived Southern Renaissance values. My argument is that reading black and white women writers outside the Southern Renaissance formula changes this formula altogether.

3. Harris argues that Big Sweet is a more conventional figure: "By constantly referring to her own sexual attractiveness, Hurston is rewriting black female sexuality even as she includes Big Sweet and other women as examples of how it is usually written" (1996, 28).

4. Spillers describes this "escape from knowledge" as both by-product and cause of the Middle Passage: "The European males who loaded and captained" ships containing African slaves "were not curious about this 'cargo' that bled, packed like so many live sardines among the immovable objects. Such inveterate obscene blindness might be denied, point blank, as a possibility for *anyone*, except that we know it happened" (1994, 462).

5. See, for example, Abel, Christian, and Moglen (1997); Ayers (1992); Branch (1988); Carby (1987); Christian (1990); Clinton (1994); Davis (1985, 1988, 1993); Dittmer (1995); Faust (1999); Foner (1988); Fox Genovese (1988); Griffin (1995); Hale (1998); Hall (1983, 1993); Hall et al. (1987); Harris (1982); Hill (1997); Howard (1997); Hull (1997); J. Jones (1985); Kelley (1994); Lott (1993); Morrison (1992, 1994); O'Brien (1979, 1993); Painter (1995); Roediger (1991); B. Smith (1994); Spillers (1994); K. Stewart (1996); Sullivan (1996); C. Tate (1992,1998); Wray and Nemitz (1997).

6. The South's habit of fractioning black subjects has been both continuous and historically variable. In 1864 the Louisiana legislature refused a "progressive" quadroon bill that would have given free men of color who possessed "three quarters white blood" the right to vote (Foner 1988, 62). For an interpretation of the ways this fractioning pertains to southern literature see Yaeger (1996).

7. See also V. Smith (1989), 39, 45; Homans (1997), 84.

8. There are numerous exceptions, including Davis (1985); Griffin and Doyle (1995); Gwin (1990); Jones and Donaldson (1997); Manning (1993); and Segrest (1985).

9. Michael O'Brien raises a similar question about southern intellectual history in his ironic comments in *The Idea of the American South*: "Since the late 1970s, I have been forced to understand that books about the South tend to get locked in a box labeled 'Southern,' whatever their authors may intend. Other Americans feel little need to assimilate what may be said therein, except when they decide to understand the South, a thing clean different from understanding the United States" (1979, xii).

10. Morrison also suggests that some white writers create distorted, encrypted symbols that are not always a means of escaping blackness but can be a means of trying to transform it "into intelligible, accessible, yet artistic modes of discourse" (1994, 380). She cites Melville as an author "overwhelmed by the philosophical and metaphysical inconsistencies of an extraordinary and unprecedented idea that had its fullest manifestation in his own time in his own country, and that idea was the successful assertion of whiteness as ideology" (382).

Chapter One

1. DuCille criticizes Adrienne Rich's arrogant transformation of her black caretaker into "my Black mother" in *Of Woman Born.* This appropriation of the mammy as "a role, a womb, a pair of hands" is not unique to Rich's prose. "Frequently when white scholars reminisce about blacks from their past it is black mammy . . . who mothers the ignorant white infant into enlightenment." DuCille comments that these reminiscences

frequently occur in "forewords, afterwords, rationales, even apologias" that white scholars habitually "affix to their would-be scholarly readings of the black Other." The white invocation of mammy both positions the white scholar as privileged outsider and uses past connections to African Americans to "insist on the rightness of their entry into and the significance of their impact on the fields of black literature and history" (1997, 41). Do similar symptoms and blindnesses drive the opening of my chapter? Others will have to decide. For a superb analysis of the ways in which African American domestics function in black literature see Harris (1982). For an example of the complexities and pitfalls for a white scholar who tries to think through his relationship with the black woman who "raised me" (an attempt that is valiant, and yet missing the strong voice of a black interlocutor who will continue to trouble the meaning of "love" across economic rifts), see Weinstein (1996).

2. In *Virtue, Commerce, and History,* J. G. A. Pocock argues that it may be interesting to get at the "*mentalité* of the silent and inarticulate majority" but that it is even more important to understand the history of public political discourse. But in this terrible assault on two women in a public space, we see that these two discourses are not so far apart. As Pocock says: "There is something unilateral about the act of [political] communication, which does not take place wholly between consenting adults. By . . . injecting script, print, or image into your field of attention, I impose on you, without your consent, information you cannot ignore. I have demanded your response, and I have also sought to determine it. I have indeed determined that it is to an act of mine . . . that you must respond." He describes such scriptive violence as an "act of verbal rape . . . penetration of your consciousness without your consent" (18–19).

3. Here the white woman cuddling a black baby is, quite literally, uncanny; as a reverse image it recalls the moment in Freud's essay on the uncanny when he fails to recognize his own reflection on a train. In Paley's text, the uncanny recurs as a bizarrely social instance of the return of the repressed—as if the dream-thoughts of an entire culture are forcing their way into one dreamer's consciousness.

4. This portrayal of white convulsion recurs in story after story, from King's "The Little Convent Girl" to Wright's *Uncle Tom's Children,* Smith's *Killers of the Dream,* Welty's *Golden Apples,* Gilchrist's "The President of the Louisiana Live Oak Society," and even Tate's *The Fathers:* A white murderer protests, "I never had any idea of killing that nigger," while the white narrator stands passively, watching him drag the dead man's body "to the edge of the rock and let it fall into the water." When the narrator goes over to look "at the black water," he panics: "And then I was running and my shins burned from the scratches" (1960, 258).

5. I want to indicate not only the importance of black biological or surrogate mothers in these texts, but their hiddenness, the ways in which white writers often create a structure of withholding, a pool of forbidden information, not only about their heroine's origins but about their emotional investments. At the end of "Everything That Rises Must Converge" we are shocked when the dying white mother who has been condescending to African Americans cries out for her forgotten black caretaker instead of her son, and he suddenly finds himself "looking into a face he had never seen before. . . . "'Tell Caroline to come get me,' she said" (O'Connor 1971, 420).

6. Glasgow reduces her black characters to "kindly" objects in "Jordan's End": "I could see nothing clearly except the ruddy glow of the wood fire in front of which two negroes were seated on low wooden stools. They had kindly faces, these men; there was a primitive humanity in their features, which might have been modelled out of the dark

earth of the fields" (1989, 170). Almost every African American writer takes exception to this, and novels such as Williams's *Dessa Rose* and Morrison's *Beloved* take special pains to create narratives about the despicable ways in which African Americans figure in the catalogues of white people.

7. Like all the preceding generalizations, this one is complex and incomplete. In Glasgow's "Jordan's End" we encounter a ruined plantation and the usual story of a dying southern aristocracy gone mad whose bodies become recognizably grotesque. But Glasgow's story is not only corrected by African American fictions; white writers such as Elizabeth Maddox Roberts also reinvent the story of plantation decay and renovation by inserting simple white country folks into stories like "The Haunted Palace"—characters who fill the plantation's great halls with the sweet cries of lamb-birthing sheep. (Both stories appear in Forkner and Samway 1989.)

8. Again, this is wonderfully complicated by the fact that Ernest Gaines, in *A Lesson Before Dying,* also makes the kitchen and the local roadhouse the best sites of political intrigue instead of the courthouse.

9. We can see this contrast by examining Tucker's memories of what remained silent in her relation with her black nanny: "the rules about race were always between us . . . unspoken. . . . The rules had been made long before for reasons no one would discuss. Children learned only that discussion of the rules was not permitted" (1988, 3). In contrast, Clifton describes her own search for her great-great-grandmother's African name: "'They called her Ca'line,' Daddy would tell us. 'What her African name was, I never heard her say. I asked her one time to tell me and she just shook her head. But it'll be forgot, I hollered at her, it'll be forgot. She just smiled at me and said 'Don't you worry, mister, don't you worry'" (1980, 228).

10. Gilchrist savors these consumables in "In the Land of Dreamy Dreams," a story about a rich local WASP who cheats in order to win a tennis game against an upstart Jewish parvenu who's just been admitted to her club. After winning (but failing to uphold the standards of "southern honor"), the WASP goes on a buying spree: "She went in . . . and bought some cocktail dresses and some sun dresses and some summer skirts and blouses and some pink linen pants and a beige silk Calvin Klein evening jacket. Then she went downstairs and bought some hose . . . and a blue satin Christian Dior gown and robe. . . . She went into the shoe department and bought some Capezio sandals and some Bass loafers" (1981, 71). Contrast this with the very different sense of the marketplace in Welty's "A Worn Path" or Hurston's "The Gilded Six-Bits."

11. See also pp. 142–43, 93, where she explains that "place does endow," or that "I feel that I learn through my roots and understand better what I have lived with and come to know, and those are the tools you write with."

12. Sometimes, as in Ellen Douglas, this gorgeousness of place is associated with the memorialization of a sacrificial white body. This is also the pattern of Thomas Dixon's *The Clansman* when a young girl joins her mother in a trip over the edge of a cliff to "the moist earth of the fields below." The mother smiles at her daughter and "the daughter answered with a smile; and then, hand in hand, they stepped from the cliff into the mists and on through the open gates of death" (1970, 308). This is a chauvinist story about the suicide of a "pure" white maiden who has been sullied not only by a rape but by her culture's ideations of race. Like Wordsworth's Lucy, she disappears into these "moist fields" to restore her fruitfulness as worthy ingenue, as a metaphor for southern splendor. For more analysis of Dixon's story, see Louise Westling, *Sacred Groves and Ravaged Gardens* (1985), 13.

13. For a powerful reading of this story, see the chapter on King in Anne Goodwyn Jones's *Tomorrow Is Another Day.*

14. See also pp. 37, 250.

15. But if this tale describes local spirits walking the South, then who are these spirits? Porter's children are haunted by other people's stories, by the unspeakable crimes of the past: "Yassuh. Dat was it. And nary a drop of watah noh a moufful of braid. . . . Yassuh, dat's it. Lawd, dey done it. Hosanna! Now take dis yere tombstone and don' bother me no more" (342). Uncle Jimbilly terrifies the children with stories that are fantastic but also true. (As Lucille Clifton's father comments when she is searching for facts to corroborate his legends about her slave ancestors: "he told me one day not to worry, that even the lies are true. In history, even the lies are true" [1980, 7].)

16. I say "hypothetical" because the characters in the story have moved from Louisiana to Texas; Uncle Jimbilly's slave stories would have taken place, and many of the buried babies would still reside, then, in Louisiana.

17. If the child can never return to make reparation, in Porter's fiction the child's psyche does become a site for *retoxifying* the past, for *de-occulting* its secrets: "Sister Maria had got freckled and Father was furious. 'Keep your bonnet on,' he said to Miranda, sternly. 'Now remember. I'm not going to have that face ruined, too.' But oh, what had made that funny sound? Miranda's ears buzzed and she had a dull round pain in her just under her front ribs. She had to go back and let him out. He'd never get out by himself, all tangled up in tissue paper and that shoebox. He'd never get out without her. 'Grandmother, I've got to go back. Oh, I've *got* to go back!'" (1972, 357).

18. Even Ellen Glasgow's "Jordan's End" (1989) gives us a portrait of white inertia and stasis in which "the young wife stood as motionless as a statue" (172) and whiteness is equated with madness: "He sat there, lost within the impenetrable wilderness of the insane . . . the inhabitant of an invisible world. . . . Distraught as he was, he still possessed the dignity of mere physical perfection . . . his hair was the color of ripe wheat, and his eyes, in spite of their fixed gaze, were as blue as the sky after rain" (170).

19. In *Delta Wedding* Welty suggests that it can be chilly riding high on "a masted green boat on the cottony sea" (1946, 38). Just before the wedding itself, Troy "was sitting there—bathed and dressed in a white suit, but having trouble with some of the hands. Shelley walked into the point of a knife" (257). "'I can't get past—there's blood on the door,' said Shelley, her voice like ice. 'Then you'll have to jump over it, my darlin',' said Troy, sing-song" (258).

20. Dittmer (1995) is especially attentive to the ways in which landscape shaped local racial practices. See, for example, his distinctions between the racism in Hattiesburg and in the Delta, and the ways in which this shaped the civil rights movements of the 1960s. See also 178–84.

Chapter Two

1. For those unacquainted with southern literary studies, *Agrarians* refers to a group of intellectuals centered in Vanderbilt (including Donald Davidson, Andrew Lytle, Frank Owsley, John Crowe Ransom, Allen Tate, and Robert Penn Warren) who, as Richard King has argued, became "the closest thing to an authentic conservative vision which America has seen. They were the party of the past, yearning for an organic, hierarchical order such as had allegedly existed in the antebellum South or the European Middle Ages. Like most defenders of aristocracy, they were literary intellectuals and displayed considerable hostility to the natural sciences, modern technology, and the philosophical

position—broadly known as positivism—they associated with the modern world" (1980, 51). Their ideas are frequently derided by southern scholars for their conservatism, and yet their work still forms the center of a number of monographs. As Michael O'Brien suggests, "recent southern literary culture is rather stuck on the themes of 1930, still recycling Faulkner and echoing Tate. While there are fresh voices, such as Walker Percy, their originality consists in the skepticism with which they use the old themes. But old themes they remain" (1996, 6). Many southerners dissented from the Agrarians' conventional right-wing charm. Sullivan reports that Clark Foreman was "'greatly depressed' by the static, repressed condition of southern intellectuals. The Nashville Agrarians were reigning over the only intellectual movement of note . . . leading the retreat from reality, pining for an agrarian utopia that was built on the backs of a cheap, inexhaustible supply of black labor. He dubbed them 'Neo-Confederates'" (1996, 37).

2. Carby also suggests the importance of contemplating this literature outside its "folk" parameters. She notes that after World War I the "movement of masses of rural black southern workers destined to become an urban proletariat" created a "distinct shift in who was represented as 'the people'" in black literature (1987, 164).

3. As Ray Marshall argues in *The Negro Worker,* "the main occupations open to Negroes after Reconstruction were those that were regarded as 'Negro' jobs (which were, by definition, hot, dirty, or otherwise disagreeable). . . . Racial job patterns had a strong caste element about them" (1967, 8–9). Harris adds that black domestics "are looked upon as sponges; they soak up confidences but very seldom put them out again. . . . The pattern is an old one. Black women have not only had their labor exploited and their bodies abused: they have additionally had to soak up the intimate slime of their employers' personal lives" (1982, 78).

4. To transpose Morrison's description of Melville's struggle with race, "I would not be understood to argue that [Lee] was engaged in some simple . . . black/white didacticism. . . . Nothing like that. What I am suggesting is that [she] was overwhelmed by the philosophical and metaphysical inconsistencies of an extraordinary and unprecedented idea that had its fullest manifestation in [her] own time in [her] own country, and that that idea was the successful assertion of whiteness as ideology" (1994, 382).

5. I want to thank Jessica Forbes Roberts for this citation. As Roberts has said via email, "In the text each ellipsis is followed by a passage in plain font describing lovemaking between Sula and Ajax. The intermingling of the clean water and equally clean soil beautifully complicates" our concepts of both dirt and cleanliness.

6. Kreyling is critiquing Simpson's *The Fable of the Southern Writer* (1994, xvii, for "southern self-interpretation").

7. In contrast, Gaines argues that he is reclaiming and rewriting a white tradition in his own terms. He suggests that white writers "who so poorly described blacks, did well with the odor of grass and trees after a summer rain." These descriptions inspired his fiction, but even more, "I wanted to see on paper those Louisiana black children walking to school on cold days when yellow Louisiana buses passed them by" ("Miss Jane and I," 27–28, quoted in Davis 1991, 107–8). Gaines's transformations of other southern writers are manifold, but I would especially note his connections to Richard Wright's ideas about black epistemology, his focus on African American invisibility ("I was there, and yet I was not there" [1]), and his understanding of Eudora Welty's telegraphic sense of community in "The Whole World Knows" as it works among black neighbors, as well as his southern spin on urban detective fiction. His themes are as relentlessly regional as those of any other southern writer.

8. Ann duCille would extend this schism to black and white academics. "I—whose earliest childhood memories include finding a snake in our mailbox shortly after we moved into an all-white neighborhood . . . did not learn my racial consciousness from reading Richard Wright's 'Big Boy Leaves Home' as an adult" (1997, 44). She suggests a difference between "critical analysis that honors the field and guilty conscience rhetoric that demeans it" with "I-once-was-a-racist confessionals" (44). It is intriguing to note that this white liberal "genre," once so common among white southerners, is still in force.

9. There are numerous and remarkable exceptions, including Sundquist's (1995) scathing analysis of Lee's *To Kill a Mockingbird* in light of the trial of the "Scottsboro boys."

10. Thadious Davis explores the southern sources of the Harlem Renaissance and notes that "Hughes, Hurston, and Brown, the major young writers to emerge from the renaissance, were all Southerners either by actual place of birth or by their own identifications with the South" (1985, 303). She also notes that "because the New Negro Renaissance was not treated as an added part of the South's Renascence, the history of Southern literature can only claim those Southern standard bearers in the New Negro Renaissance from afar" (313).

11. Hazel Carby describes the ways in which the black intellectual elite is forced to change when southern blacks move north (1987, 164–65). I'm arguing that white southern writers and intellectuals changed as well (although sometime this change can be measured through increased resistance), as they became increasingly aware of the aesthetic and intellectual breadth of the Harlem movement. Carby also suggests that the idea of the "New Negro" within the Harlem Renaissance has become a conventional way of referring to a group of intellectuals that empties this movement "of the radical working-class meaning that was established by the groups of intellectuals, leaders, organizations, and journals which were to devoted to 'economic radicalism'" (165). This is an exacting critique, but numerous critics also use the term *New Negro Renaissance* to decenter our sense of this movement's geographic locatedness in Harlem.

12. Hall contrasts the segregated ASWPL and the interracial movement, as well as the ways in which the ASWPL's timid statistical tactics differed from the NAACP's stronger program of moral outrage: "in 1937 the NAACP emphasized the debasing effects of mob violence on the white children who witnessed it by circulating photographs of a crowd of men, women, and children staring at the mutilated body of a lynch victim" (1993, 210). Nevertheless, she describes this association's crucial work as its members "sought to strike down the apologetics of lynching by disassociating the image of the [white] lady from its connotations of female vulnerability and retaliatory violence" and attacked "the paternalism of chivalry" (193).

13. See especially Claudia Tate's essay on *Seraph* in *Psychoanalysis and Black Novels: Desire and the Protocols of Race* (148 –77).

14. As Naylor says of her experience writing *Mama Day:* "I am from southern parents, so I grew up in a very southern home right here in New York City. I knew the foods, I knew the speech patterns, I knew the behavioral codes of the South, because that was my enculturation. But I did not know the Sea Islands, per se. So I had to go. I went to do what I call 'tactile research'" (1994, 161). See Davis (1993) on the need to rethink the confluences between black and white southern women's writing. See Brookhart (1993) for an argument about the southernness of northern-raised black writers.

15. If these are my criteria, *Dirt and Desire* should also include white women writers

who write about the South as a way of thinking about an ancestral whiteness. And Willa Cather's *Sapphira and the Slave Girl* does just that. In returning to Virginia, where Cather spent the first decade of her life, *Sapphira* is utterly unlike Cather's other novels in its development of character, its narrow canyons of space, its preoccupations with the grotesque and with hidden black mothers. In fact, in its invocation of grotesque bodies and its portrait of a bizarrely fragmented whiteness, *Sapphira* is closer to the fictions of Cather's white southern colleagues than it is to her canonical novels about the West or the Midwest.

16. Both Morrison's and Clifton's parents were raised in the South and preoccupied with black southern cultures that had come north with the Great Migration.

17. For a description of the power of reclaiming ancestral mythologies in black women's writing see Hull (1997). In the same volume Christian is "struck by Morrison's virtually unique accomplishment . . . her use of the African traditional religious belief that Westerners call ancestor worship" as a way of reinvoking ancestors lost to "American cultural memory" in the brutal act of "collective psychic rupture" (364) during the Middle Passage. Both Hull and Christian stress the importance of contemplating African belief systems in order to analyze black writing. Shaw (1997) becomes an interlocutor for both these essays when she distinguishes between "the separate paths that African and African American spirituality have taken" (355–61) and examines spirit mediumship in African societies as a form of social control. Taken together, these writers suggest the relative inattention of critics to Africanist spiritual history when examining a wide range of black and white southern writers.

Chapter Three

1. For example, Howard Kester's 1934 report for the NAACP, "The Lynching of Claude Neal," was widely circulated; Mencken sent copies to friends along with his Christmas cards. As Hale explains, "Kester presented white women unflatteringly detached from their pedestals. He reported how an unidentified woman at the Cannidy house drove a butcher's knife through the heart of Neal's corpse, brought to the door by some lynchers in a car. His report also described Lola's sister shouting that no possible punishment could ever fit the crime. Most importantly, however, Kester described how Lola herself, about to marry a white man, wanted to end her sexual relationship with Neal and threatened him with lynching. This alternative female image contrasted sharply with the picture of violated ladyhood drawn by the local papers " (1998, 224). Welty's story is set squarely in the midst of such highly contested southern histories.

2. I want to thank Arlene Keizer for referring me to this poem and to the Angelou autobiography—as well as for her capacious, foundational ideas.

3. Although it is Ella who disposes of this child by neglecting it, her act emanates from the alternating violence and neglect within her own life as a slave—as her owners' domestic sexual pawn.

4. Stallybrass and White have also added to Douglas's paradigm by suggesting "clean-dirty" as part of a genealogy of high-low binaries involving the disposal of waste, comparisons of humans to abject animals such as pigs and rats, and fantasies about slums, domestic servants, and bodily filth that reinforce static patterns, allowing those on top to exclude those on the bottom. In Angelou's story all these elements recur as a child is compared to a dog, defined as untouchable.

5. For a powerful reading of gender and history in *Delta Wedding* see Donaldson (1997).

6. For example, what do we make of the following passage from *Delta Wedding*? The Fairchilds "had eaten everything they could, everything there was, and lay back groaning on the plaids and rugs. . . . There was a smell of cut green wood. And a smell of smoke—Howard was wafting it gently over them from a distant fire, aided by six or eight" (319). How do we think about this "six or eight"? We need a vocabulary that acknowledges the emptiness as well as the violence inherent in having to redefine oneself, continually, against a world where one is ignored—regarded alternatively, as filth, as ambience, as number, as nonentity. Painter discovers another register for talking about this neglect in her seminal essay "Soul Murder" (1985).

7. This bizarre aphorism gets repeated in so many different contexts that it seems doubly frightening. Moreover, it is not restricted to southern stories. In Mel Brooks's *Blazing Saddles* (a parody about a western town that acquires a black sheriff), when two black railroad workers find themselves and their trolley deep in treacherous quicksand, the white foreman comes immediately to the rescue. He pulls out his lariat—and rescues the trolley, leaving the two men to fend for themselves.

8. The Creole words are juxtaposed with their English translation in just this manner in Chopin's text. The punctuation of these repeated phrases is oddly inconsistent. Clearly, Chopin uses the Creole phrases to redouble the emotional impact of this moment. Later she provides the English words first—and ends her story with a translation into Creole—in order to use the translation to summon the effects of the uncanny.

9. This passage is also quoted in Lester (1968, 70).

10. I would like to investigate the importance of rags for women writers, especially, in relation to the garments of menstruation. But I have found little textual or archival material that would support such an investigation in the terms this chapter sets out; I hope other scholars will pursue this topic. The emotional impact of Sarah's death, however, is clearly heightened by the shiver of abjection associated with the cloth rags of menstruating women.

11. In "Worn Worlds" (1993) Stallybrass reassesses the role of cloth not only in societies "in which values and exchange alike take the form of cloth" (38) but also in modern economies in which "for all our talk of the 'materialism' of modern life, attention to material is precisely what is absent" (39). In the southern economies that these stories depict, cloth is "richly absorbent of symbolic meaning"—as in a cloth economy. But cloth also emerges in what Stallybrass defines as its capitalist mode, when "the life of textiles takes on a ghostly existence, emerging to prominence, or even to consciousness, only at moments of crisis" (39).

12. Still, within Agee's text even this bedding is emancipatory. See pp. 158–59.

13. In this text I've argued that we need to think harder about the fate and formal lineage of black characters who become throwaways. But interlocutors like Jay Watson have continued to ask me whether the fate of the throwaway "happens mainly to blacks, or whether poor whites qualify" (personal communication). Of course they do, but I would argue that they are handled differently—in terms of tone, telos, and imagery. Milly Jones becomes a case in point, a figure Faulkner (with uncharacteristic directness) asks his reader to mourn. That is, *Absalom, Absalom!* is able to handle the tragedies of Sutpen's white lover and child, tragedies Faulkner can dramatize in a way that he never manages to dramatize Clytie's story. This chapter could, then, be expanded to include a comparative discussion of "white trash," albeit with controversial results. In Faulkner's "Barn Burning," dirt and the economy of cloth (for example, the dirty rug that the "linen-clad" white man forces Abner Snopes to clean) become central. But for the white

hero of this story, the rags that surround him, the "thin, rotten shirt" that fails to protect him, become emblems of heroism as cloth itself gains a quicksilver materialism when the boy seeks out the sun and does not look back (1950, 24). These examples from "Barn Burning" and *Absalom, Absalom!* suggest that the literary archive of the white throw-away looks very different from that of African Americans who have suffered the results of a white culture of neglect. Of course, the children in *Bastard out of Carolina* and the wandering white girl who, after being struck by a train, gets stuffed into a portmanteau in Welty's *Delta Wedding* suggest other stories. But in Caldwell's *Tobacco Road,* that archetypal trash text, we do not find any remnant of the melancholia that effaces the lives of the black characters I have discussed in this chapter. At the novel's finale, Jeeter's and Ada's death in a fire becomes the topic of protracted, fetishized mourning. Even Ada's meager cloth wardrobe becomes an object of heroic meditation: "Ada didn't get no stylish dress to die in, though . . . it don't make no difference now. Her old dress was burned off her in the fire, and she was buried just like God made her. Maybe that was better than having a stylish dress, after all. . . . It sort of worked out just right for her. She didn't know she didn't have a stylish dress to die in. It didn't make no difference it was the right length or not" (1962, 170).

14. Suzanne Raitt, private conversation. These are ideas from her forthcoming work on modernism and "waste."

Chapter Four

1. As quoted in Dittmer, *Local People* (1995, 57).

2. In contrast, see W. J. Cash's *The Mind of the South* (1941). See as well the excellent chapter on Cash in Richard King's *A Southern Renaissance* (1980,) 146–72. O'Brien critiques "the idea of the South" for the way it undergirds a mythological sense of "the South's coherence and reality" and allows true believers to "comprehend and weld an unintegrated social reality." That is, O'Brien is interested not in upholding the South as idea but in noting the ideological functions of this idea (1979, xxi–xxii). The association of southernness with some vaguely defined notion of "the South" as mindset, image, or idea is widespread, however. In the introduction to the *Encyclopedia of Southern Culture* Wilson and Ferris explain that "the South exists as a state of mind both within and beyond its geographical boundaries" (xv), and they extend this state of mind to sites where "southern culture" can be found, including "black Mississippians who migrated to south Chicago" and "white Appalachians and black Alabamians who migrated to Detroit." The South as idea dominates the opening pages of their introduction: "The South has nurtured important myths, and their impact on other cultures is a vital aspect of the *Encyclopedia*'s perspective" (xv). I want to challenge this gestalt, to suggest that we need to shift our focus from ways of knowing the South and southern culture to ways of knowing within the South's many cultures. The broad-based focus on the South as epistemology has given short shrift to equally important epistemological issues about diverse ways in which southerners know.

3. Sundquist has also produced an incredibly nuanced and incisive reading of the range of Faulkner's race-perceptions. See especially his comments on p. 139 about the real effects of racial fantasy and the wonderful irreverence toward the myth of America in chapter 1.

4. This does not take into account formidable new trends in Faulkner criticism or Faulkner's own excavations of white southern ways of unknowing—as in the sheriff's conversation with his wife in "Pantaloon in Black" in *Go Down, Moses* (1973, 154–59).

5. I want to step back, at least intermittently, from my critique of Faulkner and suggest that these underexamined dramas inhere in his prose as well. For example, in the opening riffs of "Dry September" racist maxims get reiterated emptily, mindlessly, until an African American man is dead. But the narrative drive of these stories—their brilliant, lyrical success as cathartic tragedy—also distracts from the very trauma of unthinking repetition that Faulkner sets out to denounce.

6. Bersani explains Freud's preoccupation with part-bodies (with the body as a series of disappearing objects) in terms of the child's fantasied analogy between the penis and other detachable objects, "especially feces and the child himself (who at birth detaches himself from his mother's body)." I want to ignore the question of whether this child actually detaches himself and note that for Bersani "a chain of symbolic equations develops, the real terms of which either in fact detach themselves from the person (for example, feces, gifts, and money), or are seen as detachable in emotionally charged and frequently violent fantasies of mutilation and incorporation (penis and breasts)" (1977, 58). This mobility of meaning threatens the self's integrity, for the body, as integer, "no longer makes sense when something drops away from it" (59).

7. These floating flour particles might also be a sign of the miller's ex-centricity, since they are associated with him, not Sapphira. In these diametrically opposed bodies, Cather seems to be searching for diverse locations for recognizing the shattering of intersubjectivity that the system of slavery purveys—the white body floating in the air, in bits and pieces, but not at all cognizant of its own disarray. In the miller's world there is too much mobility; flour operates, symbolically, like so much dead skin, falling off in bits and fragments that have to be brushed away but recur like an exponentially expanding virus and cannot be disavowed; Sapphira, in contrast, has no mobility at all but, as Toni Morrison argues, experiences utter dependence on those she disavows. See also Bersani (60).

8. Prissie is used in just the ways Morrison suggests in *Playing in the Dark* to set up Scarlett's greater carelessness, so that finally the point is not so much Prissie's maternal inadequacies as Scarlett's. As Toni Morrison argues, however, the "serviceability" of black characters' speech or action is often a transparent literary device deployed "to win admiration" for a white hero (1992, 76). "We see Africanism used as a fundamental fictional technique by which to establish character." White texts frequently "solicit our admiration" for a white character "by the comparison that is struck" between this character's "fully embodied humanity and a discredited Africanism. The voice of the text is complicit in these formulations: Africanism becomes not only a means of displaying authority but, in fact, constitutes its source" (80). The scene where Scarlett, not Prissie, delivers Melanie's baby is a case in point.

Chapter Five

1. In *Telling Memories* Tucker explains that whites frequently romanticized black female domestics as women of "exceptional strength"—a way of rationalizing "the fact that domestics labored under harsh social and economic conditions" (1988, 106). "The black domestic in literature is also frequently shown as a physically strong and robust woman, particularly by white authors. . . . Black writers, on the other hand, show more of the toll that such emotional and physical strength took. . . . Katherine Anne Porter, in 'The Last Leaf,' is one of the few white writers who shows a black domestic growing very old and tired" (107). Although this characterization seems all too accurate, I'm suggesting another dimension to the portrayal of female gigantism—one as closely allied to white characters as to black.

2. Miss Eckhart's face changes, her music seems to come from some unearthly realm. To underline this transgressive power, Welty appropriates images from Shelley's "Mont Blanc" but with this difference. While Shelley mourns—and then appropriates—Mont Blanc's grandeur and cruelty, the sublimity Shelley withholds from himself Welty gives to her heroine. Miss Eckhart becomes the mountain that stares back at Shelley and will not answer his call.

3. Although Miss Eckhart is foreign, an outsider, she is still expected to conform to the community's norms. Although her rebellion is nonnormative, it is not especially exceptional, except in its mode of aesthetic self-expression. As Robb Foreman Dew describes her own feminine cohort in "The Power and the Glory" (1987): "The kind of charm we aimed for was counterfeit, because it had nothing to do with any one of us; we were only learning how to make someone else believe that he or she was enchanting. And it turned some of the brightest girls into incredibly manipulative and secretly angry women. I meet these people still, all the time; they are certainly not all Southern, although they are all women, and there are no other social creatures of whom I'm as wary" (121)

4. Fleming is describing his grandfather's experience in New Orleans in 1915.

5. Smith has criticized attempts to rematerialize white feminism by threading it through black women's bodies and texts (1989, 38–57). Abel adds that white writers frequently cite "black women . . . to bestow a cultural authority that derives in part from [black women's] enforced experience of embodiment" (1997, 108). In this chapter I hope to rematerialize and complicate both black and white feminism by threading my analysis through white women's large bodies and by making the portrait of the "enforced experience of embodiment" that has been associated with black women more intricate.

6. We see the extent to which even Miss Eckhart has internalized this miniaturization in her response to Miss Snowdie: "What were you playing, though?" Miss Snowdie asks, "holding streams of bead curtains in both hands. "I couldn't say,' Miss Eckhart said, rising. 'I have forgotten'" (58).

7. It is generally accepted that "A Memory," the only story in A Curtain of Green narrated by a lyrical "I," functions as a memoir or fanciful redaction of Welty's own memories.

8. There are, of course, some wonderful exceptions, including Myra Jehlen's *Class and Character in Faulkner's South* (1978) and Eric J. Sundquist's *Faulkner: The House Divided* (1983).

9. Although Cassie's automatic aversion to Miss Eckhart's playing can be described as part and parcel of a southern rape complex that refuses women autonomy and power, her autonomic remembrance of Miss Eckhart's rape could be described, with equal devastation, as a matter of condoned or appropriate "taste." As Pierre Bourdieu suggests, "the ultimate values, as they are called, are never anything other than the primary, primitive dispositions of the body, 'visceral' tastes and distastes, in which the group's most vital interests are embedded" (1984, 474).

10. See Myra Jehlen's *Class and Character in Faulkner's South* (1978, 137ff.).

11. In *Class and Character* Jehlen describes the narrator's use of this framing device among the southwestern humorists: "Cultural historians who thought they were reading the other side of the Southern story in the work of the humorists, who found in it a way at last to raise 'the veil of smug respectability for a refreshing view of the real thing,' were . . . largely misled by formal differences . . . through the wise narrator whose commentary typically framed the action of the tale, the humorists projected precisely the

plantation myth's image of a cultured aristocrat who was obviously meant to rule the South" (1978, 138). (Jehlen is quoting Hoole 1952.) Welty is reenacting this framing—first by literalizing her child narrator's reliance on a framework to stabilize her vision, and second, by thrusting a set of "rude mechanicals" into her line of sight. But when her narrator's frame gets interrupted or broken, Welty is also disrupting the political assumptions of a longstanding literary tradition. She refuses to repeat a simplified story of southern yokels as "uncouth, unclean, [and] lawless"—as poor whites with the ominous power of deranging the South's best traditions—but instead asks the weird characters at the center of her story to break or call into question the narrator's frame (Jehlen 1978, 139, quoting Percy 1965).

12. As Jehlen points out, this anxiety takes a particularly elitist patriarchal shape in the American South. "Walker Percy has explained the 'spectacular' change in the South as resulting from the defeat of 'the old moderate tradition of the planter-lawyer-statesman class' and 'the consequent collapse of the alliance between the "good" white man and the Negro. . . . To use Faulkner's personae,' he wrote succinctly, 'the Gavin Stevenses have disappeared and the Snopeses have won.' The dire prophecies of Hooper and Harris have been realized; Longstreet would have concurred, shuddering. The Whig Götterdämmerung has come and in its wake the 'uncouth, unclean, [and] lawless poor whites' have successfully taken over the ruined South" (1978, 138–39).

13. This is also the subject of Peter Taylor's "The Old Forest," in which a working girl with an untold history breaks the careful framework of denial that upper-class Memphis society has constructed to maintain its wealth, security, and sense of history. The working girl's well kept secret: that she is also working-class, that her mother is the owner of a scurrilous bar (and is thoroughly frightening—a goiter ridden, dragon-like, vestigial, but monstrous grotesque). The hero's romantic desire for this working-class heroine surfaces too late, and his new knowledge about this need to disassociate himself from his own class distorts his destined career path and underlines his alienation from the very traditions his marriage to a well-bred woman works so well to uphold.

14. Although the promise of heterosexual romance—of a world to be had for the marrying—offers this young girl some longed-for stability, Welty also insists on its slenderness as a device for organizing the world.

15. From the beginning of the story this framework is, of course, already riven with contradictions: "I was at an age when I formed a judgment upon every person and every event which came under my eye, although I was easily frightened. When a person, or a happening, seemed to me not in keeping with my opinion, or even my hope or expectation, I was terrified by a vision of abandonment and wildness which tore my heart with a kind of sorrow" (148).

16. Although this woman's body comments on the southern race-plot only indirectly (see Roediger's *Wages of Whiteness* [1991]), Welty uses its violence to begin to expose the nightmarish underside of southern fantasies about race and class inferiority, fantasies that led to historic scenes of excess resembling the mob scene Joel Williamson describes in his biography of Faulkner—scenes where grown-ups and children alike were participants in communal acts of predation: "The details of the Patton lynching were specific to Lafayette County, but the pattern was general. The justification was rape or attempted rape, the crowd numbered hundreds and thousands, an active cadre of several dozen men did the actual work, and the body would be mutilated, castrated, and displayed in a public, ritualistic, and dramatic way. Afterward, white people would feel a significant measure of relief. The Patton lynching was also true to the general pattern in

that it was done not only by 'rednecks,' the lower orders of whites. It was done by everybody, and the white community found release in the event" (1993, 159).

17. We have already seen that in *The Faraway Country* Rubin makes a more general suggestion about a southern world without synthesis. In the twentieth-century South "not only have towns become cities, and cities metropolises, but the moral order of the older South, the old notions of certainty and belief, have ceased to suffice as a sufficient explanation and an adequate basis for daily experience. I speak not only of religion, but of attitudes toward the values of the community, toward history, toward society. The future novelist or poet growing up in the South in the 1900's and 1920's did not find, as his father and grandfather had been able to find, sufficient emotional scope within the life of the community" (1963, 7). I am suggesting that Welty depicts a southern world in which this malaise has spread to the community at large. She intimates that when the upper classes forfeit the logic of their modus vivendi—their rationale for life at the top—the entire social structure is in danger of crumbling. In fact, the placement of "Clytie" in *A Curtain of Green* (following "A Memory") suggests that the traditionally gendered and elitist worldview that supports the heroine of "A Memory" has already declined past the point of use.

18. In Douglas's story female gigantism is not about freeing black women but about the enormity of white guilt.

19. For more on Clifton's "ancestral muses" see Hull (1997, 340–47).

20. In the groundbreaking *From Mammies to Militants: Domestics in Black American Literature* (1982) Harris contrasts militant domestic workers (usually maids "pictured in northern settings" who are "defiant in reaction to the sixteen-hour days their mistresses may want to squeeze into eight" and "refuse to stay in the kitchen," 24) with "the true southern maid" or "mammy whose ineffective compromise in the home of the white mistress causes her to identify completely with the status quo; she believes within her heart in the rightness of the established order of which she is a part" (24). Harris's study is wonderfully informative, but it does not reflect the complexity of southern women's writing. For Harris southernness comes to mean obedience, conformity, and loss of black cultural identity. Although she describes a group of domestics who are tricksters, women on their way to becoming militants who use southernness as "a performance, a mask" (29), *mammy* becomes a term describing southern blacks' acquiescence, whereas *militant* describes the literary character of northern domestics. And yet within southern literature we find other characters such as Walker's Sofia, who talks back to her former white ward. In white fiction, a topic outside the preoccupations of Harris's study, we also encounter Porter's Old Nannie, an ex-slave and servant who moves out of her white employer's house and seeks independence.

21. Harris also defines Pilate as "a tower of selflessness" whose fall "is difficult to acquiesce to. Yet it is consistent with Pilate's prediction about who would save Milkman's life" and strengthens her role as his spiritual helper. But Harris also puts a negative spin on Pilate's sacrifice. She points out that "Pilate joins the other women in Milkman's life in being made a victim to his health [and] . . . positive sense of self." Whereas I have tried to celebrate Pilate's communal being, Harris argues quite rightly that Pilate is also "the victim of communal, familial, and individual values, brought together in [Guitar,] the man who loves community enough to kill for it and the one who loves family enough to die for it" (1991, 115). At the same time, Harris resurrects the poignancy of Pilate's death by invoking scale: "her victimization . . . might have its worth in the larger picture of familial and communal good" (115).

22. Like all strong generalizations, this one is radically incomplete. From the opening scene, where the heroine of Arnow's *The Dollmaker* (1999) prevents a military car from plunging over a precipice and saves her child's life, Gertie Nevels's great stature is turned toward her children. When she travels north she becomes increasingly isolated and lonely but attempts, with tremendous will, to mend this isolation by inventing a series of failed communities.

Chapter Six

1. The origins of this meeting are well worth contemplating. Gelders proposed a conference that would focus on racial violence, on the extraordinary terror that antiunion forces had begun to visit on New Deal activists. The Roosevelts counseled a broader (and less controversial) focus, with the goal of addressing problems plaguing the South at large, and the conference itself was planned in consultation with the Roosevelts, Lucy Randolph Macon, and Clark Foreman, among others (Sullivan 1996, 97–99).

2. See also p. 366.

3. See, for example, Kelley's *Race Rebels: Culture, Politics, and the Black Working Class* (1994).

4. As Foucault argues, any analysis of hegemony must recognize that power is always "directly connected to the body—to bodies, functions, physiological processes, sensations, and pleasures; far from the body having to be effaced, what is needed is to make it visible through an analysis in which the biological and the historical are not consecutive to one another, as in the evolutionism of the first sociologists, but are bound together in an increasingly complex fashion" (1980a,151–52).

5. See Westling, "The Loving Observer of *One Time, One Place*" (1987, 180): "Welty's emphasis on black women's lives seems to be her tribute to their special strength and community. The photographs of solitary female figures establish an overall image of competent, determined independence."

6. This reading is complicated by Welty's overly mythologized celebration of Old Phoenix's capacity to create community anywhere. This story is, of course, a romance, but like all romances, it's filled with political trouble.

7. This began to change, of course, during the war, when black women worked in factories and offices vacated by servicemen. But the majority of black women still found employment in white homes.

8. Contrasting McCullers's *The Member of the Wedding* with McCullers's Broadway play, performed in the 1950s, Davis argues that, while McCullers's novel "is expansive in its empathy and perceptions about human nature," race, class, and sexual identity, "the play is restricted and limiting." But Davis also argues that McCullers capitulates to popular racial stereotypes in the novel as well; she "complied with notions of blacks as fighting, stealing, working at menial jobs, believing in superstitions, seeking physical pleasure, and so on." Davis suggests that the play became popular precisely because McCullers betrayed the complex homosocial- homosexual impulses driving the novel "with a focus on the more sensational elements of a staged and stereotypical black southern life" (1996, 212–14).

9. Tucker dramatizes this forgetfulness in an interview with Nancy Valley, a domestic worker who was always on call; she brought the little boy of the white family she worked for home at night because he needed her company; she stayed with this family's grown daughter when her baby was born and cut the umbilical cord. "I raised that one. . . . I stay home now and I would tell you more, but I get things all mixed up, so I'd

rather not. Just with that whole family, I worked all the time, till I got too old. I didn't have no hours there, 'cause anytime I went, they wouldn't even let nobody else work but me. Such is life!" (1988, 78).

10. "A familiar surrealist tack [whose] intent was to break down the conventional 'bodies'—objects, identities—that combine to produce what Barthes would later call 'the effect of the real'" (Clifford 1988, 133).

11. The emergence of this minotaur suggests that U.S. civic history is not "in its right mind" and might benefit from the techniques that spill out of McCullers's novel.

12. See Salman Rushdie's 1992 essay on Oz in *The New Yorker.*

13. See Elizabeth Spencer, "First Dark" (1991): "Mrs. Harvey was as sound as a young beagle, and she could still weave a more interesting conversation than most people who go about every day and look at the world. She was of the old school of Southern lady talkers: she vexed you with no ideas, she tried to protect you from even a moment of silence" (358).

14. For an excellent reading of the ways in which McCullers's fiction responds to World War II, see Hannon (1996).

15. In an unpublished essay James McNaughton suggests that the publishing history of *The Member of the Wedding* makes its relation to the war even more complex. Although the novella takes place in the midst of the war, when women were widely employed in industry, by the time the novella was published in the January 1946 edition of *Harper's Bazaar,* "the predicted normalization of gender roles and reversal of wartime employment, the 'postwar gender backlash,' has, for the most part, occurred." Unlike the wartime advertisements (exploring women's temporary assumption of male roles) that surrounded the text of "The Ballad of the Sad Café" when it was published in *Harper's* in 1943, the advertisements in the 1946 *Harper's* ignore "all roles for women but the domestic and the objectified" so that the magazine's postwar ideology connects "the restrictions that Frankie's age imposes upon her" with the restricted employment opportunities available to women who had, until recently, contributed so actively to public life.

16. The Student Nonviolent Coordinating Committee was composed of activists who were responsible for, among other feats, bringing freedom riders to Alabama and Mississippi.

Chapter Seven

1. I take to heart the questions Ann duCille asks in "The Occult of True Black Womanhood" (1997) about the dangers of jumping into the field of black feminist studies without sufficient disciplinary rigor. I hope this chapter is informed not only by my interest in the South but by the work of the black feminist scholars who have preceded me, including Hazel Carby, Anne duCille, Farah Jasmine Griffin, Mae Henderson, Arlene Keizer, Deborah McDowell, Nellie McKay, Val Smith, Hortense Spillers, Claudia Tate, and Mary Helen Washington, among others

2. Of course, women's work varied from region to region. In some Mississippi counties, for example, blacks outnumbered whites and subsisted on sharecropping or others forms of agricultural labor. Elsewhere, factory work was the norm. See especially Lerner (1972) and Jacqueline Jones (1985).

3. For a distinct but similar methodology, see Valerie Smith's *Not Just Race, Not Just Gender: Black Feminist Reading.* Smith deploys "intersectionality as a mode of cultural or textual analysis," that is, reading at the intersecting "constructions of race, gender,

class and sexuality." She explores the ways in which the dominance of one category can mask "both the operation of the others and the interconnections among them" (1998, xiv–xv).

4. In "White Dirt" (forthcoming) I have argued that Cather builds complex white characters out of the object-detritus of the landscapes that surround them but that this complex relation to objects and landscapes is not available to her black characters. In fact, the landscapes that white people inhabit are more intricate than the psyches of Cather's black characters, who do create rich inner lives but possess an inert relation to space, suggesting not only an arrested spatiality but an arrested inventiveness on Cather's part. The same seems true, although in a more complex and troubled fashion, of Welty's *Delta Wedding,* where Welty continually looks askance at her characters' (and her own) consignment of African American characters to background or atmosphere.

5. To complicate this picture, I should add that Welty describes swept yards with pleasure and respect: "Here, where no grass was let grow on the flat earth that was bare like their feet, the old women had it shady, secret, lazy, and cool. A devious, invisible vine of talk seemed to grow from shady porch to shady porch, though all the old women were hidden" (*Delta Wedding,* 167).

6. Slaves possessed some things not legally but by right of use.

7. See, for example, Fox-Genovese on Fanny Kemble's dramatization of a mistress's arrival at a plantation, involving petitions to reduce the workload and requests for more clothing and things to eat: "tanks to de good Lord Almighty that missus had come, what give de poor niggar sugar and flannel." Simple requests for "sugar, rice, and baby clothes" were often denied (131ff.).

8. See, for example, Windley (1983).

9. The particulars of black economic lives, both individually and regionally, were more complex. See Foner (1988) on tenancy, land ownership, and the growing black middle class (379–411). See also his description of the South's new mercantile class and its relation to black farmers: "As for black tenants, the ability to seek supplies off the plantation enhanced their independence. . . . On the other hand, interest rates for goods purchased on credit rose to exorbitant levels (often exceeding 50 percent)," reflecting the fact that "many rural merchants faced no local competition" or were willing to inflict "outright fraud on illiterate tenants" (408). See also Hall (1998, 121–98) on the changes in southern patterns of consumption, including the freedom created by mail-order catalogues, the increasing competition among white businesses for black clients in southern cities, and white anxiety at "the shock of sameness" (195) when middle-class southern whites encountered middle-class African Americans.

10. Even Linda Brent (looking over her shoulder at her white, bourgeois audience?) is oddly apologetic about these crossover objects. She apologizes for Luke, an escaped slave who put extra money in the pockets of his dying master's trousers, and then, at his death, asked for these "'ole trousers, an dey gub 'em to me.' With a low chuckling laugh, he added, 'You see I didn't *steal* it; dey gub it to me.' . . . This is a fair specimen of how the moral sense is educated by slavery" (Jacobs 1973, 198).

11. Carby argues that Hurston's "holistic celebration of black life" also represents "'negroness' as an unchanging, essential entity" (1990, 77). Beilke argues, contra Carby, that there are two perspectives on Hurston that must be overturned: first, that "her comedy upholds racist stereotypes," and second, that her representations of race are essentialist. Instead, Beilke suggests that Hurston's characters practice signifying and other modes of "folk" comedy as ritual techniques to increase status (1998, 21–33). In the

clerk's response to his next customer we have more evidence of Hurston's canny estimations of white people's perceptions of "negroness" as an unchanging entity. Both Missie May and Joe represent the role of comic performance in maintaining the delicate balance of their status and marriage.

12. See Hale on the routine practice of going to town and the spiral of mass-produced consumer goods that created radical changes in the culture of segregation by the 1930s. (1998, 183–98).

13. For a canny reading of Clifton's project of reclaiming not simply a family of names but a mythology, see Hull (1997).

Chapter Eight

1. For a paradigm-shifting reading of the grotesque that restructures Bakhtin, tampering with his nonfeminist theories in order to spin out an interpretation of excessive feminine bodies that is at once aerial and earthy, exalted and campy, see Russo (1994).

2. Since command over space is a fundamental source of social power within everyday life, white ownership of the most mundane domestic places could instigate acute spatial and bodily crisis for southern African Americans. "It all comes back to houses," says Walker, thinking not only about the houses of her own past (among them a sharecropper's shack a few miles from Flannery O'Connor's spacious house) but also about Faulkner's black caretaker, exiled from the big house to a backyard shack. For Walker the southern power ratio is enacted through a grim domestic grid that damages the body, relentlessly fractioning its integrity.

3. Gilchrist's metaphors ring contemporary changes on traditional southern grotesques. Gus's body resembles an old catcher's mitt; Robert's mother wears a hairdo that resembles the helmets of the L.A. Rams. In addition, the trees in this story tell a story of the changing South. We move from the live oak that supports Gus's drug-dealing in Audubon park to the weak-limbed crepe myrtle that fails to support the children's falling bodies at the story's end: Gilchrist's cynical comment on an equally predatory but far less foundational South.

4. This sideshow does not fit within the narrow margins that, for Susan Stewart, describe the noncarnivalesque, nondemocratic aspect of spectacle. See *On Longing* (1984).

5. See Susan Stewart's distinctions between the carnivalesque and the grotesque in *On Longing* (1984).

6. Personal correspondence; these sentences were dropped from O'Brien's *Times Literary Supplement* review.

7. This litany could go on and on. In Alabama, during radical Reconstruction, freedmen delivered "inflammatory" speeches asserting that "the wealth of the white man had been made by negro labor, and that the negroes were entitled to their fair share of all these accumulations." "Didn't you clear the white folks' land?" asked one orator. "Yes and we have a right to it" (Foner 1988, 290).

8. Not that early Reconstruction violence wasn't brutal and frightening. Many blacks who asserted their freedom were shot on the spot. A Nashville newspaper described regulators who were "riding about whipping, maiming and killing all negroes who do not obey the orders of their former masters, just as if slavery existed." Foner adds that this period witnessed extraordinary incidents of violence against blacks, but that in very few instances did blacks attack whites, despite extraordinary waves of fear about such uprisings among the white populace. For Foner these pervasive insurrection panics

"underscored what might be called the 'politicization' of everyday life that followed the demise of slavery" (123).

9. Felman asserts that the act of bearing witness is made out of "bits and pieces of a memory that has been overwhelmed by occurrences that have not settled into understanding or remembrance, acts that cannot be constructed as knowledge nor assimilated into full cognition, events in excess of our frames of reference" (5). It is this excessiveness, this sense of the event as simultaneously fragment and impossible fullness, as well as this sense of events pressuring us toward lost cognition, that connects testimonial with the grotesque body. I'm suggesting a mode of mimesis where the fractured nature of testimony spills over into the bodiliness of the grotesque. Finally, beyond (1) testimony as vow or promise, (2) testimony as attempted or wished-for action, and (3) testimony as cognitionless fragment—as an event that ruptures or refuses everyday frames of reference—testimony is profoundly dialogic; it requires a listener. "The listener to trauma comes to be a participant and a co-owner of the traumatic event: through his very listening, he comes to partially experience trauma in himself" (57).

10. See Smith, *Killers of the Dream,* pp. 70, 71.

11. See Watson (1997) for a reading of Smith that examines the intertwining of sex and race as well and postulates the body as the ultimate site of ideological work. See also Hale (1998) on Smith's sexuality and the biracial impetus of *Pseudopodia, North Georgia Review,* and *South Today*—all names for a journal that Smith created with Paula Snelling.

12. As Foucault argues, even when history seems to offer "a closed field" inscribing play "among equals" (1977, 150), we must recognize that daily space disguises a void; it is a site that divides.

13. See p. 108, where Smith uses a striking grotesque panoply to stir up her audience's fear of the ill effects of revivalists' sermons.

Chapter Nine

1. One response would be to widen the network of texts we read as "southern" to include Juanita Harrisons's *My Great, Wide Beautiful World,* a travelogue by a black southerner who works her way around the world but never mentions the South, as well as Cuban literature coming out of Miami, or the Laurentian sweep of novels by Elizabeth Maddox Roberts. All of this is "southern," suggesting a need to widen our definitions. But the books I have described here are mostly canonical works, in the sense that most people think of them as southern, recognize the names of these authors, but haven't necessarily read them. Americanists are always turning to me and saying—I know most of American literature, except the South—as if this fiction is so minor, un-American, and anomalous that it can be sidelined so that critics can get a clear view of the rest.

2. See Faust (1996) for the transformations in women's writing practices that began with the Civil War.

3. Hurston, for example, dedicated *Seraph on the Sewanee* to Marjorie Kinnan Rawlings. But Trefzer describes the limits of this friendship. Rawlings and Hurston might spend their daytimes talking and their nighttimes drinking, but when Hurston stayed at Cross Creek, she always slept in the maid's cabin (1998, 75).

4. What writers like O'Connor and Walker do best is expose the sadism associated with this posturing; they explore the costs, across race and class boundaries, of an obsession with matter out of place. Witness Amy's father's reaction in *The Old Order* when she dresses as a shepherdess for the ball: "'No daughter of mine is going to show herself

in such a rig-out. It's bawdy,' he thundered. 'Bawdy! . . . You go upstairs this minute, and pin up that waist in front and let down those skirts to a decent length before you leave this house. And wash your face!' " (Porter 1972, 185).

5. Amy's and Edna's deaths I take as other instances of the self-excluding behavior of "polluting agents"—as are the deaths of Désirée and Margaret Copeland and their-mixed race babies.

6. This category could be elaborated to include a variety of lower-class white characters—people diffidently defined as white trash—for example, the polluting white boys who return with a vengeance and burn down the farm in O'Connor's "A Circle in the Fire" or Welty's Lilly Daw from *A Curtain of Green,* a wild child whose sexual maturity demands her exile into either an insane asylum or marriage.

7. That is, dirt becomes the medium not only of defilement but of the consecration of that which is other, outside, forbidden, unclean.

8. Porter puts equally pernicious associations to work in "The Old Order" when the grandmother returns "not to the house but to the black, rich soft land and the human beings living on it" (1972, 322).

9. From the beginning Janie risks landscapes stinging with pleasure that create an ecstatic contact with her own bodily margins: "She was stretched on her back beneath the pear tree soaking in the alto chant of the visiting bees, the gold of the sun and the panting breath of the breeze when the inaudible voice of it all came to her. She saw a dust-bearing bee sink into the sanctum of a bloom; the thousand sister-calyxes arch to meet the love embrace and the ecstatic shiver of the tree from root to tiniest branch creaming in every blossom and frothing with delight" (24). The aura of interchange between self and world imaged in the contact between dusty bee and arching tree is gorgeously sexual, but these subliminal desires suggest a shift in worldview that is more fundamental: "She was sixteen. She had glossy leaves and bursting buds and she wanted to struggle with life but it seemed to elude her" (25). The Janie who comes back to town covered with road dust and emanating danger to everyone is not simply brandishing a recovered sexuality, but a recovered capacity to struggle.

10. The dirt of the Everglades buckles the bourgeois trajectory of Hurston's novel and fills its space with a new political energy. The muck initiates a spatial economy in which the vertical mobility of the first half of the novel is exchanged for the adventure of the horizon. Janie's and Teacake's exuberance on the muck, their delight in defilement, suggests there may be unexplored, unimagined ways of inhabiting social space. (As the geographers Keith and Pile suggest: "there is more to space than merely being in the centre or confined to the margin. Indeed, space can be seen to be full of gaps, contradictions, folds, and tears. Through these, marginalized communities may be able to inscribe themselves into new geographies" [1993, 36]. Hurston resists this broad optimism, but she uses the symbolic potential of dirt to explore the gaps and contradictions, the cyborgian folds in the south's racial dramas.)

11. This dynamic is complex in *Let Us Now Praise Famous Men* because it is Agee who supersedes the ordinary rules of his "characters' " lives—they do not live within his emancipatory prose but outside of it. His attempt to give poverty the flint of heroism is always complicated by his own agenda. That is, one could argue that Agee is as pollution-obsessed as Mrs. Turpin, but that he keeps trying to give his obsession a different spin.

12. Their house is pristine; within its "gloaty, sparkly white" walls, Jody "didn't have to get up and go to the door every time he had to spit. Didn't spit on his floor neither. Had

that golded-up spitting pot right handy. But he went further than that. He bought a little lady-size spitting pot for Janie to spit in. Had it right in the parlor with litttle sprigs of flowers painted all around the sides" (75–76). Here pollution obsession enters in all its political dimensions. Jody cares not a whit about the disposition of Janie's bodily fluids, but he does care about establishing hierarchy.

13. On the uses of play and negation see Gates (1988), 180–216. For a dissenting viewpoint see Carby (1990), 71–73.

14. The mule becomes "our departed citizen, our most distinguished citizen," and Sam Watson conjures up his topsy-turvy life in mule heaven, where the devil can plow "Matt Bonner all day long in a hell-hot sun . . . laying the raw-hide to his back. With that the sisters got mock-happy and shouted and had to be held up by the menfolks." Of course Janie, once more, is forbidden to go. So there stands Jody, delivering his parodic eulogy from "the distended belly of the mule" while Janie minds the store: "you ain't goin' off in all dat mess uh commonness. Ah'm surprised at yuh fuh askin'" (94).

15. As Avery Gordon comments in *Ghostly Matters,* "To write stories concerning exclusions and invisibilities is to write ghost stories. To write ghost stories implies that ghosts are real, that is to say, that they produce material effects" (1997, 17).

References

Abel, Elizabeth. 1997. Black writing, white reading: Race and the politics of feminist interpretation. In *Female Subjects in Black and White: Race, Psychoanalysis, Feminism,* edited by Elizabeth Abel, Barbara Christian, and Helene Moglen, pp. 102–31. Berkeley: University of California Press.

Abel, Elizabeth, Barbara Christian, and Helene Moglen, eds. 1997. *Female Subjects in Black and White: Race, Psychoanalysis, Feminism.* Berkeley: University of California Press.

Adorno, Theodor. 1984. *Aesthetic Theory.* Translated by Christian Lenhardt. London: Routledge and Kegan Paul.

Agee, James, and Walker Evans. 1966. *Let Us Now Praise Famous Men.* New York: Ballantine.

Angelou, Maya. 1970. *I Know Why the Caged Bird Sings.* New York: Bantam.

Ansa, Tina McElroy. 1989. *Baby of the Family.* New York: Harcourt, Brace, Jovanovich.

Arendt, Hannah. 1958. *The Human Condition.* Chicago: University of Chicago Press.

Arnow, Harriet. 1999. *The Dollmaker.* 1954. Reprint, New York: Bard.

Ayers, Edward L. 1992. *The Promise of the New South: Life After Reconstruction.* New York: Oxford University Press.

Bakhtin, Mikhail. 1968. *Rabelais and His World.* Translated by H. Iswolsky. Cambridge: MIT Press.

Ball, Charles. 1837. *Slavery in the United States: A Narrative of the Life and Adventures of Charles Ball, a Black Man.* New York: John S. Taylor.

Barthes, Roland. 1981. *Camera Lucida: Reflections on Photography.* Translated by Richard Howard. New York: Hill and Wang.

Beilke, Debra. 1998. Yowin' and jawin': Humor and the performance of identity in Zora Neale Hurston's *Jonah's Gourd Vine. Southern Quarterly* 36:21–33.

Bersani, Leo. 1977. *Baudelaire and Freud.* Berkeley: University. of California Press.

Bollas, Christopher. 1987. *The Shadow of the Object.* New York: Columbia University Press.

Bourdieu, Pierre. 1984. *Distinction: A Social Critique of the Judgement of Taste.* Translated by Richard Nice. Cambridge: Harvard University Press.

Branch, Taylor. 1988. *Parting the Waters: America in the King Years 1954–63.* New York: Simon and Schuster.

Brookhart, Mary Hughes. 1993. Spiritual daughters of the black American South. In *The Female Tradition in Southern Literature,* edited by Carol S. Manning, pp. 125–139. Urbana: University of Illinois Press.

Burton, Orville Vernon. 1987. Foreword to *Born to Rebel: An Autobiography,* by Benjamin E. Mays. Athens: University of Georgia Press.

Caldwell, Taylor. 1962. *Tobacco Road.* 1934. Reprint, New York: Signet.

Carby, Hazel V. 1986. "It jus be's dat way sometime": The sexual politics of women's blues. *Radical America* 20:9–24.

———. 1987. *Reconstructing Womanhood: The Emergence of the Afro-American Woman Novelist.* New York: Oxford University Press.

———. 1990. The politics of fiction, anthropology, and the folk: Zora Neale Hurston. In *New Essays on* Their Eyes Were Watching God, pp. 71–93. Cambridge: Cambridge University Press.

Carson, Anne. 1990. Putting her in her place: Woman, dirt, and desire. In *Before Sexuality: The Construction of Erotic Experience in the Ancient Greek World,* edited by David M. Halperin, John J. Winkler, Froma I. Zeitlin, pp. 135–69. Princeton: Princeton University Press.

Cash, W. J. 1941. *The Mind of the South.* New York: Random House.

Casti, John L. 1997. *Would-Be Worlds.* New York: John Wiley and Sons.

Cather, Willa. 1968. *Sapphira and the Slave Girl.* 1940. Reprint, New York: Vintage.

Chambers, Ross. 1994. Mediation and the escalator principle (on Nicholson Baker's *The Mezzanine*), *Modern Fiction Studies* 40:765–806.

Chesnutt, Charles. 1969. *The Conjure Woman.* 1899. Reprint, Ann Arbor: University of Michigan Press.

Childress, Alice. 1956. *Like One of the Family . . . Conversations from a Domestic's Life.* New York: Independence.

Chopin, Kate. 1976. *The Awakening.* 1899. Reprint, New York: Norton.

———. 1979. Désirée's baby. [1894.]In *The Literary South,* edited by Louis D. Rubin Jr., pp. 403–7. New York: John Wiley and Sons.

———. 1991. La belle Zoraïde. [1894.] In *The Signet Classic Book of Southern Short Stories,* edited by Dorothy Abbott and Susan Koppelman, pp. 101–7. New York: Signet.

Christian, Barbara. 1990. What Celie knows that you should know. In *Anatomy of Racism,* edited by David Theo Goldberg, pp. 135–45. Minneapolis: University of Minnesota Press.

———. 1997. Fixing methodologies: *Beloved.* In *Female Subjects in Black and White: Race, Psychoanalysis, Feminism,* edited by Elizabeth Abel, Barbara Christian, and Helene Moglen, pp. 363–70. Berkeley: University of California Press.

Clifford, James. 1988. *The Predicament of Culture.* Cambridge: Harvard University Press.

Clifton, Lucille. 1980. *good woman: poems and a memoir, 1969–1980.* Brockport, N.Y.: BOA Editions.

Clinton, Catherine, ed. 1994. *Half-Sisters of History: Southern Women and the American Past.* Durham: Duke University Press.

Cook, Blanche Wiesen. 1992. *Eleanor Roosevelt: Volume One 1884–1933.* New York: Viking.

Cooper, Jan. 1993. Zora Neale Hurston was always a southerner too. In *The Female Tradition in Southern Literature,* edited by Carol S. Manning, pp. 57–69. Urbana: University of Illinois Press.

Csikszentmihalyi, Mihaly. 1993. Why we need things. In *History from Things: Essays on Material Culture,* edited by Steven Lubar and W. David Kingery, pp. 20–29. Washington, D.C.: Smithsonian Institution Press. Daniels, Jonathan. 1938. *A Southerner Discovers the South.* New York: MacMillan.

Davis, Thadious M. 1985. Southern standard bearers in the new negro renaissance. In *The History of Southern Literature,* edited by Louis D. Rubin Jr., Blyden Jackson, Rayburn S. Moore, Lewis P. Simpson, and Thomas Daniel Young, pp. 291–313. Baton Rouge: Louisiana State University Press.

———. 1988. Expanding the limits: The intersection of race and region. *Southern Literary Journal* 20:3–11.

———. 1991. Ernest J. Gaines. In *African American Writers' Profiles of Their Lives and Works—From the 1700s to the Present,* edited by Valerie Smith, Lea Baechler, and A. Walton Litz, pp. 105–20. New York: MacMillan.

———. 1993. Women's art and authorship in the southern region: Connections. In *The Female Tradition in Southern Literature,* edited by Carol S. Manning, pp. 15–36. Urbana: University of Illinois Press.

———. 1996. Erasing the "we of me" and rewriting the racial script: Carson McCullers's two *Member(s) of the Wedding.* In *Critical Essays on Carson McCullers,* edited by Beverly Lyon Clark and Melvin J. Friedman, pp. 206–19. New York: G. K. Hall.

de Certeau, Michel. 1984. *The Practice of Everyday Life.* Berkeley: University of California Press.

Deleuze, Gilles. 1990. *The Logic of Sense.* Translated by Mark Lester, edited by Constantin V. Boundas. New York: Columbia University Press.

Dew, Robb Foreman. 1987. The power and the glory. In *A World Unsuspected: Portraits of Southern Childhood,* edited by Alex Harris, pp. 108–26. Chapel Hill: University of North Carolina Press.

Dittmer, John. 1995. *Local People: The Struggle for Civil Rights in Mississippi.* Urbana: University of Illinois Press.

Dixon, Thomas, Jr. 1970. *The Clansman: A Historical Romance of the Ku Klux Klan.* 1905. Reprint, Lexington: University Press of Kentucky.

Donaldson, Susan. 1997. Gender and history in Eudora Welty's *Delta Wedding. South Central Review* 14:3–14.

Douglas, Ellen. 1988. *Can't Quit You, Baby.* New York: Penguin.

Douglas, Mary. 1984. *Purity and Danger: An Analysis of the Concepts of Pollution and Taboo.* London: Ark Paperbacks.

Dove, Rita. 1986. *Thomas and Beulah.* Pittsburgh: Carnegie-Mellon University Press.

Du Bois, W. E. B. 1989. *The Souls of Black Folk.* 1903. Reprint, New York: Penguin.

duCille, Ann. 1997. The occult of true black womanhood: Critical demeanor and black feminist studies. In *Female Sbjects in Black and White: Race, Psychoanalysis, Feminism,* edited by Elizabeth Abel, Barbara Christian, and Helene Moglen, pp. 21–56. Berkeley: University of California Press.

Eagleton, Terry. 1981. *Walter Benjamin, or Towards a Revolutionary Criticism.* London: Verso.

Einstein, Carl. 1929. Andre Masson, etude ethnologique. *Documents* 1 (2):93–104.

Elliott, Sarah Barnwell. 1991. The heart of it. [1890s.] In *The Signet Classic Book of Southern Short Stories,* edited by Dorothy Abbott and Susan Koppelman, pp. 115–31. New York: Signet.

Engelhardt, Tom. 1994. The morphing of the American mind. *New York Times,* 24 December, A25.

Faulkner, William. 1991. Dry September. [1930.] In *The Signet Classic Book of Southern Short Stories,* edited by Dorothy Abbott and Susan Koppelman, pp. 175–87. Reprint, New York: Signet.

———. 1972. *Absalom, Absalom!* 1936. Reprint, New York: Vintage.

———. 1973. *Go Down, Moses.* 1942. Reprint, New York: Vintage.

———. 1950. *Collected Stories of William Faulkner.* New York: Random House.

Faust, Drew. 1996. *Mothers of Invention: Women of the Slaveholding South in the American Civil War.* Chapel Hill: University of North Carolina Press.

———. 1999. Clutching the chains that bind: Margaret Mitchell and *Gone With the Wind. Southern Cultures* 5 (spring):6–20.

Felman, Shoshana, and Dori Laub. 1992. *Testimony: Crises of Witnessing in Literature, Psychoanalysis, and History.* New York: Routledge.

Fleming, Robert. 1993. The ritual of survival. *Up South: Stories, Studies and Letters of This Century's African-American Migrations,* edited by Malaika Adero, pp. 33–43. New York: New Press.

Foner, Eric. 1988. *Reconstruction: America's Unfinished Revolution 1863–1877.* New York: Harper and Row.

Forkner, Ben, and Patrick Samway, S.J., eds. 1989. *Stories of the Old South.* New York: Penguin.

Foucault, Michel. 1972. *The Archaeology of Knowledge,* Translated by A. M. Sheridan Smith. New York: Pantheon.

———. 1977. Nietzsche, genealogy, history. In *Language, Counter-Memory, Practice: Selected Essays and Reviews.* Translated by Donald F. Bouchard and Sherry Simon, pp. 139–64. Ithaca: Cornell University Press.

———. 1980a. *The History of Sexuality.* Vol. 1, *An Introduction.* Translated by Robert Hurley. New York: Vintage.

———. 1980b. *Power/Knowledge: Selected Interviews and Other Writings,* edited by Colin Gordon. New York: Pantheon.

Fox-Genovese, Elizabeth. 1988. *Within the Plantation Household: Black and White Women of the Old South.* Chapel Hill: University of North Carolina Press.

Gaines, Ernest. 1993. *A Lesson Before Dying.* New York: Vintage.

Gates, Henry Louis Jr. 1988. *The Signifying Monkey: A Theory of Afro-American Literary Criticism.* New York: Oxford University Press.

———. 1995. *Colored People.* New York: Vintage.

Gilchrist, Ellen. 1981. *In the Land of Dreamy Dreams.* Boston: Little, Brown.

Glasgow, Ellen. 1989. Jordan's end. [1923.] In *Stories of the Old South,* edited by Ben Forkner and Patrick Samway, S.J., pp. 161–75. New York: Viking Penguin.

Goodman, Susan. 1998. *Ellen Glasgow: A Biography.* Baltimore: Johns Hopkins University Press.

Gordon, Avery. 1997. *Ghostly Matters: Haunting and the Sociological Imagination.* Minneapolis: University of Minnesota Press.

Gordon, Caroline. 1990. *The Collected Stories of Caroline Gordon.* Baton Rouge: Louisiana State University Press.

Gordon-Reed, Annette. 1998. Three perspectives on America's Jefferson fixation. *The Nation,* 30 November, 23–28.

Griffin, Farah Jasmine. 1995. *"Who Set You Flowin'?" The African-American Migration Narrative.* New York: Oxford.

Griffin, Larry J., and Don H. Doyle. 1995. *The South as an American Problem.* Athens: University of Georgia Press.

Gwin, Minrose. 1990. *The Feminine and Faulkner: Reading (Beyond) Sexual Difference.* Knoxville: University of Tennessee Press.

Habermas, Jürgen. 1975. *Legitimation Crisis.* Translated by Thomas McCarthy. Boston: Beacon Press.

Hale, Grace Elizabeth. 1998. *Making Whiteness: The Culture of Segregation in the South, 1890–1940.* New York: Pantheon.

Hall, Jacquelyn Dowd. 1983. "The mind that burns in each body": Women, rape, and racial violence. In *Powers of Desire: The Politics of Sexuality,* edited by Ann Snitow, Christine Stansell, and Sharon Thompson, pp. 328–49. New York: Monthly Review Press.

———. 1993. *Revolt Against Chivalry: Jessie Daniel Ames and the Women's Campaign Against Lynching.* New York: Columbia University Press.

Hall, Jacquelyn Dowd, James Leloudis, Robert Korstad, Mary Murphy, Lu Ann Jones, and Christopher B. Daly. 1987. *Like a Family: The Making of a Southern Cotton Mill World.* Chapel Hill: University of North Carolina Press.

Hannon, Charles. 1996. "The Ballad of the Sad Café" and other stories of women's wartime labor. *Genders* 23:97–117.

Harris, Trudier. 1982. *From Mammies to Militants: Domestics in Black American Literature.* Philadelphia: Temple University Press.

———. 1991. *Fiction and Folklore: The Novels of Toni Morrison.* Knoxville: University of Tennessee Press.

———. 1996. *The Power of the Porch: The Storyteller's Craft in Zora Neale Hurston, Gloria Naylor, and Randall Kenan.* Athens: University of Georgia Press.

Harrison, Juanita. 1996. *My Great, Wide, Beautiful World.* 1936. Reprint. New York: G. K. Hall.

Harvey, David. 1990. *The Condition of Postmodernity.* Cambridge, Mass.: Blackwell.

Held, David. 1989. *Political Theory and the Modern State.* Stanford: Stanford University Press.

Hellman, Lillian. 1960. *An Unfinished Woman.* Boston: Little, Brown.

Henderson, Mae. The stories of O(Dessa): Stories of complicity and resistance. In *Female Subjects in Black and White: Race, Psychoanalysis, Feminism,* edited by Elizabeth Abel, Barbara Christian, and Helene Moglen, pp. 285–304. Berkeley: University of California Press.

Hill, Mike. 1997. *Whiteness: A Critical Reader.* New York: New York University Press.

Hobson, Fred. 1978. *Serpent in Eden: H. L. Mencken and the South.* Baton Rouge: Louisiana State University Press.

———. 1991. *The Southern Writer in the Postmodern World.* Athens: University of Georgia Press.

Homans, Margaret. 1997. "Racial composition": Metaphor and the body in the writing of race. In *Female Subjects in Black and White: Race, Psychoanalysis, Feminism,* edited by Elizabeth Abel, Barbara Christian, and Helene Moglen, pp. 77–101. Berkeley: University of California Press.

Hoole, William Stanley. 1952. *Alias Simon Suggs: The Life and Times of Johnson Jones Hooper.* University: University of Alabama Press.

Howard, John, ed. 1997. *Carryin' On in the Lesbian and Gay South.* New York: New York University Press.

Hull, Akasha [Gloria Hull]. 1997. Channeling the ancestral muse: Lucille Clifton and Dolores Kendrick. In *Female Subjects in Black and White: Race, Psychoanalysis, Feminism,* edited by Elizabeth Abel, Barbara Christian, and Helene Moglen, pp. 330–48. Berkeley: University of California Press.

Hurston, Zora Neale. 1962. *Jonah's Gourd Vine.* 1934. Reprint, London: Virago Press.

———. 1989. The gilded six-bits. [1933.] In *Stories of the Old South,* edited by Ben Forkner and Patrick Samway, S.J., pp. 224–34. Reprint, New York: Viking Penguin.

———. 1990a. *Mules and Men.* 1935. Reprint, New York: Harper Perennial.

———. 1990b. *Their Eyes Were Watching God.* 1937. Reprint, New York: Harper and Row.

Ivins, Molly. 1991. *Molly Ivins Can't Say That, Can She?* New York: Random House.

Jabès, Edmond. 1984 *The Book of Questions: El, or the Last Book.* Translated by Rosmarie Waldrop. Middletown, Conn.: Wesleyan University Press.

Jacobs, Harriet [Linda Brent]. 1973. *Incidents in the Life of a Slave Girl,* edited by L. Maria Child. 1861. Reprint, New York: Harcourt Brace Jovanovich.

Jacobus, Mary, Evelyn Fox Keller, and Sally Shuttleworth. 1990. *Body/Politics: Women and the Discourses of Science.* New York: Routledge.

Jameson, Fredric. 1972. *Marxism and Form.* Princeton: Princeton University Press.

———. 1990. *Late Marxism: Adorno, or, The Persistence of the Dialectic.* London: Verso.

Jehlen, Myra. 1978. *Class and Character in Faulkner's South.* Secaucus, N.J.: Citadel Press.

Jones, Anne Goodwyn. 1981. *Tomorrow Is Another Day: The Woman Writer in the South, 1859–1936.* Baton Rouge: Louisiana State University Press.

———. 1997. "I don't hate it. I don't hate it": Teaching southern literature. *The Heath Anthology of American Literature* 15 (spring): n.p.

Jones, Anne Goodwyn, and Susan Donaldson, eds. 1997. *Haunted Bodies: Gender and Southern Texts.* Charlottesville: University Press of Virginia.

Jones, Gayl. 1975. *Corregidora.* Boston: Beacon Press.

Jones, Jacqueline. 1985. *Labor of Love, Labor of Sorrow: Black Women, Work, and the Family, from Slavery to the Present.* New York: Vintage.

Keith, Michael, and Steve Pile. 1993. *Place and the Politics of Identity.* London: Routledge.

Kelley, Robin D. G. 1994. *Race Rebels: Culture, Politics, and the Black Working Class.* New York: Free Press.

Kester, Howard. 1934. "The Lynching of Claude Neal." New York: NAACP.

Kincheloe, Joe L., Shirley R. Steinberg, Nelson M. Rodriguez, and Ronald E. Chennault. 1998. *White Reign: Deploying Whiteness in America.* New York: St. Martin's Press.

King, Grace. 1995. The little convent girl. [1893.] In *Southern Women's Writing: Colonial to Contemporary,* edited by Mary Louise Weaks and Carolyn Perry, pp. 169–76. Gainesville: University of Florida Press.

King, Richard H. 1980. *A Southern Renaissance: The Cultural Awakening of the American South, 1930–1955.* New York: Oxford University Press.

Kreyling, Michael. 1998. *Inventing Southern Literature*. Jackson: University Press of Mississippi.

Kristeva, Julia. 1982. *The Powers of Horror*. New York: Columbia University Press.

Larsen, Nella. 1986. Quicksand *and* Passing, edited by Deborah E. McDowell. New Brunswick: Rutgers University Press.

Lee, Harper. 1982. *To Kill a Mockingbird*. 1960. Reprint, New York: Time Warner.

Lefebvre, Henri. 1991. *The Production of Space*. Translated by Donald Nicholson-Smith. Oxford: Blackwell.

Lemann, Nicholas. 1991. *The Promised Land: The Great Black Migration and How It Changed America*. New York: Vintage.

Lerner, Gerda, ed. 1972. *Black Women in White America: A Documentary History*. New York: Vintage.

Lester, Julius. 1968. *To Be a Slave*. New York: Dell.

———. 1991. Black and white together: Teaching the "Beloved Community" in today's racially divided classrooms. *Lingua Franca* 1:30–32.

Lipsitz, George. 1995. Diasporic intimacy in the art of Renée Stout. In *"Dear Robert, I'll See You at the Crossroads: A Project by Renée Stout*. Seattle: University of Washington Press.

Lorde, Audre. 1997. *The Collected Poems of Audre Lorde*. New York: Norton.

Lomax, Alan. 1993. *The Land Where the Blues Began*. New York: Delta.

Lott, Eric. 1993. *Black Minstrelsy and the American Working Class*. New York: Oxford University Press.

Manning, Carol S., ed. 1993. *The Female Tradition in Southern Literature*. Urbana: University of Illinois Press.

Marshall, Ray. 1967. *The Negro Worker*. New York: Random House.

Marx, Karl. 1977. *Selected Writings*, edited by David McLellan. Oxford: Oxford University Press.

Mays, Benjamin. 1968. *The Negro's God as Reflected in His Literature*. 1938. Reprint, New York: Russell and Russell.

Mays, Benjamin, and Joseph W. Nicholson. 1969. *The Negro's Church*. 1933. Reprint, New York: Russell and Russell.

McCullers, Carson. 1971. *The Ballad of the Sad Café and Other Stories*. 1951. Reprint, New York: Bantam.

———.1975. *The Member of the Wedding*. 1946. Reprint, New York: Houghton Mifflin.

McDowell, Deborah E. 1989. Reading family matters. In *Changing Our Own Words*, edited by Cheryl Wall, pp. 38–57. Brunswick, N.J.: Rutgers University Press.

McKay, Nellie Y. 1998. Naming the problem that led to the question Who shall teach African American literature? or, Are we ready to disband the *Wheatley* court? *PMLA* 113: 359–69.

Mitchell, Margaret. 1973. *Gone with the Wind*. 1936. Reprint. New York: Avon.

Moraga, Cherrie. 1981. *This Bridge Called My Back: Writings by Radical Women of Color*. Edited by Cherrie Moraga and Gloria Anzaldua. New York: Kitchen Table, Women of Color Press.

Morrison, Toni. 1973. *Sula*. NewYork: Knopf.

———. 1977. *Song of Solomon*. New York: Signet.

———. 1987. *Beloved*. New York: Signet.

———. 1992. *Playing in the Dark: Whiteness and the Literary Imagination.* Cambridge: Harvard University Press.

———. 1994. Unspeakable things unspoken: The Afro-American presence in American literature. In *Within the Circle: An Anthology of African American Literary Criticism from the Harlem Renaissance to the Present,* edited by Angelyn Mitchell, pp. 368–98. Durham: Duke University Press.

Myrdal, Gunnar. 1944. *An American Dilemma: The Negro Problem and Modern Democracy.* 2 vols. New York: Harper and Brothers.

Naylor, Gloria. 1994. Gloria Naylor. In *I Know What the Red Clay Looks Like: The Voice and Vision of Black Women Writers,* edited by Rebecca Carroll, pp. 158–73. New York: Crown Trade Paperbacks.

O'Brien, Michael. 1979. *The Idea of the American South, 1920–1941.* Baltimore: Johns Hopkins University Press.

———. 1993. *Rethinking the South: Essays in Intellectual History.* Athens: University of Georgia Press.

———. 1995. "Old Song of Percy." *Times Literary Supplement,* 24 March, 23.

O'Connor, Flannery. 1949. *Wise Blood.* New York: Farrar, Straus, and Giroux.

———. 1960. *3 by Flannery O'Connor.* New York: Farrar, Straus, and Giroux.

———. 1961. *Mystery and Manners,* edited by Sally and Robert Fitzgerald. New York: Farrar, Straus, and Giroux.

———. 1971. *The Complete Stories of Flannery O'Connor.* New York: Farrar, Straus and Giroux.

———. 1979a. *The Habit of Being,* edited by Sally Fitzgerald. New York: Farrar, Straus, and Giroux.

———. 1979b. *Letters of Flannery O'Connor: The Habit of Being,* edited by Sally Fitzgerald. New York: Farrar, Straus, and Giroux.

Oliver, Diane. 1991. Neighbors. [1966.] In *The Signet Classic Book of Southern Short Stories,* edited by Dorothy Abbott and Susan Koppelman, pp. 466–83. Reprint, New York: Signet.

Padel, Ruth. 1990. Making space speak. In *Nothing to Do with Dionysus? Athenian Drama in Its Social Context,* edited by John Winkler and Froma Zeitlin. Princeton: Princeton University Press.

Painter, Nell Irvin. 1995. Soul murder and slavery: Toward a fully loaded cost accounting. In *U. S. History as Women's History: New Feminist Essays,* edited by Linda K. Kerber, Alice Kessler-Harris, and Kathryn Kish Sklar, pp. 125–46. Chapel Hill: University of North Carolina Press.

Paley, Grace. 1997. "Travelling." *New Yorker,* 8 September, 42–43.

Park, Mungo. 1800. *Travels in the Interior Districts of Africa.* London: W. Bulmer.

Percy, Walker. 1965. Mississippi: The fallen paradise. *The South Today,* special supplement to *Harper's,* April.

———. 1984. "The southern imagination": An interview with Eudora Welty and Walker Percy. In *Conversations with Eudora Welty,* edited by Peggy Whiteman Prenshaw, pp. 92–114. Jackson: University Press of Mississippi.

Pocock, J. G. A. 1985. *Virtue, Commerce, and History.* Cambridge: Cambridge University Press.

Porter, Katherine Anne. 1972. *The Collected Stories of Katherine Anne Porter.* New York: Harcourt, Brace, Jovanovich.

Powell, Padgett. 1987. Hitting back. In *A World Unsuspected: Portraits of Southern*

Childhood, edited by Alex Harris, pp. 14–52. Chapel Hill: University of North Carolina Press.

Pratt, Minnie Bruce. 1984. Identity: Blood skin bones. In *Yours in Struggle: Three Feminist Perspectives on Anti-Semitism and Racism,* by Elly Bulkin, Minnie Bruce Pratt, and Barbara Smith, pp. 9–64. Ithaca: Firebrand Books.

Prown, Jules David. 1993. The truth of material culture: History or fiction? In *History from Things: Essays on Material Culture,* edited by Steven Lubar and W. David Kingery, pp. 1–19. Washington, D.C.: Smithsonian Institution Press.

Reed, Julia. 1997. The Bubba stories. *New York Times Book Review,* 30 November, sec. 7, p. 23.

Roberts, Elizabeth Maddox. 1989. The haunted palace. [1937] In *Stories of the Old South,* edited by Ben Forkner and Patrick Samway, S.J., 370–86. New York: Penguin.

Roediger, David R. 1991. *The Wages of Whiteness: Race and the Making of the American Working Class.* London: Verso.

Rose, Jacqueline. 1984. *The Case of Peter Pan, or The Impossibility of Children's Fiction.* London: Macmillan.

Rosengarten, Dale. 1987. "Row upon Row: Sea Grass Baskets of the South Carolina Lowcountry." McKissick Museum Catalogue. Columbia, S.C.: University of South Carolina.

Rubin, Louis D., Jr. 1963. *The Faraway Country: Writers of the Modern South.* Seattle: University of Washington Press.

Rubin, Louis D., Jr., and Robert D. Jacobs, eds. 1961. *South: Modern Southern Literature in Its Cultural Setting.* Garden City, N.Y.: Doubleday.

Rushdie, Salman. 1992. A Critic at Large: Out of Kansas. *New Yorker,* 11 May, 93–103.

Russo, Mary. 1994. *The Female Grotesque: Risk, Excess, and Modernity.* New York: Routledge.

Saville, Julie. 1994. *The Work of Reconstruction: From Slave to Wage Laborer in South Carolina, 1860–1870.* New York: Cambridge University Press.

Schwab, Gabrielle. 1989. Cyborgs and cybernetic intertexts: On postmodern phantasms of body and mind. In *Intertextuality and Contemporary American Fiction,* edited by Patrick O'Donnell and Robert Con Davis, pp. 191–213. Baltimore: Johns Hopkins University Press.

Segrest, Mab. 1985. *My Mama's Dead Squirrel: Lesbian Essays on Southern Culture.* Ithaca: Firebrand Books.

Shaw, Carolyn Martin. 1997. The poetics of identity: Questioning spiritualism in African American contexts. In *Female Subjects in Black and White: Race, Psychoanalysis, Feminism,* edited by Elizabeth Abel, Barbara Christian, and Helene Moglen, pp. 349–62. Berkeley: University of California Press.

Simpson, Lewis P. 1994. *The Fable of the Southern Writer.* Baton Rouge: Louisiana State University Press.

Smith, Barbara. 1994. Toward a black feminist criticism. In *Within the Circle: An Anthology of African American Literary Criticism from the Harlem Renaissance to the Present,* edited by Angelyn Mitchell, pp. 410–27. Durham: Duke University Press.

Smith, Lillian. 1978. *Killers of the Dream.* 1949. Reprint, New York: Norton.

Smith, Valerie. 1989. Black feminist theory and the representation of the "other." In *Changing Our Own Words,* edited by Cheryl Wall, pp. 38–57. Brunswick, N.J.: Rutgers University Press.

———. 1998. *Not Just Race, Not Just Gender: Black Feminist Readings*. New York: Routledge.

Spencer, Elizabeth. 1991. First dark. [1959.] In *The Signet Classic Book of Southern Short Stories,* edited by Dorothy Abbott and Susan Koppelman, pp. 351–70. New York: Signet.

Spillers, Hortense. 1984. Interstices: A small drama of words. In *Pleasure and Danger: Exploring Female Sexuality,* edited by Carole S. Vance, pp. 73–100. Boston: Routledge and Kegan Paul.

———. 1994. Mama's baby, Papa's maybe: An American grammar book. In *Within the Circle: An Anthology of African American Literary Criticism from the Harlem Renaissance to the Present,* edited by Angelyn Mitchell, pp. 454–81. Durham: Duke University Press.

Stallybrass, Peter. 1993. Worn worlds: Clothes, mourning, and the life of things. *Yale Review* 81:35–75.

Stallybrass, Peter, and Allon White. 1986. *The Politics and Poetics of Transgression.* Ithaca: Cornell University Press.

Starkey, Marion L. 1964. *Striving to Make It My Home.* New York: W. W. Norton.

Stewart, Kathleen. 1996. *A Space on the Side of the Road: Cultural Poetics in an "Other" America.* Princeton: Princeton University Press.

Stewart, Susan. 1984. *On Longing: Narratives of the Miniature, the Gigantic, the Souvenir, the Collection.* Baltimore: Johns Hopkins University Press.

Stowe, Harriet Beecher. 1966. *Uncle Tom's Cabin.* New York: Signet.

Sullivan, Patricia. 1996. *Days of Hope: Race and Democracy in the New Deal.* Chapel Hill: University of North Carolina Press.

Sundquist, Eric. 1983. *Faulkner: The House Divided.* Baltimore: Johns Hopkins University Press.

———. 1995. Blues for Atticus Finch: Scottsboro, *Brown,* and Harper Lee. In *The South as an American Problem,* edited by Larry J. Griffin and Don H. Doyle, 181–209. Athens: University of Georgia Press.

Tate, Allen. 1960. *The Fathers.* Denver: Alan Swallow.

Tate, Claudia. 1992. *Domestic Allegories of Political Desire: The Black Heroine's Text at the Turn of the Century.* New York: Oxford University Press.

———. 1998. *Psychoanalysis and Black Novels: Desire and the Protocols of Race.* New York: Oxford.

Taussig, Michael. 1992. *The Nervous System.* New York: Routledge.

Taylor, Peter. 1985. *The Old Forest and Other Stories.* New York: Ballantine.

Trefzer, Annette. 1998. Floating homes and signifiers in Hurston's and Ralings's auto biographies. *Southern Quarterly* 36:69–76.

Tucker, Susan. 1988. *Telling Memories Among Southern Women: Domestic Workers and Their Employers in the Segregated South.* New York: Schocken Books.

Turner, Bryan S. 1997. *The Body and Society.* London: Sage.

Tyler, Ann. 1992. The fine full world of Welty. In *Friendship and Sympathy: Communities of Southern Women Writers,* edited by Rosemary M. Magee, pp. 142–46. Jackson: University Press of Mississippi.

Wagner-Martin, Linda, ed. 1996. *New Essays on Go Down, Moses.* Cambridge: Cambridge University Press.

Walker, Alice. 1970. *The Third Life of Grange Copeland.* New York: Harcourt Brace Jovanovich.

———. 1976. *Meridian.* New York: Simon and Schuster.

———. 1983a. *The Color Purple.* New York: Washington Square Press.

———. 1983b. *In Search of Our Mothers' Gardens.* New York: Harcourt, Brace, Jovanovich.

———. 1984. An interview with Eudora Welty. In *Conversations with Eudora Welty,* edited by Peggy Prenshaw. Jackson: University Press of Mississippi.

———. 1988. *The Third Life of Grange Copeland.* 1970. Reprint, New York: Simon and Schuster.

———. 1991. Everyday use. [1973.] In *The Signet Classic Book of Southern Short Stories,* edited by Dorothy Abbott and Susan Koppelman, pp. 519–28. New York: Signet.

Walker, Margaret. 1965. *Jubilee.* New York: Bantam.

Watson, Jay. 1997. Uncovering the body, discovering ideology: Segregation and sexual anxiety in Lillian Smith's *Killers of the Dream. American Quarterly* 49:470–503.

Weinstein, Philip. 1995. Diving into the wreck: Faulknerian practice and the imagination of slavery. *Faulkner Journal* 10:23–54.

———. 1996. *What Else But Love? The Ordeal of Race in Faulkner and Morrison.* New York: Columbia University Press.

Welty, Eudora. 1946. *Delta Wedding.* New York: Harcourt, Brace.

———. 1949. *The Golden Apples.* New York: Harcourt, Brace, and World.

———. 1979. *A Curtain of Green and Other Stories.* 1941. Reprint, New York: Harcourt Brace Jovanovich.

———. 1980. *The Collected Stories of Eudora Welty.* New York: Harcourt Brace.

———. 1984. *Conversations with Eudora Welty,* edited by Peggy Prenshaw. Jackson: University Press of Mississippi.

Westling, Louise. 1985. *Sacred Groves and Ravaged Gardens: The Fiction of Eudora Welty, Carson McCullers, and Flannery O'Connor.* Athens: University of Georgia Press.

———. 1987. The loving observer of *One Time, One Place.* In *Welty: A Life in Literature,* edited by Albert J. Devlin. Jackson: University Press of Mississippi.

Williams, Sherley Anne. 1986. *Dessa Rose.* New York: Berkley.

Williamson, Joel. 1993. *William Faulkner and Southern History.* New York: Oxford University Press.

Wilson, Charles Reagan, and William Ferris. 1989. *Encyclopedia of Southern Culture.* Chapel Hill: University of North Carolina Press.

Windley, Lathan A. 1983. *Runaway Slave Advertisements: A Document History from the 1730's to 1790.* Vol. 2, *Maryland.* Westport, Conn.: Greenwood Press.

Wray, Matt, and Annalee Newitz. 1997. *White Trash: Race and Class in America.* New York: Routledge.

Wright, Richard. 1965. *Uncle Tom's Children.* 1940. Reprint, New York: Harper and Row.

———. 1989. Silt. [1937.] In *Stories of the Old South,* edited by Ben Forkner and Patrick Samway, S.J., pp. 161–75. Reprint, New York: Viking Penguin.

Wright, Sarah E. 1969. *This Child's Gonna Live.* New York: Delacorte Press.

Wyatt-Brown, Bertram. 1994. *The Literary Percys: Family History, Gender, and the Southern Imagination.* Athens: University of Georgia Press.

Yaeger, Patricia. 1995. The woman without any bones: Anti-angel aggression in *Wise*

Blood. In *New Essays on* Wise Blood, edited by Michael Kreyling. Cambridge: Cambridge University Press.

———. 1996. Flannery O'Connor and the aesthetics of torture. In *Flannery O'Connor: New Perspectives,* edited by Sura P. Rath and Mary Neff Shaw, pp. 183–206. Athens: University of Georgia Press.

———. Forthcoming. White dirt: The surreal racial landscapes of Willa Cather's South. In *Willa Cather's Southern Connections: New Essays on Cather and the South,* edited by Anne Romines. Charlottesville: University Press of Virginia.

Young, Thomas Daniel. 1985. A second generation of novelists. In *The History of Southern Literature,* edited by Louis D. Rubin Jr., Blyden Jackson, Rayburn S. Moore, Lewis P. Simpson, and Thomas Daniel Young, pp. 466–69. Baton Rouge: Louisiana State University Press.

Zizek, Slavoj. 1991. *The Sublime Object of Ideology.* New York: Verso.

———. 1992. *Enjoy Your Symptom! Jacques Lacan in Hollywood and Out.* New York: Routledge.

Index